FROM DISINTEGRATION
TO REINTEGRATION

FROM DISINTEGRATION
TO REINTEGRATION

Eastern Europe and the Former Soviet Union in International Trade

Edited by
Harry G. Broadman

 THE WORLD BANK

1 2 3 4 08 07 06 05

ISBN-10: 0-8213-6197-X
ISBN-13: 978-0-8213-6197-9
e-ISBN: 0-8213-6198-8
DOI: 10.1596/978-0-8213-6197-9

Cover photo of Poti Port, Georgia, by: Yuri Mechitov, The World Bank.
Cover design by: Naylor Design, Inc.

Library of Congress Cataloging-in-Publication Data
From disintegration to reintegration : Eastern Europe and the former Soviet Union in international
  trade / edited by Harry G. Broadman.
     p. cm.
   Includes bibliographical references and index.
   ISBN-13: 978-0-8213-6197-9
   ISBN-10: 0-8213-6197-X
     1. Europe, Eastern—Commercial policy. 2. Former Soviet republics—Commercial policy.
3. Europe, Eastern—Commerce. 4. Former Soviet republics—Commerce. I. Broadman, Harry G.
HF1532.7.F76 2006
382'.30947—dc22

                                                                              2005056815

Contents

Boxes

Figures

Tables

Foreword

Price liberalization was one of the very first reforms undertaken by many countries of Eastern Europe and the Former Soviet Union at the start of their transition from centrally planned to market economies a decade and a half ago. In the case of tradable goods, this meant opening up domestic markets to international prices and liberalization of the countries' trade policy regimes. In short order, external tariffs were lowered, and import quotas and other nontariff barriers (NTBs) were reduced or eliminated. At the same time, the CEMA (Council for Mutual Economic Cooperation), the central planning institution that had administratively governed these countries' trade with the rest of the world—as well as trade among themselves—was dismantled. This was often accompanied by other fundamental reforms, such as macroeconomic stabilization and privatization. These reforms revealed that many enterprises were uncompetitive at international prices and resulted in countries losing guaranteed outlets for their products, precipitating what has come to be known as the "transition recession." The recovery was characterized by an expansion of exports and the ignition of economic growth. In turn, this brought about higher incomes and reduced poverty for many people of the Region. The early—and bold—actions on the trade front proved to be critical down payments that facilitated the integration of these countries into the world economy.

Indeed, the transition from central planning to market systems could not have occurred without greater openness to international trade. This study, *From Disintegration to Reintegration: Eastern Europe and the Former Soviet Union in International Trade*, finds that over the past 15 years, the Region as a whole has experienced rapid trade flows and today trades largely in line with other regions of the world at comparable levels of income.

It appears that two new intra-Regional trade blocs are emerging, however. One largely comprises the eight new European Union (EU) member countries, which are increasingly trading with the most advanced economies in Europe and enjoying relatively high national incomes. The other bloc is generally populated by economies of the Commonwealth of Independent States (CIS), many (though not all) of which are still dominated by commodity trade, exhibit increasingly centralized and segmented trade patterns reminiscent of the planning era, and are significantly poorer, although the Russian Federation and Ukraine have experienced considerable international integration and are middle-income economies. Most of the seven countries in Southeastern Europe lie somewhere in between these two blocs, but are increasingly aligning themselves with the former. While these trends are surely evident, as the study shows, the increasing bifurcation of trade in the Region is by no means predetermined. As has happened elsewhere, countries that have not only opened trade but also systematically implemented complementary domestic or "behind-the-border" policies have been more effective in leveraging international integration to raise growth rates.

To be sure, virtually all of the countries in the Region still need to pursue further trade policy reforms, and some require fundamental liberalization of their trade regimes. In this regard, early accession to the World Trade Organization (WTO) for the 10 countries in the Region that currently are not members would be beneficial, especially to take advantage of the present Doha Round negotiations. By the same token, benefits would arise from regional trade agreements (RTAs) that create rather than divert trade. The bigger—and largely Region-wide—unfinished agenda, however, concerns behind-the-border reforms. The most critical of these are enhancing domestic interenterprise competition and governance, developing trade-facilitating infrastructure, and deregulating the services sectors. While meeting these challenges will require policy reforms (such as improving market access in agriculture) by developed countries and support for technical assistance (for example, in customs reform) from international donors, the lion's share of actions will need to come from the Region's countries themselves.

This study, part of a new series of regional studies, is intended as a contribution to the World Bank's goal to work more effectively with our partners in the Region to foster economic growth and reduce poverty through greater integration into international commerce. It complements two recent studies on growth, poverty, and inequality and on job opportunities in the Region. Forthcoming reports on migration and infrastructure will look at other key economic and social opportunities and challenges for the Region. I hope that this series of studies will stimulate debate, promote better understanding, and spur action to bring about prosperity for all.

Shigeo Katsu
Vice President
Europe and Central Asia Region

Acknowledgments

This study was prepared by a team led by Harry Broadman. The principal authors of the chapters are as follows: *Overview*—Harry Broadman; *Chapter 1: Introduction*—Harry Broadman; *Chapter 2: Trade Performance*—Harry Broadman, with the assistance of Theodora Galabova, Alia Moubayed, Francis Ng, and Olga Pindyuk; *Chapter 3: Trade Policy*—Costas Michalopoulos, with the assistance of Theodora Galabova and Gallina Vincelette; *Chapter 4: Competition and Governance*—Harry Broadman and Gallina Vincelette, with the assistance of Theodora Galabova and Olga Pindyuk; *Chapter 5: Trade Facilitation*—John Wilson, with the assistance of Naomi Aoki; *Chapter 6: Services Trade and Investment*—Bernard Hoekman and Felix Eschenbach, with the assistance of Aaditya Mattoo; *Chapter 7: Network Trade and FDI*—Bart Kaminski and Beata Javorcik, with the assistance of Francis Ng; and *Chapter 8: Conclusions and Policy Recommendations*—Harry Broadman. Harry Broadman integrated and edited the chapters. The team was assisted in the production of the manuscript by Mismake Galatis, Jenepher Mosely, and Kate Sullivan.

This work was supported by the Chief Economist of the Europe and Central Asia Region of the World Bank, Pradeep Mitra, who provided essential intellectual guidance throughout the research process. The study benefited from useful comments and suggestions provided at various stages by Asad Alam, James Anderson, Paul Brenton, Uri

Dadush, Lev Freinkman, Cheryl Gray, Daniela Gressani, Ali Mansoor, Fernando Montes-Negret, Mamta Murthi, Evgeny Polyakov, David Tarr, Peter Thomson, and Merrell Tuck-Primdahl.

The peer reviewers were Luca Barbone, Johannes Linn, Martin Raiser, and Alan Winters. The team thanks them for their very helpful comments and suggestions.

Earlier versions of this study were presented at the CASE conference, "Europe after the Enlargement," held in Warsaw on April 8–9, 2005, as well as in seminars in April 2005 at the German Agency for Technical Cooperation (GTZ) in Bonn, European Commission in Brussels, Organisation for Economic Co-operation and Development (OECD) in Paris, and Department for International Development (DfPID) and European Bank for Reconstruction and Development (EBRD) in London. The comments and insights given in these forums were helpful in sharpening the analysis.

The World Bank Office of the Publisher coordinated the book design, editing, and production. Dina Towbin was the production editor.

Acronyms
and Abbreviations

AD	antidumping
ATC	Agreement on Textiles and Clothing
BEEPS	Business Environment and Enterprise Performance Survey
BiH	Bosnia and Herzegovina
BIS	Bank for International Settlements
BOO	build-operate-own
BOP	balance of payments
BOT	build-operate-transfer
BRSA	Banking Regulatory and Supervisory Agency
CAP	Common Agricultural Policy
CEE	Central and Eastern Europe
CEFTA	Central Europe Free Trade Area
CGE	computable general equilibrium
CIS	Commonwealth of Independent States
CMEA	Council for Mutual Economic Cooperation
CPI	corruption perception index
DfID	Department for International Development (U.K.)
EAP	East Asia and the Pacific
EBRD	European Bank for Reconstruction and Development
EC	European Commission
ECA	Europe and Central Asia

ECOSOC	Economic and Social Council of the UN
EFTA	European Free Trade Association
EPZ	export processing zone
EU	European Union
EU-8	Eight new EU-member countries
EU-15	European Union before the 2004 enlargement
FBiH	Federation of Bosnia and Herzegovina
FDI	foreign direct investment
FSU	Former Soviet Union
FTA	free trade agreement
FYR	former Yugoslav Republic (of Macedonia)
GATS	General Agreement on Trade in Services
GATT	General Agreement on Tariffs and Trade
GDP	gross domestic product
GOST	Committee of the Russian Federation for Standardization, Metrology, and Certification
GSP	generalized system of preferences
GTAP	Global Trade Analysis Project
IBRD	International Bank for Reconstruction and Development
IMF	International Monetary Fund
IOSCO	International Organization of Securities Commissions
IT	information technology
LAC	Latin America and the Caribbean
LRMC	long-run marginal cost
MENA	Middle East and North Africa
NAFTA	North American Free Trade Agreement
NTBs	nontariff barriers
OECD	Organisation for Economic Co-operation and Development
P&C	parts and components
PPP	purchasing power parity
ROW	rest of the world
RTA	regional trade agreement
SAA	Stabilization and Association Agreement
SAM	Serbia and Montenegro
SAR	South Asia Region
SEE	Southeastern European
SMEs	small and medium enterprises
SOE	state-owned enterprise
SSA	Sub-Saharan Africa
TBT	technical barriers to trade
TRIMs	trade-related investment measures

UN	United Nations
UNMIK	United Nations Mission in Kosovo
UNDP	United Nations Development Programme
U.S.	United States
USSR	Union of Soviet Socialist Republics
VAT	value added tax
WDI	*World Development Indicators*
WTO	World Trade Organization

Note: All dollar amounts are U.S. dollars ($) unless otherwise indicated.

Overview

As the world marketplace becomes increasingly globalized, much is at stake for the prosperity of hundreds of millions of people in Eastern Europe and the Former Soviet Union (the Region), now in their second decade of transition from Communism to capitalism. One hallmark of the transition is the Region coming almost full circle in reintegrating into international commerce, albeit not precisely where it started with the onset of Communism near the beginning of the twentieth century. A decade and a half after the disintegration of the Soviet trade bloc, the Region as a whole has experienced rapid trade flows and now trades largely in line with comparable regions in the world. But two new intra-Regional trade blocs are emerging. One is tending toward trade with the advanced countries in Western Europe and enjoying relatively high national incomes. The other bloc is significantly poorer, and tending to pull back toward a Russia-centric sphere. Its economies are still dominated by commodity trade, and risk non-participation in the modern international division of labor. The formation of the second bloc is not inevitable, however. As has happened else-where in the world, transition countries in the Region that have opened trade and judiciously implemented complementary domestic or "behind-the-bor-der" policies have been more effective in leveraging international integration to raise growth rates. Nevertheless, virtually all of the countries in the Region need to pursue further trade policy reforms, and some still require fundamental liberalization. The bigger—and largely Region-wide—unfinished agenda, however, concerns behind-the-border reforms. These include enhancing domestic interenterprise competition and market flexibility, strengthening basic market institutions and incentives for sound governance, developing trade-facilitating infrastructure, deregulating services sectors, and attracting cutting-edge foreign direct investment (FDI). While meeting these challenges will require policy reforms by developed countries and assistance from international donors, the lion's share of actions will need to come from the Region's countries themselves.

A decade and a half have passed since the disintegration of the Soviet trade bloc. For 70 years the bloc had interrupted the Eurasian continent's long economic history of international commerce with much of the rest of the world, thus largely isolating almost half a billion people in the 27 "transition" countries of Eastern Europe and the Former Soviet Union (the Region)[1] from the modern global marketplace. With the fall of the Berlin Wall, the dissolution of the Soviet Union, and the breakup of Yugoslavia, the Council for Mutual Economic Cooperation (CMEA)—the key central planning mechanism that managed how the countries of the Region traded with each other as well as with the outside world—no longer had any obvious purpose, and was terminated.

The implication of CMEA's demise was more than symbolic. It meant that, in practice, the Region's global trade was no longer channeled through administrative functions. At the same time, transactions that had previously been essentially domestic within an integrated region suddenly became international trade, conditioned by market forces and international trading practices and rules. Where previously such transactions had been mediated across different territories through one currency and under common laws and regulations, now they cut across new national boundaries, were paid for in different currencies, and were subject to new national customs authorities and procedures.

The dismantling of the Soviet bloc brought economic chaos and a collapse of trade flows that compelled countries in the Region to begin to reintegrate into the global economy. By the mid-1990s, the transition of an increasing number of countries to market economic systems began to take hold and, today, most of the Region's countries are significantly better integrated into the global economy than at any time since the Russian Revolution. The Region now sends and receives more than two-thirds of its goods and services to and from the rest of the world (EBRD 2003) and, since the mid-1990s, trade growth has been faster than in any other region worldwide.[2] The Region's exports have tripled and imports increased two and one-half times.

Open Trade: The Critical First Step

Without open trade, none of this could have occurred. Liberal trade has propelled growth in the Region, as has been the case elsewhere in the world (Frankel and Romer 1999, Dollar and Kraay 2002).

In the early years of the transition, many countries in the Region adopted liberal import policies in short order. However, a domestic institutional bias against competition and enterprise restructuring discouraged exports, with the result that the increased flows (of imports) did little to enhance productivity and increase growth. In fact, they created distortions and exacerbated poverty. In time, however, the countries that responded to increased import flows by allowing resources to be flexibly reallocated throughout the economy, facilitating the ability of firms to compete with one another, and eliminating disincentives to export, engendered a supply response where prices of tradable goods rose, new jobs were created, and growth increased.

At present, the Region comprises economies with fairly open trade policies. On average, tariffs range from 3.3 to 11.6 percent.[3] Much of this trade policy liberalization was carried out autonomously by the countries themselves in the early years of the transition, albeit with encouragement and support (and discipline) by the international development community. In subsequent years, such liberalization has been occurring through the European Union (EU) accession process and through the fashioning of various bilateral and regional trade agreements (RTAs). Moreover, 17 countries of the Region, as well as Turkey, are now members of the World Trade Organization (WTO), with most of the others—all in the Commonwealth of Independent States (CIS)—in various stages of the WTO accession process.

Leveraging International Integration into Economic Growth: A Reciprocal Process

The most prosperous countries of the Region are those that found ways to leverage greater international trade into more rapid growth. They have not accomplished this by liberalizing formal trade policies alone, however. They have also instituted complementary behind-the-border (domestic) structural and institutional reforms that foster trade. These countries include the Czech Republic, Hungary, and Slovenia. Of such reforms, several that stand out for their effectiveness are those that promote competition between enterprises and sound governance; deregulation of services sectors; development of infrastructure systems that facilitate trade; attraction of FDI; and reallocation of labor and other resources when market conditions change.

These reforms can conflict with vested interests and have not always been easy. However, establishing trade links, especially under international commitments and agreements, has helped lock in these hard-won domestic reforms. The converse is also true: countries in the Region that have been most successful in implementing internal market reforms have also tended to be the ones that were most effective in integrating into the world marketplace. In short, growth during the transition has been engendered through a mutually reinforcing two-way effect between international integration and domestic structural reforms.

Thus, while the reform of trade policies is necessary to ensure sustainable growth, it is not sufficient. For most of the countries in the Region this leaves a significant behind-the-border reform agenda unfinished. Moreover, several, such as Belarus, Tajikistan, Turkmenistan, and Uzbekistan, are still relatively closed and have yet to put in hand fundamental trade policy reforms.

The Challenge for the Region and the World

Much is at stake for the prosperity of hundreds of millions of people of the Region. Thus, understanding the dynamics that are shaping the contours of international integration that have emerged—and are likely to emerge—in the Region is a crucial challenge for the medium-term economic development agenda. This is true not only for these countries' policy makers and trading partners, but also for international financial institutions and the donor community; indeed for the future of the world trading system as a whole.

Addressing this challenge raises several questions:

- Why have some countries in the Region integrated internationally to a greater extent and in different ways than others, and what do the current trends portend for the future? How have the Region's goods and services, their production, and trading methods changed among the countries over the course of the transition, and what are the implications for competitiveness and growth?

- How does trade performance of the Region of today compare with that of other regions of the world? What factors in the Region are most important in conditioning the relationships among greater international integration, geography, policy reforms, and growth?

- Which policy reforms are likely to be most effective in using trade as a lever to enhance growth in the Region? Is the Region's trade policy too restrictive? What is the impact of developed country protectionism? What are the priority policy issues that governments in the Region should focus on, and what can the international community do to be most effective?

This study seeks to answer these questions.[4]

Summary of Principal Findings

Two trading blocs are emerging. The countries of Eastern Europe and the Former Soviet Union are becoming more like a "typical" region regarding trade, with most of the economies registering merchandise trade flows as a share of gross domestic product (GDP) largely in line with other countries of comparable size and levels of development.[5] However, the pace, nature, and extent of the Region's international reintegration differ strikingly from its earlier historic pattern of integration—both among the constituent countries and with the rest of the world. Moreover, it is characterized by pronounced variations that, in effect, are forming the countries into two new trading blocs. One is Euro-centric, comprising the eight new members of the European Union (EU-8),[6] Turkey, and, gradually, the seven Southeastern European (SEE) countries.[7] The other is "Russia-centric," largely comprising the 12 countries of the CIS.[8]

The two blocs have begun to coalesce in terms of:

- Volume and direction of trade flows

- Commodity composition and factor intensity of trade

- Export competitiveness

- Development of trade facilitation institutions and infrastructure

- Extent of intraindustry trade, both in the services sectors and by participation in global production-sharing networks through FDI

- Extent to which trade flows enhance domestic competition and governance, and vice versa.

But the blocs' boundaries are soft. Of course this admittedly sharp binary prism masks the more complex realities. There is a sizeable difference in scale between the emerging blocs, and there is significant intra-bloc heterogeneity. Total merchandise trade flows of the EU-8 and SEE are almost twice the size of those of the CIS. At the same time, while the wealthier and larger CIS countries, such as the Russian Federation and Ukraine, have some trading attributes akin to those of the EU-8 or SEE, the smaller and poorer CIS countries show decreasing participation in the modern international division of labor. By the same token, some of the SEE countries, such as Bosnia and Herzegovina, the Former Yugoslav Republic of (FYR) Macedonia, and Serbia and Montenegro, exhibit trade patterns more along the lines of CIS economies. Indeed, while the overall group of SEE countries is increasingly gravitating toward the Euro-centric pole, in fact they are doing so at different rates. Consequently, at this point, along some dimensions the SEE countries form a "middle ground" between the two poles.

A dichotomous region is not inevitable. The emerging differences in the present pattern of international integration in the Region could continue for the foreseeable future. So, too, could differences in the countries' prospects for economic growth and prosperity. But the formation of the second bloc is not inevitable; the alternative is the direction taken by the transition countries that have already been able to leverage international integration to raise growth rates through complementary behind-the-border reforms. A detailed summary of the policy actions to achieve the desired results appears at the end of this Overview.

The unfinished policy agenda. Some actions will require significant measures by developed nations, such as improving market access in agriculture and removing the "nonmarket" designation they apply to transition countries in antidumping cases. Technical assistance is also needed from the donor community to strengthen trade-related institutions in the Region, especially for the low income CIS countries. Because they are neither classified as "least developed" countries nor have realistic prospects for EU accession, they tend to get overlooked in qualifying for certain aid.

In the end, however, much will depend on reform actions undertaken by the countries in the Region themselves. In the area of trade policy, needed reforms include further tariff reductions; elimination of nontariff barriers (NTBs); reduction of disincentives to export; aggressive pursuit of WTO accession (especially where EU accession is unrealistic); and rationalization, harmonization, and consolidation of existing RTAs.

Arguably the more challenging tasks would be vigorous implementation of economywide behind-the-border reforms. Particularly important are policies that foster greater competition and sound governance, that improve trade facilitation mechanisms, that liberalize services sectors, that improve the climate to attract FDI, and that create greater flexibility in labor and capital markets.

Coming "Full Circle?" The Reemergence of Eastern Europe and the Former Soviet Union in International Markets

In the aftermath of the dissolution of the Soviet bloc, economies conditioned by command and control regimes began a transformation into economies based on market institutions and incentives. The changes unfettered firms' and consumers' economic decisions, which increasingly came to be determined more by the forces of supply and demand than by administrative fiat. The result was to unleash a drive for international reintegration.

Two "Poles" Emerging: Trade Patterns and Performance of the Reintegrated Region

A dichotomy in merchandise trade growth. Total merchandise trade of countries in the Region since the start of the transition has grown significantly, but exhibits a highly heterogeneous pattern, both over time and across subregions; see figure 1.[9] For the Region as a whole, merchandise trade flows (in dollar value and in real terms) have grown significantly since 1993: exports almost tripled and imports increased by a factor of 2.5.[10] Trade growth was greatest for the EU-8, where exports and imports increased by factors of 3.6 and 4.1, respectively. The CIS is at the other end of the spectrum: exports and imports expanded by factors of 2.1 and 1.5, respectively. In between is SEE, where exports grew by 3.5 and imports increased 2.7 times.

Services trade growth. A similar picture emerges of the Region's growth of trade in services. Services industries were accorded low priority under central planning. They were not considered a productive activity. But as part of the process of the transition to modernized economies, the services sectors have begun to emerge as a dynamic force in economic growth in the Region. In recent years, telecommunications, transportation, and energy services, among other network industries, as well as banking, have been core targets of domestic reform in the Region. As in other regions of the world, international trade (and investment) in such services sectors also has begun to increase in countries located in the Region.[11]

The growth in the value of both exports and imports of services for the overall Region in 1993–2003 significantly exceeds that of comparable regions in the world. Not surprisingly, however, at present, the Region's volume (by $ value) of services trade as a share of global services trade of exports and imports of services generally remains small.

FIGURE 1

Eastern Europe and the Former Soviet Union's Merchandise Exports and Imports as a Share of GDP PPP, 1994–2003

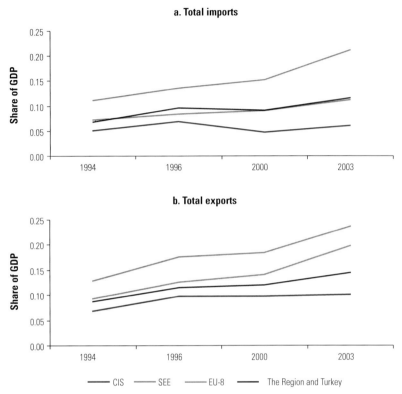

Source: International Monetary Fund (IMF) Direction of Trade (DOT) Yearbook.

Note: CIS = Commonwealth of Independent States; EU-8 = European Union-8; GDP = gross domestic product; PPP = purchasing power parity; SEE = Southeastern Europe.

There are significant differences within the Region, however. Services trade flows—whether in terms of exports or imports—grew fastest in the SEE countries between 1993 and 2003, followed by those in the EU-8. In contrast, the CIS economies' services sectors remain largely closed. Their services sectors are heavily burdened by regulation, protection from the competitive pressures that accompany exposure to international trade.

There are few data available on the direction of trade in services for the Region. But telecommunications traffic flows suggest that much of the Region's trade in services, largely by the EU-8 and SEE, is oriented toward Western Europe. More than half of all outgoing telecommunications traffic originating in the eight new EU members states and in SEE goes to the EU. This compares to less than 2 percent for Central Asia and the Caucasus, and 8 percent for Russia, Ukraine, and Belarus. This effective bifurcation of the Region's countries—in this case in terms of services trade—is a characteristic increasingly endemic along multiple dimensions of the overall pattern of international integration in the Region.

Patterns of the destination and origin of merchandise exports. Over the course of the transition there have been significant changes in the destination and origin markets of both the exports and imports of merchandise by the Region. While age-old destination and origin markets on the Eurasian continent still figure prominently for most of these countries, less traditional, newer locations have been gaining strength in certain instances. Most striking is the increasing bifurcation of the Region into two trade "poles": the geographic pattern of trade flows is moving toward a Euro-centric clustering and a Russia-centric clustering.

On a *global* basis—that is, considering the countries' trade flows *both* outside and inside the Region—for the most developed economies of Eastern Europe and the Former Soviet Union, the EU-8, the major export destination market today remains the more advanced countries in Europe (figure 2). The EU-15 comprises the 15 EU member states prior to May 1, 2004: Austria, Belgium, Denmark, Finland, France, Germany, Greece, Ireland, Italy, Luxembourg, the Netherlands, Portugal, Spain, Sweden, and the UK. Indeed the share of the EU-8's global exports sold in the EU-15 rose over the decade, while their corresponding export share within the Region fell. The EU-8's share of exports to the rest of the world (ROW) increased sizably over the decade, another indicator of the EU-8's increased international integration.

Over the course of the decade, the geographic spread of CIS merchandise exports has become more concentrated. The CIS's largest destination market for its merchandise exports in 2003 was the same as it was in 1993—the EU-15—but only marginally so. In fact, the share of CIS exports shipped to the Region's countries grew substantially, while the share of exports shipped to the EU-15 declined substantially. Latin America and the Caribbean (LAC) and, to a much lesser extent, Africa, have proven to be new markets for CIS exports, with a doubling of the export shares over the decade.

The global pattern of merchandise export penetration for the SEE countries falls somewhere in between that of the EU-8 and CIS. The largest shares of SEE exports are accounted for by EU-15 and the Region's customers. Like their wealthier EU-8 counterparts, the SEE countries sold proportionally more exports in EU-15 markets than in the Region's markets between 1993 and 2003. On the other hand, as in the case of the CIS, the share of exports from the SEE group of countries destined for the LAC markets has substantially increased. At

FIGURE 2

Eastern Europe and the Former Soviet Union's Share of Total World Merchandise Exports

Share of Total World Merchandise Exports

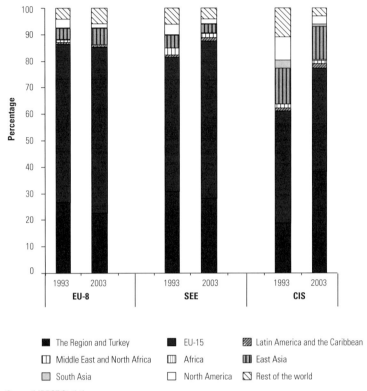

Source: IMF DOT Statistics.

the same time, SEE export shares in North America (U.S., Canada, and Mexico), South Asia, and East Asia declined.

On an *intra-Regional* basis, the destination patterns of merchandise exports of countries in the Region are particularly revealing (figure 3). While the major destination market for intra-Regional merchandise exports by the EU-8 in 1993 was the CIS, today, following a major locational shift over the decade, most of the intra-Regional exports sold by EU-8 countries are to other EU-8 countries. This natural change in the trade pattern is a hallmark of the EU-8 countries' development success, particularly the restructuring and modernization of their enterprise sectors.

The pattern of intra-Regional merchandise exports for the CIS is just the reverse. Rather than enlarging the share of their intra-Regional exports to the wealthier countries in the Region, the CIS's share of intra-Regional exports in the EU-8 market decreased while it increased in the CIS market itself. The share of CIS exports within the

FIGURE 3

Shares of Intra-Regional Merchandise Exports in Eastern Europe and the Former Soviet Union

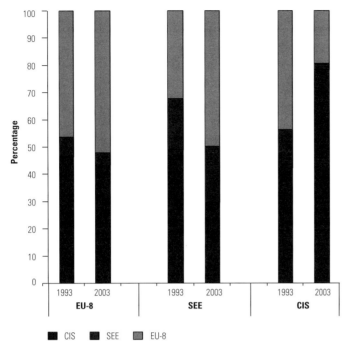

Source: IMF DOT Statistics.

Region also declined in the SEE market. Taken together, these data suggest that CIS exports within the Region have become more (sub-) regionalized and concentrated.

For the SEE economies, like the EU-8 grouping, there has been a significant shift over the period 1993–2003 as the EU-8 surpassed the CIS in being the dominant destination for intra-Regional merchandise exports originating in SEE. Indeed, the share of SEE intra-Regional exports rose in the EU-8 market and fell—even more dramatically—in the CIS market. The share of intra-Regional exports sold in the SEE market by SEE producers remained relatively the same over the decade.

Patterns of the destination and origin of merchandise imports. The emerging two-pole paradigm is equally evident on the import side of the equation. On a *global* basis, the share of EU-8 imports purchased from the EU-15 rose and purchased from the Region fell. There also was significant growth in the corresponding share of EU-8 merchandise imports from North America, which has remained the EU-8's largest non-European import market. As in exports, the CIS tends to have a pattern of global import markets that is the most diversified compared to the other country groups in the Region. But in contrast to its exports, CIS global import shares have become somewhat more diversified. Importantly, the CIS's largest origin market for imports worldwide is now the Region, whereas it used to be the EU-15. As in exports, the global pattern of merchandise import sourcing for SEE falls somewhere in between that of the EU-8 and CIS. The largest shares of SEE global imports are accounted for by EU-15 producers.

The EU-8 market remains the primary origin of *intra-Regional* EU-8 merchandise imports. However, the CIS's share of intra-Regional imports from the EU-8 market decreased and it increased in the CIS market. Again, as in exports, these data suggest that CIS trade has become more concentrated. For the SEE economies, there was a significant shift: whereas in 1993 the EU-8 was the major origin market, most SEE intra-Regional imports now come from the SEE market itself. At the same time, as is the case for their wealthier EU-8 counterparts, the share of SEE intra-Regional imports purchased from the CIS has declined.

Clustering in product concentration, commodity composition, and factor intensity of trade. Typically, with greater economic development, diversification of the composition of a country's trade increases. Has the Region's transition from central planning to market-oriented development resulted in increased diversification of exports? Overall, the Region's progress in product diversification of exports has been limited and, in some cases, commodity concentration of trade has worsened. In the aggregate, the number of exported products for the Region declined between 1993 and 2003, and the share accounted for by the largest 3 as well as the largest 10 products in total exports has increased. The CIS countries are the least diversified; indeed, their product diversification has substantially deteriorated over time, notably after 1996. This has been most striking in Azerbaijan, Georgia, Kazakhstan, and Russia, where oil and gas are increasingly the prominent exports.

Product concentration of trade has also been increasing, though in a different form, in the EU-8 countries, notably Hungary and the Slovak and Czech Republics, and particularly in heavy industries such as automotive production and parts. The Baltic countries, particularly Latvia and Lithuania, have managed nevertheless to improve their export diversification profiles. The SEE countries, on the other hand, remain the most diversified, due to an increase in low value-added exports, such as textiles, among other factors.

The concentration of exports in primary commodities remains large and is increasing in the CIS countries, where the average share of ores, metals, and fuels (oil and natural gas) in total exports increased from 38 percent to 47 percent over the period 1996–2003. With the collapse of manufacturing exports following the breakup of the Union of Soviet Socialist Republics (USSR), most of these countries had shifted toward commodity exports. In the natural resource-rich countries such as Azerbaijan, Kazakhstan, Russia, and Turkmenistan, trade in energy and raw materials experienced a boost and compensated for the decline in manufacturing trade. By the same token, Tajikistan's exports are dominated by aluminum, and Kyrgyzstan relies extensively on exports of gold.

Differences among the Region's countries in factor endowments, initial conditions, and level of development have largely conditioned the factor intensities of the Region's exports and imports. The variation in the factor composition of merchandise exports falls along two lines.[12] In less developed, resource-rich and labor-endowed countries, such as the Central Asian Republics and the Caucasus, exports of labor-intensive products tend to be dominant. Merchandise exports of the more developed economies—the EU-8—are on average more capital intensive. Indeed, many of the more developed countries in the Region have increased the technological content of their traded goods: the EU-8 countries have more capital-intensive exports than other countries in the Region.

However, some EU-8 exports, such as textiles and footwear, are, on average, more *unskilled*-labor intensive than exports of the CIS. This characteristic—if sustained—poses risks to both the wage regime of workers entering the EU-8 labor market in trade-related sectors and the incentives conditioning workers' investment in human capital. Moreover, because labor costs in these countries are relatively high, reliance on unskilled labor-intensive exports may not be sustainable in the long run, given the growing competition from low-wage countries in Asia and elsewhere.

In the main, while there has been substantial change over the course of the transition in the commodity composition and factor intensity of trade by the EU-8 and the SEE economies, relatively little has changed in these regards among the CIS countries, which effectively have been frozen in time. The result is that these countries are not active participants in the evolving international division of labor. The existing composition and factor intensity of exports puts the future growth prospects of the CIS at risk.

A dichotomy in the interactions between trade intensity and domestic competition and governance. The interactions between the extent of international integration and of domestic competition in the Region's countries over the course of the transition have manifested them-selves in several ways. On the one hand, in the countries where import penetration has been greatest, firms have been most prone to reducing production costs and innovating. This finding is strongest for firms of smaller scale and those with greater private ownership. Par-ticularly telling is that private foreign-invested firms operating in "host" markets have been more likely to react to import competition than have their domestically owned counterparts. Importantly, in the countries where there has been less progress in fostering a competi-tive market environment—especially in the CIS—the effects of imports on business decisions have been more muted than in coun-tries, such as the EU-8, where markets are more competitively struc-tured as a result of more advanced reforms (see table 1).

On the other hand, the state of competition domestically has affected the extent of international integration. Two pieces of evidence are telling in this regard. In the Region's countries where there has been greater introduction of private sector participation in the econ-omy, whether through privatization of existing firms or through de novo investment, the export intensity by businesses—the percentage of export revenues as a share of total sales revenues—is much higher (see figure 4). Moreover, the export intensity tends to be greater for foreign invested firms than for domestically owned businesses.

These pieces of evidence suggest a two-way relationship between international integration and behind-the-border conditions, such as greater competition: foreign firms investing in the Region are more prone to react to import competition than are their domestic counter-parts, and at the same time are more likely to further their host coun-tries' integration into world markets than are domestic businesses. In part, this may be due to the fact that foreign firms are more likely than domestic firms to have superior management skills.

However, the effect on domestic competition of the presence of foreign firms depends on the way they enter the market. If entry is

TABLE 1

Importance of Competition from Imports to Businesses of Eastern Europe and the Former Soviet Union

	CIS	SEE	EU-8	The Region
Domestic	27.1	37.6	30.5	31.3
Foreign	27.3	48.5	40.0	35.2

Source: Business Environment and Enterprise Performance Survey (BEEPS2).

Note: Percentage of surveyed firms in 2002 indicating that competition from imports is very or extremely important. Pre-liminary results from the new BEEPS 2005 are broadly consistent with those reported in this table. However, some changes may have occurred for individual countries or subgroups of countries in the Region.

FIGURE 4

Export Intensity of Businesses Is Greater in the More Advanced Countries of Eastern Europe and the Former Soviet Union

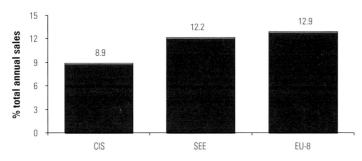

Source: BEEPS2.

Note: Average export revenues as a share of total annual sales, 2002. Preliminary results from the new BEEPS of 2005 are broadly consistent with those reported in this figure. However, some changes may have occurred for individual countries or subgroups of countries in the Region.

accomplished through establishment of wholly new ("greenfield") businesses, with all other things being equal, competition is generally enhanced, since the number of sellers operating in the domestic market has increased. But if entry occurs through the acquisition of two or more incumbent businesses that are then consolidated under one corporate roof, again, all other things being equal, competition is generally diminished, since the number of sellers in the market is reduced. (When entry results simply in a one-for-one change of ownership of a single business, all other things being equal, the effect on competition in the market is neutral.)

The interactions between the extent of international integration and of domestic governance share the same attributes. For example, the ability to resolve effectively commercial disputes associated with international trade transactions "at home" is greatest in the Euro-centric pole and weakest in the Russia-centric pole. Not surprisingly, firms in the CIS rely on bribes to overcome institutional hurdles in international transctions to a greater extent than those in the rest of the Region.[13] This evidence implies that there might be an important relationship between the sophistication and availability of instruments for dispute resolution and international integration.

The incidence of corruption among countries in the Region is quite varied. Importantly, there is now evidence that these differences appear to be associated with the extent of international integration— independent of the level of a country's development—among the countries in the Region (see figure 5). In particular, countries where corruption is more prominent tend to be those with the least amount of integration into the world economy.[14]

FIGURE 5

Corruption Perception Index and International Integration, 2003

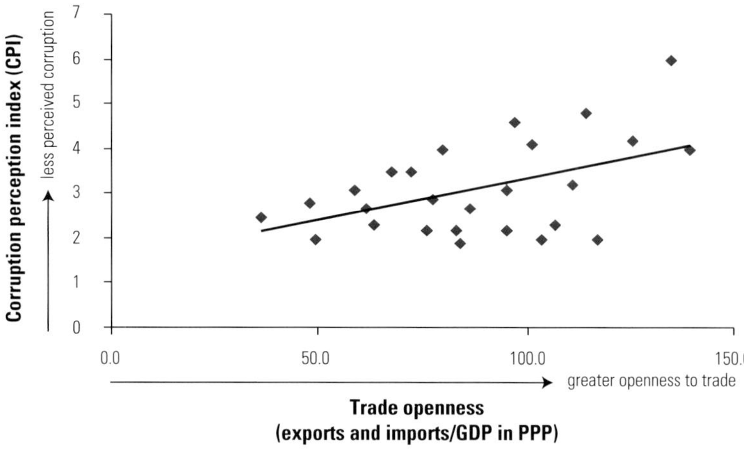

Source: CPI index from Transparency International; export and import in output (PPP) data from World Bank World Development Indicators.

Note: CPI ranks countries in terms of degree to which corruption is perceived to exist among public officials and politicians. It is a composite index, drawing on corruption-related data in expert surveys carried out by a variety of reputable institutions. It reflects the views of business people and analysts from around the world, including experts. The higher the CPI, the lower the level of perceived corruption. Each diamond represents one country in the Region.

Subregional differences in trade and transport facilitation infrastructure and institutions. The institutional and physical capacity for trade facilitation are significantly heterogenous across the Region. Broadly, the trend toward two poles is evident with respect to the state of customs, development of trade-related transport facilities, level of technical product standards, and use of modern mechanisms, such as information technology (IT), in carrying out logistical operations.[15]

The most serious problem in customs—the incidence of unofficial payments needed to move goods across national borders—is extraordinarily pernicious in Central Asia and the Caucasus, and to a lesser extent in certain areas of SEE. This handicap compounds other customs impediments, such as the lack of coordination among border-related agencies, the complexity of customs procedures, unclear customs codes and regulations, and the low utilization of IT in customs operations. Most importantly, perhaps, some of these countries are still experiencing political tensions with neighboring countries, and therefore the level of regional cooperation in trade facilitation remains low. In contrast, in the EU-8, among the "EU accession" countries (Bulgaria and Romania) and the "EU candidate countries" (Croatia and Turkey), customs administration has significantly improved over the last decade. This is at least in part due to the reforms necessary to accede to the EU, although to be sure, more progress is needed to adopt and fully implement relevant EU legislation.

In trade-related transport, much of the Caucasus and most of the CIS countries confront poor quality of service and high costs. Many of these countries are landlocked, making it important to extend their transport infrastructure to neighboring countries. For the Caucasus and the Balkans, war-damaged infrastructure and inoperable links from the transport network inherited from the Soviet period are especially problematic.

In the EU-8 countries, by comparison, the transport systems have been well maintained and have benefited from new investment over time. The result is lower transport costs and better service quality. In part, the improved quality of the transport networks in the EU-8 is rooted in the adoption of market-oriented policies, including bringing rates more in line with costs, reducing subsidies, and privatization. Nonetheless, while trade-related transport privatization has been most widespread among the EU-8 compared to other areas of the Region, the level of private sector participation in these countries is still low by global standards.

Low product standards and technical barriers to trade are also important contributors to high trade logistics costs, especially as they relate to border crossing procedures and administrative rules. On a cross-country basis, there is empirical evidence that they play a key role in export performance in the Region. By dint of complying with EU accession requirements, the EU-8 countries have adopted world class standards. Increasingly, the two EU accession and two EU candidate countries will also do so. In contrast, the remaining SEE countries, the Central Asian Republics, and the Caucasus are still at an early stage of reform in standardization.

The development of e-commerce and adoption of IT in trade transactions are low in the Region relative to other regions of the world. But, again, there is a marked bifurcation among the countries. While significant advances have been made in the EU-8, the development of trade-related Internet infrastructure in the CIS, and to a more limited extent in SEE, is subpar to support effective use of e-commerce in international trade.

Can FDI enable mobility between the two trade poles? Intraindustry trade and participation in global production-sharing networks. As in other regions, the increasing globalization of the world economy and the fragmentation of production processes have changed the economic landscape facing the nations, industries, and individual firms in Eastern Europe and the Former Soviet Union. Through FDI, multinational corporations have been key agents in this transformation, creating international production and distribution networks spanning the globe. In essence, network trade in parts and components, where countries complete different stages of final products, is the internationalization of the manufacturing process.

Production sharing involves the development of specialized and often skilled-labor-intensive activities within a vertically integrated international network. Such production sharing has been growing rapidly on a global scale, with growth rates that have exceeded other dimensions of manufacturing trade. The result has been the growth of intraindustry or increasingly intraproduct trade at the expense of traditional interindustry trade.[16]

Trade in parts and components (P&C) in the Region has increased in importance in the Region's global trade. The Region's trade in goods used in production sharing grew at an annual rate of 17 percent from 1996 to 2003. Today, trade in parts and components by countries in the Region accounts for 9 and 12 percent of total exports and imports, respectively, up from 5 and 10 percent in 1996. While most of the EU-8 and, to a lesser extent, SEE countries, have been heavily involved in network trade, most successor countries of the Former Soviet Union (FSU)—the CIS—have been left out of this process.[17]

The Czech Republic, Estonia, Hungary, Poland, the Slovak Republic, and Slovenia, for example, have become successful in network trade. During the initial phase of the transition, most of these countries relied on unskilled-labor-intensive exports associated with "buyer-driven" production chains in clothing and furniture. However, rising wages have prompted these countries to shift toward skilled-labor and capital-intensive exports conducted through "producer-driven" networks encompassing automotive and information technology industries. The sizeable FDI inflows to these countries have been instrumental in this shift. In fact, the countries that experienced the largest FDI inflows have registered the largest increases in exports of network products, components, and parts. Indeed, as is the case elsewhere in the world, trade and FDI flows in the Region are complements (see figure 6).

Most other countries in the Region have been active in buyer-driven production chains but have not managed to make a transition toward producer-driven supply chains. Countries in this group largely include the SEE economies, along with Armenia (which is engaged in the diamond supply chain), Belarus (which participates in the furniture network), and the Kyrgyz Republic, Moldova, and Turkmenistan (all of which are still heavily involved in the clothing network). The remaining CIS countries have largely stayed outside any network trade.

FIGURE 6

Trade and FDI Inflows Are Complements in Eastern Europe and the Former Soviet Union

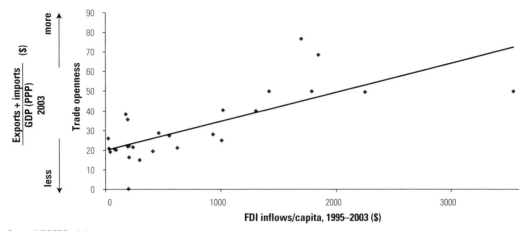

Source: IMF DOT Statistics.

Note: Each diamond represents one country in the Region; Turkey is also included.

These stylized facts suggest once again that the Region has an emerging bifurcated pattern of international integration: the countries that have integrated more into the global economy through producer-driven production-sharing networks have significantly advanced developmentally, whereas those not participating in such networks and hence less integrated internationally are generally poorer. Participation in producer-driven production-sharing networks has enabled countries in the Region to shift output from lower to higher skilled-labor-intensive products. It has also provided gains to these economies in terms of transfers of advances in technology and productivity growth.

Importantly, global production sharing can provide the opportunity for mobility from the Russia-centric to the Euro-centric pole. By attracting FDI, countries can engage in network trade, capitalize on their comparative advantage, and proactively break out from their trade block. While, many countries in the Region have attracted sizeable inflows of FDI, the cross-country differences in the amount of FDI received are striking. While Tajikistan received only $35 of FDI per capita at the end of 2003, for example, the corresponding figure for Estonia is 138 times larger, at $4,823. Generally the EU-8 countries have attracted the largest stock of FDI per capita within the Region, while among CIS countries, only Azerbaijan and Kazakhstan have managed to attract significant FDI, albeit mainly in their oil sectors.

This suggests an important policy challenge for the less developed countries in the Region is to attract FDI. For this to happen, several critical ingredients are needed. Industry investment location decisions to engage in international production sharing depend on countries' having in place market-oriented, open-trade policy regimes. In this regard, it is important for countries to provide for ease of exportation and importation of parts and components, as well as assembled, "final" products. Well-developed trade-facilitation systems and related institutions (such as customs) as well as modernized services sectors (such as the transport and communication infrastructure) also will be key. But, perhaps most important, countries need to create a favorable behind-the-border business environment. This means establishing incentives and institutions that will foster domestic markets that are competitively structured, with low barriers to entry and exit, rules-based checks on anticompetitive conduct and undue government interference in commercial decisions, and adherence to the rule of law, protection of property rights, and good governance.

Qualifications on the two-bloc paradigm. Overall, the portrait that emerges of the Region's international trade landscape is one depicting a movement from "integration" to "disintegration," and now "reintegration." But the "new" integration differs significantly from the old. Virtually all of the EU-8 have substantially integrated into the global marketplace and moved away from the old structures. An increasing proportion of the SEE countries are not far behind, although some, notably Bosnia and Herzegovina, FYR Macedonia, and Serbia and Montenegro, are much less internationally integrated. In contrast, the CIS has, with a few important exceptions, such as Russia and Ukraine, largely tended to stay together. Indeed, in several respects there is actually an *increasing* amount of subregionalized trade among the CIS.

To be sure, the reality is more complicated than this simple dichotomized portrait. There is a sizeable difference in scale between the two trade blocs. Total merchandise trade flows for the EU-8 and SEE are almost twice the size of those of the CIS. Moreover, there is significant heterogeneity *within* each bloc. For example, some of the larger CIS countries, such as Russia and Ukraine, have trading attributes akin to those of the EU-8 or SEE. At the same time, some of the SEE countries exhibit trading patterns that resemble those of the CIS countries. Indeed, while the overall group of SEE countries is increasingly gravitating toward the Euro-centric pole, they are in fact doing so at different rates. Consequently, at this point, along some dimensions, the SEE countries form a "middle ground" between the two poles. Nonetheless, there are unmistakable trends toward a "bifurcated Region" in international trade among the countries of Eastern Europe and the Former Soviet Union.

The Region's Openness to Trade Today: How Does It Compare with the Rest of the World?

In light of the rapid growth in trade flows for the Region over the last decade, how significant today is trade in the overall economic activity of the Region's countries? One way to measure this is through the conventional "output-based" metric of "trade openness," calculated as the sum of a nation's total exports and imports as a percentage of GDP.

In terms of merchandise trade, on average the Region's total merchandise exports and imports today account for more than 25 percent of GDP, as compared to about 15 percent in 1994.[18] But there is significant variation across the countries, with trade openness in the EU-8 reaching almost 45 percent, while the corresponding measure for the CIS is only 5 percent; openness in the SEE countries lies somewhere in between (see figure 7).

In services trade, the extent and pattern of openness is quite different (see figure 8). Today, on average, services trade accounts for about 4 percent of GDP in the Region. But SEE's services trade accounts for about 8 percent of GDP on average—the highest in the Region. Until 2000, the EU-8's services trade openness was the highest. For the CIS countries, services trade stayed more or less flat over the decade; today, on average, services trade among the CIS accounts for only about 3 percent of GDP.

How open are the Region's countries compared to other nations worldwide? A rigorous assessment of this question comes from an econometric "openness model" developed for 149 countries, including the 27 countries in the Region (plus Turkey). The model was designed to determine the broad association between a country's trade openness in the aggregate—that is, its gross trade flows, regardless of their

FIGURE 7

Openness in the Region's Merchandise Trade

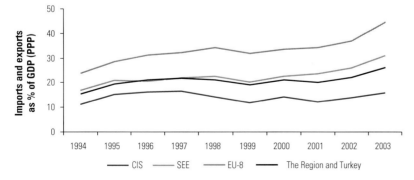

Source: IMF DOT Statistics.

FIGURE 8

Openness in the Region's Services Trade

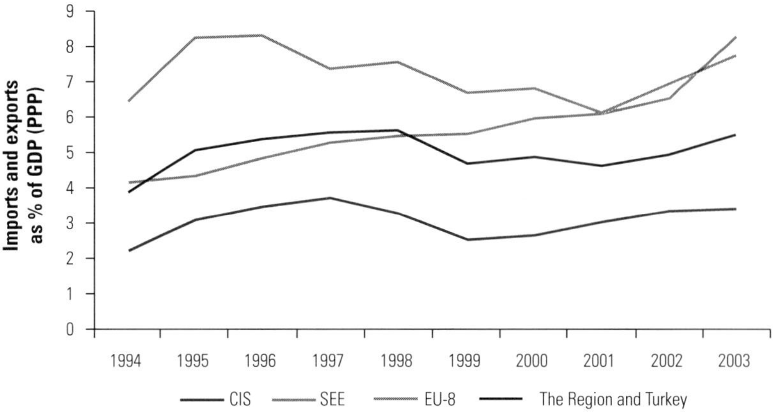

Source: IMF DOT Statistics.

destination or origin[19]—and the level of its national income. In the model, trade openness is regressed on GDP per capita as well as population (which is a proxy for country size) and geographic distance to major markets (a measure of market access). The hypothesis underlying this approach is that richer countries trade more (as a percentage of their GDP), while larger counties and those that are relatively far away from major markets trade less.

Both the theoretical and the empirical literature suggest a positive correlation between openness (trade integration) and income levels. This positive correlation can be attributed to the increasing diversification of an economy and its deepening international specialization in the course of development. At the same time, as the recent literature suggests, both income and trade are dependent on the quality of local institutions. Thus, income level may be viewed as a proxy for institutional variables that underlie trends in both overall economic development and international trade.[20] On the other hand, a country's large size (the number of domestic economic agents and consumers) creates larger opportunities for within-country trade, so these countries will be less open.

The empirical results confirm that, for all 149 countries, all other things being equal, larger countries and those further from major markets on average tend to trade less, and countries that are more advanced economically and institutionally tend to trade more. With respect to the Region, the results indicate that most of the 27 transition economies, on average, tend to trade largely in line with other countries worldwide that have similar income levels, size, and geographic distance from major markets; the only exception is many (though not all) countries in SEE, where there is evidence of "undertrading." In other words, more than a decade into the transition, most of the Region's countries as a whole trade generally in line with the global cross-country norm: they neither under- nor overtrade.

How does the actual trade openness of the Region's countries, which reflects their actual income level, size and access to markets, compare with their "theoretical" openness, which is based on the estimates corresponding to the regression line in the model? (See table 2.)

The data show that there is significant variation among the countries within the Region. The CIS countries—as a group, not necessarily every country individually—are actually trading broadly in line with their current potential (as reflected by the estimated model). On the other hand, most of the EU-8 countries appear to be measurably overtrading; on average the subregion overtrades by one-third. In contrast, the estimation results suggest that a core group of the SEE countries— especially Albania, Bosnia and Herzegovina, and FYR Macedonia—are undertrading such that, on average, SEE is trading at just over three-quarters of its potential.[21]

A similar pattern emerges from a "gravity model" where the units of analysis are the bilateral trade flows between the origin and destination countries (rather than the aggregate trade flows of a country as just discussed). Despite theoretical controversies surrounding gravity models since their inception (which have been somewhat alleviated recently),[22] they have proven to be the most accurate tool for the explanation and prediction of bilateral trade flows. A number of studies have applied gravity models to assessing trade flows among various countries in the world, including the Region.[23] In this study, we perform a new analysis applying the gravity model developed by Frankel (1997).

Based on this analysis, although total world trade flows of the CIS were significantly lower than their potential in the early 1990s (owing to the collapse of CMEA), over the course of the decade, the CIS countries steadily and sizably exploited their global trade opportunities. The bulk of these trade flows, as noted earlier, have been largely in the natural resources sectors. In contrast, the results suggest that

TABLE 2

The Region's Actual vs. Theoretical Trade Openness

Merchandise Exports plus Imports to GDP in PPP $

Averages	2003 Realization Ratios (actual/predicted by the model)
The Region	1.37
CIS	0.96
SEE	0.77
EU-8	1.33
The Region and Turkey	1.35

Source: Author's calculations.

the EU-8 and SEE countries largely maintained their pattern of total world trade flows during the same period.

Importantly, the "reconstitution" of a Russia-centric CIS trading bloc that has been taking place over the course of the decade is also clearly discernable in the gravity model empirical results. In contrast to the EU-8 and SEE countries, where the ratio of actual to potential trade among the countries within each of these two subregions declined over the 1994-2003 period, for the CIS countries, the comparable ratio steadily increased; that is, the ratio of actual to potential intra-CIS trade flows has been rising over time.

Interpretation of empirical results of openness and gravity models—both in the literature and in this study—must be done with care. In part this stems from the complexity of the reality that is being modeled econometrically. In particular, it is important to realize that institutional and policy-related variables do not likely play an exogenous role; rather, such variables are often endogenous and directly related to the level of trade. Some steps have been taken in this analysis to deal with this problem, but data availability limits the sophistication of the approach that can be taken.

Moreover, as is the case in almost all similar analyses in the literature, institutional and policy-related variables in such models have very strong—sometimes the greatest—explanatory power. This suggests that the most acute barriers to trade expansion may not rest in "fixed" factors, such as geography. Rather, trade performance may be more greatly influenced by actions taken (or not taken) at home. It is in this context that policy makers need to interpret these empirical results and recognize that behind-the-border reforms are likely to be critical in complementing trade-related policy actions if international integration of the Region is to deepen.

All this is not to suggest that improving most of the Region's countries' *trade* policy regimes is unlikely to induce greater international integration to facilitate increased growth. On the contrary, the evidence points to the importance of improving these countries' *behind-the-border* production structures and institutional regimes and to do so in concert with further reform of trade policies.

How Have the Region's Countries Opened Trade and Increased International Integration? The Role of Trade Policy

Many countries in the Region—either early on in the transition process or over time—have cut tariffs and reduced or eliminated non-tariff barriers. As a result, at present, the Region as a whole comprises economies with relatively liberal formal *trade policies*. By easing policy restrictions at the border, governments have shaped the incentive framework that affects trade flows. Today, the weighted average applied tariff rate on all goods for all of the Region's countries is 5.8 percent. These tariff rates compare favorably with those of developing countries at comparable income levels. Very few of the countries have maintained the patterns of trade control that characterized central planning. Nonetheless, some countries in the Region still maintain high tariffs and appreciable NTBs. This includes some Central Asian Republics and others in the CIS such as Belarus.

The basic reforms in the Region's countries' trade policies have taken place through three avenues: (i) *unilateral* trade policy reforms; (ii) *bilateral or regional* trade agreements; and (iii) *multilateral* trade commitments.

Virtually all of the countries have undertaken formal tariff reductions *unilaterally* as part of achieving national economic reform objectives rather than as a result of specific bilateral/regional or multilateral trade commitments. Importantly, much of this liberalization was carried out autonomously by the countries, albeit with the encouragement and support (and discipline) of the international development community in the early years of the transition. In comparison to developing countries of similar income levels, the Region's tariff protection of domestic industry and agriculture is on average lower, the extent of protection through nontariff barriers appears to be no greater, and there is less recourse to contingent protection. On the other hand, most countries in the Region have done little to encourage and have often discouraged exports. This remains a major item on the trade policy reform agenda.

All of the Region's countries are party to (sometimes several) *bilateral or regional* trade agreements—including free trade areas and customs unions—that have provided for reciprocal tariff reductions, preferential market access, and other forms of trade policy liberalization. Of course the most prominent example of regional trade liberalization is that provided through EU accession, which eight of the Region's countries completed in May 2004. Two more of the Region's countries (Bulgaria and Romania) are "EU accession countries" and one other (Croatia) is an "EU candidate country." (Turkey is also an "EU candidate country.") In Southeast Europe, most other countries are participating in a stabilization and association process that ultimately is expected to lead them to EU membership.

Myriad other regional free trade agreements or customs unions has also been forged, among them the 29 bilateral free trade agreements (FTAs) among the SEE economies and the various trade agreements within the CIS, such as the CIS FTA, the Eurasia Economic Community, and the Central Asian Cooperation Organization. The agreements in the SEE appear to involve greater mutual trade liberalization than those of the CIS. Both, however, are complex and are focused primarily on the exchange of trade preferences. The main challenges faced by both groups of countries are how to rationalize the large number of bilateral FTAs to regionwide agreements, as well as how to extend regional cooperation beyond preferences in merchandise trade, and include such matters as transit facilitation as well as liberalization of services.

To date, the majority of the Region's countries have liberalized trade policies *multilaterally* by becoming members of the WTO, with most of the others—all in the CIS—in various stages of the WTO accession process. Accession to the WTO has generally meant liberalized market access for the Region's firms in global markets and, conversely, significant reductions in NTBs, as well as adherence to internationally accepted rules-based disciplines for dispute settlement regarding dumping, intellectual property protection, and government procurement, among others. Market access is not a serious, generalized problem affecting most of the Region's countries' exports—especially in comparison to domestic, behind-the-border restraints to international trade. There are, however, serious market access problems in particular sectors stemming in part from extensive use of antidumping actions against transition economies, as well as developed countries' protectionist agricultural policies. Some of these market access problems will be addressed by WTO accession and hopefully by progress achieved in the ongoing Doha Round of WTO negotiations. In that regard, WTO accession is important in order to improve and secure market access abroad. However, it is even more important because it forces countries in the Region to strengthen their domestic institutional capacity to trade, introduce stability in their trade regimes, and lock in internal reforms.

Overall, for most of the Region's countries, large-scale liberalization of "first-generation" merchandise trade policies, including lower tariffs, reduction of NTBs, and eased market access, has been accomplished, resulting in greater openness. But for a few countries, such as Belarus, Turkmenistan, and Uzbekistan, even these "first-generation" trade-policy reforms are still needed. Yet even for the Region's countries that have already substantially liberalized, greater fine-tuning of merchandise trade policy is in order. There is still a large gap between bound and applied tariff rates in some countries, and in certain cases, for example Russia, tariff rate schedules are greatly dispersed, creating opportunities for discretion and corruption. There also remain disincentives to exporting, which results in lost opportunities for growth and job creation. In numerous instances, overlapping bilateral or sub-Regional free trade agreements incorporating complex rules of origin reduce clarity of trade rules, hindering commercial decisions by traders and investors. While preferential provisions of some of these agreements in the Region create trade, some also divert trade. Greater harmonization and consolidation of such agreements into a uniform agreement, such as the one being pursued among the SEE economies, would be highly beneficial.

How has increased openness to trade enhanced growth and reduced poverty in the Region? Trade performance is one of many factors that affect GDP growth, and through growth, the reduction of poverty. Trade performance in turn is affected, in part, by trade policy. The beneficial effect of trade policy on poverty via its effect on growth is, necessarily, more complicated. The transmission is indirect and manifests generally only over a relatively long term. At the same time, however, trade policy results in changes in relative prices, which will have a short-term impact on the welfare of the poor, by affecting their employment and income prospects as well as the prices of the goods they consume. Based on experiences of trade policy reform in developing countries, a great a deal of analysis has been carried out in recent years exploring the impact of liberal trade regimes on economic growth. The preponderance of empirical evidence from developing countries worldwide suggests that, on average, growth will be enhanced in the long run as a consequence of liberal trade regimes.[24]

As is the case elsewhere in the world, disentangling the linkages between trade and poverty reduction in the Region is complex. As is well known, there was, for several reasons, a massive increase in poverty in the Region at the onset of the transition.[25] Despite the fact that most of the Region's countries adopted early on (and have largely maintained) relatively liberal formal trade regimes and that, moreover, substantial progress in poverty reduction has been made in the Region in recent years, nevertheless, today, more than a decade after the onset of transition, widespread poverty persists in several the Region's countries, especially, but not exclusively, in Central Asia and the Caucasus.[26]

There have been some efforts to analyze through simulations the implications of specific trade policy reforms on poverty in individual countries in the Region. However, there is no aggregate assessment of the experience for the group as a whole. The individual countries for which assessments have been made are Bulgaria, Moldova, Romania, and Russia.[27] These analyses generally find that the effect of trade liberalization on the poor as a group would tend to be positive.[28] However, there is also evidence that trade liberalization would likely reduce the well-being of some people, at least in the short term, and some of these would be the poor, who can ill afford it.[29]

On the other hand, the absence of trade liberalization does not always translate into the poor becoming better off. The case of the slowest reforming countries—such as Belarus and Uzbekistan—is instructive in this regard. Although their declines in output and increases in poverty have been more limited than those of other countries in the Region, in part because of the maintenance of relatively closed trade regimes, they have nonetheless engaged in policies, such as the protection and state control of the cotton sector in Uzbekistan, which in fact have been adverse to the welfare of the poorest elements of society.

Although the assessment of the implications of trade reform on poverty in the Region's transition economies is sobering—in the sense that in the short run poverty will likely increase in certain segments of society—it is not inconsistent with the analysis in other countries worldwide. Retrospectively, greater exposure to trade may well have exacerbated poverty in the CIS countries. The situation was much better in EU-8 and SEE economies, however, probably because many of these countries quickly pursued policies that provided for greater flexibility in resource allocation. These policies permitted workers displaced by imports as well as labor force entrants to be employed in new labor-intensive activities; they also focused on facilitating exports. Thus, in the absence of effectively flexible product and factor markets, the adjustment to trade reforms in the CIS has been very protracted. In consequence, the "short run" for these countries may still be lingering.

There is a general consensus that, for the poor to gain from trade liberalization, actions that complement trade reform are needed. The main conclusions of individual country case studies—as well as cross-country econometric studies—that have looked at experiences with trade liberalization at the country level worldwide point to the importance of enhancing flexibility in labor markets and facilitating the flow of investment from sectors that are contracting to those that are expanding. In short, a policy of import liberalization alone is not sufficient to promote the strong trade performance that could be beneficial to output growth and indirectly to poverty reduction.

Overall, without open trade, the Region's transition to market economic systems could not have transpired. As illustrated in figure 9, as has been the case elsewhere in the world, trade and behind-the-border reforms in the Region have been mutually reinforcing. The economies that have had the most international integration have made more progress in implementing enduring domestic structural and institutional policy reforms and vice versa.

Beyond Trade Policy: The Pivotal Role of Behind-the-Border Reforms in the Region's International Reintegration

If international integration of the Region's countries is not solely the result of changes in trade policy at the border, which behind-the-border policies and market institutions have been most important in furthering integration and harnessing the ways in which trade can leverage growth and reduce poverty? The evidence from the Region suggests a multifaceted set of such reforms is key, notably: (i) ensuring competitively structured domestic markets, reinforced by a policy regime that disciplines anticompetitive behavior and attracts investment—from both domestic and foreign sources—as well as promotes sound governance; (ii) developing a modern infrastructure and related institutions for trade facilitation; and (iii) liberalizing private investment in and regulatory reform of backbone and network services sectors.

Domestic market competition, investment climate, and governance. Vibrant domestic competition and favorable conditions for business investment have played an important role in fostering the international

FIGURE 9

Trade Openness and Transition: A Mutually Reinforcing Relationship

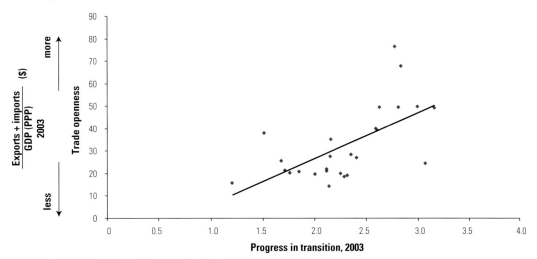

Source: World Bank, using IMF DOT data and EBRD Transition Index.

Note: Each diamond represents one country in the Region; Turkey is also included.

integration of the Region over the course of the transition. Among other pieces of evidence, statistical analysis covering all of the Region's countries between 1995 and 2003 suggests a positive association between a country's trade performance and its competition regime and the extent of FDI inflows as a percentage of GDP, after controlling for tariff levels.[30]

How do the underlying structural parameters that determine the intensity of competition in domestic markets relate to the extent of international integration by businesses in the Region? The countries that have relatively high barriers to entry for business start-ups or high barriers to exit for money-losing firms tend to be less integrated internationally and less able to capitalize on the reallocation of capital and human resources that stem from exposure to trade in order to promote growth and reduce poverty.

The empirical evidence suggests that in the Region's countries where the cost of *entry* is highest—measured, for example, by the time and resources required to get a new business license and registration—international integration is being hindered: import and export performance as well as FDI inflows are relatively low (see figure 10). Importantly, different factors appear to give rise to barriers to entry for domestically owned firms than for foreign-owned firms in the Region. Data collected through recent business surveys suggest that, while economic policy uncertainty, macroeconomic instability, high tax rates, and poor access to financing are seen as the most severe entry barriers by domestic firms, anticompetitive business behavior, contract violations, lack of skilled labor, and delays and complexities in obtaining business licenses and permits are the greatest barriers to entry for foreign firms. This finding suggests important policy implications for deepening integration in the Region: an emphasis on different reforms to reduce barriers to entry may well be needed if countries are to be more successful in attracting foreign investors.

There is abundant evidence over the course of the transition suggesting that where the *exit* of money-losing firms in the Region is likely to be impeded most is where there are "soft budget constraints" arising from two factors: (i) sizeable arrears in taxes, wages, utility payments, and payables to input suppliers, and (ii) subsidies to businesses. Recent data indicate that the incidence of arrears is greatest among firms in Central Asia and other CIS countries. Across firms of different ownership forms, arrears are least among firms with significant private ownership, including foreign-invested businesses. Significantly, there is new evidence that in the countries where arrears are largest, export performance (measured by the share of exports in

FIGURE 10

Export Levels and Cost of Entry in the Region, 2003

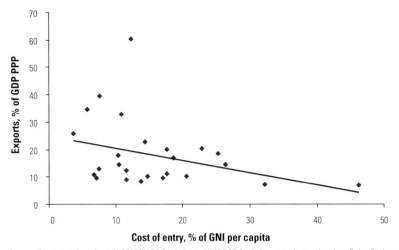

Sources: Export data based on UN COMTRADE Statistics and IMF DOT Statistics; cost of entry data from Doing Business (2004).

Note: GNI = gross national income. Each diamond represents one country in the Region; Turkey is also included.

GDP) is worst. This suggests another direct linkage between behind-the-border conditions and success in the Region in international integration: where there is a lack of domestic competition, firms' ability to penetrate foreign markets is dulled. Among firms in the Region, the incidence of direct business subsidies is greatest in the CIS, with average direct subsidies amounting to more than 20 percent of sales revenue.[31]

These findings corroborate the notion that the CIS countries have been much less vigorous than other countries in the Region in implementing measures to induce competitive restructuring and ownership change in the enterprise sector. Given that the CIS countries on average have privatized fewer corporate assets than other countries in the Region, it is not surprising that available evidence indicates that the least competitively structured markets in the Region are those that are heavily populated by state-owned firms, whereas the most competitively structured markets are those in which a greater number of de novo private and foreign firms operate. Firms' commercial ties with the state, for example through participation in "state orders" or public procurement, are also more extensive in the CIS countries, compared with other parts of the Region.

At the same time, from a sectoral perspective, the Region's markets in energy and natural resources as well as in infrastructure tend to have the fewest competitors. To be sure, this is due to the fact that it is in these sectors where state ownership is dominant and private sector entry is blocked. Of course on the other hand, in a small number of these sectors, such as the local distribution of electricity or natural gas, the scarcity of competitors may well be socially desirable due to inherent "natural monopoly" conditions; nevertheless, these market segments are decreasing in number worldwide as a result of technological changes. In contrast, markets in the trade and retail sectors, where private ownership is the rule and state ownership the exception, are populated by the greatest number of competitors.

An important linkage between the extent of behind-the-border competition and international integration of the Region's countries confirmed by empirical evidence is that firms that have achieved larger market shares in their domestic markets have a higher propensity to engage in exports. As observed above, this finding suggests that "competitive success at home breeds competitive success abroad," a conclusion consistent with the broader economics literature. Indeed, as new econometric analysis suggests, the Region's firms that have achieved relatively dominant market positions tend to be more profitable, holding constant other factors, including overall scale, ownership form, softness of budget constraints, and technological prowess.

Moreover, consistent with the evidence that less competition exists in CIS domestic markets are data indicating that, over the past decade, firms located in the EU-8 countries have exported to more numerous "new" markets than have firms in Central Asia and the Caucasus. By the same token, countries in the Region whose markets are more competitively structured—measured by the number of competitors—tend to have more firms integrating into global markets through outward direct investment than do countries where markets are less competitively structured; in addition, on average, foreign-owned firms located in "host" markets in the Region have more extensive direct investments abroad than do counterpart domestic firms.

Enhancing domestic competition in the Region's markets is thus likely to be an important element not only to enhance deeper international integration but also to capitalize on and leverage the economywide benefits that integration can engender. If this conclusion is correct, the implication for domestic policy makers is clear: in an increasingly globalized economy, where competition among countries for investment resources and international market share for business is ever more intense, steps to increase national welfare should focus squarely on policies to: reduce barriers to entry and exit; prevent restrictive and anticompetitive business practices; privatize incumbent state-owned firms where little or no rationale for public ownership exists; and take concrete steps to improve the climate for investment—from domestic as well as foreign sources.

Moreover, a central policy lesson from the experiences of the successfully reforming countries in the Region (and elsewhere in the world) is that governments should design reforms to improve domestic competition so that they are mutually reinforcing with international trade agreements and commitments. This will help to lock in such reforms, to ensure that greater integration fosters the competitiveness of businesses located behind the border and vice versa. This objective should be pursued at a variety of levels: globally through WTO accession; regionally through EU membership and other RTAs; or bilaterally through free trade agreements.

In pursuit of the goal of encouraging entry, the Region's governments also should work toward eliminating not only barriers to establishment of a business and the entry of new rivals, but also barriers to the ongoing challenges that businesses face behind the border on a day-to-day basis. Reducing "administrative barriers" for business start-ups and postestablishment operations is still an important "first-generation" reform for certain countries in the Region, largely in the CIS, but also in some SEE countries. For other countries in the Region, such barriers have either been largely implemented or are well into the process of being so. For these countries there is now the need for "second-generation" competition reforms—ones that actually deal with the fundamental challenges in the industrial structure of the national economy.

Although an increasing number of the Region's countries have sound competition laws, there is almost universally weak enforcement of these instruments. Thus, competition authorities in every country should have sufficient competencies to assess and penalize dominant firms' structures and behavior, as well as restrictive business practices that harm competition.

With respect to exit, the restructuring or liquidation of large loss-producing enterprises that take up resources and economic space have not been sufficiently facilitated—particularly, but not exclusively in the CIS—in part because sound legislation has not been implemented or because vested interests, including the politically well-connected, stand to lose. Developing an effective bankruptcy process is critical to improving the competitiveness of viable firms and to liquidating or reorganizing firms that are no longer commercially viable. This will strengthen creditor rights, which in turn will improve the climate for investment. Equally important, it will facilitate the reallocation of resources—human as well as financial—to engender greater flexibility in the economy, which is the key to ensuring growth as well as poverty reduction as the process of international integration continues.

Some of the Region's governments have extended preferential treatment to select market participants to encourage development of "strategic sectors." While such industrial policies need not be always harmful to economic development, depending on how they are designed and implemented (including their longevity), they can undermine the competitive nature of markets and ultimately distort the pattern and extent of a country's international integration. Although the opposition of political and vested interests may be considerable, government reform in various countries in the Region should focus on eliminating tax support, tolerance of arrears, subsidies, and distortionary investment or export incentives—not only to incumbent domestic firms but also to foreign entrants. The long-run net benefits to the domestic economy from the establishment of special export-processing zones or preferential tax concessions in the Region—as elsewhere in the world—may be limited, in part because such regimes can—but need not—result in enclave markets with limited positive spillovers to the rest of the economy and the creation of opportunities for corruption.

Related to industrial policy is the manner in which the Region's governments conduct their public procurement with, and grant contracts to, the "outside" business world. Adherence to WTO-based rules regarding government procurement that provide for open competition, transparent procedures, and nondiscriminatory treatment to domestic and foreign firms alike can be an important reform in minimizing existing distortions in international trade and investment in the Region and fostering international integration.

Weak governance and corruption are also critical behind-the-border impediments to the international integration of the Region's countries. At the end of the day, consumers pay higher prices as the costs of corruption are internalized into the final cost of internationally traded products or services. In addition, corruption affects the end user not only by increasing prices, but also by reducing the quality and diversity of available products and services.

Asymmetric information among market players caused by a lack of transparency in transactions negatively affects international exchange. To this end, it is important to investigate how the quality of domestic governance institutions relates to international integration. There is a statistically significant positive association between government effectiveness/quality of institutions and trade openness. Stated differently, countries that engage in freer trade tend to have better quality of institutions, which leads to better governance (see figure 5).

While progress has been made in some of the Region's countries regarding the establishment of relatively well-functioning, market-based legal institutions that facilitate resolution of domestic commercial problems associated with international trade and investment, in many countries this is an unfinished agenda item. There is throughout the Region a general lack of security in the commercial contracting process. Businesses—not only foreign, but also domestic—have "voted with their feet" and traded or invested elsewhere to get around this obstacle, but in so doing, there also has been a loss of efficiency in the transactions process and, ultimately, resources have been diverted from more productive activities.

Trade facilitation infrastructure and institutions. Integration into global markets will, over time, involve reform in trade facilitation and logistics. Meeting the behind-the-border trade-facilitation challenge places enormous importance on the need for setting priorities if for no other reason because of the resources often required. EU membership, for example, will make it possible to move goods freely between member states without the need to complete formal import and export documentation or pay import value added tax (VAT) or customs duties. But the harmonization and implementation of the EU's *acquis communitaire* require new member countries to make major improvements in their overall economic environment—both at the border and behind the border.[32] As countries in the Region—and the international donor community—decide on how best to deploy resources, a critical policy question arises: what is the relative impact of improvements in trade facilitation compared with gains from lowering traditional trade barriers, such as tariffs and quotas?

New empirical analysis provides one indication of the potential benefits of reform in trade facilitation. Estimates, on a global basis, suggest that improvements in four areas—port efficiency, customs regimes, regulatory policy, and information technology infrastructures—can lead to significant trade gains. The global analysis indicates that, for 75 sample countries, raising capacity halfway to the world average would yield a $377 billion gain to world trade.[33]

Region-specific work has been carried out, building on the global analysis, incorporating the indexes utilized for measuring trade facilitation development.[34] It focuses on simulation of improvements in trade facilitation in 15 countries in the Region (plus Turkey) which are fairly representative of the Region and comprise about 95 percent of the Region's GDP.[35] As a group, the countries exhibit a much lower level of performance in all four areas of trade facilitation relative to the EU-15. The analysis projects the gains in trade that could be realized in two situations: how would *intra-Regional* trade change if all of the Region's countries improved their capacities in trade facilitation and how would trade with the *rest of the world* change? In both cases it was postulated that the Region's countries would improve their trade facilitation capacities to half of the EU-15 average.

In the first case, the total estimated gain from capacity building in all four categories of trade facilitation would be approximately $94 billion in the Region. The country with the largest projected gains would be Russia, where trade flows would be expected to increase by $19 billion, and improvements in IT would contribute the most to those gains. Trade volumes of Lithuania, Poland, (as well as Russia), and Ukraine would rise more than 100 percent. Improvements in port efficiency would raise trade volumes significantly in Croatia, the Czech Republic, FYR Macedonia, Serbia, the Slovak Republic, and Slovenia. In contrast, improvements in IT would generate trade gains in Bulgaria, Hungary, Latvia, Lithuania, Poland, Russia, and Ukraine. Improvements in customs would yield the second largest trade gains.

In the second case, the total gains to the Region are estimated at approximately US$178 billion (see figure 11). This represents about 50 percent of the Region's trade with the rest of the world. Eighty-seven percent of the total gains to the Region are generated from the Region's own moves to upgrade infrastructure in ports and information technology, harmonize regulations, and improve customs.

Overall, the results demonstrate the importance of capacity building in trade facilitation in the Region as a means of strengthening trade ties globally—as well as fostering intra-Regional trade. Gains would be greatest from improvements in IT infrastructure and port efficiency. The results from the simulation suggest that the principal

FIGURE 11

Gains from Improving Trade Facilitation in Eastern Europe and the Former Soviet Union

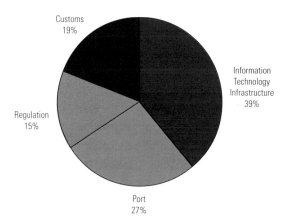

Source: Wilson, Luo, and Broadman 2004.

priorities should focus on port and IT infrastructure improvements, complemented by reforming customs and streamlining regulations.

Services sector liberalization and regulatory reform. An increasing number of countries in the Region—notably the EU-8 and, to a much lesser extent, SEE—have come to recognize that greater and more sustainable growth will come from liberalization of their services sectors. Indeed, in some of these countries the increased efficiency in the services needed for export production has been a contributing factor to the rapid expansion in merchandise exports, for example, the liberalization of Hungary's financial sector. At the same time, certain countries have embraced a strategy of boosting trade and investment in the services sectors in their own right and have experienced significant services export growth; these include, for example Croatia's and FYR Macedonia's software sectors. Other countries in the Region, however, typically the less developed ones in the CIS, still treat services as "nonproductive" activities, a legacy from the mindset during the era of central planning.

Policy developments (or the lack thereof) help explain the differences in services-related trade performance and FDI flows. In many FSU countries (with the exception of the Baltics), bureaucratic impediments, the lack of competition as a result of public or newly established private monopolies, and slow progress in privatization have impeded services trade and FDI. Most lagging are Belarus, Tajikistan, Turkmenistan, and Uzbekistan. As FDI is an important source of new technologies and know-how, and the cost and variety of services that are available in an economy are an important determinant of the competitiveness of firms, the greater service intensity is likely to help explain the differential growth performance among countries in the Region.

This proposition is supported by econometric evidence that assesses the links between investment, services sector development and economic growth using cross-country growth regressions. The analysis reveals the importance for economic growth of sound policies that promote the efficient functioning of the services sectors.

The reform challenges today are not as simple in many services sectors as they used to be, however. Scale economies and high sunk costs of investing in infrastructure or banking do not necessarily call for regulated monopolies. New technologies often make large fixed investment either reversible or allow for a separate role of service provision (for example, in telecommunications). The ensuing policy challenge is the need for achieving a balance between traditional regulation and the introduction of competition.

In the telecommunications sector, the EU-8 countries have reformed the most extensively, including significant private participation in service delivery, followed by Southeastern Europe. Regulatory reform, including rate setting and establishment of independent regulatory authorities, however, is still very much underway, with further progress required. In the CIS, fixed-line services are still quite underdeveloped, and state control and monopolies still prevail. Where privatization of incumbents has occurred in the CIS, its objective has often been the maximization of revenue. As a result, some private investors have been granted monopoly status for significant periods of time. Armenia, for instance, provided a Greek investor with a 15-year exclusivity clause.

In the banking sector, a similar pattern is observed. In the EU-8, the sector is generally characterized by only small shares of credit allocated through state-owned banks, high foreign participation, and stronger regulatory regimes. Evidence from these countries indicates that foreign banks have been contributing to the modernization of the sector. However, bottlenecks relevant to sustained financial development often persist in the legal framework (within the tax system, creditor rights, and, the bankruptcy code, for example). Banking markets in the CIS tend to be relatively closed, in both formal and informal aspects. In this regard, Belarus, in spite of its relative proximity to the EU in terms geographic location, is one of the least advanced countries, as are most Central Asian republics. Actual and potential limits on foreign participation (both economywide and in individual banks) play an important role, but bureaucratic impediments seem to play a more prominent role in inhibiting foreign participation; these include limitations on bringing in foreign staff, lengthy licensing procedures, financial repression, public ownership of dominant banks, and inadequate regulatory practices. In general, the banking sector in these countries suffers from weak capital bases and lack of confidence.

The picture is not very different in rail and road and rail transport. Progress in the reform of railways is greatest in the EU-8, with the SEE countries not too far behind. Estonia, for instance, has fully privatized its railway system, and network maintenance is carried out privately in the Czech Republic, Poland, and Romania. With few exceptions, such as Russia and Kazakhstan, the CIS countries have, by far, done the least to improve the policy framework for such services. Reforms in road transport are lagging behind the railway sector in most countries of the Region and private sector participation remains limited. Only some EU-8 and SEE countries, such as Croatia, Hungary, and Poland, have introduced private sector participation through toll roads. Success, however, has been mixed so far due to traffic diversion to alternative roads and high risks associated with private investment. Toll-based concessions in Hungary have therefore been converted into payments to the private investors via the public budget. This transfers traffic risk back to the state while maintaining the character of the public-private partnership.

The incentive to adhere to international trade commitments, especially the EU *acquis*, has been a key driver in bringing about behind-the-border liberalization and deregulation of the services sectors in the Region. Indeed, for the EU accession countries, the *acquis* sets a relatively strict policy framework for acceding countries to abide by in a short time with little flexibility. In contrast, countries without the prospect of EU accession have made much less progress on liberalization of services trade and FDI regimes, thereby lowering growth prospects. Emulating the liberalization that has been implemented by the other countries in the Region is therefore a priority, all the more so as the environment for FDI and investment generally is now much more competitive than it was at the beginning of the transition.

The WTO's General Agreement on Trade in Services (GATS) can be used as a substitute instrument to drive services reform. However, the evidence to date suggests that the countries that have joined the WTO have not made significant commitments on services. Moreover, WTO membership is not sufficient, in part because the disciplines currently imposed by the WTO are relative weak, relying on dispute settlement for enforcement. Most of the countries concerned are too small to make this attractive. The result is that the burden of reform of the services sectors falls squarely on individual governments. However, deeper regional cooperation among countries, as is beginning to occur in transport and energy in SEE, could help reduce implementation costs and increase the benefits of regulatory reform.

Overall, pursuing services sector reforms in the Region in parallel with merchandise trade liberalization and trade facilitation will facilitate entry by new firms and generate employment opportunities for both skilled and unskilled workers who currently may be employed by the public sector or in import-competing private manufacturing, or who are unemployed. Because certain services cannot be traded, despite the increasing impact of the Internet, obtaining access to new technologies and products by necessity must involve FDI in services. Many countries in the Region have proceeded to liberalize their FDI policy regimes to this end, but prevailing policies in many countries outside the EU-8 continue to be unduly restrictive.

Conclusion: Policy Agenda, Reform Linkages, and Action Plan

Market opportunities for trade in the world economy will no doubt continue to grow for the countries of Eastern Europe and the Former

Soviet Union as the transition process in the Region continues. But as the international economy continues to globalize, market competition from other regions in the world will only become stronger. This poses a challenge to the Region's countries' abilities to use trade and international integration as an engine for growth and the reduction of poverty.

Absent policy reforms, the differences in the present pattern of international integration within the Region could continue for the foreseeable future. So, too, could the countries' prospects for economic growth and prosperity, with the attendant emergence of a bifurcated region—punctuated by a bloc of relatively wealthy countries and a bloc of relatively poor countries. But the formation of the second bloc is not inevitable. Experience in the Region to date, as well as in other regions of the world, shows that success in this environment requires a *combination* of not only implementing sound, market-based trade policies and trade-related related institutions, but also establishing a strong, complementary behind-the-border incentive framework in the domestic sphere.

To this end, the study of which this *Overview* is a part develops a detailed set of such policy recommendations. Below, the principal recommendations that deserve priority attention are outlined, as well as linkages among the reforms and how they might best be sequenced in their implementation. The division of labor for the responsibilities of the various stakeholders with policy-making roles in furthering the Region's transition is identified, as is an action plan. A one-page Policy Matrix that summaries this information is found at the end.

Priority Policy Recommendations

Priority Trade Policy Reforms

- *WTO accession is a critical policy objective for the 10 countries in the Region that are not yet members.* Many countries in the Region—especially in the CIS and SEE—must *address the challenge of how to rationalize the large number of existing bilateral FTAs* and to *broaden them to include such matters as trade facilitation as well as liberalization of services.*

- In a few countries—notably in the CIS—trade is restricted by high average tariffs and nontariff barriers (NTBs). *These should be appreciably reduced over the medium term.*

- In several other countries, there is still a large gap between "bound" and "applied" tariff rates: *all tariffs in the Region should be bound closer to the level of applied tariffs.* Not doing so undermines the economic effectiveness of commitments already made in trade agreements.

- *Tariff regimes also should be simplified and the structure of rates reduced in dispersion*. This will make customs administration more transparent and improve the predictability of the trade policy regime. It will also reduce opportunities for discretionary behavior and incentives for corruption.

- Reforms are needed to reduce the bias in investment decisions across sectors and reduce disincentives for greater product diversification. To this end, *the widespread practice of discrimination against export activities that exists in many countries of the Region should be eliminated.*

- To improve market access, reforms are needed in developed countries' *extensive use of "nonmarket"-designated antidumping actions against the Region's economies*, as well as in their *protectionist agricultural policies*.

Priority Behind-the-Border Reforms

Enhancing Competition and Governance

- The Region's governments should work toward *eliminating fundamental economic and policy barriers to new business entry, especially structural conditions that engender a lack of or weak competition among businesses.*

- *Barriers to exit of commercially nonviable firms also need to be eliminated,* through reducing subsidies and eliminating the practice of tolerating arrears (with the government, banks, and among firms).

- *Competition authorities should be given greater authority and competencies to assess, penalize, and, if necessary, remedy dominant firm structures, as well as other forms of restrictive business practices, such as collusion, anticompetitive mergers and acquisitions, and predatory pricing.*

- Improving governance will require efficient institutions that facilitate effective resolution of commercial disputes. *Policies aimed at the simplification and cost reduction of formal legal procedures as well as bolstering out-of-court mechanisms will strengthen contract sanctity and property rights and improve the level of investor confidence in the Region.*

- Sound governance will also require mechanisms to ensure *greater transparency and accountability of public officials' conduct.*

Improving Trade Facilitation

- In trade facilitation institutions, the priority reforms are *to improve coordination among agencies, both within and across countries; simplify customs procedures; make customs codes and associated regulations, rules-based, transparent and commercially oriented, with proper incentives for employees; and introduce the use of IT into customs systems.*

- As to further development of trade-related infrastructure, the critical areas for improvement are *modernization of ports and IT capacity. Meeting this challenge will require continued privatization or private-public partnerships* to entice new investments.

Liberalization of Services Sectors

- *Deregulation of services* should be the rule rather than the exception, and include the implementation of market-reinforcing reform of regulatory procedures and rules, including rate levels and structures. Where regulation is warranted, *independent regulatory authorities* with the proper competencies and resources should be established.

- *Territorial restrictions or other artificial barriers to competition either within a services sector or across services sectors, for example for intermodal competition, should be eliminated.*

- *Private participation in the provision of services*, either through greenfield investment or privatization of incumbent providers should be encouraged. This will require reductions in or elimination of limits or prohibitions on trade and private investment (whether from domestic or foreign sources) in network services.

- Deeper cooperation between the countries in the Region, such as in *regional approaches to deregulation (or more efficient regulation) of utility services*, could help reduce implementation costs and increase the overall benefits of regulatory reform.

Enhancing Intraindustry/Network Trade through Greater FDI

- The policy regime governing FDI should be *brought in line with international best practice,* which typically includes (i) adhering to "national treatment" for foreign investors; (ii) prohibiting the imposition of new, and the phasing out of existing, trade-related investment measures (TRIMs), for example, local content measures; and (iii) providing for binding international arbitration for investor-State disputes.

- Actions should be taken that ensure *transparency, predictability, and consistency of the FDI policy framework across different levels of government* and different industry sectors.

Fostering Resource Flexibility in Markets

- To reduce poverty impacts from changes in prices and outputs engendered by trade flows, measures should be implemented to *promote labor mobility* (for example, enhancing wage differentiation and adaptability and improving the effectiveness of social safety nets) *and to facilitate the reallocation of capital* so as to encourage new investment and job-creating opportunities.

Linkages Between and Sequencing of Reforms

- Many of the *policy reforms are mutually supportive and reinforcing.* Their implementation should capitalize on these linkages. For example, further tariff reform will enhance import competition, which in turn improves efficiency and increases export penetration.

- *Some policy actions can be done in the short term.* These include, for example, increasing Technical Assistance (TA) for institutional capacity building in the poor CIS countries.

- *Other reforms require balancing "winners and losers" or the marshaling of significant resources. These necessarily can be implemented only in the medium term.* For example, a few powerful vested interests will stand to lose from competition as liberalization in certain services sectors takes place and these losses must be balanced against the diffused gains enjoyed by the public. Investment in the modernization of ports will require large amounts of capital resources.

- *Sequencing of reforms can be critical, not only for their proper implementation, but also to build public support for the reform program and to maintain its momentum.* For example, steps should be taken to enhance labor mobility and strengthen social safety nets while liberalizing imports, or regulatory reform and strong competition policy institutions should be established as services sectors are liberalized.

Division of Labor among Stakeholders

What the Developed Countries Can Do

- Improve market access for many of the Region's countries' agricultural products through reform of the EU's Common Agricultural Policy (CAP) program and of other related Organisation for Economic Co-operation and Development (OECD) programs; rationalizing the Generalized System of Preferences (GSP) program.

- Change the "nonmarket" designation for several of the Region's countries—primarily in the CIS—in enforcement of antidumping (AD) policies to reduce excessive, protectionist use of AD procedures.

- Facilitate WTO accession for current non-Members. The CIS countries have fewer trade preferences from the EU, for example. However, the solution is not enlargement of the number of such preferences. Rather, it is for these countries to liberalize multilaterally through WTO accession and thus enjoy the benefits of "most favored nation" (MFN) treatment.

What the International Community (Donors and International Organizations) Can Do

- Many countries in the Region, apart from the EU-8 and the two EU accession and EU candidate countries, are in need of technical assistance and capacity building to strengthen trade-related institutions and policy implementation and management, for example, in customs regimes; in WTO and EU accession; in the harmonization of regional trade agreements (for example the 29 bilateral FTAs in SEE); in competition policy; and in governance reform.

- Special attention for TA should be paid to the poor countries in the CIS, which "fall through the TA cracks." Because they are neither classified as "least developed countries" nor have realistic prospects for EU accession, they are often overlooked in qualifying for such assistance.

What the Region's Governments Can Do

- Virtually all of the remainder of the reform agenda will largely depend on the implementation efforts of the Region's countries themselves.

- In the area of trade policy, this would include tariff reductions; termination of NTBs; elimination of disincentives to exporting; pursuit of WTO accession; and rationalization, harmonization, and modernization of existing RTAs.

- The more challenging tasks will be the vigorous implementation of economywide behind-the-border reforms to: enhance competition and governance in domestic markets and foster greater flexibility in labor and capital markets; improve trade facilitation infrastructure and institutions; liberalize the services sectors and reform of associated regulation; and improve the climate to attract FDI.

SUMMARY OUTLINE OF PRIORITY POLICY RECOMMENDATIONS

Region's Subregion*	REFORM AREAS I. Trade Policy Regime		
	Reform	Principal Responsibility	Term
EU-8	As part of EU WTO negotiation objectives, push proactively to reduce global trade barriers in manufacturing, services, and agriculture in Doha Round	EU-8 governments	S/M
SEE	Bosnia and Herzegovina and Serbia and Montenegro: pursue WTO accession vigorously	BiH/SaM governments	S/M
	Bulgaria, Croatia, and Romania: align tariffs with EU/pursue EU accession vigorously	BG/CR/RM governments	S
	Bind *all* tariffs at applied levels	SEE governments	S
	Eliminate remaining NTBs; also policies that create anti-export bias	SEE governments	S
	Rationalize, consolidate, and modernize 29 bilateral FTAs	SEE governments, w donor TA	S
	Strengthen regional cooperation on Trade and Transport Facilitation (TTF) utilization (for example, customs)	SEE governments, w donor TA	M/L
CIS	AZ, BEL, KZ, RU, TAJ, TKM, UKR,UZ: pursue WTO accession vigorously	Named CIS gov'ts w donor TA	S/M
	Non-WTO members: appreciably reduce tariffs; bind at applied levels; simplify tariff design; and reduce dispersion of rates	CIS governments	S
	Eliminate NTBs; also policies that create anti-export bias	CIS governments	S
	Rationalize, consolidate, and modernize CIS/CAR (Central Asian Republics) RTAs and bilateral FTAs	CIS governments w donor TA	S/M
	Establish mechanism for regional cooperation on TTF development and utilization	CIS governments w donor TA	M/L
	Reform of nonmarket antidumping designation and reduce protectionist policies (for example, in agriculture)	EU, OECD, other governments	S

	II. Behind-the-Border Policy Regime		
	Reform	Principal Responsibility	Term
EU-8	Continue to strengthen competition policy agencies' competencies and resources; focus on anticompetitive conduct (for example, mergers, pricing)	EU-8 governments	S/M
	Continue to improve judicial-legal institutions to protect property rights and resolve commercial disputes and public administration reform to reduce corruption	EU-8 governments	S/M
	Continue modernization of TTF infrastructure	EU-8 governments	S/M
SEE	Increase removal of economic and policy barriers to entry and exit (for example, subsidies; arrears)	SEE governments	S
	Strengthen competition policy agencies' competencies and resources; focus on anti-competitive structures (for example., dominant firms) as well as on conduct (mergers; pricing)	SEE governments	S/M
	Ensure public procurement is transparent and open to foreign competition	SEE governments	S
	Improve judicial-legal institutions to protect property rights and enhance public administration reform to reduce corruption	SEE governments w donor TA	S/M
	Implement reforms for greater labor and capital mobility to enhance flexibility in factor markets (for example, wage-setting rules/social benefits/pension and corp. governance)	SEE governments	S
	Further develop TTF infrastructure (esp. ports and IT applications to customs)	SEE governments	S/M
	Cont. reg. reform, public-private partnerships, privatization/liberalization of services	SEE governments	S/M
	Establish mechanisms for regional cooperation in infrastructure/services regulation	SEE governments	S/M
	Improve FDI policy regime to comport w. int'l. best practice (for example, national treatment)	SEE governments	S
CIS	Systemic removal of economic and policy barriers to entry and exit (for example, subsides; arrears)	CIS governments	S
	Establish modern bankruptcy/insolvency institutions, including judges, trustees	CIS governments w donor TA	M
	Build independent competition policy agencies w. political teeth, legal basis, adequate competencies/resources: focus on anticompetitive structures as well as conduct	CIS governments w donor TA	M
	Establish judicial and legal institutions to protect property rights and resolve disputes	CIS governments w donor TA	M
	Reform public administration system to reduce corruption	CIS governments w donor TA	M
	Open up public procurement to competition—private domestic and foreign vendors	CIS governments	S
	Develop and implement reforms for labor and capital mobility for flexible factor markets (for example, reform wage-setting rules/social benefits/pension and corp. governance)	CIS governments	S
	Develop TTF infrastructure (esp. ports and IT applications to customs) and institutions	CIS governments	M
	Establish independent regulatory agencies; liberalize/deregulate services sectors	CIS governments w donor TA	M
	Privatize "nonstrategic" services sectors (for example, telecom, transport, energy, banking)	CIS governments	S
	Reform FDI policy regime to comport w. int'l. best practice (for example, national treatment)	CIS governments	S

Note: * Summary policy recommendations do not necessarily apply equally to all countries in each group. S=short-term (1-2 yrs); M=medium term (3-5 yrs); L=longer term (5-10 yrs). AZ = Azerbaijan; BEL = Belarus; BiH = Bosnia and Herzegovina; FDI = foreign direct investment; FTA = free trade agreement; IT = information technology; KZ = Kazakhstan; NTB = non-tariff barriers; OECD = Organisation for Economic Co-operation and Development; RTA = regional trade agreement; RU = Russian Fed.; SaM = Serbia and Montenegro; TA = technical assistance; TAJ = Tajikistan; TKM = Turkmenistan; UKR = Ukraine; UZ = Uzbekistan; WTO = World Trade Organization.

Notes

1. In addition to the 27 countries of Eastern Europe and the Former Soviet Union in (various stages of the) "transition" from Communism to capitalism specified below—which we define as "the Region"—the analysis in this monograph also covers Turkey. This coverage is done to be consistent with the World Bank Group's organizational definition of the "Europe and Central Asia Region" (ECA), which includes the full set of 28 countries. Therefore, when we use the term "Region" or "Transition countries," we are referring only to the group of 27 countries, and when we use the term "ECA" we are referring to all 28 countries.

2. Unless otherwise indicated, the most recent data cited pertain to year-end 2003. International Monetary Fund 2004.

3. See chapter 3.

4. Systematic cross-country analyses of international trade in the transition economies of Eastern Europe and the former Soviet Union have been surprisingly few in number (see, for example, EBRD 2003). This study contributes to the small stock of knowledge in several ways. First, the country coverage in the analysis is comprehensive, and is based on the most recent and complete trade data available for the entire Region. Second, previous studies of the Region's international integration have given only relatively limited attention to assessing behind-the-border institutions and how they interact with trade policies to affect the process of transition and the prospects for growth. Third, although the study's findings on whether or not the Region is overtrading or undertrading relative to countries in other regions mirror earlier assessments, the evidence presented that two trade blocs appear to be emerging is a new insight. Finally, the policy recommendations developed in this study are more comprehensive and given greater specificity than heretofore has been the case in analyses of this kind.

5. The statistical analysis undergirding this point is presented below.

6. The EU-8 are the Czech Republic, Estonia, Hungary, Latvia, Lithuania, Poland, the Slovak Republic, and Slovenia.

7. SEE comprises Albania, Bosnia and Herzegovina, Bulgaria, Croatia, FYR Macedonia, Romania, and Serbia and Montenegro. Kosovo, although part of Southeastern Europe, is not covered in the analysis.

8. The CIS includes Armenia, Azerbaijan, Belarus, Georgia, Kazakhstan, the Kyrgyz Republic, Moldova, Russia, Tajikistan, Turkmenistan, Ukraine, and Uzbekistan.

9. It is important to bear in mind that the data for the pre-1993 period are necessarily fraught with imperfections and based, in large part, on estimates precisely because market valuations were not made during that period.

10. In comparison, over the same period, exports and imports for the EU-15 roughly doubled; in Latin America and the Caribbean, exports rose two and one-half times while imports doubled, and in East Asia, exports and imports doubled.

11. Trade and investment in services are the focus of chapter 6.

12. With respect to the factor composition of the Region's merchandise imports, roughly the same broad dichotomy holds, but the differences across the country groupings is less significant.

13. This conclusion draws from data in chapter 4, which focuses on competition and governance.

14. The scatter plot indicates a positive association between greater international integration and less (perceived) corruption. These results are bolstered by multivariate regressions that indicate this positive association remains statistically significant even when the level of a country's development (measured by GDP per capita) is taken into account.

15. Chapter 5 focuses on trade facilitation and logistics.

16. Globally, the many industries where major parts of a production process have been internationalized include television and radio receivers, sewing machines, calculators, office equipment, electrical machinery, power and machine tools, typewriters, cameras and watches, among others.

17. Global production sharing and network trade are the focus of chapter 7.

18. Trade openness is calculated using GDP in purchasing power parity (PPP).

19. We also assess the Region's countries' trade performance based on the specific destination and origin of trade flows bilaterally (see below).

20. We note the likely critical role of institutional and policy factors as determinants of trade performance *apart* from income. Indeed, our estimation methodology employs an approach that uses institutional variables to combat endogeneity problems. The empirical analysis presented her draws from chapter 2.

21. These results are in line with earlier statistical analysis of the determinants of openness for the CIS countries alone by Freinkman, Polyakov, and Revenco, 2004. Statistical analysis carried out by the EBRD, 2003 on most of the Region's countries yields roughly similar conclusions to those of this study with respect to the CIS and SEE countries. However, the EBRD analysis does not find evidence of overtrading by the EU-8.

22. See Bergstrand 1985; Helpman and Krugman 1985; Deardorff 1997; and Feenstra, et al. 2001 for different theoretical justifications of the gravity model.

23. See Wang and Winters (1991), Hamilton and Winters (1992), Baldwin (1994), Frankel (1997), EBRD (2003), and Freinkman et al. (2004).

24. Over the 1990s, the proposition that trade openness is good for economic growth was advanced by a number of cross-country studies (Sachs and Warner 1995; Edwards 1998; Dollar and Kraay 2001). But the findings of some of these studies have been subjected to serious criticism: restrictiveness of trade policy is difficult to measure and the openness indicators used to show links to growth are not good proxies for trade policy. Institutional development, in a broad sense, has been proposed as a factor that explains both trade and output growth (Rodriguez and Rodrik 2001). Experience has shown that in the long term, countries need an open economy to sustain growth. But developing country experience has shown that, for a time, countries have expanded their exports and trade under different kinds of trade regimes. Some, like China, the Republic of Korea, and Taiwan (China), have done so under complex trade regimes that provided extensive import protection while at the same time providing very substantial stimulus to export industries. Successful implementation of such complex policies involving both import protection and

stimulus to exports places great demands on foreign trade policy design and trade institutions, which few developing or transition countries can meet (World Bank, 2002d). Others, like Chile, Hong Kong (China), and Singapore, have expanded exports while maintaining a very liberal regime on imports. Still others, like Mauritius and El Salvador, have used export processing zones to stimulate growth in trade, while maintaining substantial import controls.

25. World Bank 2005b and World Bank 2000b.
26. World Bank 2005b.
27. See Rutherford, Tarr, and Shepotylo 2004; Porto 2004a; Csaki et al. 2000; Csaki et al. 2002.
28. See, for example, Winters et al. 2004.
29. See, for example, IIED 2004; World Bank 2003c; Nicita 2004; Chen and Ravallion 2004.
30. The analysis is reported in chapter 4.
31. Importantly, these data show that the majority of such subsidies come from regional or local, rather than central, governments, making the task of their reduction more challenging.
32. The *acquis* is the body of EU legislation that candidate countries must adopt to become EU members.
33. Wilson, Mann, and Otsuki 2004.
34. Wilson, Luo, and Broadman 2004 which serves as the basis for the empirical core of chapter 6.
35. The EU-8 countries, the four EU candidates, and FYR Macedonia, Russia, Serbia and Montenegro, and Ukraine.

PART I

THE TRADE RECORD OF
EASTERN EUROPE AND THE
FORMER SOVIET UNION
SINCE THE TRANSITION

CHAPTER 1

Introduction

For centuries, greater openness to the international marketplace has been a central element of economic development. Nations that have integrated into the world economy through market-oriented means have benefited in a multiplicity of ways. International integration has meant greater export access for the output of a country's firms, leading to increased opportunities at home for business expansion, new investment, and job creation. Increased access to imports of goods and services has allowed consumers to enjoy greater choice of products, generally purchased at lower cost and often embodying new technologies that enhance product quality. Through greater exposure to interenterprise competition, enjoying the transfer of advances in technology, and adopting modern management practices, the businesses of countries that have vigorously engaged in the international marketplace have become more efficient and induced to keep pace with—indeed outperform—counterparts located in trading partners' countries. Indeed, country participation in international trade has borne much fruit: significant improvements in the allocation of domestic resources, enhanced productivity, and more rapid and sustained growth.

Since the early 1900s, the world economy has been increasingly integrating—the result of modern industrialization and significant technological breakthroughs that, among other consequences, have

51

led to steadily decreasing transportation and communications costs. In the past two decades, especially, the pace and extent of the world economy's integration have accelerated greatly, ushering in the age of "globalization." In fact, global trade has expanded much more quickly than has world output.[1] The process under way since the late 1980s of transition from command and control regimes to market-based incentives and institutions and open trade regimes in the countries of Eastern Europe and the Former Soviet Union (the Region) epitomizes in many respects the dramatic increase in international economic integration that recently has been taking place worldwide. Indeed, without the liberalization of trade policies that many of the countries in the Region have undertaken, the transition would not have taken place.

For decades, most of the 27 "transition" countries that currently make up the Region constituted in varying degrees an almost unified trade and investment bloc that functioned separately from, had dif-

BOX 1.1

Trade under Central Planning

Trade within the Council for Mutual Economic Assistance (CMEA)[a] was conducted as an outgrowth of the central planning process. Under the planning mechanism, in Eastern European countries and the Soviet Union, enterprises were given quantity targets, and prices played more of a redistributive than an allocative role. Imports and exports were coordinated, since trade according to market forces would be disruptive to the plan, given that prices were so misaligned with world prices. Foreign trade organizations (FTOs) were established and given a state monopoly on the import and export of goods, which prevented arbitrage on the distorted prices.

The essential feature of trade within the CMEA was the bilateral agreements (or protocols) between the countries that participated in the CMEA. These negotiated agreements obligated the two signing governments to export and import to each other specified quantities of particular goods. Trade was planned to be balanced in TR ("transferable rubles") and the prices of goods were denominated in TR. (The TR was an abstract unit of account, which had no physical presence.) Prices were negotiated at the government-to-government level. In principle, these negotiations started with a Western market world price of the product and were adjusted for quality. Then, starting from a list of import demands and export possibilities from its own economy, each government negotiated the most desirable package of imports in return for exports that would bilaterally balance its import demand. A bilateral surplus in TR with country A could not be used to finance a bilateral deficit with country B within the CMEA.

Enterprises were required by their governments to supply goods for the purpose of meeting the export requirement of the protocol. Upon delivery of the goods, the "commercial" bank account

ferent rules from, and had limited access to the rest of the international marketplace.[2] With the collapse of many of these countries' central planning systems—notably the Council for Mutual Economic Assistance (CMEA), which these countries used to manage international trade with the rest of the world and with each other—this isolated trade and investment bloc largely disintegrated; box 1.1 describes how trade was conducted under CMEA.

These changes were supported by or reflected in concomitant changes in political institutions and regimes. They included the fall of the Berlin Wall; the formal termination of the Soviet Union, which led to the establishment of 15 new independent countries; and the dissolution of Yugoslavia into 7 states. The result was a breakdown—at least de jure—of the many links between businesses and economic institutions located in the territories of the new states that, for the most part, were rooted in the political events of 1917 and in those during the decades immediately thereafter.

of the exporting enterprise was credited in domestic currency by its own central bank. Consequently, the customer of the producing enterprise was not a foreign firm in the conventional Western manner, but was so in a partial sense because its own government, which would pay the enterprise independent of the receipt of payment from abroad, made the final decision on which enterprises would have the right to export. Moreover, if the firm was obligated under the plan to provide goods for export, it felt justified in asking for subsidies if it incurred losses in production.

Each country had an exchange rate between the TR and its domestic currency, which implied a price in domestic currency for its exports in the CMEA. If the exporting enterprise received a higher price (in domestic currency) for exporting than the price of the good on the domestic market, it was taxed to equalize the export and domestic price. Similarly, it was subsidized if the export price was below the domestic price. Moreover, a similar tax and subsidy scheme for imports applied, so that enterprises were insulated from price differences on all trade within the CMEA.

Clearly the CMEA was not a customs union like the European Union (EU), since the essential feature of a customs union is that trade barriers are either eliminated or preferential within the union. Trade between firms in the customs union occurs according to decentralized optimizing decisions by firms, where the preferential tariff structure encourages intraunion trade. CMEA trade, however, consisted of trade that was quantity managed by the central government. The lack of access to hard currency by importers necessarily involved the government in the import decision.

Source: World Bank 1991.

a. The CMEA was founded in 1949 by Bulgaria, Czechoslovakia, East Germany, Hungary, Poland, Romania, and the Soviet Union. Cuba, Mongolia, and Vietnam joined in later years.

The ensuing transformation of these countries has increasingly unfettered production, investment, and consumption decisions by firms and consumers and engendered incentives for trade flows to be determined more by market forces than by administrative fiat. The result is an international reintegration of the Region—both on an intraregional and an extraregional (or global) scale. Today, the Region as a whole (albeit with some important exceptions, an issue that is one of the focal points of this study) is characterized as generally comprising formally open economies and exhibiting trade flows that are reoriented toward the "outside" world, especially, but not exclusively, toward the advanced countries of Europe.

In some respects, the pattern of integration that is emerging portends a return to a unified Eurasian continent, whose centuries-long economic history of international commerce dates back to the Silk Road. From this perspective, the Region's 70-year period of central planning, in which almost half a billion people were isolated from the world economy, can be thought of as an interruption. Yet, at the same time, "new" patterns of integration are being forged both among the countries in the Region and with those outside. The disintegration of the Region's isolated trade bloc has been followed by both reintegration and new patterns of integration.

Scope of the Study

As the world marketplace becomes increasingly globalized, much is at stake for the prosperity of hundreds of millions of people in Eastern Europe and the Former Soviet Union, now in their second decade of transition. Understanding the dynamics shaping the contours of international integration that have emerged—and will continue to emerge—in the Region is a crucial challenge for the medium-term development agenda, not only for policy makers in the Region's countries themselves, but also for their trading partners, the international financial institutions, the donor community, and the future of the world trading system as a whole.

Addressing this challenge raises several questions:

- Why have some countries in the Region integrated internationally more and in different ways than others, and what do the current trends suggest for the future? How have the commodity composition and factor intensity of trade changed among the countries over the course of the transition, and what are the implications for competitiveness and growth?

- How does trade performance in the Region today compare with that in other parts of the world? What factors in the Region are most important in conditioning the relationship between greater international integration, geography, policy reforms, and growth?

- Which policy reforms are likely to be most effective in using trade as a lever to enhance growth and reduce poverty in the Region? Is the Region's trade policy too restrictive? What is the impact of developed-country protectionism? What are the priority issues that policy makers in the Region should focus on, and what can the international community do to be most effective?

This monograph seeks to answer these questions.

Structure of the Study

The study is structured into four parts. Part I comprises this chapter—the Introduction—as well as chapter 2. Chapter 2 analyzes the nature and extent of the international integration of the Region's countries that has been taking place since 1993 and assesses determinants of countries' trade performance in a variety of dimensions. In so doing it develops the context and sets the stage for the analyses in the succeeding chapters of the study. As the chapter indicates, today, most of the countries in the Region are significantly reintegrated into the global economy, far more so than at the start of the transition. The Region now sends and receives more than two-thirds of its goods and services to and from the rest of the world.[3]

Despite these changes, chapter 2 also suggests that the pace, nature, and extent of the Region's international reintegration—both among the constituent countries and with the rest of the world—differ strikingly from the earlier pattern of integration and are characterized by pronounced variations across the Region. Two "new" trading blocs are emerging: one—a "Euro-centric" bloc—largely comprising the eight new members of the European Union (EU-8); and the other—a "Russia-centric" bloc—largely comprising the 12 Commonwealth of Independent States (CIS) countries.[4] Most of the seven countries in South Eastern Europe lie somewhere in between these two blocs, but are increasingly aligning themselves with the former.

As illustrated in the chapter, and as buttressed by further evidence presented in later chapters, these two blocs have begun to coalesce in terms of a variety of dimensions of trade and trade-related institutions and activity: direction of trade flows; commodity and factor intensity of trade; export competitiveness; development of trade facilitation institutions and infrastructure; extent of intraindustry trade and participation in global production-sharing networks through foreign direct investment (FDI); and the extent to which open trade enhances domestic competition and governance. Of course this admittedly sharp binary prism masks the more complex realities, and the chapter discusses the qualifications to this "two-bloc" paradigm. Still, taken together, the evidence suggests a clear trend that the countries in the Region that have integrated more effectively into international commerce are those that have also achieved a greater level of development. At the same time, the countries that have remained relatively closed and continue to embrace the old structures are less developed and are being left out of the global economy's modern "division of labor."

Chapter 2 closes with an analysis of how "open" the Region's economies have become. The econometric evidence suggests that the "reintegrated" Region has largely become a more "typical" region regarding trade, with most of the economies registering merchandise trade flows as a share of gross domestic product (GDP) largely in line with other countries around the world of comparable levels of development, size, and geographical characteristics (the only exception involves some of the SEE countries). In other words, the observed differentials in trade performance among the Region's countries are not rooted principally in artificial factors leading the countries to either "overtrade" or "undertrade."

To what extent do differences in trade policies account for the variation in trade performance observed among the Region's economies? How have the countries in the Region been opening their trade regimes? These are the questions addressed in part II, which comprises chapter 3. As that chapter indicates, at present, the Region as a whole comprises economies with fairly open formal trade policies, with average "Most Favored Nation" (MFN) tariffs for the Region's transition countries ranging from about 3 to 12 percent. These rates compare favorably with the tariffs of high-income developing countries worldwide. More important, much of this tariff liberalization was carried out autonomously by countries in the Region, albeit with the encouragement and support (and discipline) of the international development community in the early years of the transition. Notwithstanding the progress made in tariff liberalization, in many countries in the Region there still remain nontariff barriers (NTBs) and biases against exports.

In addition to lowering tariffs and NTBs, trade policy liberalization by most countries in the Region has also been proceeding along other lines. Beyond the eight countries in the Region that already have joined the European Union (on May 1, 2004), three other countries in the Region are poised for EU accession.[5] At the same time, a myriad of other regional trade agreements (RTAs) has been forged, including, for example, the 29 bilateral RTAs among the SEE economies. In addition, 17 countries in the Region have become members of the World Trade Organization (WTO), with most of the other 10 countries—all in the CIS—in various stages of the WTO accession process. Nonetheless, a few countries in the Region, such as Belarus and most of the Central Asian Republics, are still relatively closed and have yet to implement even basic trade policy reforms.

Overall, despite the level of openness achieved Regionwide, most countries in the Region are in need of "second-generation" trade policy reforms. Reducing trade protectionism thus remains a priority on the agenda for the Region, and chapter 3 closes with a list of policy recommendations to that end. These focus on, among other things, further tariff reform, elimination of NTBs and disincentives to exporting, aggressive pursuit of multilateral liberalization, and rationalizing and modernizing RTAs.

The upshot of the analysis in part II is that, without open trade, the Region's transition to market economic systems would not have transpired. However, trade liberalization is only a necessary and not a sufficient policy reform to enhance international integration. Indeed as part III, which comprises chapters 4, 5, 6, and 7, demonstrates, the countries in the Region that have pursued *both* trade policy reforms and complementary domestic structural and institutional reforms (the so-called "behind-the-border" reforms) have been the most effective in leveraging greater international integration into more rapid growth. The critical behind-the-border challenges that need to be addressed in most of the Region's countries are the focus of part III.

Chapter 4 concentrates on the ways in which international integration is influenced by the extent of domestic interenterprise competition, the state of the national business climate, and the institutions and incentives for sound governance. Using new firm-level survey data, numerous case studies of businesses located in the Region, and other sources, the chapter shows how high barriers to entry and exit, unchecked market dominance by incumbent firms, excessive state involvement in the commercial business sector through subsidies and other forms of "soft budget constraints," and weak governance and protection of property rights can impede international integration and reduce the ability for the countries of the Region to capitalize on the efficiency and productivity growth effects of trade.

As the chapter indicates, there is a "two-way street" between increased trade openness and domestic structural reforms that bring about a competitive business environment and good governance. The countries in the Region that have integrated substantially into the world economy, especially through commitments under international trade agreements, have been the most effective in "locking in" hard-won domestic institutional reforms, with the result that they exhibit more vigorous interenterprise competition and greater discipline to adhere to the "rule of law." At the same time, evidence presented in the chapter suggests that the more competitive the domestic economy, the greater the ability of firms to penetrate foreign markets and thus integrate internationally; in other words, success at home breeds success abroad. Chapter 4 closes with a set of policy recommendations that emphasize reforms that could enhance competition and governance in the Region's markets so as to help leverage the effects on growth of increased trade flows.

The challenges to enhancing trade flows of the Region's countries where underdeveloped national trade facilitation infrastructure networks and weak related institutional capacities, such as in customs, remain, is the focus of chapter 5. The chapter describes in detail the extent and nature of the differences among the EU-8, the SEE, and the CIS in terms of the development of such infrastucture and institutions. The core of the chapter is a simulation analysis of the gains to trade that would arise from improvements in trade facilitation capacity and institutions within the Region. The empirical results suggest there would be significant gains if the Region's countries made improvements that brought the quality and capacity of their trade facilitation systems up to 50 percent of the current average EU-15 level. Although a common overall agenda for reform across the Region would include streamlining and reforming customs services and border clearance procedures; improving capacity to meet international standards; and investing in infrastructure, especially in ports and transport and telecommunications networks that facilitate trade, the empirical evidence presented in chapter 5 shows that the priorities for reform differ significantly across the Region.

The topic on which chapter 6 concentrates is the crucial role played by domestic services sectors in fostering international integration, both through trade and investment in services per se, as well as the ways in which the regulatory and ownership regime that governs domestic services sectors affects trade in goods. While an increasing number of countries in the Region—notably the EU-8 and, to a much lesser extent, most SEE[6] countries—have come to recognize that greater and more sustainable growth will come from liberalization of their services sectors, other nations in the Region—typically the less-developed ones in the CIS—still treat services as "nonproductive" activities, a legacy from the mind-set during the era of central planning.

Empirical evidence presented in the chapter suggests that policy developments (or the lack thereof) help explain the differences in services-related trade performance. However, the reform challenges today are not as simple in many services sectors as they used to be. Scale economies and high sunk costs of investing in infrastructure or banking do not necessarily call for regulated monopolies. New technologies often either make large fixed investment reversible or allow for a separate role of service provision (for example, in telecommunications). The ensuing policy challenge is the need for achieving a balance between traditional regulation and the introduction of competition. The chapter concludes with an assessment of the roles played by international trade commitments, especially the EU *acquis* and WTO accession, in bringing about behind-the-border liberalization and deregulation of the services sectors in the Region and makes recommendations for reform.

Chapter 7 focuses on the ways in which attracting multinational corporate investment into the national economy through FDI can affect the Region's countries' abilities to participate in high value added global production-sharing networks and intraindustry trade. Such trade, an outgrowth of the increasing globalization of the world economy and the fragmentation of production processes, is changing the traditional economic landscape of interindustry trade facing the nations, industries, and individual firms in the Region, as it is in much of the rest of the world.

To this end, chapter 7 analyzes the characteristics of "buyer-" and "producer-driven" networks and the degree to which countries in the Region have been involved in network trade. The analysis shows that the countries that have experienced the largest FDI inflows have also seen the largest increase in exports of network products, components, and parts. However, there is significant heterogeneity within the Region between those countries that have been able to be active in "buyer-driven" production chains versus those that are involved in lower value added "producer-driven" supply chains and those that are not involved in network trade at all. Chapter 7 concludes with a discussion of the policy implications of how the different performances in terms of network trade can be attributed to the large variation in the amount of FDI attracted by different countries in the Region and recommends actions that the countries can undertake to improve this increasingly important aspect of trade performance.

Absent certain policy changes—which are the focus of this study— the differences in the present patterns of international integration of the Region's countries are likely to continue for the foreseeable future and with them their influence on growth and poverty reduction in the Region. Part IV is the study's conclusion, which contains chapter 8. This chapter summarizes the principal policy recommendations that were detailed in the individual chapters. Although many of the countries in the Region have achieved much in the way of formal liberalization of their trade policy regimes, a number of important reforms are still needed in this area. Yet, in light of the study's conclusion that reform of trade policies is necessary but not sufficient to ensure sustainable growth, there is, not surprisingly, a significant unfinished behind-the-border reform agenda. For both areas, chapter 8 discusses the interrelationships, sequencing, and priorities among the suggested reforms. There is also an outline of a "reform action plan" and a "division of labor" for the various stakeholders, including the international donor community, the developed countries, and the Region's countries themselves, to use in implementing the reforms. The chapter closes with a policy matrix, which briefly summarizes the policy recommendations.

Endnotes

1. See, for example, International Monetary Fund 2004.
2. In addition to the 27 countries of Eastern Europe and the Former Soviet Union in "transition" from Communism to capitalism listed below— which we define as "the Region"—the analysis in this monograph also covers Turkey. This coverage is done to be consistent with the World Bank Group's organizational definition of the "Europe and Central Asia Region," which includes the full set of 28 countries. When we use the term "transition countries," we are referring only to the group of 27 countries.
3. EBRD 2003.
4. The EU-8 are the Czech Republic, Estonia, Hungary, Latvia, Lithuania, Poland, the Slovak Republic, and Slovenia. SEE comprises Albania, Bosnia and Herzegovina, Bulgaria, Croatia, FYR Macedonia, Romania, and Serbia and Montenegro. Kosovo, although part of Southeastern Europe, is not covered in the analysis. The CIS includes Armenia, Azerbaijan, Belarus, Georgia, Kazakhstan, the Kyrgyz Republic, Moldova, Russia, Tajikistan, Turkmenistan, Ukraine, and Uzbekistan.
5. Bulgaria and Romania are "EU accession countries"; Croatia is an "EU candidate country." Turkey is also an "EU candidate country."
6. However, as shown below, services trade has grown fastest in the Region in some SEE countries.

CHAPTER 2

Trade Patterns and Performance of Eastern Europe and the Former Soviet Union since the Transition

Introduction

This chapter documents and assesses the trade patterns and performance of the countries of Eastern Europe and the Former Soviet Union over the course of the transition. The analysis focuses on not only the historical evolution but also the emerging trends of the extent, nature, and direction of international integration in the countries of the Region.

The Region's trade flows are examined from several perspectives: by geography, including intra-Regional as well as global dimensions; by product and sector composition, including primary commodities, manufacturing products, and other industrial sectors, including services; and in terms of labor, capital, and other factor intensities. The analysis covers both trade in goods and services and, to the extent of its impact on trade, foreign direct investment. The data reveal the two "trading blocs" emerging in the Region—one Euro-centric and the other Russia-centric—which manifest themselves along several dimensions of trade flows and other significant aspects of trade-related activity.

The chapter also investigates how the openness of the trade flows of the countries in the Region—both in goods and services—has evolved. Our metric for trade openness is "output-based" (in the next chapter we assess trade openness from the policy [or "input-based"] perspective). We explore how the extent of a country's trade openness compares with that of other countries and regions in the world. This is done by estimating econometrically the determinants of merchandise trade flows, on both multilateral and bilateral bases, using an "openness model" and a "gravity model," respectively. The empirical evidence suggests that most of the economies in the Region today register merchandise trade flows as a share of GDP largely in line with other countries of comparable levels of development, size, and geographical characteristics around the world.

Taken together, the evidence suggests a clear trend that the countries in the Region that have integrated more effectively into international commerce are those that have also supervised greater economic development. At the same time, the countries that have remained relatively closed and continue to embrace the old structures have lower national incomes and are being left out of the global economy's modern "division of labor."

The chapter concludes by highlighting the key factors likely to influence the extent to which the Region's trade performance can leverage growth in the future. Trade policy can play only part of the role. Equally, if not more, important will likely be behind-the-border policies and institutions that promote vigorous domestic interenterprise competition and sound governance; flexibility in factor markets that will facilitate labor and capital mobility as market conditions evolve as a result of changes in trade flows (as well as other factors); well-developed trade facilitation systems; vibrant services sectors open to international trade and investment; and FDI flows that provide links to global production networks. This sets the stage for the more detailed discussion of these factors that is the focus of subsequent chapters.

It is important to bear in mind that the data on this Region for the pre-1993 period are necessarily fraught with imperfections. They are based in large part on estimates because market valuations—by definition—did not exist under central planning (see box 2.1). Therefore, where there is a paucity of economically meaningful data, the focus is necessarily on the last decade and, in some cases, on even more recent periods.

Regional Dichotomy in the Growth of Merchandise and Services Trade Flows

Trends in Merchandise Trade

Merchandise trade flows of the countries in the Region over the years since the start of the transition have grown overall, but have exhibited

BOX 2.1

Quality of Foreign Trade Statistics for the Region

The statistics on foreign trade issued by the Soviet Union were always distorted. In the 1980s the USSR Goskomstat estimated trade volumes based on information collected from enterprises and trade organizations about the destination of their shipments to other Soviet republics and the rest of the world. Foreign trade transactions were then recorded in valuta rubles at the official exchange rate, set for a long period at $1.70 per valuta ruble, which grossly overvalued the ruble. Little had changed in the system by 1990. The subsequent switch to world prices and market exchange rates, starting in 1991, resulted in the gross overestimation of the contraction of Soviet trade.

The breakup of the Soviet Union in late 1991 had disastrous effects on the quality of the already shaky statistical information on trade. Enterprises stopped reporting because they were either unable or unwilling to do so, resulting in serious underreporting, especially of imports. New enterprises sprang up to conduct foreign trade, and their transactions were never recorded. High inflation rates and rapidly depreciating market exchange rates made it difficult to estimate changes in the volume of trade. Capital outflows led to overinvoicing of imports and underinvoicing of exports. Mirror statistics were used to estimate trade with the rest of the world. Even the mirror statistics were seriously flawed because of misreporting of transshipments, especially of energy: in 1992, Latvia's biggest export to Organisation for Economic Co-operation and Development (OECD) countries was reported to be oil, although the country produces none; for a long period in the 1990s, Turkmenistan's exports of natural gas were attributed to Russia, since its natural gas is transported through pipelines to Russia and commingled there with Russian natural gas.

The problems were greater in estimating trade among the CIS countries. Until 1994, customs controls among the countries were not in place throughout their borders; a great deal of trade was conducted in barter either through formal "interstate trade" agreements or privately, and the prices charged by various countries, especially by Russia, for energy exports varied significantly from each other and from the world price.

Accurate information on trade flows was critical to estimating financing needs by the International Monetary Fund (IMF) and the World Bank, the institutions entrusted by the international community to play a leading role in assisting with CIS transition. In the World Bank, the work was undertaken by a small statistical unit led by a Lithuanian statistician. The focus was on getting better estimates of volumes and prices of trade transactions among the CIS members in order to estimate net trade positions and changes in the terms of trade faced by many CIS countries as a consequence of moving trade to international prices.

This work yielded, among other things, estimates of trade among the countries of the Former Soviet Union and total trade, in the period 1990–1994, valued at the implicit exchange rates used in the barter transactions that governed trade among many of these countries (except the

(Box continues on the following page.)

BOX 2.1 (continued)
_____

Baltics). It also yielded intra-CIS trade valued in constant 1990 ruble prices, recognizing that until 1994, the bulk of the trade among the CIS was denominated in rubles. These analyses provide several measures of the great overestimation of the reduction in foreign trade, using the official dollar exchange rates, reported in table 2.1. Using the official exchange rates, intra-CIS
trade declined by 90 percent between 1991 and 1992, but "only" about 25 percent using implicit exchange rates or valued in constant rubles. At the same time, using these estimates for
intra-CIS trade gives a different picture of total CIS trade flows over time: using the official rates,
total CIS trade hit bottom in 1992 and rose thereafter. Valuing the intra-CIS trade at the prevailing implicit exchange rates results in total trade declining through 1994 and rising after that.

Source: Belkindas and Ivanova 1995.

a highly heterogeneous pattern, both over time and across subregions.
Table 2.1 and figure 2.1 present the latest, most complete data available on merchandise exports and imports—in absolute value and as a
proportion of GDP—for the Region over the period 1990–2003.

The data illustrate clearly the well-known collapse of trade that
occurred before 1993 in the aftermath of the breakup of CMEA and the
related command and control institutions that governed international
transactions in the transition countries. Among the three large groups
of countries that are the main focus of this monograph—the EU-8, the

TABLE 2.1
The Region's Merchandise Trade Flows, 1990–2003

Group	Total trade (goods, $ millions)						
	1990			1993			
	Exports	Imports	Balance	Exports	Imports	Balance	
CIS	400,600	412,924	−12,324	89,791	76,001	13,790	
SEE	33,405	22,483	10,922	17,804	12,381	5,423	
EU-8	57,697	62,419	−4,722	62,330	49,669	12,661	
EU-15	1,370,890	1,538,964	−168,074	1,319,720	1,394,886	−75,166	
LAC	128,325	105,171	23,154	160,864	185,752	−24,888	
MENA	171,789	131,342	40,447	151,656	151,758	−102	
Africa	38,172	38,437	−265	34,360	40,968	−6,608	
East Asia	698,293	527,224	171,069	949,419	663,356	286,063	
South Asia	27,361	38,871	−11,511	33,917	39,980	−6,063	
Memo Items							
Region	434,005	429,283	4,722	429,372	442,033	−12,661	
CIS less Russian Fed.	193,073	215,983	−22,910	30,139	32,355	−2,216	
Turkey	13,384	23,147	−9,763	15,346	29,355	−14,009	

Sources: IMF DOT statistics; data for CIS 1990–93 from Michalopoulos and Tarr 1994.

SEE, and the CIS—the CIS countries experienced the deepest decline in merchandise trade flows as a percentage of GDP. Today, on an aggregate basis, all of the countries in the Region generate a level of merchandise exports as a share of GDP that is higher than it was in 1993. The same is true for imports, except for the SEE countries.

For the Region as a whole, trade flows in 2003 (in dollar value and in real terms) had grown significantly since 1993; exports almost tripled and imports increased by a factor of two and one-half. In comparison, over the same period, exports and imports for the EU-15 roughly doubled; in Latin America and the Caribbean (LAC), exports rose two and one-half times while imports doubled; and in East Asia, exports and imports doubled.

Growth in trade flows was greatest for the EU-8, where exports and imports increased by a factor of 3.6 and 4.1, respectively. The CIS is at the other end of the spectrum: exports and imports expanded by a factor of 2.1 and 1.5, respectively. In between is SEE, where exports grew by three and one-half times and imports increased 2.7 times.

Another perspective is provided by examining how the share of world trade accounted for by the countries of the Region—either as an entire region or in terms of various subgroupings of countries—has evolved since the advent of the transition. The data in table 2.2 and figure 2.2 illustrate that the overall Region generated a significantly large increase in the world share of exports and imports. The rate of increase in the Region's share of world exports (almost 39

Total trade (goods, $ millions)								
1996			2000			2003		
Exports	Imports	Balance	Exports	Imports	Balance	Exports	Imports	Balance
119,098	84,027	35,071	144,904	69,588	75,316	191,649	113,068	78,581
29,521	19,156	10,365	36,247	22,482	13,765	62,654	35,673	26,981
112,272	86,784	25,488	149,583	123,230	26,353	224,483	200,670	23,813
1,899,930	1,956,314	−56,384	2,286,920	2,291,360	−4,440	2,896,280	2,800,565	95,715
262,891	275,243	−12,352	371,007	396,929	−25,922	400,782	387,629	13,153
211,393	175,149	36,244	302,294	199,883	102,411	342,013	300,517	41,496
51,177	49,496	1,681	88,402	78,396	10,006	110,046	112,170	−2,124
1,306,000	1,015,084	290,916	1,612,140	1,134,332	477,808	1,882,730	1,366,085	516,645
49,557	62,189	−12,632	63,438	78,826	−15,388	84,975	102,689	−17,714
379,430	404,918	−25,488	342,119	368,472	−26,353	267,219	291,032	−23,813
35,119	39,523	−4,404	41,906	35,735	6,171	60,195	56,391	3,804
23,100	42,462	−19,362	27,769	54,502	−26,733	47,255	69,458	−22,203

FIGURE 2.1

The Region's Merchandise Exports and Imports as a Share of GDP, 1994–2003

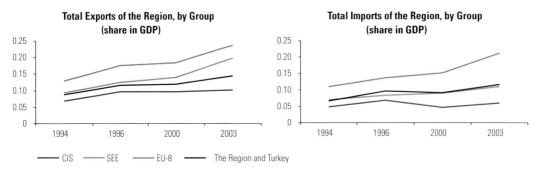

Source: IMF DOT statistics.

Note: Gross domestic product (GDP) in purchasing power parity (PPP).

percent) was considerably larger than that of its imports (about 23 percent).

The data bear out quite strikingly that, while the share of world exports generated by each of the three country groupings increased between 1993 and 2003, there is a great deal of variation. The CIS countries have performed the worst: the rate of increase in their collective share of world exports over the period was only 5 percent. However, if Russia is netted out, the CIS share of world exports has

TABLE 2.2

Shares in World Trade of the Region's Countries, 1990–2003

| Group | Share of world merchandise trade (%) | | | | | | | | | | Rate of increase (decrease) in share change (%) 1990–2003 | |
| | 1990 | | 1993 | | 1996 | | 2000 | | 2003 | | | |
	Exports	Imports	Exports	Imports	Exports	Imports	Exports	Imports	Exports	Imports	Exports	Imports
CIS	11.9	11.8	2.4	2.0	2.3	1.6	2.3	1.1	2.6	1.5	5.2	−27.9
SEE	1.0	0.6	0.5	0.3	0.6	0.4	0.6	0.3	0.8	0.5	70.5	27.5
EU-8	1.7	1.8	1.7	1.3	2.1	1.6	2.3	1.9	3.0	2.6	77.5	95.9
EU-15	40.8	44.0	35.7	37.0	36.0	36.5	35.9	34.7	38.7	36.0	8.2	−2.6
LAC	3.8	3.0	4.4	4.9	5.0	5.1	5.8	6.0	5.4	5.0	22.8	1.2
MENA	5.1	3.8	4.1	4.0	4.0	3.3	4.7	3.0	4.6	3.9	11.2	−4.0
Africa	1.1	1.1	0.9	1.1	1.0	0.9	1.4	1.2	1.5	1.4	57.9	32.8
East Asia	20.8	15.1	25.7	17.6	24.8	18.9	25.3	17.2	25.1	17.6	−2.2	−0.1
South Asia	0.8	1.1	0.9	1.1	0.9	1.2	1.0	1.2	1.1	1.3	23.5	24.6
Region	14.6	14.2	4.6	3.7	4.9	3.5	5.2	3.3	6.4	4.5	38.9	22.7
CIS less Russia	5.8	6.2	0.8	0.9	0.7	0.7	0.7	0.5	0.8	0.7	−1.5	−15.5
Turkey	0.4	0.7	0.4	0.8	0.4	0.8	0.4	0.8	0.6	0.9	51.8	14.7

Sources: IMF DOT statistics; data for CIS 1990–93 from Michalopoulos and Tarr 1994.

FIGURE 2.2

Shares in World Merchandise Trade of the Region's Countries, 1990–2003

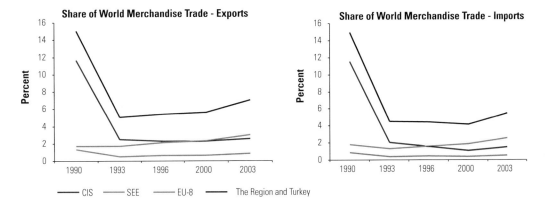

Sources: IMF DOT statistics; data for CIS 1990–1993 from Michalopoulos and Tarr 1994.

actually declined. The rates of increase in the world share of exports of the SEE and the EU-8 economies were virtually identical (71 percent and 78 percent, respectively).

The pattern that emerges on the import side is more mixed. In contrast to the other groupings in the Region, where the share of world merchandise imports rose during 1993–2003, the level of imports to the CIS as a share of world imports declined overall, and did so at a rate of approximately 28 percent. (Netting out Russia reduces this rate of decline to 15.5 percent.) The most advanced countries in the Region, the EU-8, registered the greatest increase in the share of world imports—their share rose almost 96 percent.

Trends in Trade in Services

Services industries were accorded low priority under central planning. Indeed, in many cases they were not considered "productive" activity. However, the increasingly globalized marketplace that is characterized by rapid technological advances has changed things. The services sectors have begun to emerge as a dynamic force in economic growth in an increasing number of counties in the Region. Especially in recent years, telecommunications, transportation, and energy services, among other network industries, as well as banking, are examples of services sectors that have been core targets of domestic reform in some countries. As in other regions of the world, international trade (and investment) in such services sectors also has begun to increase.[1]

Table 2.3, figure 2.3, and annex table 2.1 detail the trends in services trade in the Region based on the most complete data currently available. Although the tables contain some data beginning in 1990, because of the lack of any meaningful data on services in the CIS in the early 1990s, the focus of our discussion is on the period beginning in 1993. The growth in the value of services exports and imports for the Region in 1993–2003 significantly exceeds other regions, including Latin America and the Caribbean, the Middle East and North

TABLE 2.3

The Region's Trade in Services: Exports and Imports

	Export value of services ($ billion)							
	1990	1991	1992	1993	1994	1995	1996	
CIS	n.a.	n.a.	n.a.	n.a.	12	15	20	
SEE	1	1	2	4	5	5	6	
EU-8	6	6	10	16	21	29	31	
Region	1	1	2	4	17	20	27	
EU-15	372	384	435	408	421	495	523	
LAC	31	32	36	38	42	44	46	
MENA	23	23	28	29	30	32	34	
Africa	11	11	11	12	11	13	13	
East Asia	99	108	123	138	167	200	221	
South Asia	7	8	8	8	10	11	12	
	Import value of services ($ billion)							
	1990	1991	1992	1993	1994	1995	1996	
CIS	n.a.	n.a.	n.a.	n.a	17	24	23	
SEE	1	1	2	3	4	5	5	
EU-8	5	5	8	13	15	20	22	
Region	n.a.	n.a.	n.a.	n.a.	21	28	28	
EU-15	349	362	421	395	411	484	506	
LAC	36	39	44	49	54	56	58	
MENA	48	69	63	57	49	50	57	
Africa	20	21	21	22	22	25	25	
East Asia	145	153	172	188	220	272	294	
South Asia	10	10	11	11	13	16	17	

Source: IMF balance of payments statistics.

Note: n.a. = not available.

Africa (MENA), East Asia, and South Asia. However, and more important, within the Region there are significant differences. Services trade flows—whether in terms of exports or imports—grew fastest in the SEE countries over the 1993–2003 period, followed by the EU-8. In contrast, the CIS economies' services sectors remained largely closed to international trade. This is likely due to the fact that their services sectors are heavily burdened by regulation, which provides protection from the competitive pressures that accompany exposure to international trade.

In terms of services exports, the growth in value over the period for the overall Region (about 22 percent) was about quadruple the growth of services exports for the next-fastest-growing services-export-comparable region—East Asia (at 5.5 percent). The growth in the value of imports of services to the total Region in 1993–2003 was about 8 percent, twice that for the next fastest-growing comparator region, again, East Asia. Within the Region, services trade flows—whether in terms of exports or imports—grew fastest in the SEE countries over the

Export value of services ($ billion)							Growth
1997	1998	1999	2000	2001	2002	2003	1993–2003
22	19	16	17	19	23	26	7.6%
7	8	8	9	10	11	16	13.1%
29	32	28	31	29	34	39	8.3%
29	27	23	25	29	34	42	22.6%
528	555	581	591	614	711	844	6.8%
49	53	53	59	57	54	54	3.2%
36	37	37	40	38	37	41	3.3%
13	13	14	13	12	12	12	0.2%
231	229	237	262	257	274	249	5.5%
13	16	19	23	25	30	4	−6.6%
Import value of services ($ billion)							
1997	1998	1999	2000	2001	2002	2003	1993–2003
25	22	19	23	30	34	39	7.6%
6	6	6	6	7	8	10	10.5%
21	23	23	25	24	29	35	9.1%
32	28	24	29	36	42	49	7.9%
506	548	572	581	596	683	808	6.7%
65	68	66	74	73	66	67	2.9%
61	52	52	60	52	52	52	−0.7%
25	25	24	19	20	19	14	−3.6%
299	282	297	319	311	326	283	3.8%
18	20	23	22	22	23	5	−7.1%

FIGURE 2.3
The Region's Shares in World Trade in Services

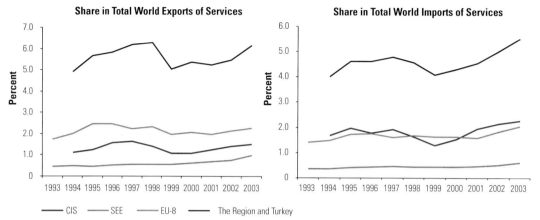

Source: IMF balance of payments statistics.

1993–2003 period, followed by the EU-8 and then the CIS. For all three of the Region's transition country groupings, the flows of services exports and imports grew faster than those in the EU-15.

Not surprisingly, as a share of world services trade, however, today the volume (by $ value) of exports and imports of services in the Region is generally still smaller than (or about equal to) that of most comparator regions (see annex table 2.1). The world shares of services exports and imports by all of the Region's countries in 2003 were 2.5 percent and 2.9 percent, respectively. East Asia's world shares of services exports and imports in 2003 were 14.5 percent and 16.5 percent, respectively, while for Latin America and the Caribbean, the analogous shares were 3.2 percent and 3.9 percent.

Bifurcation in the Destinations and Origins of the Region's Trade Flows

Over the course of the transition, there have been significant changes in the global destination and origin markets of both the merchandise and services trade of the Region. While age-old destination and origin markets on the Eurasian continent still figure prominently for most of the countries, newer, less traditional, locations have also been gaining strength in certain instances. Most striking about this phenomenon, however, is the emerging bifurcation of the Region into two trade "poles": the geographic pattern of trade flows is becoming characterized by a "Euro-centric" clustering and a "Russia-centric" clustering.

Merchandise Trade

Global merchandise trade flows among the Region's countries. On a *global* basis—that is, considering the countries' trade flows both outside and inside the Region—for the most developed economies, the EU-8, the major merchandise *export* destination market today remains the more advanced countries in Europe—the EU-15 (figure 2.4 and table 2.4). Indeed, the share of the EU-8's global merchandise exports sold in the EU-15 rose over the decade, while their corresponding export share within the Region fell. Among the country groups in the Region, the global share of exports sold in the EU-15 by the EU-8 is still the largest.

The increased international integration of the EU-8 countries has been also manifested in significant growth since 1993 in the share of their merchandise exports to East Asia, their largest export market outside the European continent. On the other hand, the shares of EU-8 countries' exports sold in the markets of North America (NAFTA), Latin America and the Caribbean, the Middle East and North Africa, and

FIGURE 2.4

Global Destinations of the Region's Merchandise Exports

Distributional Shares of Merchandise Exports of the Region's Groups, by Destination

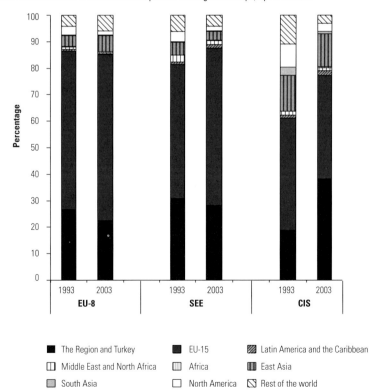

Source: IMF DOT statistics.

TABLE 2. 4
Global Geographic Destination of the Region's Merchandise Exports (%)

Group	Year	Region	Of which CIS	Of which SEE	Of which EU-8	EU-15	LAC	MENA	Africa	East Asia	South Asia	NAFTA	ROW
CIS	1993	21.0	37.6	12.9	36.7	46.2	1.1	1.7	0.2	14.7	3.3	9.4	12.0
	1996	47.7	70.2	4.5	19.0	32.5	1.1	2.2	0.1	8.6	1.2	5.2	2.8
	2000	47.6	78.0	2.8	14.3	33.6	1.4	1.2	0.3	8.3	1.6	4.6	2.9
	2003	39.3	73.7	2.3	18.2	39.6	1.9	1.1	0.5	12.4	0.9	3.1	3.1
SEE	1993	30.9	44.0	16.7	31.7	53.9	0.8	2.9	0.1	5.0	0.2	4.1	6.4
	1996	27.7	29.9	21.4	37.0	59.3	1.4	2.1	0.2	4.3	0.2	2.6	7.5
	2000	28.4	28.1	21.1	40.9	61.2	1.0	2.1	0.2	3.3	0.1	2.1	5.2
	2003	27.9	22.3	18.4	45.9	62.2	1.3	1.7	0.2	3.6	0.2	1.7	4.3
EU-8	1993	27.5	45.2	7.0	45.4	61.7	0.6	1.0	0.2	4.2	0.3	3.4	4.2
	1996	25.1	46.0	4.9	47.3	65.1	0.6	0.5	0.3	4.6	0.2	2.2	6.0
	2000	25.0	52.0	4.1	42.5	65.3	0.5	0.4	0.1	5.0	0.2	2.1	5.5
	2003	23.7	42.3	4.5	50.7	65.4	0.4	0.4	0.3	6.5	0.2	1.6	6.2
Memo Items Region	1993	25.7	42.9	10.3	40.6	55.2	0.8	1.5	0.2	8.0	1.4	5.6	6.8
	1996	34.6	58.0	6.3	30.5	51.2	0.9	1.4	0.2	6.2	0.6	3.5	4.4
	2000	32.2	60.8	5.4	29.9	55.3	0.8	0.9	0.2	5.8	0.6	2.8	4.4
	2003	29.3	53.4	5.4	35.9	56.6	1.0	0.8	0.3	8.0	0.4	2.1	4.6
CIS less Russian Fed.	1993	36.3	48.1	7.8	27.7	41.2	0.5	2.3	0.0	8.3	1.3	8.7	4.1
	1996	68.0	78.6	2.7	14.1	19.1	0.3	3.0	0.1	4.0	0.5	4.1	1.3
	2000	64.6	81.3	1.8	12.2	21.8	0.7	2.0	0.4	6.0	0.6	3.2	1.3
	2003	58.6	79.9	1.5	13.7	25.1	0.5	1.8	0.4	9.7	0.6	2.4	1.4
Turkey	1993	9.0	70.7	13.8	15.2	51.7	1.3	10.3	0.0	11.1	0.9	12.8	32.4
	1996	8.9	67.7	24.0	8.1	57.2	1.3	10.7	0.3	9.5	1.0	7.8	37.9
	2000	13.2	70.7	18.8	10.3	56.0	1.0	7.6	0.4	10.6	1.0	8.1	15.9
	2003	15.5	68.0	17.5	14.5	52.6	1.3	9.8	0.9	11.1	1.3	5.1	15.6
EU-15	1993	6.0	22.2	11.5	48.2	62.2	1.8	5.1	1.2	8.6	0.8	9.5	4.9
	1996	7.5	18.6	11.9	53.1	62.3	2.0	3.8	1.0	9.2	0.7	8.8	4.8
	2000	7.8	12.2	12.8	58.8	61.9	1.7	3.6	1.3	7.3	0.6	11.8	3.9
	2003	9.5	14.9	15.0	57.2	61.6	1.3	4.1	1.4	6.9	0.6	10.5	4.0

Source: IMF DOT statistics.

South Asia all have declined. (Apart from NAFTA, the initial EU-8 export shares for these regions were small to begin with.) The EU-8's share of exports to the rest of the world (ROW), however, increased sizably over the decade, another attribute reflecting the EU-8's increased international integration.

In 2003, as in 1993, the CIS countries arguably had the greatest diversification in location of global merchandise export markets compared with other country groups of the Region. Over the course of the decade, however, the geographic spread of CIS exports' global shares had become more concentrated. The largest destination market for CIS merchandise exports in 2003 was the same as it was in 1993—the EU-15— but only marginally so: the share of CIS exports shipped to countries in the Region grew substantially, while the share of exports shipped to the EU-15 declined substantially. LAC and, to a much lesser extent, Africa, proved to be new markets for CIS exports, with a doubling of the export shares over the decade. In contrast, the shares of exports from the CIS group of countries to South Asia, East Asia, and North America all declined, particularly for the NAFTA and South Asian markets.

The global pattern of merchandise export penetration for the SEE countries falls somewhere between those of the EU-8 and the CIS. The largest shares of SEE exports are accounted for by customers in the EU-15 and in the Region and, like their wealthier EU-8 counterparts, the SEE countries sold proportionally more exports in EU-15 markets than in the Region's markets over the 1993–2003 period. On the other hand, as is the case for the CIS, the share of exports from the SEE group of countries destined for LAC markets increased substantially. At the same time, SEE export shares in NAFTA, South Asia, and East Asia declined.

The two-pole paradigm is becoming equally evident with respect to imports. The global merchandise *import* side of the story is presented in figure 2.5 and table 2.5. Globally, for the most developed economies—the EU-8—the dominant merchandise import origin market was still the EU-15. As in exports, the share of the EU-8's global merchandise imports purchased from the EU-15 rose over the 1993–2003 period, while their corresponding import share within the Region fell. Among the three country groupings in the Region, the global share of merchandise imports bought in the EU-15 was still the largest for the EU-8.

Outside the European continent, the change in the share pattern of EU-8 global imports is largely the reverse of what happened regarding exports. There was significant growth since 1993 in the share of EU-8 merchandise imports from North America, which remained its largest non-European import market. On the other hand, the share of EU-8 merchandise imports purchased in the markets of East Asia declined. The share of EU-8 imports from MENA and LAC also declined between 1993 and 2003.

As in the case of exports, the CIS countries tend to have a pattern of global import markets that is more diversified in comparison with the other country groups of the Region. Unlike the changes exhibited in CIS export destinations, however, over the course of the decade the geographic spread of CIS import shares became somewhat more diversified.

The CIS' largest origin market for its merchandise imports in 2003 was the Region; this differs from 1993, when it was the EU-15. The share of CIS imports shipped from the Region grew substantially, while the share of imports shipped from the EU-15 declined, albeit by a modest amount. LAC, NAFTA, and MENA all have become more

FIGURE 2.5

Global Distribution of the Region's Merchandise Imports

Distributional Shares of Merchandise Imports of the Region's Groups, by Destination

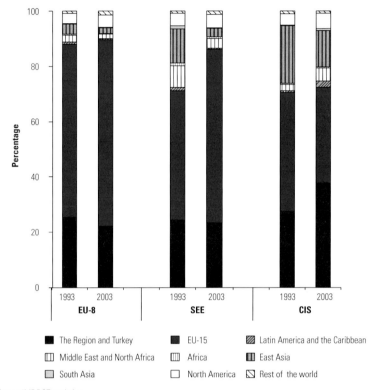

Source: IMF DOT statistics.

significant import source markets for the CIS. In contrast, the share of imports to the CIS from East Asia declined. This is a different pattern from the one that evolved for CIS exports.

As in exports, the global pattern of merchandise import sourcing for the SEE countries falls somewhere between those of the EU-8 and the CIS. The largest shares of SEE imports are accounted for by EU-15 and Regional producers and, like their wealthier EU-8 counterparts, SEE bought proportionally more imports in EU-15 markets than in the Region's markets over the 1993–2003 period. On the other hand, as is the case for the CIS, the share of imports by the SEE group of countries bought in East Asian markets decreased substantially. At the same time, SEE import shares from LAC, MENA, South Asia, and North America declined.

Intra-Regional merchandise trade flows. The patterns of the *intra-Regional* destination of the countries' merchandise *exports* are particularly

TABLE 2.5
Global Geographic Origin of the Region's Imports (%)

Country Group	Year	Region	Of which CIS	Of which SEE	Of which EU-8	EU-15	LAC	MENA	Africa	East Asia	South Asia	NAFTA	ROW
CIS	1993	27.7	23.4	20.8	40.2	42.9	0.7	2.2	0.4	20.8	0.3	4.0	1.0
	1996	47.9	63.6	7.9	23.3	28.7	0.8	2.4	0.2	13.5	1.0	4.3	1.1
	2000	39.0	53.1	8.2	28.8	33.1	1.9	3.3	0.4	12.3	0.7	7.0	2.3
	2003	37.8	53.3	8.3	28.0	34.8	2.1	4.7	0.4	13.0	0.8	5.6	0.8
SEE	1993	22.8	22.7	29.5	36.0	47.9	1.1	7.9	1.1	12.5	1.2	4.6	0.9
	1996	24.3	20.3	34.9	26.5	52.0	1.1	6.7	2.5	7.2	1.7	3.7	0.8
	2000	24.6	9.5	40.7	28.0	61.1	0.3	3.9	1.3	2.3	0.3	5.4	0.8
	2003	22.2	7.6	40.2	30.5	63.7	0.4	3.6	0.6	3.1	0.3	4.8	1.4
EU-8	1993	25.3	26.2	12.0	60.9	62.6	0.8	2.5	0.4	3.5	0.3	3.7	0.8
	1996	26.1	25.9	12.7	59.6	64.1	0.7	1.4	0.2	2.7	0.3	3.3	1.1
	2000	19.9	16.7	16.5	63.6	68.6	0.7	1.0	0.3	2.2	0.1	5.9	1.3
	2003	22.1	17.2	17.4	61.3	67.5	0.4	1.5	0.3	2.0	0.2	4.7	1.4
Memo Items													
Region	1993	26.2	24.5	18.0	48.2	51.7	0.7	2.9	0.5	12.8	0.4	4.0	0.9
	1996	37.6	51.3	10.7	32.9	44.1	0.8	2.4	0.4	8.9	0.8	3.9	1.1
	2000	30.1	40.5	12.5	38.1	49.8	1.3	2.4	0.4	7.4	0.4	6.4	1.8
	2003	29.4	38.2	13.4	39.4	51.9	1.2	3.2	0.3	7.2	0.5	5.1	1.1
CIS less Russian Fed.	1993	45.3	41.7	19.5	23.0	29.2	0.6	5.0	0.0	15.3	0.3	3.9	0.4
	1996	71.5	82.0	3.7	9.8	12.2	0.9	3.4	0.3	7.5	0.8	3.2	0.2
	2000	54.7	74.6	5.3	11.4	21.1	4.3	4.6	0.4	9.0	0.9	4.7	0.3
	2003	50.1	67.8	7.3	16.4	20.6	5.3	8.2	0.6	10.9	1.2	2.6	0.4
Turkey	1993	10.3	76.0	12.4	11.6	51.5	0.7	17.1	0.1	9.7	0.7	8.6	1.2
	1996	10.5	67.1	19.2	13.7	56.8	0.6	14.1	0.5	6.1	0.8	9.1	1.5
	2000	9.8	49.1	28.7	22.2	59.9	0.9	10.8	1.0	2.8	0.7	12.7	1.4
	2003	13.5	35.7	34.4	29.8	56.6	0.5	14.1	1.0	3.0	0.5	9.2	1.6
EU-15	1993	6.0	22.2	11.5	48.2	62.2	1.8	5.1	1.2	8.6	0.8	9.5	4.9
	1996	7.5	18.6	11.9	53.1	62.3	2.0	3.8	1.0	9.2	0.7	8.8	4.8
	2000	7.8	12.2	12.8	58.8	61.9	1.7	3.6	1.3	7.3	0.6	11.8	3.9
	2003	9.5	14.9	15.0	57.2	61.6	1.3	4.1	1.4	6.9	0.6	10.5	4.0

Source: IMF DOT statistics.

revealing (see figure 2.6). While the major destination market for intra-Regional merchandise exports by the EU-8 in 1993 was the CIS, in 2003, following a major locational shift over the decade, most of the intra-Regional exports sold by EU-8 countries were to other EU-8 countries themselves.

This change in trade patterns is a hallmark of the EU-8 countries' development progress, particularly regarding the restructuring and modernization of the enterprise sector. Although the SEE market remained the smallest for EU-8 intra-Regional exports, there was also a decline in the share of the EU-8's intra-Regional merchandise exports sold in SEE.

FIGURE 2.6
Intra-Regional Distribution of Merchandise Exports
Share of Intra-Regional Merchandise Exports

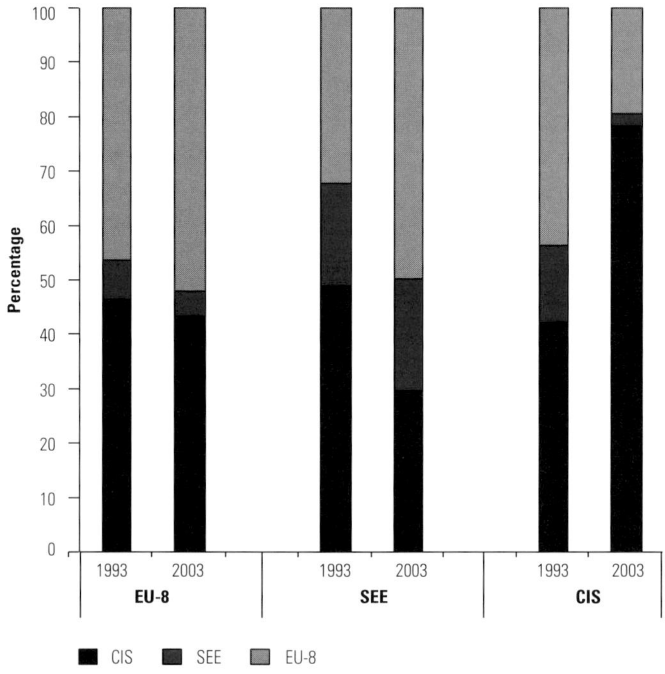

Source: IMF DOT statistics.

The dynamics of the pattern of intra-Regional merchandise exports for the CIS is just the reverse. Rather than enlarging their share of exports to the wealthier countries as development in the overall Region has proceeded, the CIS' share of intra-Regional exports in the EU-8 market decreased while it increased in the CIS market itself. The share of CIS exports within the Region also declined in the SEE market. Taken together, these data suggest that CIS exports within the Region became more (sub-) regionalized and concentrated.

For the SEE economies, there was a significant shift between 1993 and 2003 from the CIS to the EU-8 becoming the dominant destination for intra-Regional merchandise exports. Indeed, the share of SEE's intra-Regional exports rose in the EU-8 market and fell—even more dramatically—in the CIS market. The share of intra-Regional exports sold in the SEE market by SEE producers remained relatively the same over the decade.

The pattern of merchandise *imports* for the EU-8 within the Region is different from that for exports (see figure 2.7). Although the share of EU-8 intra-Regional imports from the CIS declined and the share from the EU-8 rose (as did the share of imports from SEE), the EU-8

FIGURE 2.7

Intra-Regional Distribution of Merchandise Imports

Share of Intra-Regional Merchandise Imports

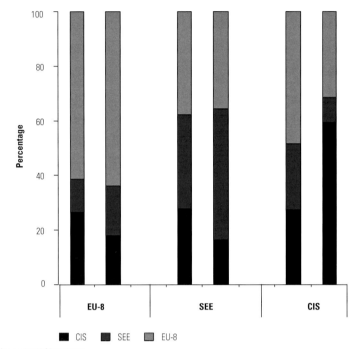

Source: IMF DOT statistics.

market remains the dominant origin for EU-8 merchandise imports.

On the other hand, the story for the shares of the CIS' intra-Regional imports is not different from that for exports. The CIS' share of intra-Regional imports from the EU-8 market decreased, while it increased in the CIS market itself. The share of CIS imports from the SEE market also declined within the Region. Again, as in exports, these data suggest that the CIS' intra-Regional imports have become more (sub-) regionalized and concentrated.

For the SEE economies, there was a significant shift over 1993–2003. Whereas in 1993 the EU-8 was the major origin market for intra-Regional merchandise imports for SEE, by 2003, the share of SEE intra-Regional imports was greater from the SEE market itself. At the same time, as it did for their wealthier EU-8 counterparts, the share of the SEE's intra-Regional imports purchased from the CIS declined.

Services Trade

While there are few systematic data available on the direction of trade in services, telecommunications traffic flows suggest that much of the trade in services that occurs is oriented toward Western Europe. More than half of all outgoing telecommunications traffic originating in the eight new EU member states and in SEE goes to the EU. This compares with less than 2 percent for Central Asia and the Caucasus and 8 percent for Belarus, Russia, and Ukraine. This bifurcation of the Region's countries—in this case in terms of services trade—is a characteristic increasing along multiple dimensions of the overall pattern of international integration in the Region.

A similar dichotomy is present regarding services sector FDI in the Region. Indeed, largely as a result of growing inflows of FDI in the services sectors, the share of domestic economic activity accounted for by services in the EU-8 and SEE economies has rapidly converged on that of the EU. For example, the Baltic countries of Estonia and Lithuania have attracted significant inflows of FDI in services, and in the coastal countries of the Balkans, FDI in tourism services has become increasingly predominant. In other countries of the Region, however, especially Central Asia and the Caucasus, services account for only 40 percent of economic activity. In these countries there are extremely limited FDI flows in services and an absence of private sector participation in services delivery.

Liberalization of foreign investment in services in the Region—usually capitalized on by the privatization of deregulated incumbent businesses—has been most pronounced in network and backbone industries, such as telecommunications, energy, and banking, as well as in tourism, wholesale and retail commerce, and business services. In contrast, many new, higher-technology services activities, such as the information technology (IT) and software development sectors, have developed from the start within relatively liberalized frameworks. (A more detailed discussion of trade and investment in the services sectors in the Region is the focus of chapter 6.)

Bipolar Clustering in Product Concentration, Commodity Composition, and Factor Intensity

Product Diversification vs. Concentration

It is often assumed that with greater development of a market economy and overall economic prosperity, diversification of the composition of a country's trade increases. In this case, has the transition from central planning to market-oriented development resulted in increased diversification of the Region's exports? Analyses of the magnitude and effects of export diversification in various regions of the world have typically employed three types of indices: (a) a count of the number of products exported, (b) the share of a country's total exports accounted for by a set number of the largest products (a simple measure of export concentration), and (c) the index of export concentration (a more sophisticated measure of concentration than the second).[2] Analysis of these indices calculated for the Region's trade provides valuable insights into the evolution of trade diversification in these countries since the start of transition.

As figure 2.8 shows, the Region's progress in diversification of export products has been generally limited, with concentration of trade worsening markedly for the CIS countries. The number of products exported generally declined between 1993 and 2003, and the share of the largest 3 or 10 products in total exports generally increased. The Hirschman concentration index for most of the Region increased only slightly, while for the CIS countries it rose significantly, reflecting a decrease in the diversification of export products.

FIGURE 2.8

Changes in Product Concentration of the Region's Merchandise Exports in Global Markets

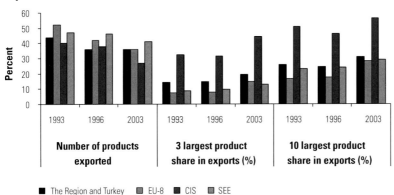

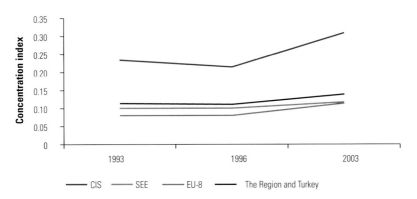

Source: Computations based on UN COMTRADE statistics.

Overall, across all of the indices, the CIS countries score the worst. Indeed, their indices have deteriorated substantially over time, especially since 1996. This has been most striking in Azerbaijan, Georgia, Kazakhstan, and Russia, where oil and gas are increasingly the prominent exports.

Concentration of trade has also been increasing, though taking a different form, in the EU-8 countries, notably in Hungary and the Slovak and Czech Republics, particularly in heavy industries such as automotive and parts. The Baltic countries, particularly Latvia and Lithuania, have nevertheless managed to improve their export diversification profile. The SEE countries, on the other hand, remain the most diversified, most likely the result of a relative specialization in low value added exports, such as textiles.

Commodity Composition

Export prospects are affected by the commodity composition of trade.[3] Important negative effects from a high concentration of exports may take place depending on the nature of the commodities exported. Some studies show that countries with highly concentrated exports may experience relatively unstable export earnings, a factor that makes economic planning difficult.[4] This can occur if the commodities exported see their prices fluctuate in an unpredictable manner, which is often the case with primary commodities such as oil and gas and many agricultural products.

What does the commodity composition of exports in the Region look like? As depicted in table 2.6, a common feature for almost all the countries in the Region is the relative decline in the importance of

TABLE 2.6

The Structure of the Region's Exports by Major Product Category, 1996 and 2003

Exporter	Year	Total exports ($ millions)	Food & feeds	Agric. raw materials	Ores & metals	Fuels	All manuf.	
Region and Turkey	1996	247,493	17.1	4.9	6.3	13.2	56.5	
	2003	461,051	12.3	4.4	7.4	15.7	56.6	
EU-8	1996	83,456	11.5	5.7	3.2	5.5	71.5	
	2003	195,259	7.0	5.9	2.7	5.1	78.9	
CIS	1996	119,813	19.2	5.3	8.2	26.6	38.4	
	2003	182,718	14.1	4.7	12.1	31.4	30.3	
SEE	1996	20,687	16.4	4.6	8.5	4.9	64.7	
	2003	35,408	11.8	3.3	6.3	5.3	71.8	

Source: Computations based on UN COMTRADE statistics.

agricultural products in exports. The share of food and agricultural raw material exports of the total of the Region's exports has declined from 22 percent in 1996 to 16.7 percent in 2003. This decline was paralleled by an increase in the share of manufacturing exports for some of the countries, which was offset by a reallocation toward primary commodities (namely ores, minerals, and fuels) by other countries, the export shares of which increased from 19.5 percent to 23.1 percent.

The concentration of the Region's exports in (nonagricultural) primary commodities, however, remains large and is increasing. This is particularly the case for the CIS countries, where the shares of ores, metals, and fuels in total exports increased from 38 percent to 47 percent over the period 1996–2003. With the collapse of manufacturing exports following the breakup of the Union of Soviet Socialist Republics (USSR), most of these countries had shifted toward exports of natural resources. Exports of manufactures declined by 10 percentage points over the period 1996–2003. In the natural resource-rich countries like Azerbaijan, Kazakhstan, Russia, and Turkmenistan, trade in energy and raw materials experienced a boost and compensated for the decline in manufacturing trade. These are universal commodities that can easily be sold on international markets. By the same token, Tajikistan's exports are dominated by aluminum, and the Kyrgyz Republic relies extensively on exports of gold. As discussed below (and in chapter 7) in the analysis of intraindustry trade and buyer- versus producer-driven global production-sharing networks, Armenia managed to develop inward processing in its diamond-cutting industry that cushioned the decline in the more traditional food, light, and machinery industries. In the Kyrgyz

Chemical	Wood & papers	Leather & rubber	Textiles & clothing	Machinery excl. auto	Motor veh. & parts	Misc. manuf.
8.7	2.4	2.3	13.0	11.2	3.2	6.2
5.7	2.5	2.5	11.7	13.9	4.4	6.2
9.5	5.2	2.1	12.1	17.0	6.6	9.3
7.0	5.4	2.1	8.0	26.5	10.7	10.4
7.6	0.7	0.9	7.4	8.0	2.0	3.0
3.5	0.7	0.5	6.9	6.9	1.3	2.0
9.7	1.7	5.4	18.2	10.2	1.3	7.6
5.6	2.1	7.1	22.9	12.7	1.4	8.2

Republic, however, gold exports have generated only limited positive spillovers into the local economy.

Factor Intensity

Differences among the Region's countries in factor endowments, initial conditions, and levels of development have largely conditioned the observed factor intensities of the countries' exports and imports. Figure 2.9 and tables 2.7 and 2.8 present the most recent and complete data available on this score, across various groupings of countries in the Region, by individual country, and over time. (Annex tables 2.2 and 2.3 show the distribution of factor use in value terms for exports and imports.)

FIGURE 2.9

Factor Intensity of Merchandise Exports and Imports in the Region, 1993 and 2003

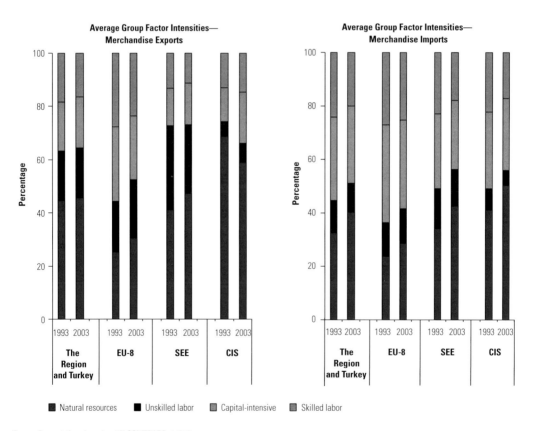

Source: Computations based on UN COMTRADE statistics.

Note: The import share of the CIS may be exaggerated by trade deflection; see Freinkman et al. 2004.

At present, the variation in the factor intensity of merchandise exports of the Region's countries generally falls along two lines. In less developed, resource-rich, and labor-endowed countries such as the Central Asian Republics and the Caucasus, exports of natural-resource-intensive and labor-intensive products tend to be dominant on average. Merchandise exports of the more developed economies, such as the EU-8, are on average more capital-intensive and less natural-resource-intensive. Indeed, many of the more developed countries in the Region have increased the technological content of their traded goods: the EU-8 countries, and to a much lesser extent only a few of the SEE countries, have more capital-intensive exports than the other countries in the Region. However, the EU-8's merchandise exports are, on average, *more* unskilled-labor-intensive than the exports of the CIS, but *less* unskilled-labor-intensive relative to SEE exports—an issue that has implications of potential importance for prospective employment trends in the EU-8, a topic addressed below.

On the other hand, a core portion of the SEE countries, mostly in the Western Balkans, has exports with relatively low capital intensity and relatively high unskilled-labor intensity. In large part, this is the result of these countries' not attracting significant amounts of FDI, especially in greenfield (or wholly new) investments. This leaves them with a pattern of trade specialization that does not correspond to their competitive position. (This point is further reinforced by the empirical evidence on determinants of trade openness presented below.)

On an individual country basis the pattern generally holds, with the aggregate share of skilled-labor-intensive and capital-intensive exports highest for the most developed economies in the Region, as well as for Croatia. At the other extreme, Moldova, the poorest country in Europe in terms of GDP per capita, has the lowest share of such products in its exports. A substantial deviation from the pattern appears to be Serbia and Montenegro, with a share very close to that of Croatian exports. This, combined with a very low share of unskilled-labor-intensive products in its exports, may point to weaknesses in the economic policy regime of Serbia and Montenegro in preventing allocation of resources to sectors with potential comparative advantage.

With respect to the factor intensity of the Region's merchandise imports, roughly the same broad dichotomy holds, but the differences across the country groupings is less significant.[5] Merchandise imports into the CIS countries on average tend to be more natural-resource-intensive and less capital-intensive than the EU-8's imports. Although

TABLE 2.7

Factor Intensity of Merchandise Exports by Country in the Region, 1996, 2000, and 2003

	Share of total exports (%)[a, b]									
	1996					2000				
Country	Total exports	Natural resources	Unskilled labor	Capital-intensive	Skilled labor	Total rxports	Natural resources	Unskilled labor	Capital-intensive	
Albania	100.0	59.7	33.0	3.4	3.9	100.0	50.3	42.8	2.2	
Armenia[c]	100.0	70.0	5.8	16.8	7.4	100.0	71.1	3.4	18.3	
Azerbaijan	100.0	45.3	10.7	38.2	5.8	100.0	92.3	1.9	5.0	
Belarus[c]	100.0	17.7	19.4	29.0	33.9	100.0	19.5	18.6	29.8	
Bulgaria	100.0	37.7	17.1	28.3	16.9	100.0	35.2	27.1	21.5	
Croatia	100.0	32.8	35.1	24.0	8.1	100.0	33.3	34.3	23.3	
Czech Rep.	100.0	20.8	18.3	30.0	30.8	100.0	15.0	16.6	32.3	
Estonia	100.0	36.3	24.4	22.1	17.2	100.0	30.4	17.8	39.0	
Georgia	100.0	63.9	3.2	14.7	18.3	100.0	71.3	3.0	21.9	
Hungary	100.0	31.1	19.3	30.2	19.3	100.0	13.2	11.7	51.1	
Kazakhstan	100.0	72.4	1.3	15.3	11.0	100.0	83.0	0.3	6.4	
Kyrgyz Rep.	100.0	64.3	8.8	22.1	4.8	100.0	70.1	5.4	16.6	
Latvia	100.0	45.3	24.2	14.4	16.1	100.0	52.8	22.9	11.8	
Lithuania	100.0	43.2	20.2	21.9	14.7	100.0	43.7	25.9	20.0	
Macedonia, FYR	100.0	43.3	34.7	10.3	11.7	100.0	35.4	31.4	7.9	
Moldova	100.0	80.7	8.8	6.5	4.0	100.0	67.6	23.6	5.8	
Poland	100.0	30.0	28.3	19.1	22.6	100.0	23.8	24.1	23.3	
Romania	100.0	22.7	39.0	19.9	18.4	100.0	22.3	41.3	21.4	
Russian Fed.	100.0	70.7	3.0	11.9	14.4	100.0	71.8	3.5	12.0	
Serbia & Montenegro	100.0	54.4	12.1	17.7	15.8	100.0	44.9	17.2	17.9	
Slovak Rep.	100.0	21.2	18.3	28.0	32.5	100.0	14.2	15.5	25.2	
Slovenia	100.0	16.5	22.4	24.9	36.3	100.0	15.6	19.7	26.4	
Tajikistan	n.a.	n.a.	n.a.	n.a.	n.a.	100.0	86.7	3.6	8.9	
Turkmenistan[c]	100.0	92.5	6.3	0.7	0.6	100.0	91.2	7.5	1.2	
Ukraine	100.0	34.5	5.2	24.5	35.8	100.0	32.3	5.7	21.9	

Source: Computations based on UN COMTRADE statistics.

Note: a. Because of missing data, Bosnia and Herzegovina and Uzbekistan are excluded.
a. Sum of individual country shares may not exactly equal totals because of rounding methodology.
b. Calculated based on SITC four-digit products.
c. Armenia and Turkmenistan are using 1997 data, and Belarus is using 1998 instead of 1996 data.
n.a. = not available.

the EU-8's imports are on average more unskilled-labor-intensive than the CIS' imports, the differences in this factor intensity are much smaller than the similar pattern exhibited regarding exports.

How have the development and greater modernization of the Region's economies shifted the factor composition of trade since the start of transition? Looking over the 1996–2003 period, the merchandise imports of most of the Region's economies at lower levels of development—largely, but not exclusively, the CIS—are now importing relatively more skilled-labor-intensive and capital-intensive products and fewer natural-resource-intensive products. At the same time, the merchandise exports of the CIS countries have become even

	Share of total exports (%)[a, b]								
		2003					Change 1996–2003 (%)		
Skilled labor	Total exports	Natural resources	Unskilled labor	Capital-intensive	Skilled labor	Unskilled labor	Capital-intensive	Skilled labor	
4.6	100.0	48.1	40.8	3.8	7.3	24	13	88	
7.2	100.0	92.8	0.9	3.2	3.1	−84	−81	−58	
0.8	100.0	93.6	0.5	4.4	1.5	−95	−89	−74	
32.1	100.0	23.8	16.7	28.9	30.5	−14	0	−10	
16.2	100.0	34.0	32.2	18.9	14.9	88	−33	−12	
9.0	100.0	29.0	33.6	26.4	10.9	−4	10	35	
36.1	100.0	12.5	14.6	37.1	35.8	−20	24	16	
12.7	100.0	33.5	19.4	28.0	19.1	−20	27	11	
3.8	100.0	75.0	1.3	19.2	4.4	−59	31	−76	
24.0	100.0	13.2	10.3	53.9	22.7	−47	78	17	
10.3	100.0	86.1	0.3	4.8	8.8	−76	−69	−20	
7.8	100.0	66.3	15.6	11.6	6.5	78	−48	35	
12.5	100.0	51.6	22.3	12.3	13.8	−8	−15	−14	
10.4	100.0	40.1	28.5	18.2	13.2	41	−17	−10	
25.3	100.0	37.3	37.1	7.8	17.8	7	−24	53	
3.1	100.0	69.3	20.9	5.4	4.4	137	−17	10	
28.8	100.0	21.5	23.8	24.0	30.7	−16	25	36	
15.0	100.0	22.7	40.5	19.0	17.8	4	−4	−4	
12.7	100.0	77.1	1.2	11.6	10.1	−59	−3	−30	
20.1	100.0	48.2	15.4	17.4	19.0	27	−1	20	
45.0	100.0	15.4	14.3	21.7	48.6	−22	−23	50	
38.3	100.0	14.9	17.9	29.8	37.5	−20	20	3	
0.8	n.a.	n.a.	n.a.	n.a.	n.a.	n.a.	n.a.	n.a.	
0.1	n.a.	n.a.	n.a.	n.a.	n.a.	n.a.	n.a.	n.a.	
40.1	100.0	36.5	6.0	19.5	38.0	15	−21	6	

more natural-resource-intensive and less skilled-labor-intensive on average, although among individual countries there are exceptions.

Over the same period, the SEE countries on average recorded a significant increase in exports of labor-intensive products and a slight decline in capital-intensive exports. Indeed, SEE exports remain largely concentrated in unskilled-labor-intensive products, the intensity of which grew between 1996 and 2003. For the EU-8, over the 1996–2003 period, both merchandise exports and imports became more skilled-labor-intensive and capital-intensive.

Overall, while there has been substantial change over the course of the transition in the commodity composition and factor intensity of

TABLE 2.8

Factor Intensity of Merchandise Imports by Country in the Region, 1996, 2000, and 2003

	Share of total imports (%)[a, b]								
	1996					2000			
Country	Total exports	Natural resources	Unskilled labor	Capital-intensive	Skilled labor	Total exports	Natural resources	Unskilled labor	Capital-intensive
Albania	100.0	50.0	13.8	21.8	14.3	100.0	45.2	16.3	18.7
Armenia[c]	100.0	62.7	5.5	21.5	10.3	100.0	57.7	6.1	24.0
Azerbaijan	100.0	49.7	4.7	25.0	20.7	100.0	32.0	8.3	40.3
Belarus[c]	100.0	42.8	6.4	28.0	22.8	100.0	50.7	6.2	25.6
Bulgaria	100.0	53.2	9.7	23.2	14.0	100.0	40.3	14.5	25.8
Croatia	100.0	31.4	15.7	29.4	23.7	100.0	29.7	15.5	28.4
Czech Rep.	100.0	24.1	11.7	39.9	24.5	100.0	22.5	11.4	41.3
Estonia	100.0	26.0	16.2	30.2	27.8	100.0	21.4	12.0	43.4
Georgia	100.0	77.1	4.4	12.7	5.9	100.0	40.3	7.6	35.5
Hungary	100.0	28.0	14.0	35.7	22.5	100.0	14.0	10.6	50.9
Kazakhstan	100.0	37.6	5.6	28.6	28.3	100.0	23.6	6.0	40.8
Kyrgyz Rep.	100.0	54.0	3.6	28.6	13.9	100.0	40.2	4.9	40.8
Latvia	100.0	29.8	14.6	31.3	24.5	100.0	25.5	15.1	32.5
Lithuania	100.0	39.4	10.6	25.8	24.5	100.0	39.5	13.9	26.2
Macedonia, FYR	100.0	35.0	19.6	23.2	22.3	100.0	42.7	6.7	26.5
Moldova	100.0	53.8	8.3	23.1	14.9	100.0	43.5	15.3	27.2
Poland	100.0	26.0	13.5	37.2	23.5	100.0	24.3	12.1	38.9
Romania	100.0	36.9	15.8	32.0	15.5	100.0	28.8	20.8	34.5
Russian Fed.	100.0	36.6	8.9	34.6	20.2	100.0	36.3	8.0	37.6
Serbia & Montenegro	100.0	38.2	12.7	28.5	21.0	100.0	29.3	9.9	33.1
Slovak Rep.	100.0	30.0	9.4	34.5	26.3	100.0	30.4	11.0	33.4
Slovenia	100.0	25.9	14.3	31.6	28.3	100.0	26.8	12.7	33.1
Tajikistan	n.a.	n.a.	n.a.	n.a.	n.a.	100.0	42.2	2.0	49.1
Turkmenistan[c]	100.0	32.3	6.0	41.9	19.9	100.0	17.1	7.3	43.7
Ukraine	100.0	61.0	5.3	21.3	12.5	100.0	55.3	6.6	24.4

Source: Computations based on UN COMTRADE statistics.

Note: Because of the missing data, Bosnia and Herzegovina and Uzbekistan are excluded,
a. Sum of individual country shares may not exactly equal totals because of rounding methodology.
b. Calculated based on SITC four-digit products.
c. Armenia and Turkmenistan are using 1997 data, and Belarus is using 1998 instead of 1996 data.
n.a. = not available.

trade in the EU-8 and the SEE economies, relatively little has changed in these regards among the CIS countries, which effectively have been almost "frozen in time." The result is that these countries are not active participants in the evolving modern international division of labor.

The existing composition and factor intensity of exports put the future growth prospects of the CIS at risk. Skilled-labor-intensive and capital-intensive industries tend to pay higher wages, and growth of exports in these sectors can lead to expanded production, an increase in economic growth. On the other hand, excessive reliance on exports of natural-resource-based products that involve little processing—

		Share of total imports (%)[a, b]						
		2003				Change 1996–2003 (%)		
Skilled labor	Total exports	Natural resources	Unskilled labor	Capital-intensive	Skilled labor	Unskilled labor	Capital-intensive	Skilled labor
19.9	100.0	42.9	16.4	20.1	20.6	19	−8	44
12.3	100.0	62.3	6.5	17.4	13.8	18	−19	34
19.4	100.0	29.0	12.1	31.3	27.5	160	25	33
17.4	100.0	47.1	6.9	27.8	18.1	8	−1	−21
19.4	100.0	22.9	20.2	31.9	25.0	108	37	79
26.5	100.0	24.2	15.8	31.1	28.9	1	6	22
24.8	100.0	19.5	11.0	42.8	26.7	−6	7	9
23.1	100.0	24.6	11.5	33.9	30.1	−29	12	8
16.6	100.0	39.5	6.3	28.7	25.5	46	126	328
24.5	100.0	15.5	10.0	51.5	23.0	−29	44	2
29.5	100.0	24.6	7.5	37.1	30.8	33	30	9
14.1	100.0	45.0	9.6	25.2	20.2	169	−12	46
26.8	100.0	28.5	14.2	30.2	27.1	−3	−4	11
20.3	100.0	31.5	15.9	28.5	24.0	51	11	−2
24.2	100.0	42.4	7.2	27.2	23.2	−63	17	4
14.0	100.0	43.2	14.8	23.3	18.7	80	1	25
24.7	100.0	21.6	14.2	36.8	27.4	5	−1	17
15.9	100.0	27.9	20.4	30.9	20.8	29	−3	34
18.1	100.0	29.5	8.3	37.5	24.7	−6	8	22
27.8	100.0	36.5	9.2	31.0	23.3	−27	9	11
25.2	100.0	23.8	11.7	34.6	30.0	24	0	14
27.3	100.0	25.6	12.2	34.0	28.2	−15	8	−1
6.7	n.a.	n.a.	n.a.	n.a.	n.a.	n.a.	n.a.	n.a.
31.9	n.a.	n.a.	n.a.	n.a.	n.a.	n.a.	n.a.	n.a.
13.7	100.0	53.2	6.0	24.3	16.5	13	14	32

such as is the case of many CIS countries—will not have the same effect on wages. While the concentration of trade patterns in natural-resource and unskilled-labor-intensive activities acted as a short-run cushion for job losses for unskilled workers in the CIS in the early to mid-1990s, in the aftermath of the collapse of CMEA, this is not a sustainable growth strategy. Over the long term, increased international competition from other low-price labor countries means that these countries would be unlikely to retain a strong comparative advantage, making it all the more important to focus on upgrading exports and shift into higher value added goods. Indeed, in such a situation, increased international competition in the face of little or stalled economic reform could well exacerbate poverty in these already poor countries, a topic that is further explored in chapter 3.

At the same time, the increase in unskilled-labor-intensive merchandise exports in the EU-8—if persistent—poses risks to the wage regime of workers entering the labor market in trade-related sectors and to the incentives affecting workers' investment in human capital in these countries. Moreover, since labor costs in these countries are relatively high, reliance on unskilled-labor-intensive exports, such as textiles and footwear, may not be sustainable in the long run, given the growing competition from low-wage countries, in Asia and elsewhere.

Sub-Regional Variation in Sources of Intertemporal Change in the Region's Export and Import Market Shares

It is informative to analyze the extent to which the changes in the observed patterns of the Region's trade flows over the past decade are the result of variations in (a) demand, (b) export competitiveness, or (c) product diversification (or lack thereof). We examine this decomposition over 1996–2003 for trade both among the Region's countries and between the Region's countries and the EU-15. (For information about the methodology used for this decomposition, see annex box 2.1.)

Decomposing Intra-Regional Trade, by Country

Growth of intra-Regional trade since 1996 has been largely driven by *demand* for exports from the Czech Republic, Hungary, Poland, Russia, the Slovak Republic, Turkmenistan, and Ukraine. (As table 2.9 illustrates, for Russia, Turkmenistan, and Ukraine, the overwhelming bulk of exports comprised natural gas and oil products.) The same pattern holds for the more recent portion of the period (that is, since 2000), except that the demand for Turkmenistan's exports has significantly declined.

More important, the vast majority of the countries did not improve their *competitiveness* in intra-Regional trade over the 1996–2003 period; of the seven that did improve their ability to be more competitive in intra-Regional trade, three (Hungary, Poland, and Lithuania) are in the EU-8; two (Georgia and Tajikistan) are in the CIS; and one (Romania) is in the SEE. However—yet not surprisingly—intra-Regional trade competitiveness improved markedly for most countries in the years following the Russian economic crisis and ruble devaluation in August 1998 (although the three CIS and SEE coun-

TABLE 2.9

Role of Demand, Export Competitiveness, and Product Diversification in Intra-Regional Merchandise Trade

	Exports to the Region ($ millions)			Factors underlying the 1996–2003 export change ($ millions)			Factors underlying the 2000–3 export change ($ millions)		
	1996	2000	2003	Demand factor	Competitive factor	Diversi-fication	Demand factor	Competitive factor	Diversi-fication
Albania	37	10	19	25	–42	–2	4	4	0
Armenia	108	85	108	125	–78	–47	54	–31	–1
Azerbaijan	339	445	570	534	–280	–23	152	51	–78
Belarus	4,098	5,122	6,206	986	–709	1,832	423	94	567
Bosnia & Herzegovina	319	373	391	225	–145	–8	159	–112	–29
Bulgaria	1,386	1,430	1,749	1,051	–692	3	552	22	–256
Croatia	995	805	1,601	823	–343	127	402	272	122
Czech Rep.	6,066	5,964	9,763	4,680	–693	–290	3,025	846	–73
Estonia	485	598	768	346	–25	–38	285	–104	–10
Georgia	149	295	471	83	214	25	258	–103	22
Hungary	2,976	3,745	6,338	2,230	1,156	–24	2,010	576	8
Kazakhstan	3,673	3,772	3,507	715	–776	–105	668	–1,050	117
Kyrgyz Rep.	274	158	189	169	–253	–1	43	–12	–1
Latvia	598	595	655	471	–369	–46	308	–214	–34
Lithuania	815	1,087	1,846	611	576	–156	514	417	–172
Macedonia, FYR	474	319	195	340	–610	–10	140	–256	–8
Moldova	1,059	503	600	696	–1,149	–6	359	–261	0
Poland	3,570	4,867	9,135	4,829	6,336	–5,599	4,630	3,933	–4,294
Romania	1,311	1,983	2,783	988	399	86	1,010	–39	–171
Russian Fed.	28,429	36,907	37,561	62,601	–54,643	1,174	12,950	–11,634	–661
Serbia & Montenegro	522	606	803	456	–188	14	291	–98	4
Slovak Rep.	4,297	3,962	5,942	4,101	–2,329	–127	2,024	71	–115
Slovenia	1,797	1,907	3,422	1,698	–59	–13	1,106	414	–5
Tajikistan	158	320	341	139	42	1	96	–77	1
Turkmenistan	2,056	1,649	509	11,364	–12,890	–21	1,214	–2,316	–38
Ukraine	9,299	7,706	10,695	5,748	–4,449	97	4,165	–977	–199
Uzbekistan	1,290	1,435	778	1,086	–1,561	–37	543	–1,133	–67
The Region and Turkey	78,782	89,241	112,717	108,422	–71,264	–3,224	38,498	–9,604	–5419
EU-8	20,604	22,726	37,870	16,608	1,387	–729	11,890	3,682	–428
CIS	50,932	58,395	61,534	4,047	–76,532	2,887	20,925	–17,448	–337
SEE	4,524	4,920	6,739	3,452	–1,433	184	2,268	–109	–341
Turkey	1,979	2,452	5,546	1,165	2,416	–14	1,011	2,106	–23

Source: Computations based on UN COMTRADE statistics.

Note: The demand factor isolates the effects of the increase or decrease in Regional demand for exports from other countries in the Region. This factor shows the increase or decrease in exports that would have occurred had there been no change in the country's market shares from the 1996 or 2003 base period. The competitive factor shows the change in exports, *over or under that associated with demand changes,* resulting from changes in a country's import market shares. Any difference between the change in the total exports and the sum of these two factors is the result of product diversification.

tries that gained competitively in the years before the crisis actually became less competitive in the postcrisis period).

Virtually none of the countries in the Region were able to garner any intra-Regional trade gains through greater *product diversification.* This has been the case most starkly for Poland, Russia, and Ukraine.

Decomposing the Region's Trade with the EU-15, by Country

A different picture emerges with regard to trade between the Region and the EU-15 (see table 2.10). Not only is *demand* for exports from the EU-8 countries—especially the Czech Republic, Hungary, Poland, and Slovenia—largely responsible for the growth in trade flows between the EU-15 and the Region between 1996 and 2003, but so is the competitiveness of these countries' exports. In other words, successful export penetration into EU-15 markets has required countries in the Region to exploit any cost-effective advantages they have—in addition to capitalizing on the market opportunities that have arisen as a result of income growth.

While, again, demand for Russian exports has been a prominent element in the growth of the Region's trade with the EU-15, such demand was not sustained over the entirety of the 1996–2003 period (this stands in contrast to the role of demand for Russia's exports in the growth of intra-Regional trade flows noted above); indeed the demand for Russian exports has declined significantly since 2000. On the other hand, Russia's export competitiveness has contributed substantially to the country's trade growth, especially in the post-2000 period (as would be expected, in light of the devaluation of the ruble in late 1998).

Increased product diversification has played a more positive role in the growth of trade between the Region and the EU-15 than in intra-Regional trade. This is particularly the case for Croatia and Ukraine. On the other hand, Russia's trade growth has been constrained considerably as a result of limited export product diversification, and the extent of diversification improved only marginally following the devaluation of the ruble. Lithuania, Poland, and Slovenia also have experienced losses in trade growth rersulting from restricted export product diversification.

Overall, these results suggest that "fixed" factors, such as geographic proximity, may not have been predominant in influencing changes in export and trade performance for many of the Region's countries. Some non-EU-8 transition economies have been able to increase their exports because of improved competitiveness and higher demand in the more distant markets of the EU-15, rather than among themselves. (The role of geography in explaining the Region's trade flows is explored in greater detail below.)

Decomposing Intra-Regional Market Share Changes, by Product Category

In order to better understand the reasons behind the loss of market share in "home" markets by the countries in the Region, an exami-

TABLE 2.10

Role of Demand, Export Competitiveness, and Product Diversification in Merchandise Trade between the Region and EU-15

	Exports to EU ($ millions)			Factors underlying the 1996–2003 export Change ($ millions)			Factors underlying the 2000–3 export change ($ millions)		
	1996	2000	2003	Demand factor	Competitive factor	Diversi-fication	Demand factor	Competitive factor	Diversi-fication
Albania	251	267	426	98	74	3	75	82	2
Armenia	57	110	274	8	209	0	−9	173	0
Azerbaijan	38	904	1,193	−15	1,171	−1	−43	339	−7
Belarus	527	693	1,194	213	460	−6	140	369	−8
Bosnia & Herzegovina	87	477	804	36	677	5	96	229	3
Bulgaria	2,204	2,840	4,272	929	1,083	57	546	827	59
Croatia	2,248	1,913	2,806	1,251	−900	207	586	64	243
Czech Rep.	12,380	19,726	33,482	7,422	13,593	87	5,853	7,878	25
Estonia	1,581	3,094	3,575	494	1,502	−1	645	−144	−20
Georgia	52	258	298	15	230	2	−4	43	1
Hungary	11,357	19,896	28,219	8,760	7,465	637	6,128	1,552	642
Kazakhstan	512	2,869	3,873	11	3,352	−2	72	951	−19
Kyrgyz Rep.	42	119	14	6	−36	2	−4	−102	1
Latvia	1,868	1,918	2,366	178	354	−35	263	196	−11
Lithuania	1,535	2,126	3,448	344	1,575	−6	276	1,113	−67
Macedonia, FYR	545	700	732	199	−11	0	94	−61	−1
Moldova	114	177	305	28	162	2	45	82	2
Poland	15,688	21,817	35,756	9,691	10,437	−59	7,657	6,388	−106
Romania	4,666	7,153	12,723	2,351	5,612	95	2,042	3,433	95
Russian Fed.	30,173	36,895	48,448	9,141	12,670	−3,536	1,501	12,799	−2,747
Serbia & Montenegro	616	737	1,452	229	605	2	192	522	1
Slovak Rep.	4,300	6,513	13,741	2,628	6,708	105	2,100	5,004	124
Slovenia	5,502	5,579	7,365	4,041	−2,275	98	1,966	−244	64
Tajikistan	120	40	98	−64	42	0	−7	65	0
Turkmenistan	91	205	240	−54	203	0	−119	155	0
Ukraine	1,836	2,575	3,972	303	1,814	20	306	969	124
Uzbekistan	670	453	279	−367	−24	−1	−113	−61	0
The Region and Turkey	112,198	156,992	239,464	55,147	74,369	−2,250	36,370	47,623	−1,522
EU-8	54,212	80,671	127,953	33,558	39,358	826	24,889	21,743	652
CIS	34,232	45,297	60,188	9,219	20,253	−3,521	1,766	15,781	−2,654
SEE	10,001	13,351	21,764	4,863	6,533	366	3,438	4,573	400
Turkey	12,579	16,267	27,441	7,047	7,756	59	5,767	5,347	61

Source: Computations based on UN COMTRADE statistics.

Note: The demand factor isolates the effects of the increase or decrease in Regional demand for exports from other countries in the Region. This factor shows the increase or decrease in exports that would have occurred had there been no change in the country's market shares from the 1996 or 2003 base period. The competitive factor shows the change in exports, *over or under that associated with demand changes,* resulting from changes in a country's import market shares. Any difference between the change in the total exports and the sum of these two factors is the result of product diversification.

nation of the underlying statistics by product category (four-digit SITC level) is warranted. The extent to which different countries outside the Region have expanded their shares of the Region's imports and therefore displaced home country suppliers by product category is depicted in table 2.11.

TABLE 2.11

Changes in Market Share of the Region's Imports, by Major Product Category and by Source of Imports

SITC	Major export product	Total imports of Region,[a] as of end-2003 ($ millions)	1996–2003 market share changes (%)							
			The Region[a]	EU-15	NAFTA	East Asia incl. Japan	South Asia	Latin America and the Caribbean	MENA	ROW
3330	Petroleum oils and crude oils	16,849	14.0	−3.0	0.0	0.0	0.0	0.0	−12.0	1.0
7810	Passenger motor cars, for transport	16,907	6.2	1.5	−1.0	−4.4	−0.1	0.0	0.0	−2.2
3341	Motor spirit and other light oils	7,357	7.3	−8.0	−0.3	−1.9	−0.4	0.2	0.9	2.2
7849	Other parts and accessories of motor veh.	10,078	−6.6	9.7	−0.8	−2.0	0.0	0.3	0.0	−0.5
7132	Int. combustion piston engines	2,777	6.3	1.1	0.5	−7.7	0.3	0.1	0.0	−0.7
7731	Insulated, electric wire, cable	3,160	4.6	−10.6	−1.3	4.4	0.1	0.1	1.6	1.0
8211	Chairs and other seats and parts	1,670	17.3	−13.8	−2.2	1.3	0.0	0.1	−0.1	−2.5
7611	Television receivers, color	1,278	35.4	0.2	−0.7	−33.8	0.0	0.0	0.0	−1.1
8462	Undergarments, knitted of cotton	880	12.3	−18.8	−0.8	1.8	2.7	0.1	1.4	1.2
8439	Other outer garments of textile fabrics	686	13.0	−32.0	−1.7	18.4	1.4	0.0	2.1	−1.2
8219	Other furniture and parts	1,823	8.2	−8.9	−0.9	1.9	−0.1	0.2	−0.1	−0.3
7721	Elec. appl. such as switches and relays	6,052	−1.4	−3.1	0.1	5.1	0.1	0.2	0.0	−1.0
8451	Jerseys, pull-overs, twinsets	724	19.6	−30.8	−0.5	11.1	−0.4	0.1	0.5	0.4
8510	Footwear	1,760	−4.3	−16.9	−1.0	22.9	−0.6	0.0	0.4	−0.7
3414	Petroleum gases	8,277	−10.5	3.6	0.0	0.0	0.0	0.0	0.2	6.8
6841	Aluminum and alum. alloys	1,776	6.3	−10.4	−0.9	0.0	0.0	1.7	−1.3	4.5
8423	Trousers, breeches of textile fabric	435	9.9	−25.3	−1.0	10.5	3.2	−0.1	3.3	−0.6
7643	Radiotelegraphic and radiotelephonic	5,633	6.5	−29.1	−11.4	35.2	0.0	0.1	0.0	−1.4
7649	Parts of apparatus of telecom	3,451	3.2	−16.0	−2.4	17.0	0.0	0.7	0.0	−2.6
2482	Wood of coniferous species, sawn	603	−2.3	3.7	−1.5	0.1	0.0	0.1	0.0	−0.1
7523	Complete digital central processing	1,143	8.1	−9.7	−12.0	13.4	0.0	0.1	0.1	−0.1
8459	Other outer garments, knit	570	8.7	−11.9	−0.9	5.8	0.0	0.0	0.3	−2.0
7821	Motor vehicles for transport of goods	4,441	−14.0	25.2	−1.2	−7.8	0.0	−0.1	0.0	−2.2
3222	Other coal, whether/not pulverized	2,018	−2.3	−0.2	−2.6	3.8	0.0	3.3	0.1	−2.1
6842	Aluminium and alum. alloys	2,520	−2.9	4.2	−1.3	0.8	0.0	0.2	−0.2	−0.8
7139	Parts of int. comb. piston engines	3,612	−18.0	23.0	−3.9	−0.5	0.2	0.6	−0.1	−1.1
8939	Plastic articles	5,642	0.4	0.4	−1.7	2.3	0.0	0.0	−0.1	−1.3
2820	Waste and scrap metal of iron or steel	2,301	36.2	−29.1	−7.8	0.0	0.0	0.0	2.0	−1.3
6821	Copper and copper alloys, refined	500	−24.6	−1.2	−0.9	−2.0	0.0	29.8	1.7	−2.7
6584	Bed linen, table linen toilet, kitchen	288	3.9	−14.5	−0.2	6.0	6.8	0.3	−0.3	−2.0
	All above products	115,214	−7.5	9.4	−1.0	3.0	0.1	0.3	−4.3	0.1

Source: Computations based on UN COMTRADE statistics.

Note: UN COMTRADE statistics do not include data on Bosnia and Herzegovina, Tajikistan, and Uzbekistan.

a. Region includes Turkey.

Changes in import shares are reported for the 30 largest four-digit products that the Region imports globally, which together account for around a quarter (25 percent) of the Region's total imports. The data show that, on average, the countries lost their Regional market share across all the product categories by about 7.5 percent. In five product categories, the loss exceeded 10 percent. The erosion of market shares of producers based in the Region was greater than that registered by producers from NAFTA and MENA, the only other producers that also saw their market shares decline in the Region's markets. The largest competitive gains by the Region's suppliers occurred within a limited number of product groups, notably waste and scrap metal of iron and steel; televisions; sweater garments; and petroleum products.

EU-15 and East Asian suppliers made the greatest market share gains in imports into the Region. On average, the EU-15 increased its market share by more than 9 percent, with the largest gains recorded in motor vehicles, engine parts, and motor accessories. East Asian producers increased their market shares by an average of 3 percent. They realized the greatest increases in radio electronics, footwear, garments, and digital processing equipment.

The CIS as a group enjoyed competitive gains in EU markets mainly from the largest oil and gas CIS producers; such market share gains reached around $20 billion and were largely accounted for by Azerbaijan, Kazakhstan, Russia, and Ukraine. These gains exceeded those associated with higher demand by about $10 billion, reflecting the critical importance of larger shares in EU markets for the oil and gas products originating in these countries.

A Dichotomy in the Interactions between Trade Intensity and Domestic Competition and Governance

There are several ways in which the relationship between greater integration and domestic competition and governance conditions have been manifested in the countries of the Region throughout the transition, as discussed in detail in chapter 4. In the countries where import penetration has been greatest, firms have been most prone to reduce production costs and innovate. This finding is strongest for firms of smaller scale and those with greater private ownership. Particularly telling is that private foreign-invested firms operating in "host" markets have been more likely to react to import competition than have their domestically owned counterparts. More important, in the countries where there has been less progress in fostering a competitive market environment—especially in the CIS—the effects of imports on business decisions have been more muted than in countries, such as the EU-8, where markets are more competitively structured as a result of more advanced reforms.

The state of competition in the domestic sphere also affects international integration on the export side. Two pieces of evidence are significant here. First, in the Region's countries where there has been greater introduction of private sector participation in the economy, export intensity by businesses—measured by the percentage of export revenues as a share of total sales revenues—is much higher. This is true whether the increased private sector participation is the result of the privatization of existing firms or de novo investment. Moreover, the export intensity tends to be greater for foreign invested firms than it is for domestically owned businesses. This is evidence of a two-way relationship between international integration and behind-the-border conditions, such as greater competition: foreign firms investing in countries in the Region are more prone to react to import competition than are their domestic counterparts and at the same time are more likely to further their host countries' integration into world markets than are domestic businesses.

The ability to effectively resolve commercial disputes associated with international trade transactions "at home" is greatest in the emerging Euro-centric pole and weaker in the emerging Russia-centric pole. This evidence implies that there might be an important relationship between the sophistication and availability of instruments for dispute resolution and institutional development. Not surprisingly, firms in the CIS have relied on bribes to overcome institutional hurdles to a greater extent than those in the rest of the Region.

The incidence of corruption in the Region's countries is quite varied. More important, there is now evidence that these differences appear to be strongly related to the extent of international integration achieved—whether in terms of exports or imports—among the countries in the Region. In particular, the countries where corruption is more prominent tend to be those with the least amount of integration into the world economy.

Uneven Development of Trade-Facilitation Infrastructure and Institutions

Over the course of the transition, the institutional and physical capacity in trade facilitation have varied significantly across the Region; it has also been shaped by different local geographical, political, and economic conditions, as detailed in the discussion in chapter 5.

Broadly, the trend toward two poles is evident in regard to the state of customs, the development of trade-related transport facilities, the level of technical product standards, and the use of modern mechanisms, such as IT, in carrying out logistical operations.

The most serious problem in customs—the incidence of unofficial payments in order to move goods across national borders—is extraordinarily pernicious in Central Asia and the Caucasus, and to a lesser extent in certain areas of SEE. This handicap compounds other customs impediments, such as the lack of coordination among border-related agencies, the complexity of customs procedures, unclear customs codes and regulations, and the low utilization of IT in customs operations. Most important perhaps, some of these countries are still experiencing political tensions with neighboring countries, and therefore the level of regional cooperation in facilitating trade remains low.

For the EU-8 and EU accession and candidate countries—Bulgaria and Romania, and Croatia and Turkey, respectively—in contrast, customs administrations have significantly improved over the last decade, at least in part because of the reforms necessary to accede to the EU. Still, more progress is needed in adopting and fully implementing relevant EU legislation.

In trade-related transport, much of the Caucasus and most of the CIS countries confront poor quality of service and high transportation and handling costs. Many of these countries are landlocked, making it important to extend their transport infrastructure to transit neighbors. For the Caucasus and the Balkans, war-damaged infrastructure and inoperable links from the transport network inherited from the central planning period are especially problematic.

With respect to the EU-8 countries, by comparison, the transport systems have been well maintained and have benefited from new investment over time. The result is lower transport costs and better service quality. In part, the improved quality of the transport networks in the EU-8 is rooted in the relatively early adoption of market-oriented policies, including bringing rates more in line with costs, reducing subsidies, and privatization. While privatization of trade-related transport has been most widespread among the EU-8 compared with other portions of the Region, the overall level of private sector participation in these countries is still low by global standards.

Low product standards and technical barriers to trade are also important contributors to high trade logistics costs, especially as they relate to border-crossing procedures and administrative rules. On a cross-country basis, there is empirical evidence that they play a key role in export performance in the Region. By dint of complying with

EU accession requirements, the EU-8 countries have adopted world-class standards. Increasingly the EU accession and candidate countries will also do so. In contrast, the remaining Balkans, the Caucasus, and the Central Asian Republics are still at an early stage of reform in standardization.

The development of e-commerce in trade transactions and adoption of IT are low in the Region relative to other regions of the world. Here again, there is a marked bifurcation among the countries. While significant advances have been made in the EU-8, the development of trade-related Internet infrastructure in the CIS, and to a more limited extent in the Balkans, is not adequate to support effective use of e-commerce in trade transactions.

Intraindustry Trade and Global Production-Sharing Networks: Can FDI Enable Mobility between the Two Poles?

As in other parts of the world, the increasing globalization of the international economy and the fragmentation of production processes have changed the economic landscape facing the nations, industries, and individual firms of the Region. Through FDI, multinational corporations have been key agents in this transformation, creating international production and distribution networks spanning the globe. In essence, network trade in parts and components, where countries complete different stages of final products, is the internationalization of the manufacturing process.

Production sharing usually involves the development of specialized (and often) skilled-labor-intensive activities within a vertically integrated international network. Such production sharing has been growing rapidly on a global scale, with growth rates that have exceeded other dimensions of manufacturing trade. Worldwide, the many industries where major parts of a production process have been internationalized include television and radio receivers, sewing machines, calculators, office equipment, electrical machinery, power and machine tools, typewriters, cameras, and watches, among others. The result has been the growth of intraindustry or increasingly intraproduct trade at the expense of traditional interindustry trade.

As is the case elsewhere in the world, in the Region, trade and FDI are largely complements (see figure 2.10). Trade in parts and components (P&C) has increased in importance in the Region's global trade. In the aggregate, the Region's trade in goods used in production sharing grew at an annual rate of 17 percent from 1996 to 2003 (see table 2.12). Today, trade in parts and components by the Region's countries

FIGURE 2.10

Trade and FDI Inflows in the Region Are Complements, 1995–2003[a]

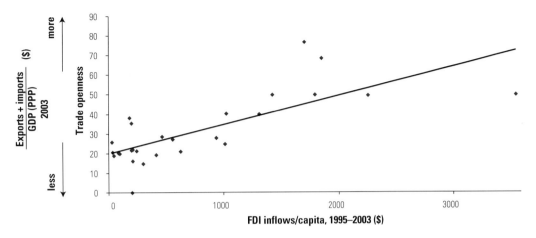

Source: IMF DOT statistics.

Note: a. Includes Turkey.

accounts for 9 and 12 percent of total exports and imports, respectively, up from 5 and 10 percent in 1996.

As discussed in detail in chapter 7, many EU-8 and some SEE countries have been heavily involved in network trade. During the initial phase of the transition, most of these countries relied on unskilled-labor-intensive exports associated with "buyer-driven" production chains in clothing and furniture. However, rising wages have prompted these countries to shift toward skilled-labor-intensive and capital-intensive exports conducted through "producer-driven" networks, especially in the automotive and IT industries. The other SEE economies and a few CIS countries—notably those active in natural-resource trade—have been active in buyer-driven production chains but have not managed to make a transition toward producer-driven supply chains. The remaining CIS countries have effectively remained outside network trade of any form.

Sizable FDI inflows have been instrumental in participation in network trade. In fact, the countries that experienced the largest FDI inflows have registered the largest increase in exports of network components and parts. Many countries in the Region have attracted sizable inflows of FDI, but the cross-country differences in the amount of FDI received are striking (see table 2.13). While Tajikistan received only $35 of FDI per capita as of end-2003, for example, the corresponding figure for Estonia is 138 times larger at $4,823. Generally the EU-8 countries have attracted the largest stock of FDI per capita within the Region,

TABLE 2.12

Trade in Parts and Components in the Region, 1996–2003

Country	Year	Total exports of P&C ($ millions)	Total imports of P&C ($ millions)	Exports of P&C as % of total exports	Imports of P&C as % of total imports	Share of P&C as % of manufacturing exports	Share of P&C as % of manufacturing imports
Region[a]	1996	10,984	25,716	4.6	9.5	10.0	16.1
	2000	20,324	37,493	6.5	12.4	13.2	20.0
	2003	38,058	53,694	8.8	12.4	15.8	19.0
EU-8	1996	7,653	13,432	9.2	12.0	13.6	18.8
	2000	15,656	22,603	13.2	15.9	17.8	23.8
	2003	31,062	31,919	16.7	15.9	21.7	22.9
CIS	1996	1,719	6,062	1.5	6.8	6.3	13.2
	2000	1,865	5,433	1.3	7.3	6.0	13.9
	2003	2,032	10,966	1.2	9.4	5.5	15.4
SEE	1996	653	1,774	3.7	6.8	6.2	11.3
	2000	1,272	2,611	5.9	8.8	9.3	13.6
	2003	2,232	4,098	6.8	8.7	9.6	12.6

Source: Computations based on UN COMTRADE statistics.

Note: a. Includes Turkey.

while among CIS countries, only Azerbaijan and Kazakhstan have managed to attract significant FDI, mainly in their oil sectors.

These data suggest, again, that the Region has been evolving toward a bifurcated pattern of international integration: the countries that have integrated more into the global economy through producer-driven production-sharing networks have significantly advanced developmentally, whereas those not participating in such networks and hence less integrated internationally are generally poorer. Participation in producer-driven production-sharing networks has enabled countries in the Region to shift output from unskilled-labor-intensive to skilled-labor-intensive products. It has also provided gains to these economies in terms of transfers of advances in technology, which have engendered productivity growth. By fostering greater product diversification, global production sharing has strengthened the "virtuous cycle" between trade and growth. In this regard, it has helped avoid the deterioration in countries' export prices resulting from expansion of exports of the same products.

One important feature of global production sharing is that through FDI, the Region's countries may be able to create opportunities to engage in network trade, capitalize on certain aspects of their comparative advantage that otherwise might not readily present themselves in traditional interindustry trade, and achieve some mobility across trading blocs. In other words, increasing the prospects for trade in parts and components could facilitate the international integration

TABLE 2.13

Stock of Foreign Direct Investment in Countries in the Region, End–2003

Country	Cumulative FDI per capita 2003 ($)
Albania	344
Armenia	275
Azerbaijan	1,049
Belarus	192
Bosnia & Herzegovina	279
Bulgaria	650
Croatia	2,547
Czech Rep.	4,022
Estonia	4,823
Georgia	202
Hungary	4,241
Kazakhstan	1,178
Kyrgyz Rep.	99
Latvia	1,430
Lithuania	1,436
Macedonia, FYR	500
Moldova	186
Poland	1,365
Romania	572
Russian Fed.	- 366
Serbia & Montenegro	410
Slovak Rep.	1,904
Slovenia	2,184
Tajikistan	35
Turkmenistan	270
Ukraine	144
Uzbekistan	36

Source: UNCTAD FDI database.

of the Region's countries that to date have not effectively done so and further their growth potential.

Therefore, a significant policy challenge for the less-developed countries in the Region is to attract FDI. For this to happen, several ingredients are key. For one, industry decisions regarding investment location depend on countries in the Region having in place market-oriented, open-trade policy regimes, so as to permit ease of exportation and importation of parts and components, as well as assembled, "final" products. Well-developed trade facilitation systems and related institutions (such as customs), as well as modernized services sectors (such as the transport and communication infrastructure), also will be critical. But most important, countries need to create favorable behind-the-border business environments. This means establishing incentives and institutions to foster domestic markets that are competitively structured; that have low barriers to entry and exit; that have rules-based checks on anticompetitive conduct and on undue government interference in commercial decisions; and that have adherence to the rule of law, protection of property rights, and good governance. These are the focus of chapter 4.

How Does the Region's Openness to Trade Compare with That of Other Regions?

The Region's Progress in Openness to Trade

Against the backdrop of the rapid growth in trade flows for the Region over the last decade, how significant is trade in the overall economic activity of the Region's countries today? Using the conventional "output-based" metric of "trade openness," calculated as the sum of a nation's total exports and imports as a percentage of GDP, on average for the Region (as well as Turkey), total merchandise exports and imports today account for about 40 percent of GDP, as compared with about 35 percent in 1994.[6] That said, there is significant variation in trade performance across the countries, with trade openness in the EU-8 reaching 65 percent, while the corresponding measure for the CIS is only 24 percent; openness in the SEE countries lies somewhere in between (see figure 2.11).

In services trade, not surprisingly, the extent and pattern of openness are different (see figure 2.12). Today, on average, services trade accounts for about 14 percent of GDP in the Region (as well as Turkey). But SEE's services trade accounts for about 18 percent of GDP on average—the highest in the Region. Until 1999, the EU-8's services trade openness was the highest. For the CIS countries, although openness in services trade has more or less continued to rise over the decade, today, on average, services trade among the CIS accounts for about 11 percent of GDP.

The Region's Trade Performance in the Global Context: Determinants of Aggregate Trade Openness

In order to understand how the Region's members compare with other countries worldwide in terms of trade openness, an empirical model was developed for 149 countries, including the 27 countries in the Region and Turkey. This model of trade performance is designed to determine broadly, other things being equal, the average association between a country's national income level and its *aggregate* (or multilateral) trade openness—that is, its gross trade flows, regardless of their destination or origin. (We assess in the next section the coun-

FIGURE 2.11

Merchandise Trade Openness in the Region, 1994–2003

Imports and Exports as Percentage of GDP PPP

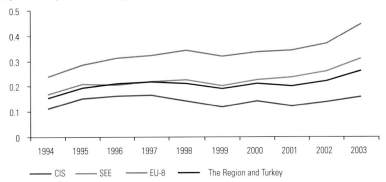

— CIS — SEE — EU-8 — The Region and Turkey

Source: IMF DOT statistics.

FIGURE 2.12

Services Trade Openness in the Region, 1994–2003

Imports and Exports as Percentage of GDP PPP

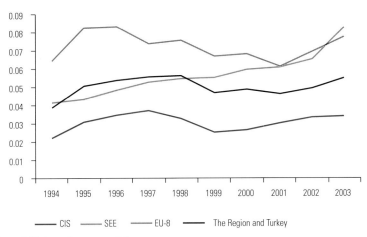

— CIS — SEE — EU-8 — The Region and Turkey

Source: IMF balance of payments statistics.

tries' trade performance based on destination and origin of *bilateral* trade flows.) Openness, as measured by the share of trade in goods in GDP, was regressed on the country's population (which was used as a proxy for country size), geographic distance to major markets (which was used to measure market access), and GDP per capita.

The hypothesis underlying this approach is that richer countries trade more (as a percentage of their GDP), while larger countries and those that are relatively far away from major markets trade less. The theoretical and empirical literature suggests a positive correlation between openness (trade integration) and income levels.[7] This positive correlation can be attributed to the increasing diversification of an economy and to deepening international specialization in the course of development. At the same time, as the recent research suggests, both income and trade are dependent on the quality of institutions. In this regard, a country's income level may be viewed as a proxy for institutional variables that underlie trends in both overall economic development and international trade.[8] On the other hand, a country's large size (the number of domestic economic agents and consumers) creates larger opportunities for within-country trade, so these countries will be less open, all other things being equal.

The empirical results, summarized in table 2.14, suggest that, for all 149 countries, larger countries and those farther from major markets on average tend to trade less, and countries that are more advanced economically and institutionally tend to trade more.[9]

How does the trade openness of the Region's countries compare with that of other regions of the world? The estimated model suggests that the vast majority of the countries tend to trade largely in line with countries elsewhere in the world having similar income levels, size, and geographic distance from major markets. The only exception is many (though not all) SEE countries, where there is evidence of "undertrading."[10] In other words, more than a decade into the transition, most of the countries in the Region, as a whole, trade generally in line with the global cross-country norm: they neither "under-" nor "overtrade."[11]

TABLE 2.14

The Region's Merchandise Trade Openness in Comparison with That of Other Regions, 1994–2003

Explanatory variable	Dependent variable Ratio of exports and imports to GDP in PPP ($)			
	Base Model	Model 1	Model 2	Model 3
Ln population	−3.45 (0.9)***	−5.29 (1.2)***	−5.40 (1.3)***	−5.40 (1.3)***
Ln GDP per capita (PPP)	11.44 (2.0)***	11.62 (4.1)***	12.67 (4.4)***	12.82 (4.0)***
Ln distance to major market	−6.06 (2.79)**	−5.30 (3.0)*	−5.15 (3.1)*	−5.28 (3.1)*
The Region			−2.66 (3.2)	
EU-8				−2.16 (3.5)
SEE				−7.29 (3.8)*
CIS				4.66 (4.9)
East Asia		18.20 (7.7)**	18.36 (7.6)**	19.76 (8.8)**
Latin America		−1.23 (3.7)	−1.54 (3.8)	0.12 (4.5)
OECD		7.62 (8.1)	5.92 (8.4)	6.93 (7.5)
Sub-Saharan Africa		—	—	—
Intercept	34.92 (30.5)	55.16 (46.3)	46.84 (46.2)	45.06 (42.8)
R^2	0.56	0.61	0.61	0.61
Number of countries	122	79	79	79

Source: Author's calculations.

Note: Standard errors in parentheses. Significance level: *** 1 percent; ** 5 percent; * 10 percent. IV (2SLS) regressions with robust standard errors.

How does the *actual* trade openness of individual countries in the Region compare with the *expected* openness that reflects their actual size, access to markets, and income level (that is, the "theoretical openness" estimates being those corresponding to the regression line in the model)? The data show that there is significant variation among the countries within the Region (table 2.15).

As the table demonstrates, two features are prominent. Actual openness increased from 1995 to 2003 for the Region overall. But

TABLE 2.15
Actual vs. Theoretical Trade Openness in the Region
Merchandise exports plus imports to GDP in PPP ($)

	Actual openness (%)		2003 realization ratios (actual/predicted by the model)
	1995	2003	
Albania	10.5	15.8	0.53
Armenia	19.0	15.9	0.74
Azerbaijan	9.5	16.2	0.96
Belarus	31.2	36.2	1.35
Bosnia & Herzegovina	14.6	20.6	0.56
Bulgaria	21.8	29.6	0.94
Croatia	39.6	40.5	0.98
Czech Rep.	33.2	62.3	1.41
Estonia	45.0	75.4	1.63
Georgia	7.3	12.2	0.61
Hungary	30.2	61.0	1.78
Kazakhstan	17.3	21.8	0.83
Kyrgyz Rep.	17.0	14.9	1.32
Latvia	24.2	35.1	1.04
Lithuania	28.8	43.7	1.09
Macedonia, FYR	27.7	23.9	0.61
Moldova	25.9	34.4	b
Poland	19.3	27.4	0.92
Romania	14.5	25.9	1.02
Russian Fed.	14.1	14.3	0.88
Serbia & Montenegro	a	a	a
Slovak Rep.	39.2	60.5	1.40
Slovenia	74.2	70.1	1.33
Tajikistan	40.5	23.7	b
Turkmenistan	27.1	20.8	0.90
Ukraine	17.3	18.3	1.07
Uzbekistan	20.5	10.0	b
Averages:			
The Region	25.8	31.9	1.37
CIS	20.6	19.9	0.96
SEE	21.5	26.0	0.77
EU-8	36.8	54.4	1.33

Source: Author's calculations.

Note: Coefficients from model with dummy variables used.
a. data unavailable.
b. Moldova, Tajikistan, and Uzbekistan are outliers because of large measurement errors.

while it increased for SEE and (quite dramatically) for the EU-8, it actually decreased for the CIS. Thus, for most of the countries where international integration increased markedly, especially in the EU-8—notably the Czech Republic, Estonia, Hungary, Latvia, Lithuania, Poland, and the Slovak Republic—economic growth was relatively fast. Where integration declined, largely in the CIS—especially Armenia, the Kyrgyz Republic, Tajikistan, Turkmenistan, and Uzbekistan—growth was considerably slow or stagnant. This is part of the evidence that international integration can spur growth.

At the same time, the results once again suggest that the CIS countries—as a group, not necessarily every country individually—are actually trading broadly in line with their current potential (as reflected by the estimated model). On the other hand, most of the EU-8 countries appear to be measurably overtrading; on average the sub-Region overtrades by one-third. In contrast, the estimation results suggest that a core group of the SEE countries—largely the Western Balkans nations of Albania, Bosnia and Herzegovina, and FYR Macedonia—are undertrading, such that on average SEE is trading at just over three-quarters of its potential.[12] This evidence concerning the CIS and the SEE is consistent with that presented above.

The Region's Trade Performance: The Gravity Model Approach to Determinants of Bilateral Trade Flows

A similar pattern emerges from analysis of a gravity model of bilateral trade openness, that is, one where the units of analysis are the trade flows between the origin and destination countries. (In contrast, the openness model presented earlier measures a country's aggregate [or multilateral] flows of trade, that is, trade flows irrespective of the origin and destination of trade.) Despite controversies surrounding the gravity model since its inception (which have been somewhat alleviated recently),[13] the gravity model has proven to be the most accurate tool for the explanation and prediction of bilateral trade flows. A number of studies have applied the gravity model to assessing trade flows among various countries in the world, including some of those in the Region.[14] Following the recent analysis of Freinkman et al. (2004), who examine trade flows within the 12 CIS countries, applying the gravity model developed by Frankel (1997), we perform a similar analysis for all 27 countries in the Region and Turkey.[15]

Sub-Regional groupings. The intertemporal dynamics of the bilateral realization ratios—that is, the ratios of actual-to-predicted trade flows—aggregated at the sub-Regional level over 1994–2003 are depicted in table 2.16. There is a marked pattern in the data. Although total world trade flows of the CIS were significantly lower than their potential in the early 1990s (owing to the collapse of CMEA), over the course of the decade, the CIS countries steadily and sizably exploited their global trade opportunities. The bulk of these trade flows, as noted earlier, have been largely in the natural resources sectors. In contrast, the results suggest that the EU-8 and SEE countries largely maintained their pattern of total world trade flows during the same period.

More important, the "reconstitution" of a Russia-centric trading bloc that has been taking place over the course of the decade is clearly discernible in table 2.16. In contrast to the EU-8 and SEE countries, where the ratio of actual-to-potential trade among the countries *within* each of these two sub-Regions declined over the 1994–2003 period, for the CIS countries, the comparable ratio steadily increased; that is, the ratio of actual-to-potential intra-CIS trade flows has been rising over time.

TABLE 2.16

Gravity Model Bilateral Trade Openness Realization Ratios (Sub-Regional)

Actual bilateral trade/potential trade

	CIS	EU-8	SEE
1994			
World total	0.72	0.80	0.85
CIS	0.78	2.34	3.72
EU-8	1.97	0.86	1.38
SEE	2.87	1.18	3.54
EU-15	0.60	0.80	0.82
1997			
World total	0.83	0.90	0.96
CIS	1.02	2.31	4.10
EU-8	2.04	0.76	1.29
SEE	3.32	1.25	3.43
EU-15	0.67	0.98	1.02
2001			
World total	1.11	1.00	1.24
CIS	1.20	2.62	4.88
EU-8	2.28	0.70	1.42
SEE	3.96	1.21	3.72
EU-15	1.08	1.19	1.45
2003			
World total	1.64	0.80	0.85
CIS	1.89	1.82	2.70
EU-8	3.06	0.53	0.90
SEE	5.17	0.88	1.83
EU-15	1.56	0.94	0.89

Source: Author's calculations using new data applied to Frankel (1997).

Country-level analysis. Disaggregating the gravity model analysis to the country-level (table 2.17)[16] reveals a pattern of individual countries' trade performance that largely parallels the sub-Regional perspective shown above. For example, the generally consistent increase in trade openness of the CIS countries over time is again evident. Indeed, in contrast to the EU-8 and SEE countries, all CIS countries, without exception, increased their trade openness between 2001 and 2003.

The country-level analysis also shows the heterogeneity among countries *within* the two trading blocs. For example, Russia and Georgia are prominent among the CIS countries that have steadily increased their ratios of actual-to-potential trade flows toward the CIS. They are at the forefront of the re-creation of the "Russia-centric" trading bloc. By comparison, the already relatively significant orientation of trade flows to the CIS by Tajikistan and Uzbekistan did not change much between 1997 and 2003.

At the same time, within SEE, in 2003, Bulgaria and Romania registered relatively strong trade performances on both a global basis and

TABLE 2.17

Gravity Model Bilateral Trade Openness Realization Ratios (by Country)

Actual bilateral trade/potential trade

Sub-Region / Country	CIS											
	Arm	Azr	Bel	Geo	Kaz	Kyr	Mol	Rus	Taj	Trm	Ukr	Uzb
1994												
World Total	0.63	1.09	0.41	0.40	0.99	1.76	1.02	0.78	0.78	1.31	0.57	0.54
CIS	0.99	1.07	0.57	0.52	1.25	2.14	1.87	0.76	0.79	1.67	0.75	0.66
EU-8	0.34	1.08	0.82	0.40	2.70	1.06	0.93	2.43	2.46	2.07	1.29	1.32
SEE	0.26	0.63	0.83	1.36	2.65	0.82	4.76	3.68	1.22	0.18	1.61	0.33
EU-15	0.17	0.30	0.19	0.12	0.63	0.68	0.20	0.73	0.86	0.79	0.25	0.46
1997												
World Total	1.16	0.89	1.08	0.71	1.12	1.52	1.86	0.77	3.64	2.14	0.75	1.24
CIS	1.08	0.78	1.51	0.58	1.27	1.88	2.78	0.92	5.38	3.31	0.78	1.42
EU-8	1.54	1.27	1.76	2.27	2.05	2.24	3.19	2.07	10.63	1.19	1.88	3.83
SEE	5.58	1.66	2.01	11.89	1.13	1.48	9.55	3.38	11.49	2.10	2.68	2.37
EU-15	0.94	0.46	0.50	0.48	0.98	0.67	0.80	0.69	2.37	0.64	0.51	0.98
2001												
World Total	0.96	1.09	0.91	0.83	1.49	1.33	1.88	1.08	3.22	1.77	1.13	1.02
CIS	0.87	0.58	1.24	0.62	1.62	1.53	2.57	1.05	5.35	2.83	1.19	1.39
EU-8	0.61	0.54	1.83	1.22	1.85	1.21	2.58	2.42	7.41	0.63	2.14	2.50
SEE	1.54	2.34	1.44	7.35	3.45	1.00	7.28	4.05	6.56	4.08	4.13	1.64
EU-15	0.94	1.91	0.63	0.81	1.70	1.09	1.35	1.10	1.68	0.81	0.93	0.87
2003												
World Total	1.59	1.68	1.97	1.22	2.11	1.81	2.93	1.57	3.95	2.24	1.63	1.08
CIS	1.26	0.94	3.03	0.99	1.99	2.18	4.06	1.75	5.21	3.56	1.63	1.31
EU-8	1.31	3.86	2.37	1.59	3.31	1.73	3.60	3.09	15.02	0.72	3.41	1.52
SEE	4.11	1.08	2.44	9.54	8.14	2.35	10.49	4.98	31.03	2.72	5.86	1.05
EU-15	2.01	2.43	1.13	1.15	2.25	0.72	2.25	1.58	2.10	1.08	1.41	0.69

Source: Author's calculations using IMF DOT data applied to Frankel (1997).

with respect to trade with the EU-15. In contrast, the analogous trade flows during the same period for the core of the Region, the Western Balkan countries (Albania, Bosnia and Herzegovina, Croatia, FYR Macedonia, and Serbia and Montenegro) were significantly below their potential, reinforcing the earlier evidence that this sub-Region is not fully exploiting its competitive advantage.

Capturing the roles of institutional and policy-related factors. Interpretation of empirical results of openness and gravity models—both in the literature and in this study—must be done with care. In part this stems from the complexity of the reality that is being modeled econometrically. In particular, it is important to realize that institutional and policy-related variables do not likely play an exogenous role; rather, such variables are often endogenous and directly related to the level of trade itself. Some steps have been taken in this analysis to deal with this problem, but data availability limits the sophistication of the approach that can be taken.

	EU-8							SEE						
Cz	Est	Hu	Lat	Lit	Pol	Slk	Slv	Alb	BH	Bul	Crt	Mac	Rom	SM
0.80	1.33	0.83	1.04	1.40	0.59	1.27	1.16	0.65	0.60	1.32	0.95	1.41	0.97	0.02
2.38	2.86	5.86	2.87	4.51	1.04	4.63	4.02	0.07	16.58	5.40	3.52	5.19	3.89	0.21
1.26	1.42	0.31	1.39	1.84	0.25	8.22	2.58	0.59	3.95	0.30	3.49	14.48	0.98	0.00
1.16	0.53	0.69	0.57	1.19	0.23	1.82	5.23	2.17	16.72	4.65	5.20	13.02	1.19	0.00
0.70	1.38	0.99	0.90	0.99	0.70	0.65	1.19	0.76	0.35	1.48	0.98	1.04	0.94	0.02
0.88	2.19	1.07	1.60	1.46	0.64	1.32	1.30	0.87	2.22	1.24	1.04	1.21	1.07	0.27
2.02	3.59	5.77	3.48	3.81	1.22	4.52	5.10	0.30	2.48	7.08	4.63	5.95	3.97	0.03
0.94	2.29	0.32	2.18	1.62	0.34	5.77	2.98	0.81	18.20	0.23	3.57	5.65	0.96	0.60
1.42	0.33	1.09	0.46	0.65	0.28	1.98	5.67	2.44	33.91	2.02	9.02	5.64	0.85	0.43
0.89	2.48	1.45	1.57	1.26	0.76	0.88	1.35	1.11	2.19	1.36	1.10	1.10	1.19	0.31
1.19	2.45	1.03	1.34	1.39	0.67	1.70	1.45	1.44	3.29	1.33	1.05	1.27	1.46	0.42
2.57	4.76	5.96	2.82	3.52	1.52	6.21	6.18	2.39	7.80	6.21	7.57	8.25	4.55	0.03
0.85	2.21	0.27	2.04	1.58	0.38	5.23	3.44	0.91	25.87	0.27	3.13	4.33	1.61	1.30
1.87	0.50	0.94	0.35	0.51	0.37	2.58	6.37	2.94	31.26	2.67	8.32	5.43	1.71	1.42
1.41	2.75	1.54	1.50	1.41	0.83	1.39	1.54	1.87	3.48	1.81	1.12	1.30	1.81	0.46
0.84	1.68	0.90	1.10	0.86	0.58	1.30	0.84	0.50	0.68	0.90	0.63	0.74	1.13	0.28
1.54	3.08	3.95	2.01	1.95	1.20	3.34	3.47	1.97	1.34	3.14	2.86	2.14	3.33	0.06
0.59	1.72	0.27	1.58	1.08	0.30	3.37	1.87	0.32	4.78	0.19	1.53	2.86	1.17	0.81
1.13	0.26	0.81	0.27	1.38	0.32	1.67	2.56	0.81	5.47	1.52	3.87	2.80	1.00	0.47
0.97	1.83	1.28	1.17	0.80	0.72	1.09	0.84	0.60	0.70	1.21	0.65	0.73	1.33	0.30

FIGURE 2.13

**Trade Openness and Behind-the-Border Reforms in the Region:
A Mutually Reinforcing Relationship[a]**

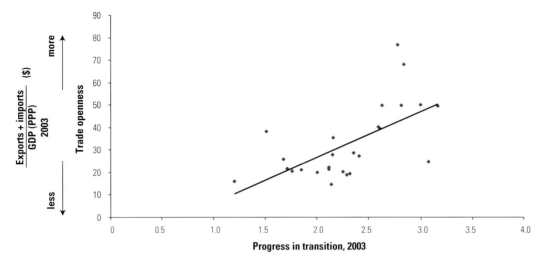

Source: World Bank, using IMF DOT data and EBRD transition index.

Note: a. Includes Turkey.

Moreover, as is the case in almost all similar analyses in the literature, institutional and policy-related variables in such models have
very strong—sometimes the most—explanatory power. This suggests
that the most acute barriers to trade expansion probably do not rest in
"fixed" factors, such as geography. Rather, trade performance is likely
to be greatly influenced by actions taken (or not taken) at home.

In fact, countries in the Region that have been most successful in
implementing domestic market reforms over the course of the transition have also tended to be the ones that were most effective in integrating into the world marketplace (see figure 2.13). It thus appears
that growth in the Region has been engendered through a mutually
reinforcing two-way effect between international integration and
domestic structural reforms. In effect, while reform of trade policies is
necessary to ensure sustainable growth, it is not sufficient. Consequently, for most of the countries in the Region, this leaves unfinished a significant behind-the-border trade reform agenda.

It is in this context that policy makers need to interpret these
empirical results. Behind-the-border factors are likely to be critical in
complementing trade-related policy actions if international integration of the Region is to deepen. These factors are the focus of subsequent chapters of this book.

Conclusions

The portrait that emerges of the Region's international trade landscape today is one depicting a movement from "integration" to "disintegration," and now "reintegration." More important, however, the "new" integration differs significantly from the old. Virtually all of the EU-8 countries have substantially integrated into the global marketplace and moved away from the old structures. And some SEE countries are not far behind. In contrast, the vast majority of the CIS countries, with a few important exceptions (such as with respect to the large increase in oil and gas exports by a few countries), have tended to stay together. Indeed, there is actually an increasing amount of sub-Regionalized trade among the CIS, arguably driven more by political imperatives than by fundamental economic dynamics.

The result is that two "new" trading blocs are emerging: one, a "Euro-centric" bloc, and the other, a "Russia-centric" bloc. As illustrated in this chapter, and as buttressed by further evidence presented in later chapters, these two blocs have begun to coalesce in a variety of dimensions of trade and trade-related institutions and activity. These include the direction of trade flows, the commodity and factor intensity of trade, the degree of export competitiveness, and the state of development of trade facilitation institutions and infrastructure. Other important dimensions in which this bifurcation is apparent are the extent of intraindustry trade, both in the services sectors and in participation in global production-sharing networks through FDI; and the interaction between trade flows and domestic competition and governance.

To be sure, the reality is more complicated than this dichotomized portrait. For example, there is a sizable difference in scale between the two blocs. In addition, total merchandise trade flows for the EU-8 and SEE are almost twice the size of those of the CIS. At the same time, however, there is intra-bloc heterogeneity. Some of the larger CIS countries, such as Russia and Ukraine, have certain trading attributes akin to those of the EU-8 or SEE, while some of the slower-reforming countries in SEE, such as Bosnia and Herzegovina and Serbia and Montenegro, resemble portions of the CIS. Nonetheless, there are unmistakable trends toward a bifurcated Region in international trade. Further, the countries in the Region that have integrated more effectively into international commerce are those that have higher national incomes. At the same time, the countries that have remained relatively closed and embracing the old structures have lower national incomes, and are being left out of the global economy's modern "division of labor."

The econometric evidence suggests that the "reintegrated" Region has largely become more like a typical region regarding trade, with most of the economies registering merchandise trade flows as a share of GDP largely in line with other countries of comparable levels of development, size, and geographical characteristics around the world. But, taken together, the data are sober evidence that the relatively limited openness of trade by most of the CIS—the poorest countries in the Region—reflects the already substantial utilization of their existing production structure and underlying institutional parameters. Taking into account their geographic location, the CIS appears to be trading in line with their peer groups of poor developing countries in other regions of the world. Against this backdrop, it would be difficult to claim that the CIS members—as a group—are either being adversely affected by severe market-access restrictions imposed by their trading partners or suffering greatly from highly distortive domestic trade policies.

By the same token, the fact that the evidence points to undertrading by some of the SEE countries suggests that, in part, domestic policy and institutional distortions are present. These distortions may well be preventing some of these countries from registering larger trade volumes in line with their favorable geographic access to the major markets in Europe, production potential, relatively well-educated workforce (but reflective of the countries' relatively low levels of FDI). It is unlikely to be coincidental that it is in the poorer countries in the group—Albania, Bosnia and Herzegovina, FYR Macedonia, and Serbia and Montenegro—where undertrading is most severe.

All of this is not to suggest that improving trade policy regimes in most of the countries of the Region is unlikely to induce greater international integration to facilitate increased growth; quite the contrary. Rather, as elaborated in greater detail below, the conclusion from this analysis is that enhancing and transforming domestic, behind-the-border production structures and institutional regimes of many countries in the Region are critical to bringing about this goal and that these should be done in concert with further reform of trade policies.

ANNEX

ANNEX TABLE 2.1
Share in Total World Exports of Services (%)

	1990	1991	1992	1993	1994	1995	1996	1997	1998	1999	2000	2001	2002	2003	Share change 1993–2003
CIS	n.a.	n.a.	n.a.	n.a.	1.1	1.3	1.6	1.6	1.4	1.1	1.1	1.3	1.4	1.5	35.0
SEE	0.2	0.1	0.2	0.5	0.5	0.4	0.5	0.5	0.6	0.6	0.6	0.7	0.7	1.0	113.6
EU-8	0.8	0.7	1.1	1.7	2.0	2.5	2.5	2.2	2.3	2.0	2.0	2.0	2.1	2.3	31.3
EU-15	46.7	45.9	46.6	43.4	40.9	41.9	41.3	40.1	40.7	40.9	39.3	40.9	44.8	49.2	13.5
LAC	3.9	3.9	3.9	4.1	4.0	3.7	3.6	3.7	3.9	3.8	4.0	3.8	3.4	3.2	−22.2
MENA	2.9	2.8	3.0	3.1	2.9	2.7	2.7	2.7	2.7	2.6	2.7	2.5	2.4	2.4	−21.3
Africa	1.4	1.3	1.2	1.2	1.1	1.1	1.0	1.0	1.0	1.0	0.8	0.8	0.8	0.7	−43.7
East Asia	12.5	12.9	13.1	14.7	16.2	16.9	17.5	17.5	16.7	16.7	17.5	17.1	17.3	14.5	−1.2
South Asia	0.9	0.9	0.9	0.9	1.0	0.9	0.9	1.0	1.1	1.3	1.5	1.7	1.9	0.2	−74.0
The Region and Turkey	n.a.	n.a.	n.a.	n.a.	1.6	1.7	2.1	2.2	2.0	1.6	1.7	1.9	2.1	2.5	53.2

Share in Total World Imports of Services (%)

	1990	1991	1992	1993	1994	1995	1996	1997	1998	1999	2000	2001	2002	2003	Share change 1993–2003
CIS	n.a.	n.a.	n.a.	n.a.	1.7	2.0	1.8	1.9	1.6	1.3	1.5	2.0	2.1	2.3	34.6
SEE	0.2	0.2	0.2	0.4	0.4	0.4	0.4	0.5	0.4	0.4	0.4	0.5	0.5	0.6	65.2
EU-8	0.7	0.6	0.9	1.4	1.5	1.7	1.7	1.6	1.7	1.6	1.6	1.6	1.8	2.0	43.6
EU-15	43.8	43.3	45.1	42.0	39.9	41.0	39.9	38.5	40.1	40.3	38.7	39.6	43.1	47.2	12.3
LAC	4.6	4.7	4.8	5.3	5.2	4.7	4.6	4.9	5.0	4.7	4.9	4.9	4.2	3.9	−25.2
MENA	6.0	8.3	6.7	6.0	4.7	4.3	4.5	4.6	3.8	3.7	4.0	3.5	3.3	3.0	−49.4
Africa	2.6	2.5	2.2	2.3	2.1	2.1	2.0	1.9	1.8	1.7	1.3	1.3	1.2	0.8	−63.3
East Asia	18.2	18.3	18.5	20.0	21.4	23.0	23.2	22.7	20.6	20.9	21.2	20.7	20.5	16.5	−17.5
South Asia	1.2	1.1	1.2	1.2	1.3	1.3	1.4	1.4	1.3	1.4	1.4	1.4	1.5	0.3	−74.5
The Region and Turkey	n.a.	n.a.	n.a.	n.a.	2.1	2.4	2.2	2.4	2.0	1.7	2.0	2.4	2.6	2.9	38.7

Source: IMF balance of payments statistics.

ANNEX TABLE 2.2

Factor Use in Exports by Country in the Region, 1996, 2000, and 2003

Country	Export value ($ millions)				
	1996				
	Total exports	Natural-resources intensive	Unskilled-labor intensive	Capital-intensive	Skilled-labor intensive
Albania	211	123	68	7	8
Armenia	213	145	12	35	15
Azerbaijan	631	104	25	87	13
Belarus	7,070	1,139	1,246	1,864	2,183
Bulgaria	4,890	1,680	763	1,259	752
Croatia	4,512	1,478	1,582	1,085	366
Czech Rep.	21,882	4,562	4,009	6,561	6,750
Estonia	2,078	730	489	444	345
Georgia	199	127	6	29	36
Hungary	13,138	3,813	2,366	3,707	2,369
Kazakhstan	5,911	4,169	73	883	636
Kyrgyz Rep.	507	325	44	112	24
Latvia	1,443	636	340	202	226
Lithuania	3,356	1,450	678	734	493
Macedonia, FYR	1,147	492	395	117	132
Moldova	653	527	58	42	26
Poland	24,387	7,273	6,841	4,634	5,467
Romania	8,084	1,698	2,918	1,489	1,380
Russian Fed.	88,703	52,821	2,218	8,903	10,743
Serbia & Montenegro	1,842	971	216	315	281
Slovak Rep.	8,824	1,501	1,298	1,989	2,304
Slovenia	8,309	1,370	1,861	2,066	3,012
Tajikistan	n.a.	n.a.	n.a.	n.a.	n.a.
Turkmenistan	751	694	47	5	4
Ukraine	14,400	4,790	729	3,409	4,975

Source: IMF balance of payments statistics.

Note: n.a. = not available.

	Export value ($ millions)									
	2000					2003				
	Total exports	Natural-resources intensive	Unskilled-labor intensive	Capital-intensive	Skilled-labor intensive	Total exports	Natural-resources intensive	Unskilled-labor intensive	Capital-intensive	Skilled-labor intensive
	261	132	112	6	12	447	215	182	17	33
	195	132	6	34	13	540	482	5	17	16
	1,745	1,611	33	88	13	2,592	2,422	13	114	40
	7,331	1,124	1,073	1,723	1,853	9,964	1,817	1,274	2,206	2,327
	4,822	1,397	1,075	855	641	7,540	2,420	2,291	1,343	1,060
	4,431	1,476	1,521	1,034	400	6,156	1,663	1,929	1,517	626
	29,028	4,350	4,823	9,383	10,472	48,660	6,087	7,091	18,058	17,424
	3,830	1,127	660	1,445	469	5,622	1,882	1,091	1,577	1,073
	330	231	10	71	12	455	341	6	87	20
	28,082	3,597	3,192	13,953	6,548	43,007	5,599	4,355	22,872	9,618
	8,621	7,063	24	544	879	12,793	11,005	39	615	1,126
	454	182	14	43	20	322	211	50	37	21
	1,869	967	420	215	230	2,893	1,490	642	354	399
	3,809	1,660	986	761	394	7,162	2,866	2,037	1,301	942
	1,323	467	413	104	334	1,363	508	505	106	242
	456	307	107	26	14	776	537	162	41	34
	31,610	7,512	7,617	7,380	9,101	53,535	11,332	12,556	12,655	16,204
	10,367	2,148	3,977	2,064	1,446	17,618	3,973	7,097	3,331	3,116
	103,008	57,175	2,782	9,539	10,108	133,717	88,874	1,417	13,351	11,661
	1,711	751	287	299	336	2,275	1,071	342	387	422
	11,883	1,581	1,720	2,805	5,004	21,544	3,324	3,076	4,664	10,480
	8,731	1,363	1,713	2,301	3,335	12,762	1,896	2,274	3,792	4,774
	668	579	24	59	6	n.a.	n.a.	n.a.	n.a.	n.a.
	2,506	1,774	145	24	2	n.a.	n.a.	n.a.	n.a.	n.a.
	14,573	4,477	793	3,040	5,556	17,927	6,460	1,071	3,450	6,741

ANNEX TABLE 2.3

Factor Use in Imports by Country in the Region, 1996, 2000, and 2003

	Import value ($ millions)				
	1996				
Country	Total imports	Natural-resources intensive	Unskilled-labor intensive	Capital-intensive	Skilled-labor intensive
Albania	921	461	127	201	132
Armenia	645	404	36	139	66
Azerbaijan	949	472	44	237	196
Belarus	8,282	3,541	533	2,320	1,888
Bulgaria	4,841	2,571	471	1,123	676
Croatia	7,434	2,331	1,163	2,184	1,756
Czech Rep.	27,760	6,679	3,254	11,043	6,784
Estonia	2,997	777	486	902	832
Georgia	687	529	30	87	41
Hungary	15,795	4,412	2,208	5,628	3,547
Kazakhstan	4,181	1,571	235	1,193	1,182
Kyrgyz Rep.	838	452	30	240	116
Latvia	1,998	594	292	624	488
Lithuania	4,448	1,749	468	1,143	1,088
Macedonia, FYR	1,585	555	310	367	353
Moldova	1,070	575	88	248	159
Poland	36,338	9,425	4,885	13,512	8,516
Romania	10,900	4,015	1,720	3,478	1,687
Russian Fed.	41,950	15,311	3,705	14,488	8,446
Serbia & Montenegro	3,828	1,457	484	1,087	800
Slovak Rep.	9,328	2,789	875	3,216	2,448
Slovenia	9,397	2,431	1,346	2,961	2,659
Tajikistan	0	n.a.	n.a.	n.a.	n.a.
Turkmenistan	1,170	378	70	490	232
Ukraine	16,465	10,032	876	3,505	2,052

Source: IMF balance of payments statistics.

Note: n.a. = not available.

| Import value ($ millions) | | | | | | | | | |
| 2000 | | | | | 2003 | | | | |
Total imports	Natural-resources intensive	Unskilled-labor intensive	Capital-intensive	Skilled-labor intensive	Total imports	Natural-resources intensive	Unskilled-labor intensive	Capital-intensive	Skilled-labor intensive
1,089	492	177	203	217	1,864	799	306	374	385
750	433	45	180	92	1,164	725	76	203	160
1,172	375	98	472	227	2,626	761	319	823	723
8,133	4,125	508	2,081	1,419	10,599	4,995	735	2,951	1,918
6,153	2,479	894	1,584	1,196	9,198	2,106	1,861	2,936	2,295
7,884	2,341	1,219	2,236	2,088	13,791	3,340	2,177	4,295	3,979
32,231	7,243	3,686	13,306	7,996	51,227	9,967	5,650	21,920	13,690
4,743	1,015	570	2,060	1,098	7,944	1,952	914	2,691	2,387
578	233	44	205	96	1,133	447	72	325	289
30,379	4,241	3,229	15,471	7,438	46,268	7,161	4,631	23,814	10,662
4,743	1,119	286	1,937	1,401	8,396	2,065	629	3,117	2,585
557	224	27	227	79	716	322	69	180	145
2,954	754	447	961	792	5,242	1,492	746	1,582	1,422
5,311	2,100	740	1,394	1,077	9,649	3,041	1,536	2,754	2,318
1,565	668	104	414	379	1,851	785	133	504	429
669	291	102	182	94	1,398	604	207	326	261
48,833	11,864	5,916	18,993	12,060	67,097	14,508	9,526	24,673	18,390
12,766	3,674	2,658	4,405	2,029	23,942	6,687	4,875	7,389	4,991
29,269	10,631	2,339	10,992	5,307	52,101	15,347	4,345	19,544	12,865
2,919	854	288	966	811	5,975	2,181	550	1,853	1,391
12,664	3,847	1,389	4,231	3,197	22,170	5,269	2,593	7,662	6,646
10,100	2,707	1,285	3,347	2,761	13,837	3,544	1,688	4,706	3,899
555	234	11	273	37	0	n.a.	n.a.	n.a.	n.a.
1,658	283	121	725	529	0	n.a.	n.a.	n.a.	n.a.
12,265	6,785	804	2,992	1,684	16,751	8,911	1,007	4,072	2,761

ANNEX BOX 2.1

Methodology for Decomposing Factors Affecting Trade Performance

GATT (1966) lays down the methodology for the decomposition of factors affecting trade performance between demand and competitive factors:

- **The influence of demand** for a specific product can be measured by the change in the total (global) value of regional imports of the item. In calculating the influence of this factor, one assumes that a given country maintains its regional trade share for the commodity. Specifically, if $D_{o,j}$ and $D_{i,j}$ represent regional trade in product j, at time period o and t, respectively, the change in a specific country's exports attributed solely to demand $DE_{d,i}$ is

$$\Delta E_{d,i} = \Sigma(s_{o,j}) \times (D_{t,j} - D_{o,j})$$

where $s_{o,j}$ is the share of country i in regional imports of product j (defined at the four-digit level of the Revision 2 SITC) from all countries in the base period o, and the summation is over all goods traded.

- **The change in the competitive position** of country i is measured by the difference between the exports that would have occurred if the country's market share had not changed and those regional exports that were in fact realized. This competitive factor ($\Delta E_{c,i}$) is

$$\Delta E_{c,i} = \Sigma(s_{t,j} - s_{o,j})(D_{t,j})$$

where $s_{t,j}$ is the share of the country in regional imports of the product in period t, and the summation is over all goods imported.

- Any differences between changes in a country's total exports and the sum of these two "demand" and "competitive" factors are the result of **product diversification**.

An illustrative example may help explain this approach. Assume country i exports one product j and has a 20 percent share of the regional markets with exports of $20 million in 1996 and a 25 percent share with exports of $37.5 million in 2003. During this period regional demand for j rose from $100 to $150 million. The change in i's exports attributed solely to changes in demand would be $\Delta E_{d,i} = .20(\$150 - \$100) = \$10$ million; while the change resulting from the competitive factor is $\Delta E_{c,i} = (.25 - .20) \times \$150 = \$7.5$ million. This example assumes that the country experiences no diversification in its exports.

Source: Ng and Yeats 2003.

Endnotes

1. Trade and investment in the services sectors and the regulatory regimes governing them are discussed in greater detail in chapter 7.
2. These concentration indexes are based on those typically used in the field of industrial organization when measuring product market concentration. The Hirschman index is defined as $H_j = \sqrt{(\Sigma(x_i/X)^2)}$ where x_i is the value of exports of commodity i (normally defined at the four-digit SITC level) and X is the total value of country j's exports; see Ng and Yeats (2003).
3. If exports are concentrated in goods with low income elasticities of demand, export prospects are likely to be limited (Ng and Yeats 2003).
4. For an earlier related analysis, see Macbean (1966); Labys and Lord (1990) stress the need for many developing countries to diversify their exports.
5. The import share of the CIS may be exaggerated by trade deflection; see Freinkman et al. (2004).
6. Trade openness is calculated using GDP in purchasing power parity (PPP).
7. Although the direction of causality is unclear. See Kormendi and Meguire (1985), Fischer (1991), Dollar (1992), Edwards (1993), Harrison (1996), and Rodrik et al. (2002).
8. We note the likely critical role of institutional and policy factors as determinants of trade performance *apart from* income. Indeed, our estimation methodology employs an approach that uses institutional variables to combat endogeneity problems; see below.
9. In order to combat apparent endogeneity between the measures of openness and GDP, an instrumental variables estimator (two-stage least squares) was used. GDP was instrumented by the following variables: infant mortality rate (per 1,000 live births); telephone lines (per 1,000 people); and the Heritage Foundation Index (HFI) of Economic Freedom as a proxy for policy and institutions (ranging from 1 to 5; the higher the HFI value, the lower the economic freedom in a country). All 149 countries for which trade and income data are available from the World Development Indicators database have been included in the pool. The model was estimated on the averages for 1994–2003. In addition, dummies for regional country groupings were included as independent variables. Since the dummy for Sub-Saharan Africa has been insignificant in all specifications, the table presents specifications without the Sub-Saharan Africa dummy.
10. This interpretation derives from the fact that across Models 1, 2, and 3, the estimated coefficients on all of the "dummy" variables depicting the Region—except for SEE in Model 3—are never statistically significant.
11. In contrast, the results suggest that the East Asian countries tend to overtrade.
12. These results are in line with earlier statistical analysis of the determinants of openness for the CIS countries alone by Freinkman et al. (2004). Statistical analysis carried out by the EBRD (2003) on most of the Region's countries yields roughly similar conclusions to those of this study with respect to the CIS and SEE countries. However, the EBRD analysis does not find evidence of overtrading by the EU-8.

13. See Bergstrand (1985), Helpman and Krugman (1985), Deardorff (1997), and Feenstra et al. (2001) for different theoretical justifications of the gravity model.

14. See Wang and Winters (1991), Hamilton and Winters (1992), Baldwin (1994), Piazolo (1996), Frankel (1997), EBRD (2003), and Freinkman et al. (2004).

15. The applied gravity equation is the following (with standard errors in parentheses):

$$\log(T_{ij}) = -12.146 + 0.930 \log(GNP_i\, GNP_j) + 0.128 \log(GNP/pop_i\, GNP/pop_j)$$
$$\quad\;\;(0.469)\;(0.018)\qquad\qquad\qquad(0.019)$$

$$-0.770 \log(Dist_{ij}) + 0.445\,(Adj_{ij}) + 0.768\,(Lang_{ij}) + \gamma(Bloc_{ij})$$
$$(0.038)\qquad\qquad(0.157)\qquad(0.090)$$

$$+ u_{ij}\,,$$

where T_{ij} is the trade turnover between countries i and j (that is, exports from country i to country j plus imports of country i from country j), GNP is Gross National Product, GMP/pop is per capita GNP, Dist is the great circle distance between the main commercial centers (countries' capitals, with a few exceptions), Adj is the adjacency dummy (equals one for adjacent countries and zero otherwise), Lang is the language dummy (equals one for countries sharing the same language), Bloc is the bloc dummy (equals one for countries in the same trading bloc), and u_{ij} is the error term.

16. The following abbreviations are used in table 2.17: Arm = Armenia; Azr = Azerbaijan; Bel = Belarus; Geo = Georgia; Kaz = Kazakhstan; Kyr = Kyrgyz Republic; Mol = Moldova; Rus = Russian Federation; Taj = Tajikistan; Trm = Turkmenistan; Ukr = Ukraine; Uzb = Uzbekistan; CZ = Czech Republic; Est = Estonia; Hu = Hungary; Lat = Latvia; Lit = Lithuania; Pol = Poland; Slk = Slovak Republic; Slv = Slovenia; Alb = Albania; BH = Bosnia and Herzegovina; Bul = Bulgaria; Crt = Croatia; Mac = Macedonia, FYR; Rom = Romania; SM = Serbia and Montenegro.

PART II

THE ROLE OF THE TRADE REGIME

CHAPTER 3

Trade Policies and Institutions

Introduction

The demise of central planning in Eastern Europe and the former Soviet Union over the period 1989–1992 resulted in the disintegration of the domestic mechanisms of control, such as the Council for Mutual Economic Assistance, that these countries had used to manage international trade with the rest of the world and with each other. At the same time, the political disintegration of the Soviet Union leading to the establishment of 15 new independent states and the breakup of Yugoslavia into 7 states resulted in a breakdown of the traditional links between economic units located in the territories of the new states: what had been domestic transactions in the same currency governed by the same laws and procedures became international trade requiring goods to cross national frontiers into different customs territories, be subject to different regulations, and involve payments in different currencies.

The combined effect of the transition from central planning to market rules and the political disintegration of the Soviet Union and Yugoslavia forced major adjustments to the trade patterns, both among the countries in the Region and with the rest of the world. The pace of the adjustment and reintegration of these economies into the world markets varied considerably and depended on both

the countries' original situation and the breadth and speed of introduction of market-oriented reforms.

As trade policy is a key link in the transmission of price signals
from the world market to domestic resource allocation, trade reforms
were an important component of broader market reforms introduced
by the early reforming countries in Central and Eastern Europe and
the Baltics, as well as in some CIS countries like the Kyrgyz Republic
and Georgia. In other countries, such as Uzbekistan and Turkmenistan, trade reforms have lagged because overall market reforms
have been slow. Integration in the world trading system requires
much more than trade policy, however. The establishment of macroeconomic stability; effective, trade-related and, more generally, market-based institutions; the rule of law; and a supportive business
climate are essential to effective participation in international trade
and have markedly affected the reintegration of these economies into
world markets.

A country's integration into world markets depends also on the
trade policies of its trading partners and the access it obtains to their
markets. There are three important market-access relationships for
the transition countries in Central and Eastern Europe and the CIS
that affect their overall integration in world trade: (a) the trade relationships among each other at the Regional and sub-Regional level;
(b) their relationships with the European Union, the main external
market for most of them; and (c) their relationships with the rest of
the world, including China, the United States, and other developed
and developing countries.

Integration at the Regional, European, and world levels requires
countries to abide by the rules of conduct that govern the multilateral
trading system. These rules have been established and are being
implemented in the context of agreements administered by the World
Trade Organization (WTO). Regional and sub-Regional arrangements
and, to some extent and on a temporary basis, relationships with the
EU, can be based on special rules and provisions. However, membership in the WTO and abiding by the rules that are globally set in that
organization and that govern all trade relationships are essential elements, perhaps even necessary conditions, for full integration into
the world trading system. In recognition of this, all but one of the
transition countries (Turkmenistan) have either become members of
the WTO or are involved in the often-lengthy process of acceding to
the organization.

In the 15 years since the fall of the Berlin Wall, the degree of integration into the world markets achieved by the transition countries in
Europe and the CIS varies enormously. There are three broad groups:

the first group of eight countries of Central and Eastern Europe (CEE-8) have become members of the EU and have thus completed integration into the world economy. The second group of the 12 CIS countries has achieved much less integration, and many of these countries are still not members of the WTO. And there is a third group of countries in Southeastern Europe that is participating in a stabilization and association process that will ultimately lead them to EU membership, and whose integration into the world economy is in between the other two groups.

In addition, there are other groupings of countries that cut across these three classifications: for example, there are countries such as Armenia, Azerbaijan, Bosnia and Herzegovina, Georgia, Moldova, Serbia and Montenegro, and Tajikistan that have experienced significant internal or external political conflict that has impeded reforms. There are also differences in the degree of integration within each group: Armenia, Georgia, and the Kyrgyz Republic have very liberal trade regimes, while Belarus and Turkmenistan have essentially maintained the patterns of trade control that characterized central planning. Many countries are participating in a variety of multiple but often ineffective bilateral or regional trade relationships. Turkey, part of the World Bank's Europe and Central Asia (ECA) Region and thus included in parts of this study, is different: it is not a transition economy, in the sense of having had to move away from a system of central planning, though it continues to grapple with problems in a large and inefficient state enterprise sector. It is also well integrated into the world trade system, as it is in a customs union with the EU.

The purpose of this chapter is twofold: to assess how trade policies and institutions, as well as market access issues, have affected the trade performance of transition economies in Eastern Europe and the Former Soviet Union over the last decade and a half; and to look into the future in order to analyze the challenges these economies face in achieving fuller integration in the international trading system, at the Regional, European, and global levels. The analysis will deal primarily with trade in goods. But the chapter foreshadows analyses of a variety of other factors affecting trade performance, such as policies on trade in services, foreign direct investment, and other behind-the-border policies, which are discussed in detail elsewhere in the volume.

The chapter focuses on the countries of Southeastern Europe (SEE) and the CIS of the Region.[1] This is a group of 19 countries, plus Kosovo, that, although part of Serbia and Montenegro, has a separate customs territory. The eight countries of Central and Eastern Europe that have recently become members of the EU have had to adopt the EU *acquis*, including all aspects of EU trade policy, rules, and institutions; their policies and future challenges, following accession, are not discussed in detail in this chapter. The main questions regarding these countries that are addressed here relate to the implications of their EU accession for the remaining transition countries in the region. Turkey, a special case, will be dealt with separately.

Trade Policy

The formal trade policy regimes of the 20 transition economies in SEE and the CIS, especially the 17 that have become WTO members (see table 3.1), compare, on the whole, quite favorably with the trade regimes of developing countries at similar levels of income.[2] Tariff protection of domestic industry and agriculture in the transition economies is on average lower; the extent of protection through non-tariff barriers appears to be no greater; there is less recourse to contingent protection; and, unlike many developing countries in Africa and Asia, transition economies that are WTO members have bound 100 percent of their tariff schedules (see table 3.2). WTO accession by a number of these countries in the near future can be expected to result in further liberalization and increased stability of their trade regimes.

TABLE 3.1
WTO Members in the Region (as of December 2005)

Country	Date of accession
Czech Rep.	1 January 1995
Hungary	1 January 1995
Poland	1 January 1995
Romania	1 January 1995
Slovak Rep.	1 July 1995
Slovenia	30 July 1995
Bulgaria	1 December 1996
Kyrgyz Rep.	20 December 1998
Latvia	10 February 1999
Estonia	13 November 1999
Georgia	14 June 2000
Albania	8 September 2000
Croatia	30 November 2000
Lithuania	31 May 2001
Moldova	26 July 2001
Armenia	5 February 2003
Macedonia, FYR	4 April 2003

Source: WTO.

TABLE 3.2

Average Applied Tariffs and Bound Rate by Country or Group in the Region in the Most Recent Available Year

| Country/group | Average applied tariff rate (%) | | | | | | Average bound rate (%) | | |
| | All goods | | Agricultural goods | | Industrial goods | | All goods | | |
	Simple avg.	Wght. avg.	Simple avg.	Wght. avg.	Simple avg.	Wght. avg.	Simple avg.	Wght. avg.	Binding coverage
EU-8	5.1	4.5	13.5	12.8	4.5	4.0	10.6	7.9	99.1
CIS-12	8.0	7.1	11.2	9.7	7.7	6.8	7.6	8.4	33.3
SEE-8	9.8	7.5	26.4	18.1	8.4	6.3	19.3	24.6	71.4
The Region	7.8	5.8	16.4	13.0	7.1	5.2	12.4	10.4	59.0
The Region and Turkey	7.5	5.1	16.7	13.0	6.7	4.5	14.2	12.0	59.6
Developing countries	11.9	9.2	16.6	16.7	11.5	8.5	38.1	19.4	58.9
EU-15	4.4	3.1	6.2	5.2	4.2	3.0	3.9	3.0	100.0
Memo:									
Turkey	3.0	2.0	21.8	12.7	2.0	1.3	28.6	19.8	49.9
Russian Fed.	10.8	8.9	9.8	8.9	10.9	8.9	n.a.	n.a.	n.a.

Sources: UNCTAD TRAINS and WTO IDB databases.

Note: n.a. = not available.

There are of course substantial differences among the trade regimes of the transition economies. At the one extreme are three very protectionist regimes in Belarus, Turkmenistan, and Uzbekistan.[3] At the other extreme are recent WTO members like Albania, Armenia, Croatia, Georgia, the Kyrgyz Republic, and Moldova with very liberal trade regimes, especially when compared with developing countries at similar levels of per capita income. In between are some of the larger transition economies such as Russia and Ukraine.

Throughout the Region, trade is also impeded by lingering political conflicts resulting from the breakup of the Soviet Union and Yugoslavia. The unresolved conflict over Nagorno-Karabakh has resulted in a breakdown of economic relationships between Armenia and Azerbaijan, and Turkey has closed its border to Armenia. There are two quasi-independent entities, Abkhazia and Transdniester, whose administrations survive through support from Russia, but which have received no international recognition and continue to exist in a state of political confrontation with Georgia and Moldova, respectively. Both entities have become "black holes" in terms of formal trade transactions and the location of enterprises or individuals engaging in criminal economic activity; illegal arms transactions; and smuggling of cigarettes, liquor, and oil products (World Bank 2004f). This illegal trade results in significant revenue losses for the Georgian and Moldovan authorities. In the Balkans, there are still no significant economic relationships between Serbia and Montenegro and Kosovo, Serbian territory temporarily being administered by the United Nations.

Policies on Imports

Tariffs

Average Most Favored Nation (MFN) tariffs for countries in transition range from a low simple average of 3.3 percent in Armenia to a high of 11.5–11.6 percent in Belarus and Romania (see annex table 3.1). Averages weighted by imports are lower in all countries. Following a worldwide pattern, tariffs in general are much higher in agricultural than in nonagricultural sectors.[4]

Countries that have joined the EU (the EU-8) had on average lower tariffs than did other transition economies (table 3.2). Indeed, Estonia and Latvia had some of the most liberal trade regimes in the world. In contrast, tariffs in the CIS and the SEE are on average slightly higher. Still, their applied tariffs are on average somewhat lower than those of developing countries as a whole. On the other hand, tariffs on agriculture in the Southeastern European countries are on average higher than those in developing countries as a group. Turkey has increased its international integration as a result of its close interaction with the EU; see box 3.1.

BOX 3.1

Turkey's Trade Policies and Institutions

Turkey's integration into the world economy is strongly influenced by its increasingly close links to the European Union. In 2004, Turkey, already a WTO member, formally became a candidate for EU accession. Turkey has already established a customs union with the EU, and its trade policies and institutions are shifting in order to harmonize better with those of the EU. Turkey has initiated a number of macroeconomic stabilization programs in recent periods. While macro stability has been restored, the situation continues to be fragile, as inflation rates and the public debt continue to be at high levels.

Turkey's MFN tariffs are relatively high, averaging 11.8 percent in 2003. Because of the customs union with the EU, however, Turkey applies the much lower EU external tariff on industrial imports. Turkey also has a free trade agreement (FTA) on industrial products with the European Free Trade Association (EFTA) and has signed 14 other bilateral FTAs, as it tries to harmonize its trade regime with that of the EU. In agriculture, protection is quite high, with ad valorem rates ranging up to 227.5 percent for animal products. State support for agriculture is also substantial, and, as a consequence, the agricultural sector has become insulated from the world market. The government is in the process of implementing a wide-ranging five-year program (2001–2005) to restructure the sector by phasing out some of the more distorting measures such as administered prices, as well as production and export subsidies.

Broadly speaking, tariffs in most countries do not provide for a large degree of protection, although there is, of course, significant variation by country and sector. Armenia, Croatia, Georgia, and the Kyrgyz Republic, for example, have low average tariff rates with relatively little dispersion. Russia's average applied tariff rates average 10.8 percent, with highs of 50 percent in beverages. Import-weighted applied tariff rates average 8.9 percent. The tariff schedules for Belarus, Kazakhstan, and Russia are very close to the Russian tariff schedule because of the proposed customs union among these countries. The highest tariff protection in agriculture appears to be present in Bulgaria and Romania, while the highest tariff protection in manufacturing is in Belarus, Romania, and Uzbekistan (annex table 3.1). However, the tariff data are in some cases incomplete, as they do not include specific tariffs present in many countries' agricultural schedule.[5] Also, it is unclear whether the "applied" tariffs in table 3.2 and in the annex take into account the preferential rates applied by many countries as part of their participation in preferential trade arrangements.

The main nontariff barriers (NTBs) are in textiles, where Turkey maintained a quota regime based on the international Agreement on Textiles and Clothing (ATC), which, however, expired in 2005. Since 1995, Turkey has initiated 46 antidumping (AD) investigations and taken definitive measures in 33 cases. AD actions have focused on textiles (China), plastics (EU), and steel (Russia, Ukraine). Turkey itself has also been the target of a slightly smaller number of antidumping actions over the same period.

The government operates a number of schemes to promote exports in the form of finance, insurance, guarantee, promotion, and marketing assistance. Several export credit programs are operated by the Central Bank, as well as several schemes providing incentives to small and medium enterprises (SMEs).

Services is the largest sector in terms of contribution to the GDP (about 65 percent); it faces a number of structural problems, including the existence of a number of inefficient, loss-making public sector enterprises. The government has taken some measures to extend privatization and liberalization in several sectors, notably banking and telecommunications. However, public companies continue to dominate most service provision and either operate as monopolies or hold exclusive rights. And foreign direct investment inflows are much lower than they could be.

Turkey faces major challenges in the near term as it attempts to deal with deep-seated structural problems in its state enterprise sector, harmonize its policies with the EU, and maintain macroeconomic stability. Further privatization and reforms of the services and agricultural sectors can make important contributions to its future growth and competitiveness; they will also help pave the way for EU accession.

Source: WTO Trade Policy Review 2003.

Many of the countries have a relatively small number of tariff bands, and low dispersion of tariff rates. Indeed, in the early 1990s, under the influence of advice from international financial institutions (IFIs), a few of the countries (Georgia, the Kyrgyz Republic, and, most recently, Kosovo) had established uniform tariff regimes that were subsequently differentiated as a result of pressure from domestic interests to raise tariffs on final goods; this was also a response to external demands for tariff reductions ("zero for zero" and other specific requests) on raw materials and intermediates at the time of WTO negotiations. The Kyrgyz Republic had a flat 10 percent tariff that applied to all products, but while maintaining a liberal trade regime, it ended up with several bands following WTO accession. Until recently, Kosovo also had a flat 10 percent tariff; however, under pressure from domestic interests seeking to obtain higher rates of effective protection for final goods, this is in the process of changing to provide for lower tariffs in selected raw materials and intermediate inputs. Ukraine had 50 tariff bands in 2003 compared with seven a decade before.

For the nine economies of SEE and the CIS that are WTO members,[6] tariff schedules have been bound 100 percent; in most cases (the exceptions are Bulgaria and Romania), bound levels have been established that are close to those applied.[7] Binding tariffs at close to applied levels provides stability to the trade regime, which is an important attraction for foreign direct investment, as well as a good defense against future domestic pressures to increase protection. In the case of Georgia, for example, domestic pressures resulted in increases in applied tariffs to closer to the bound levels after WTO accession (World Bank 2003c).

Taxation of imports is a significant source of revenue for most countries (for example, 71 percent of revenue in Armenia). The bulk of this taxation involves value added taxes (VAT) and excise taxes that are collected on imports. Tariffs are but a small percentage of the total, usually amounting to less than a quarter of trade taxes. Most tariff regimes yield far fewer revenues than the average MFN tariff level would suggest, however. For example, in Ukraine, the yield is about half the weighted average applied tariff rate. In Georgia, the yield is about a quarter. There are several reasons for this: first, there are many preferential arrangements that result in large segments of international trade entering duty-free; second, there are frequent ad hoc exemptions and exceptions; third, highly differentiated tariff structures, combined with weak and corrupt customs authorities, yield little revenue, and in some territories (for example, Albania, Bosnia and Herzegovina, Kosovo, and Tajikistan, there is widespread smuggling. A simpler and less differentiated tariff structure would be easier to enforce and would yield more revenues.

In most countries, there is tariff escalation, usually resulting in significantly higher effective rates of protection for final products than for intermediates and raw materials. Examples of such high rates abound in the wood, leather, and textiles sector (World Bank 2004q). These high effective rates of protection for domestic industry result in inefficient resource allocation as well as in reduced incentives to export.

Nontariff Barriers

The Region's economies that have become members of the WTO have eliminated formal nontariff barriers (NTBs) on imports, except as allowed by the WTO. This means that some of them (Bulgaria, Romania) have imposed tariff quotas in agriculture, and all are using licensing procedures for imports aimed at maintaining sanitary, phyto-sanitary, and safety standards, as well as protecting the environment.

NTBs on imports are more common in non-WTO members in the Region. For example, Uzbekistan has nonautomatic licensing procedures for foreign exchange allocation through the banking system aimed at controlling both the overall level and the composition of imports, depending on the degree of "essentiality" of the imports. Ukraine uses its technical standards system as a vehicle for controlling imports into various sectors (World Bank 2004q). Serbia and Montenegro have a combination of licensing and quotas on steel imports (EC 2004). And several CIS members have used temporary import bans against selected neighbors as weapons in a variety of bilateral trade disputes or as emergency measures. For example, Russia and Ukraine have engaged in a number of bilateral disputes involving mutual bans of trade in certain commodities (see box 3.2); Uzbekistan has cut off imports from the Kyrgyz Republic in retaliation for nondelivery of electricity; and Kazakhstan has imposed prohibitive duties on trade with neighboring countries to deal with balance of payments problems. Using trade as a weapon in settling disputes is counterproductive and tends to hurt both countries in the dispute.

The IMF calculates an index of NTB restrictiveness ranging from open to moderate to restrictive; such categories are based mainly on the number of sectors covered by NTBs, the number of stages of production covered by NTBs, and the severity of the NTBs (see table 3.3). NTBs are defined to include quantitative restrictions, state trading monopolies, restrictive foreign exchange practices, quality or standards controls, and customs procedures. Over the period 1997–2003,

BOX 3.2

Russo-Ukrainian Trade Wars

In 1999, Ukraine imposed special quotas on imports of electric filaments, artificial furs, and worsted canvas from Russia. In 2000, some polyurethane products were added to the list. The same year, Ukraine replaced the quota on filaments with an antidumping tariff of 97.5 percent for a period of five years. Russia responded with imposing antidumping tariffs on Ukrainian metal pipes. In 2001, after bilateral negotiations, the Russian antidumping measures on pipes were lifted and replaced with negotiated quotas. In 2002, Ukraine imposed an antidumping tariff on crossing pieces and threatened to impose tariff quotas on a variety of Russian products from the light and chemical industries, if Russia reintroduced a special tariff on Ukrainian metal pipes, which it was considering. That year, Russia introduced higher tariffs on Ukrainian zinc, steel, some metal products, and candies. In retaliation, Ukraine introduced a higher tariff on automobiles with an engine capacity of 1,000–1,500 cc, the engine capacity of most Russian automobile production and exports to Ukraine. In 2003, the informal agreement between the presidents of the two countries to lift all contingent protection measures affecting mutual trade was disavowed by the governments of both countries (World Bank 2004q).

Belarus, Turkmenistan, and Uzbekistan were assessed as having the most restrictive NTB policies; Armenia, Croatia, the Kyrgyz Republic, FYR Macedonia, Moldova, and Tajikistan received ratings indicating the least restrictive policies.

While formal nontariff barriers to trade continue to be a problem in several countries in the Region that are not members of the WTO, a far greater problem is posed by informal barriers that impede trade in all countries. Many of these barriers result from institutional weaknesses or weak infrastructure, for example in transport or finance, and are discussed below in part III of this study. However, many other impediments that result from government policies involving the issuance of licenses and other permits for the movement of goods across frontiers act as formidable, albeit informal, barriers to trade. A recent study of nontariff measures that impede trade in SEE found that there were few formal NTBs in the Region. However, trade was impeded significantly by a variety of government rules, procedures, and other requirements that caused delays and impeded trade (EC 2004). Similar problems have been identified in other countries, such as Armenia, Georgia, Moldova, and Ukraine, where this issue has been addressed (World Bank 2002a, World Bank 2003c, World Bank 2004f).

TABLE 3.3
IMF NTB Trade Restrictiveness Ratings: 1997–2003

Country name	NTB rating		
	1997	2000	2003
Albania	2	1	1
Armenia	1	1	1
Azerbaijan	2	1	1
Belarus	3	3	3
Bosnia & Herzegovina	2	1	1
Bulgaria	2	1	1
Croatia	1	1	1
Czech Rep.	1	1	1
Estonia	1	1	1
Macedonia, FYR	1	1	1
Georgia	2	1	1
Hungary	2	2	2
Kazakhstan	2	2	2
Kyrgyz Rep.	1	1	1
Latvia	1	1	1
Lithuania	1	1	1
Moldova	1	1	1
Poland	1	1	1
Romania	2	1	1
Russian Fed.	1	2	2
Serbia & Montenegro	...	3	2
Slovak Rep.	1	1	1
Slovenia	1	1	1
Tajikistan	1	1	1
Turkmenistan	3	3	3
Ukraine	2	2	2
Uzbekistan	3	3	3
Turkey	2	2	2

Source: International Monetary Fund.

Note: The data for the EU-8 are for barriers that existed before their EU accession.

Contingent protection involves protection that a country imposes in response to actions by its trading partner(s) that are supposed to have an adverse impact on its domestic production, employment, or trade. The main forms are safeguards against an influx of imports that threaten to cause serious injury to domestic industry, counter-vailing duties against export subsidies, and antidumping measures against practices of dumping. In the last decade, antidumping has been the favorite instrument of protection of industry worldwide (see table 3.4). Compared with other instruments of protection, antidumping actions are less transparent and can lead to reduced competition and cartelization of the affected sectors (Finger 1993). Transition countries have introduced the necessary legislation, but

TABLE 3.4

Number and Share of Antidumping Investigations by Initiating Country, 1995–2003

Initiated by	Initiated against				
	Industrial countries[a]	Developing countries[b]	Of which: China[c]	Transition countries[d]	All countries
Number of antidumping investigations					
Industrial countries[a]	226	574	129	132	932
Developing countries[b]	453	827	225	173	1,453
Transition countries[d]	4	7	2	20	31
All countries	683	1,408	356	325	2,416
Share of antidumping investigations					
Industrial countries[a]	0.24	0.62	0.14	0.14	1
Developing countries[b]	0.31	0.57	0.15	0.12	1
Transition countries[d]	0.13	0.23	0.06	0.65	1
All Countries	0.28	0.58	0.15	0.13	1

Source: WTO Antidumping Committee.

Note:
a. Includes Australia, Canada, 15 European Union members, Iceland, Japan, New Zealand, Norway, Switzerland, and the United States.
b. Includes all other countries and China, excluding industrial and transition countries.
c. Excludes Hong Kong (China), Macao, and Taiwan (China).
d. Refers to the 27 transition countries in the Region, and excludes Turkey, with 61 initiations.

until recently had relatively limited recourse to antidumping or other contingent protection remedies. Until 1997, only Poland had initiated a number of antidumping investigations (in 1991), but did not actually impose antidumping measures (Miranda et al. 1998). Since 1995, six countries (Bulgaria, the Czech Republic, Latvia, Lithuania, Poland, and Slovenia) initiated a total of 31 antidumping investigations (see annex table 3.2). All of these countries except Bulgaria have by now become EU members, and the measures have been terminated. More than two-thirds of their investigations were directed against neighboring transition economies, most commonly Belarus. Cement (Latvia and Lithuania), rubber products (Lithuania), and pocket lighters (Poland) were among the items most frequently protected. The above data do not include antidumping measures taken by some CIS countries (for example, Ukraine and Russia), which are not members of the WTO, against each other, as well as against the EU and the United States; these measures are typically in retaliation for antidumping or other measures taken against their own exports (World Bank 2004q). To the extent that these actions are still in place at the time of these countries' accession to the WTO, they would have to be reviewed for their conformity to WTO provisions.

Policies on Exports

Export performance of the Region's economies has suffered simply because production of traditional export commodities has declined as part of the overall decline of production following the onset of transition. Compared with the 1980s, production of traditional exports of wine, fruits, and vegetables declined by more than 70 percent in Georgia and Moldova. Sheep exports virtually disappeared in the Kyrgyz Republic. In other cases, whole sectors turned out to be uncompetitive in market conditions: Bulgaria's computer industry, which was thriving in the sheltered environment of the CMEA, disintegrated in the face of international competition.

Other than the EU-8, most countries in the Region found it difficult to develop new exports. This was due to many factors, but in part it was a result of their own policies. Governments of transition economies, especially non-WTO members, on the whole have exhibited a tendency of taxing rather than subsidizing or supporting exports. Policies discouraging exports are in part a legacy of their planned economy days, when "keeping the goods at home" was given the highest priority and exporting was focused on disposing of surplus production. These taxes and controls have had an adverse impact on export performance for countries that have employed them.

Most transition economies tax exports of fuels and raw materials. They do this for two reasons: first, for revenue purposes, to compensate for the absence of an effective system of taxing the exploitation of natural resources; and second, in order to promote domestic industry by permitting it to obtain raw material inputs at lower than world prices. Export taxes on raw materials—and in some cases on food—exist in Belarus, Bosnia and Herzegovina, Russia, Serbia and Montenegro, and Ukraine. There are also licensing requirements or other controls on the export of natural-resource-based products such as timber (in George and Moldova). A number of countries (for example, Azerbaijan, Georgia) ban the export of scrap metal. In the case of Georgia, these controls do not appear to affect the overall level of exports, but simply to drive some of the exports underground.

The most restrictive export controls are operated by Uzbekistan. In that country, there is a system of forced government procurement of cotton, which effectively taxes producers by giving them substantially less than world prices, and state monopolies on exports of cotton, minerals, and precious metals. State trading activities in Azerbaijan (oil), Tajikistan (aluminum), and Turkmenistan (oil and gas) are used as the main instrument of control and regulation of exports.

Export taxes and other controls on raw material exports also introduce inefficiencies in the allocation of resources and need to be progressively phased out. When the main objective is capturing rents
from natural resource exploitation, taxes on resource depletion are
more efficient and need to be introduced. When the objective is to
stimulate industry, assistance can be provided in ways that do not discriminate between the domestic and external markets.

Exporters are also disadvantaged by the lack of effective and timely
rebates on tariffs, VAT, and other taxes affecting imported inputs.
While most countries in the Region have put such systems in place,
they have not operated efficiently. For example, rebates are provided
with significant time lags, with the result that exporters are penalized
and put at a competitive disadvantage with foreign suppliers, who
can obtain their inputs at world prices (World Bank 2003c, World
Bank 2004d, World Bank 2004f, World Bank 2004q).

While on the whole, the Region's policies have tended to disadvantage exporters, some countries that are not WTO members have
provided subsidies to important export industries. This has been
the case for steel in Ukraine and a number of products in Serbia
and Montenegro. Similarly, Tajikistan's aluminum exports would
not be viable without significant subsidies to electricity. Subsidizing
exports is a drain on the budget and cannot be afforded by many of
these countries, which have been facing serious budgetary constraints. In any case, many of these subsidies are not WTO-consistent and will have to be eliminated when these countries accede to
that organization.

Finally, a number of countries in the Region have introduced Export
Processing Zones and similar arrangements to provide tax-and-duty-
free arrangements for exports. Such arrangements have been shown to
have the potential for providing a stimulus to exports in several developing countries. Unfortunately, there is little evidence that these
arrangements have been effective in stimulating exports from transition economies in the Region that have them (see chapter 4).

There are, nevertheless, a few bright spots in the export performance of economies in the Region that are worth discussing in some
detail because of the implications they have for other economies in
the Region. Romania is one example of a very impressive export performance, both in terms of reorienting its trade to the European market and in sustaining its expansion in the presence of significant
competition from low-cost international suppliers in such sectors as
textile and shoes. The key to its success appears to be its ability to participate effectively in international networks of production and distribution. Falling transportation and communication costs create

opportunities for outsourcing. Value chains are becoming increasingly split, with individual production stages moving to countries to exploit their comparative advantage. In the case of Romania, the driving force has been Italian firms that have organized the insertion of Romanian firms into global networks of production and distribution of footwear and clothing (World Bank 2004i). Their efforts have been able to overcome a strongly protective tariff regime that acts as a general disincentive to exports. Many other successes in the region are discussed in detail in chapter 7.

Future Challenges

Although, overall, the existing trade regime is not a major problem of trade policy for most of the Region's countries, there is still room for improvement and a variety of challenges. On imports:

- Countries acceding to the WTO can use the accession process to further liberalize their tariff schedules and bind them at levels that are close to applied. To the extent possible, such countries need to resist domestic pressures to raise protection on final goods (or seek to establish bindings for tariffs at substantially higher levels than previously applied), as well as external pressures to reduce tariffs on a variety of raw materials and intermediates, which would result in raising effective rates of protection in various product chains.

- Countries that are already WTO members need to use the ongoing WTO multilateral trade negotiations as an opportunity to further reduce their applied and bound tariffs in exchange for improved market access for their own products. While autonomous tariff liberalization can be beneficial to any country that undertakes it, multilateral trade liberalization through international agreements has the potential of yielding even greater benefits and may be easier to accomplish domestically in light of the political-economy power of vested interests "behind the border."

- Nontariff barriers are of importance in a number of countries that are not WTO members. These barriers should be substituted by tariffs as early as possible; they will have to be dismantled as part of the WTO accession process, in any case.

- The challenge for the many countries in the Region that have so far avoided using antidumping measures is to continue this policy because, while antidumping is a popular instrument of protection worldwide, it entails large costs to the domestic economy.

- All of the Region's countries would benefit from measures that increase revenue yields from existing tariff regimes through strengthening the customs service and reducing corruption and smuggling, as well as eliminating formal exemptions to tariffs.

The main challenges transition economies face in promoting their integration into the world economy through an expanding export sector are to

- establish efficient taxation of raw material exploitation at the source and phase out export taxes;

- provide support, where appropriate, for industrial development through WTO-consistent measures that do not discriminate between domestic and export markets;

- establish efficient tariff, VAT, and other import tax-rebate systems; and

- attract export-oriented FDI to help them integrate into worldwide production and distribution chains.

Institutional and Other Domestic Constraints

The preceding analysis of trade policies in the Region suggests that, aside from a general bias against exports, in most countries the formal trade regime has not hindered their integration into the world economy. Yet, in some countries with very liberal regimes toward imports, the question, "We have done everything to liberalize our trade. Why is our trade performance worse than it was under central planning?" is frequently heard. The response to this question is multifaceted and has to do in part with the bias against exports mentioned above. Mainly, however, it is because serious weaknesses in market- and trade-related institutions and infrastructure continue to undermine effective participation of these countries in international trade. They also undermine the opportunities that trade policy reform can increase growth and reduce poverty; see box 3.3. Subsequent chapters will analyze these institutional and domestic constraints in detail. Here we develop the context for that discussion and highlight some of the more salient issues.

A fundamental problem is an interventionist attitude on the part of governments. Such an attitude is pervasive in practically all aspects of market activities, but it has a very stultifying effect on international trade and has been identified as a key constraint in export development in virtually all of the countries in the Region. In the Kyrgyz

BOX 3.3

The Interrelationships between Trade, Growth, and Poverty Reduction in the Region

Trade performance is one of many factors that affect GDP growth and, through growth, the reduction of poverty. Trade performance in turn is affected, in part, by trade policy. The effect of trade policy on poverty via its effect on growth is, necessarily, more complex. The transmission is indirect and manifests generally only over a relatively long term. At the same time, however, trade policy results in changes in relative prices, which will have a short-term impact on the welfare of the poor, by affecting both their employment and income prospects as well the prices of the goods they consume. Based on the outcomes of trade-policy reform in developing countries, a great deal of analysis exploring the impact of liberal trade regimes on economic growth has been carried out in recent years. The preponderance of empirical evidence from developing countries worldwide suggests that, on average, growth will be enhanced in the long run as a consequence of liberal trade regimes.[a]

As is the case elsewhere in the world, disentangling the linkages between trade and poverty reduction in the Region is more complex. As is well known, there was, for several reasons, a massive increase in poverty in the Region at the onset of the transition.[b] Despite the fact that most of the Region's countries early on adopted (and have largely maintained) relatively liberal formal trade regimes and that, moreover, substantial progress in poverty reduction has been made in the Region in recent years, today—more than a decade after the onset of transition—widespread poverty persists in several of the Region's countries, especially, but not exclusively, in Central Asia and the Caucasus.

There have been some efforts to analyze through simulations the implications of specific trade-policy reforms on poverty in individual countries in the Region. However, there is no aggregate assessment of the experience for the group as a whole. The individual countries for which assessments have been made are Bulgaria, Moldova, Romania, and Russia.[c] These analyses generally find that the effect of trade liberalization on the poor as a group would tend to be positive.[d] However, there is also evidence that trade liberalization would likely reduce the well-being of some people, at least in the short term, and that some of these would be the poor, who can ill afford it.[e]

On the other hand, the absence of trade liberalization does not always translate into the poor becoming better off. The case of the slowest-reforming countries—such as Belarus and Uzbekistan—is instructive in this regard. Although their decreases in output and increases in poverty have been more limited than those of other countries in the Region, in part because of the maintenance of relatively closed trade regimes, they have nonetheless engaged in policies, such as the protection and state control of the cotton sector in Uzbekistan, which have been adverse to the welfare of the poorest elements of society.

(*Box continues on the following page.*)

BOX 3.3 (*continued*)

If the assessment of the implications of trade reform on poverty in the Region's transition economies is sobering—in the sense that in the short run, poverty will likely increase in certain segments of society—it is not inconsistent with the analysis in other countries worldwide. Retrospectively, greater exposure to trade may well have exacerbated poverty in the CIS countries. The situation was much better in the EU-8 and SEE economies, however, probably because many of these countries quickly pursued policies that provided for greater flexibility in resource allocation. These policies permitted workers displaced by imports, as well new labor force entrants, to be employed in new labor-intensive activities; they also focused on facilitating exports. Thus, in the absence of effective product and factor markets, the adjustment to trade reforms in the CIS has been very protracted. In consequence, the "short run" for these countries may still be lingering.

Despite the variations in these findings, there is a general consensus that, for the poor to gain from trade liberalization, actions that complement trade reform are needed. The main conclusions of individual country case studies—as well as cross-country econometric studies—that have looked at experiences with trade liberalization at the country level worldwide are the importance of enhancing flexibility in labor markets and facilitating the flow of investment from sectors that are contracting to those that are expanding. In short, a policy of import liberalization alone is not sufficient to promote the strong trade performance that could be beneficial to output growth and indirectly to poverty reduction. A variety of additional reforms needs to be implemented for such a policy to have meaningful and enduring salutary effects.

a. Over the 1990s, the proposition that trade openness is good for economic growth was advanced by a number of cross-country studies (Sachs and Warner 1995; Edwards 1998; Dollar and Kraay 2001). But the findings of some of these studies have been subjected to serious criticism: restrictiveness of trade policy is difficult to measure, and the openness indicators used to show links to growth are not good proxies for trade policy. Institutional development, in a broad sense, has been proposed as a factor that explains both trade and output growth (Rodriguez and Rodrik 2001). Experience has shown that, in the long term, countries need an open economy to sustain growth. However, developing country experience has shown that, for a time, countries have expanded their exports and trade under different kinds of trade regimes. Some, like China, Korea, and Taiwan (China), have done so under complex trade regimes that provided extensive import protection while at the same time providing very substantial stimulus to export industries. Successful implementation of such complex policies involving both import protection and stimulus to exports places great demands on foreign trade policy design and trade institutions, which few developing or transition countries can meet (World Bank 2002d). Others, like Chile, Hong Kong (China), and Singapore, have expanded exports while maintaining a very liberal regime on imports. Still others, like Mauritius and El Salvador, have used export processing zones to stimulate growth in trade, while maintaining substantial import controls.
b. World Bank 2000b and 2005b.
c. See Rutherford, Tarr, and Shepotylo (2004); Porto (2004a); Csaki et al. (2000); Csaki et al. (2002).
d. See, for example, Winters et al. 2004.
e. See, for example, IIED (2004); World Bank (2003c); Nicita (2004); Chen and Ravallion (2004).

Republic, the majority of businesses are required to obtain more than 30 permits in a six-month period after start-up to legally conduct their operations (World Bank 2004d). In Moldova, trade can play an important role in alleviating poverty, but this can happen only when the range of informal barriers to both imports and exports—such as cumbersome and restrictive customs procedures, corruption, and burdensome and inappropriate regulation—are significantly reduced (World Bank 2004f). The business climate is seen as the major factor constraining Ukraine's integration into world trade (World Bank 2004q). Similar conclusions apply to virtually all transition economies where the role of trade in development has been analyzed.

At the same time, there are serious institutional weaknesses both of a general nature (for example, concerning enforcement of contracts and property rights), as well as in particular areas critical to international trade, such as the availability of trade finance and insurance, or the transparency of customs procedures. Because of weaknesses in government and judicial system enforcement, there are problems, even when the laws and regulations are in conformity with international standards. These weaknesses in the market mechanism tend to discriminate more against foreign suppliers and imports—just as they do against foreign investors. In addition, most countries in the Region face serious problems in their transport systems, which in some cases are combined with issues of remoteness as well as transit problems created by their neighbors; all of these raise the costs of imports and exports and undermine the countries' capacity to integrate into world markets.

Trade-Related Policies and Institutions

Macroeconomic and Exchange-Rate Policies
Macroeconomic instability and ineffective exchange-rate policies can pose serious constraints to international trade performance. In the period immediately following the breakup of the Soviet Union, macroeconomic instability and payments issues were a serious problem for international trade in the CIS countries and in the Baltics (Michalopoulos and Tarr 1996). Following the 1998 financial crisis in Russia, however, most countries restored macroeconomic stability. While there have been some problems, macroeconomic instability has not been a major issue affecting trade performance in most countries in the Region in recent years. Moreover, all countries, except Turkmenistan and Uzbekistan, have relatively liberal exchange-rate regimes, and several (Armenia, Georgia, the Kyrgyz Republic, and Moldova) have met IMF Article VIII standards.[8]

In the aftermath of the 1998 crisis, Russia found itself with a substantially devalued exchange rate, which resulted in giving strong incentives to production for export and import substitution. At the same time, countries dependent on the Russian market encountered some difficulties. Several countries (Moldova, Kazakhstan, and the Kyrgyz Republic) had to devalue as well, after a period of real exchange-rate appreciation. In others (Armenia, Georgia), the overall real exchange rate appears to have remained relatively constant over the five-year period (1995–2000); in Armenia, however, the exchange rate continued to appreciate in relation to the ruble after 1998, contributing to the decline in competitiveness of Armenian products in the Russian market.

Real exchange-rate appreciation or fluctuating real rates or both have adversely affected competitiveness and the development of new export industries in some of the Region's countries at some points in time. For example, there is strong evidence that the Serbian exchange-rate policy of the last few years, while beneficial to maintaining domestic price stability, has adversely affected the competitiveness of the economy and that a different mix of macroeconomic policies is desirable (World Bank 2004k). In Azerbaijan, rapidly expanding oil exports were accompanied by a depreciation of the exchange rate after 1997, thus apparently avoiding the "Dutch disease" phenomenon, which adversely affects the development of new export products and the competitiveness of others (World Bank 2003a). On the other hand, other traditional export products—like cotton—have all but disappeared. Again, however, the exchange rate does not appear to have been a general problem for most countries in the Region.

Taxes

The tax system and tax administration are also important impediments to exports in many of the Region's countries. In Georgia and elsewhere, many firms complain that tax administration is arbitrary and unpredictable. The tax code is complex and changes frequently. Its administration is opaque, leading to opportunities to extract bribes (World Bank 2003b; World Bank 2003c; World Bank 2004d).

While, as discussed above, formal trade barriers are not very high, they often involve some cascading of tariffs. In addition, they always involve a VAT paid by all imports, usually in the neighborhood of 20 percent. As noted earlier, where exports depend on imported inputs, both tariffs and the VAT on inputs need to be promptly refunded or credited to the enterprises. This rarely happens, as evidence in country after country suggests (World Bank 2002d; World Bank 2003c; World Bank 2004d; World Bank 2004q). As a consequence, exporters are penalized and lose competitiveness. In the case of the Kyrgyz Republic, this factor alone (nonrefund of tariffs and VAT) is estimated to have raised total costs by 9 percent on 44 firms surveyed (Cuthberson and Jones 2000).

Another problem present in the Kyrgyz Republic, and other countries in the Region as well, is the continued presence of high payroll taxes.[9] These taxes lead to a variety of problems, including depression of official wages in order to avoid payment of the payroll taxes (World Bank 2004d). In the context of international trade, however, they have an especially distorting effect: arguably, an important comparative advantage of these countries lies in their supply of large numbers of educated and qualified labor. Taxing the use of this labor is a sure way of diminishing the competitiveness of their exports, current or potential.

Customs

The problems faced by the customs services of all economies in the Region are well known (see chapter 5).[10] Customs services are only a relatively few years old and have not had adequate time to develop expertise. Customs officers are paid low salaries, both absolutely and relative to the private sector. Not only do they lack the resources of a modern customs service, including fully computerized systems and communications procedures such as mobile phones and e-mail networks, in Georgia, they even lacked uniforms for some time! Customs services are also expected to administer a complex and frequently changing set of rules and regulations including, but not limited to, the tariff. In Bosnia and Herzegovina, Georgia, Moldova, and elsewhere, they are not able to control large parts of the border. Even where there are customs posts (for example, in the Caucasus), the physical infrastructure is weak and probably would not be able to cope with significant increases in trade.

These difficulties are compounded in some cases by internal management problems. In the case of Georgia, there have been very frequent changes in the top customs administrator. In Azerbaijan, there are problems of coordination and communication among the different agencies involved in clearance of imported merchandise. In a number of countries in the Region (including Azerbaijan and the Kyrgyz Republic), approvals by the standards or health agencies take a long time and sometimes rules are capriciously enforced. Dispute settlement procedures are lengthy and nontransparent, leading participants to resort to bribes in an effort to resolve them. In the Kyrgyz Republic, approvals are needed from different agencies, which are physically situated in different parts of the country. In Armenia and Serbia and Montenegro, there is evidence that customs uses reference prices on imports, which is inconsistent with WTO provisions (World Bank 2002a).[11]

The principal border crossings vary significantly in terms of staffing and facilities. In the Caucasus, even the best seem to have little additional capacity to deal with any future increases in traffic volume and are likely to be the source of recurrent and substantial delays. In the case of Moldova, the problems do not seem to arise on the Moldovan side, but on the side of Ukraine. In the case of Central Asia, there appear to be few problems in the rail network crossings between Tajikistan and Uzbekistan, but there are serious issues in road transport that are discussed below, in connection with transit issues. Tajikistan has a long border with Afghanistan, which was patrolled by Russian troops; this, however, did not prevent significant smuggling.

The lack of coordination among the customs authorities in various territories that constitute the Region, such as the Caucasus, Central Asia, and Southeastern Europe, is a critical bottleneck to international integration. Some progress has been made in this regard in Southeastern Europe and, to a lesser extent, in Central Asia, through the establishment of mechanisms for periodic consultations among transport authorities, although many border crossing and transit problems persist. In the Caucasus, more collaboration is needed, even between the customs authorities not directly affected by the Armenia-Azerbaijan conflict.

In some countries (Georgia, Moldova, Uzbekistan), preshipment inspection (PSI) services have been put in place. These services have not been generally successful, however. In Georgia, the service was cancelled because it was not perceived to be cost-effective. In Moldova, there were complaints about the service that had been put in place in December 2001, and the decision was made to apply PSI only to final products. Firms complained about delays and costs, while customs officials complained of misclassifications. These problems may simply reflect the initial reactions of individuals who perceive the PSI as limiting either their authority or their freedom of action. And, clearly, PSI will fail if it does not have the support of the government and customs. Nevertheless, experience in many countries suggests that PSI is not a magic bullet that will solve all problems—it has to be supported by a thoroughgoing customs reform.

As discussed in greater detail in chapter 5, there are many elements to a customs reform, including internal organization of the customs authority; staffing; remuneration; performance management and accountability; automation and modernization of operational procedures consistent with international practices; introduction of internal/external control and audit procedures; physical infrastructure, both in terms of equipment for automated procedures and communication, and also for customs posts; simplification of approval procedures for various standards and health organizations; and more effective coordination between customs and other organizations involved in controlling imports.

Services

In addition to customs, effective integration into the world trading system requires the support of a variety of other institutions and policies. The availability of low-cost, high-quality services is a critical determinant of export competitiveness. Research has shown that policies and projects that aim at decreasing the costs of services that facilitate trade produce economywide benefits that are a multiple of the benefits that result from trade liberalization (Hoekman 2002). The key services that facilitate trade are those involving banking and finance, marketing, and standards organizations, as well as telecommunications and transportation.

The economies of the Region emerged from the period of central planning with even more government controls and monopolies in the services sectors than those traditionally exercised by market economies. As discussed in detail in chapter 6, in the last decade, the introduction of market-oriented reforms in the services sectors has proceeded at a different pace in the various countries, as has the liberalization of merchandise trade. However, many service sector deficiencies remain in practically all of the transition economies, including the largest and strongest. In Russia, the realization is growing that almost all service sectors, including financial services, insurance, accounting, and business services, as well as legal services and construction, are in need of competitive restructuring. The same is true for transport, telecommunications, and utilities, which traditionally have been considered as reserved for government monopolies. In many of these sectors, technology change has made it possible to introduce competition; this leads to improved efficiency, a key to long-term competitiveness in international trade (Broadman 2004).

Countries in the Region that have joined the WTO have had to review their policies that affect international trade in services when they made commitments under the General Agreement of Trade in Services (GATS) in the context of their accession; others that are in the process of accession will have to do so in the future. Box 3.4 describes the GATS.

A useful taxonomy for describing international transactions in services is provided by the notion that they can be mediated through four supply modes. One case is where the user receives the service from the provider located in another country; this mode is referred to as "cross-border supply." An example is the provision of architectural

BOX 3.4

The General Agreement on Trade in Services (GATS)

The GATS accord was part of the Uruguay Round of negotiations, which began in 1986 under the auspices of the General Agreement on Tariffs and Trade (GATT) and concluded with the establishment of the WTO in 1995. The GATS represents the first attempt to devise a multilateral, legally enforceable understanding covering trade and investment in the services sector. Like the GATT, which was updated as part of the Uruguay Round and still forms the WTO's principal rule book for trade in goods, the GATS provides a legal basis on which to negotiate the multilateral elimination of barriers that discriminate against foreign services providers and otherwise deny them market access. The GATS differs from the GATT in several respects. Perhaps the most important difference is that the principles of national treatment (that is, nondiscrimination) and market access (that is, freedom of entry and exit) are provided automatically under the GATT, but are negotiated rights and obligations in the GATS. The negotiations on national treatment and market access for services in the GATS constitute the equivalent of tariff negotiations for goods in the GATT. In services trade, there is effectively no "border," as there is in goods trade. The restrictions on international transactions in services are embedded in countries' domestic laws, regulations, and other measures. Under the GATS obligations, these restrictions are liberalized (in varying degrees), thus creating for services a regime that is the equivalent of a duty-free regime for goods.

The GATS comprises two principal components. The first is a framework that sets out general multilateral rules governing trade and investment in services. The second complements the rules framework. It is the set of binding commitments to market access and national treatment for the individual services industries; countries append these commitments to the agreement in the form of a "schedule." Like tariff negotiations in goods, these multilateral services commitments result from iterative bilateral "request and offer" negotiations conducted seriatim on a country-by-country basis. Supplementing the rules framework are sectoral annexes and under-

blueprints via fax. A second mode is the case where a service can be provided through "consumption abroad," that is, with the consumption of the service taking place outside the user's home country and in the country of the supplier. An example of this is tourism. A third case is where the provision of the service requires sustained interaction between the user and the supplier of the service, and thus the service provider establishes a facility, or otherwise attains a "commercial presence" in the user's country. Typically, though not always, this mode means that foreign direct investment is part of the provision of the service. An example is the establishment of a foreign law practice in the host country. The final mode involves the need for close inter-

standings that contain specific rules dealing with, among other things, issues affecting financial services, aviation services, and access to telecommunications networks.

While some of the provisions of the overall rules framework apply to all services industries regardless of whether they are "scheduled," many pertain only to industries for which market access or national treatment commitments are assumed. As a result, on balance, the GATS employs what has become known as a "positive list" approach: unless an industry is scheduled, it is, in the main, automatically excluded from the most meaningful terms of the agreement.

The fundamental mechanism of the GATS, which engenders the agreement's multilateral liberalizing character, is the rule that also serves as the basis of the GATT: Most Favored Nation (MFN) treatment. Like the GATT, the MFN principle—that a signatory treat all countries in a manner no less favorable than its treatment of a particular country—generally applies to all services included in the GATS, regardless of whether a particular industry is included in a country's schedule of commitments. However, the GATS allows for flexibility in the application of MFN. In particular, it permits exemptions to MFN for specific laws, regulations, and administrative practices. Such flexibility is essential because of the need to be able to maintain existing regulations or agreements not consistent with MFN, or the need to preserve the prospective use of reciprocal or unilateral measures, particularly when a country has concluded, as a tactical matter, that the GATS commitments offered by other countries for a specific industry generally are not sufficiently liberalizing.

In addition to the negotiated rights and obligations of market access and national treatment, as well as the MFN rule, other core provisions of the GATS include the requirement for countries to publish all domestic laws and regulations affecting services: these include assurances for due process in notifying interested services providers of the status of license applications; disciplines on public monopolies; rights governing the mutual recognition and harmonization of regulatory standards; consultation procedures on competition matters; and exceptions for national security, safety, and health, and the enforcement of tax laws.

Source: Broadman 1994.

action of user and provider, with the supplier located in the user's country; however, it involves only the temporary presence of "natural persons" (usually referred to as "business persons") for the delivery of the service. This situation can occur, among other ways, as an intracorporate transfer of a professional or on the basis of an individual entrepreneur operating under a contract. An example of the latter would be a foreign computer software consultant.

Of course, these various modes of supplying services are not mutually exclusive. All the modes of supply described above, taken together, can be usefully summarized as "cross-border trade and investment" in services. As the analysis above makes clear, barriers to foreign investment, as well as barriers to temporary movement of personnel, can be tantamount to barriers to services trade (see Broadman 1994).

In general, the SEE and CIS countries that have become WTO members have made more commitments to liberalize their services sectors in comparison to other countries at similar levels of economic development (Michalopoulos and Panousopoulos 2002). In terms of their overall commitments, these countries have made more commitments regarding national treatment than market access, a tendency common to virtually all WTO members worldwide. In addition, as in other countries, there were far fewer commitments for the provision of services through "mode four," presence of natural persons, than for the other three modes of supply. The sectors in which countries in transition made the fewest commitments are health, recreational, and transport services, while extensive commitments for liberal access were made for construction, distribution, tourism and travel, financial, business, and communication services (for further details, see chapter 6). In some cases (Bulgaria, Romania), the countries have liberalized sectors such as banking and finance *subsequent* to WTO accession, and their policies are in fact more liberal than their bound WTO commitments would indicate.

Banking and Finance

Despite these liberalization commitments, most of the financial institutions in many countries in SEE and the CIS do not appear capable of financing trade flows at present. Financial markets are poorly developed, and letters of credit, bills of exchange, and other modern payment instruments are unavailable. Payments between traders in the Central Asian countries can only be cleared through settlement accounts in commercial banks of neighboring countries. However, governments collect tax revenue on these accounts, and international clearing is tightly controlled.

Access to domestic credit by exporters is basically nonexistent. This is part of a general problem of unavailability of credit to small and medium enterprises, both because the banks see other, easier, and more profitable investment opportunities and because the creditworthiness of any company seeking credit is difficult to establish. As a consequence, credit has to be provided from the importing side, something that is obviously easier to do when selling to developed countries with well-developed financial sectors than when selling to Regional partners.

While trade finance is important, its provision should be part of an overall strengthening of the commercial banking system. International experience suggests that directed credit lines that are specifically designed for short-term trade finance do not have a lasting impact in the absence of a strong banking sector; further, there are a very few product lines in these countries that would require longer-term export credits. At the same time, given the weaknesses in the domestic banking sector, perhaps the best way of developing credit lines for trade is to promote the operation of foreign banks, which, with their international contacts, can help in trade finance.

Marketing Institutions

Marketing institutions are basically absent from much of the Region, and exporters have to rely on their own resources to market their products. For traditional raw material exports (for example, Uzbekistan cotton, Tajikistan aluminum), this is not a problem. Russia and, to some extent Ukraine, inherited much stronger marketing capabilities for traditional exports, which helped them preserve some high-value niches (for example, arms, nuclear, and space technologies). Russian suppliers also effectively substituted for other CIS enterprises that were parts of traditional Soviet chains (World Bank 2004p). The difficulties arise when a new product line has to be introduced. In such cases, marketing is easier when the export is based on a joint venture with an international partner who has established commercial links abroad. This has been a problem for many smaller CIS and SEE economies, as there have been few joint ventures in general and fewer yet outside the extractive industries.

Standards Organizations

Standards organizations operate in all of the countries in the Region. Traditionally, these organizations used Soviet-era standards, which increasingly have been modified to make them compatible with international standards. This is something that the countries in the Region that have become members of the WTO have had to do and that will have to be done by the others in the Region before they become members. Currently, the operations of many of these organizations in the CIS and SEE are generally ineffective. On the import side, they tend to delay shipments, sometimes extensively, sometimes intentionally. In the case of Ukraine, for example, the standards regime has been identified as an explicit NTB designed to selectively constrain import flows (World Bank 2004q). On the export side, standards organizations are not able to provide the information needed to exporters to ensure that the latter meet the requirements in export markets.[12] Assistance to these organizations has typically been offered by donors in connection with WTO accession. There is a continuing need for strengthening these institutions even after WTO accession has been secured (World Bank 2004d).

Transport

Transport costs are a major determinant of competitiveness, as the cost of international transport is often higher than the applicable tariff in external markets. Transport problems faced by these countries are both internal and external, related to the question of transit, which is a major issue discussed in chapter 5.

During the period of central planning, there was substantial investment in transport infrastructure. At the same time, the infrastructure was designed to service the trade flows established with and within the former Soviet Union. After independence, demand for transport services declined, pari passu with the substantial decline in economic activity. At the same time, existing infrastructure has been poorly maintained, and little new infrastructure has been added to address the needs for changing trade patterns; in addition, reform of the transport sector management and financing has been slow. As a consequence, in many of the countries in the Region, especially in SEE and the CIS, the transport infrastructure is a significant impediment to expanded trade. The many problems identified in various country studies include (a) freight charges that are frequently highly subsidized, resulting in poor financial condition of transport enterprises (which in many cases continue to be publicly owned); (b) the poor condition of the road infrastructure, as well as a trucking fleet that is aging and not being renewed; (c) antiquated rolling stock and lack of shunting stock and essential maintenance; and (d) limited airfreight services, which are useful only for the few high-value/low-weight exports of the Region's countries.

In addition to these problems, there are large costs resulting from corruption and unofficial payments (see chapter 4). For example, in the Caucasus, moving a generic containerized consignment by road from Northern Europe to Tbilisi—the Georgian leg—accounts for nearly 46 percent of total costs, with unofficial payments to border agencies, the road police, and other agencies representing more than 90 percent of the costs inside Georgia. Moving a similar consignment by road to Yerevan—the Caucasus leg—accounts for 67 percent of total costs, with unofficial payments accounting for almost half of total costs (World Bank 2002d; World Bank 2003c).

In many of the Region's countries, especially in the CIS and SEE, there is a need for substantial institutional strengthening of the various road funds and railway companies; there is also a need for substantial investment in maintenance and repair; there is a need for a reassessment of demand and supply for various transport services, in the light of the emerging pattern of economic activity and international trade; and there is a need for simplifying procedures, strengthening the border agencies, and eliminating corruption. Such improvements should be viewed as an important component of any effort to strengthen the integration of these economies into world trade. For a more detailed discussion of transport costs and international integration, see chapter 5.

Transit Issues

As with other issues, there are distinctly different transit problems in Southeastern Europe, Central Asia, and the Caucasus. Moldova appears to face serious transit problems as a consequence of substantial delays on the border with Ukraine. In Central Asia, the problems are concentrated in the Kyrgyz Republic and Tajikistan, with each facing transit problems—in the former through Kazakhstan and in the latter through Uzbekistan. In both cases, the problems relate primarily to road transport and not to rail. Indeed, all Central Asian railways use the same rolling stock, track standards, and rule books, and there appears to be significant cooperation among the rail authorities in the three countries. In the Caucasus, the problems derive from the Armenia-Azerbaijan conflict and the Turkish blockade of Armenia, as described in box 3.5.

The Challenges Ahead

As suggested in chapter 2, the fundamental constraints limiting the trade performance of countries in the Region relate to weaknesses in their trade-related policies and behind-the-border institutions. The experience of these economies over the last 15 years suggests that liberal trade policies affecting imports are necessary but not sufficient for these countries' effective integration into the world economy. Also, most of these countries have done little to encourage, and have often discouraged, exports.

The main challenges they face, however, relate to other behind-the-border policies and institutions. Some of these factors, such as fostering greater competition, improving governance, and adhering to the rule of law, are intimately linked to more general improvements in economic management and the performance of market institutions (these issues are discussed in chapter 4). Others, such as strengthening of the customs service, improving standards and marketing organizations, overhauling the transport system, and facilitating trade and transit are directly linked to external trade (for more, see chapter 5).

To be sure, these problems have been identified in recent years (Michalopoulos 1999), and some countries in the Region have made progress in addressing them. Unfortunately, however, the increasing attention paid to these issues has not yet resulted in Region-wide improved performance. Much more needs to be done on a sustained basis in all of the countries before trade performance can improve. Part III of this study examines the behind-the-border impediments, institu-

BOX 3.5

Transit Problems in the CIS

Kyrgyz Republic. The destination of a high percentage of the exports is Russia and the EU. Road transport costs are typically 10–15 percent of total costs, of which only about one-third are fuel costs. The remainder involves different kinds of fees and payments to be made officially and un-officially at various points in transit countries. The main problems arise in connection with transit through Kazakhstan.[a] Many of these barriers are being addressed through an Agreement on Transit that started to be implemented in early 2004. However, some barriers are still in place, including various road taxes and fees imposed by local authorities, as well as harassment by local police, bureaucratic delays created to extract bribes, and weak capacity in customs administration (World Bank 2004d; see also Molnar and Ojala 2004). Transporters also complain that axle weight limitations are set differently and are biased against their trucks, and that slight deviations above weight limitations attract draconian penalties, which force them to carry inefficiently small loads (Cuthberson and Jones 2000).

Tajikistan. The geographic location of Tajikistan is as difficult as it gets, and as a consequence, Tajik trade is burdened with one of the highest logistics costs in the world (World Bank 2004l). About 80 percent of Tajikistan's exports must be routed through Uzbekistan, in part because of the topography and in part because Tajikistan's northern and southern rail networks, which carry most of the exports, are not connected. At the same time, Uzbekistan depends on transit through Tajikistan for access to the Fergana Valley. Cooperation is working better on rail than on road traffic. In the latter case, Tajik drivers complain that current border fees are higher for exports than they are for imports, and that customs regulations are often complex and vague, leaving a great deal of leeway for harassment and bribery (World Bank 2004l). Also, Tajik truck drivers need a visa to enter Uzbekistan, and obtaining or renewing one can be problematic and time-consuming (World Bank 2004l).

tions, and policies in the Region in detail and provides suggestions for reform so as to make concerted, Region-wide progress on this front.

The international community also has responsibilities: the poorer countries in transition need technical and financial assistance to strengthen their trade-related institutions. The World Bank and other multilateral and bilateral donors have a number of assistance programs in place for this purpose, for example, to support customs reform, to improve trade-facilitation institutions, and to strengthen the overall country trade-related capacity to meet WTO-related commitments. However, although they share many of the characteristics, none of these countries formally qualify as "least developed countries" under the UN definition; this means that they cannot benefit from the many programs that the international community has

The Caucasus. Transport costs account for about 10 percent of the total value of merchandise in Armenia and slightly less in Azerbaijan and Georgia. They have been declining in recent periods, as there has been increased transit through Georgia and Iran. All countries levy high transit fees on foreign vehicles, but the fees appear to be substantially lower than those levied by the countries in Central Asia. Armenia has been the country most affected by the blockade, as it has to reroute its trade through Georgia. This has had a significant adverse effect on Armenia's exports. It is estimated that opening the Turkish border will halve the trucking costs between Armenia and Turkey. There would also be substantial savings if Turkish ports were used for transshipments of sea freight, and there would be significant, if somewhat lower, savings in freight costs to Iran. In addition to savings in money, the direct link between Armenian and Turkish road systems would increase the availability, predictability, and reliability of shipping services. By comparison, Azerbaijan transport costs would decrease only by about 10 percent as a consequence of opening up the road between Armenia and Turkey. Georgia, on the other hand, would lose transit fees if the blockade on Armenia were lifted. Nevertheless, as noted earlier, all of the countries would gain from the increased trade and growth that would result from the normalization of political relations (Polyakov 2001).

Moldova. Despite a free transit provision included in its FTAs with Russia and Ukraine, Moldova experiences serious problems with the transit of goods destined for Russia, its main market, through Ukraine. The transit environment remains chaotic, and a regime of free transit has never been achieved (World Bank 2004f).

Source: World Bank staff.

Note: a. See Cuthberson and Jones 2000. While the ratio of transport costs to merchandise value for these countries is high, it does not come close to the problems faced by a developing country like Malawi, where the ratio of transport cost to merchandise value was as high as 50 percent (UNCTAD 2001).

organized to strengthen the trade-related capacity of certain countries (see box 3.6).

Global Integration

WTO Accession

All eight of the countries in the Region that have recently become members of the EU are WTO members. Only 9 of the other 19 countries in the Region have acceded to the WTO. Romania became a contracting party to the GATT in 1983 under a special protocol and despite serious concerns as to whether its commitments at that time, for example regarding tariffs, were meaningful in the context of

---

BOX 3.6

Least Developed Countries (LDCs) and Transition

The official recognition of a country as "Least Developed" by the United Nations provides it with access to a number of assistance programs, as well as to preferential treatment in trade. To be added to the list, a country must meet a number of criteria based on a UN triennial review. In its latest review of the list of Least Developed Countries in 2003, the Economic and Social Council (ECOSOC) of the United Nations used the following three criteria for the identification of LDCs, as proposed by the Committee for Development Policy (CDP):

1. A low-income criterion, based on a three-year average estimate of the gross national income per capita (under $750 for inclusion, above $900 for graduation)

2. A human resource weakness criterion, involving a composite Augmented Physical Quality of Life Index (APQLI)

3. An economic vulnerability criterion, involving a composite Economic Vulnerability Index (EVI)

To be added to the list, a country must satisfy all three criteria. To qualify for graduation, a country must meet the thresholds for two of the three criteria in two consecutive triennial reviews by the CDP. Based on the CDP report, the ECOSOC makes recommendations to the General Assembly, which is responsible for the final decision on the list of LDCs.

As of 2004, 50 countries were designated as LDCs. None were transition economies, although some may have met at least two of the three criteria for inclusion. As a consequence, no transition economy could benefit from a number of international initiatives such as the Integrated Framework for Trade-Related Technical Assistance for LDCs, aimed to strengthen these countries' institutional capacity and become better integrated into the world trading system.

Source: United Nations.

central planning. Subsequently, it renegotiated its GATT protocols and became a founding member of WTO. Bulgaria applied for admission to the GATT in the 1980s and eventually became a member of WTO in 1996. Albania, Armenia, Croatia, Georgia, the Kyrgyz Republic, FYR Macedonia, and Moldova became WTO members in the last five years. All remaining countries, with the exception of Turkmenistan, are in various stages of the accession process. Some, like Russia and the related application for accession of Kazakhstan, as well as Ukraine, are relatively advanced. Others lag behind (see table 3.5).[13]

WTO membership results in greater integration into world trade. Trade among WTO members is on average 25 percent higher than

TABLE 3.5

Timetable of Accessions to the WTO

Government	WP establishment	Memorandum	Tariff offers (latest)	Service offers (latest)	Draft working party report
Russian Fed.	06/93	03/94, 01/01	02/01	06/02	05/03
Belarus	10/93	01/96	03/98	—	—
Ukraine	12/93	07/94	03/02	07/03	09/04
Uzbekistán	12/94	09/98	—	—	—
Kazakhstan	02/96	09/96	04/01	05/03	—
Azerbaijan	07/97	04/99	03/03	04/03	—
Bosnia & Herzegovina	07/99	11/03	—	—	—
Serbia & Montenegro	01/01	06/02	—	—	—
Tajikistan	07/01	02/03	—	—	—

Source: WTO.

Note: — = not applicable.

trade among nonmembers (EBRD 2003). WTO membership is important for a number of reasons: first, because membership promotes the establishment of the legal framework and market-based institutions in support of international trade that were absent under central planning. Second, membership is important because it provides better guarantees for market access through the provision of unconditional MFN status—something that some transition economies do not enjoy in all markets—and through the avoidance of arbitrary measures that limit market access to nonmembers. Third, because the WTO has established a binding dispute settlement mechanism, which has proved effective in adjudicating trade disputes. This is especially important for a number of the smaller countries in transition, who have in the past been victims of their larger neighbors, who used trade measures as a weapon in settling a variety of economic disputes.

Relations with the EU

The eight transition economies in Eastern Europe that have recently become EU members—the EU-8—have accepted the EU *acquis* in its totality and are in the process of implementing the myriad new obligations that come with membership. Included in these new obligations is the adoption of the common EU external tariff and all of the EU regulations governing external trade, including the preferential agreements the EU has signed with many countries worldwide. These countries have had to abandon all of the bilateral preferential agreements they had signed with other countries in the Region and all of their own trade protection immediately upon accession, with the exception of a short transition period for a few Polish products. Undoubtedly, EU accession will have a profound, and in the long term, positive impact on their economies. It will also have both a short-term and a longer-term impact on the remaining economies in transition.

The biggest challenge for transition countries in Southeastern Europe is posed by their own future membership and integration with the EU. With few exceptions, these countries have already signed Association Agreements—which involve free trade arrangements in many sectors and preferential treatment in others—with the EU. Bulgaria and Romania are in advanced stages of negotiations for EU accession, and Croatia has been approved as a candidate country. FYR Macedonia has signed, and Albania is well along in the process of negotiating a Stabilization and Association Agreement (SAA) with the EU, which envisages both free trade arrangements and an alignment of their policies to those of the EU, with a view to their future accession. Bosnia and Herzegovina and Serbia and Montenegro are also engaging in consultations with a view to signing similar agreements with the EU. The bulk of these countries' imports (more than 70 percent) are covered by preferential European arrangements, and a significant portion of the remainder involve energy and raw materials, which are not protected by the EU. Indeed, with the possible exception of the LDCs, these countries seem to occupy the top of the EU preference pyramid (Stevens et al. 1999). The average tariff on their imports to the EU (weighted or unweighted) is less than half of that applied by the EU on imports from the CIS (EBRD 2003, table 4.3).

At present, MFN tariffs on industrial products in all of these countries are substantially different—usually higher—than those of the EU. Because they already have or will have free trade arrangements with the EU that would cover most, if not all, industrial products, the current situation results in significant trade diversion that yields high rents to EU producers but no benefits to these countries (Kaminski and La Rocha 2003a). These countries would be better off by progressively realigning their overall MFN tariff schedule to that of the EU, even in advance of EU accession. However, the EU tariff will itself likely be changing as a consequence of the WTO multilateral trade negotiations. The transition economies of SEE would need to coordinate their position on the multilateral trade negotiations with the EU, but they can also use these negotiations as a means of making further adjustments to their tariff schedule so that it can be aligned to that of the EU at the earliest possible opportunity.

EU membership would require the realignment of a vast number of other policies and institutions and give rise to a large and complex set of social and economic adjustment issues, which would include, but not be limited to, trade. It is a huge task that is currently occupying a large number of policy makers and analysts both in the EU and in the countries themselves.

The EU relationship with the CIS members is fundamentally different. In most cases, the relationship is governed by so called "Partnership and Cooperation Agreements" (PCAs), which are in force with all CIS countries except Belarus, Tajikistan, and Turkmenistan. The PCAs are basic commercial treaties. The major benefits afforded by these treaties are the provision of MFN and, in some cases, GSP (Generalized System of Preferences) treatment and adherence to basic commercial rules and practices. These treaties have been especially important for the transition economies while they have not been WTO members. Once they become WTO members, the mutual commitments undertaken in the context of accession far exceed anything contained in the PCAs. It is for this reason, for example, that Russia's negotiations with the EU over pricing of natural gas in the context of WTO accession have been so protracted and difficult.

The benefits derived from EU preferences under the GSP have been modest. In Ukraine, it is estimated that roughly 30 percent of total Ukrainian exports are eligible for GSP coverage. Of the total eligible for coverage, roughly 50 percent of imports actually received preferential treatment. In Moldova, the eligibility and utilization rates were slightly higher. However, Moldova's main export, wine, was not included (World Bank 2004f). These results are in line with the results obtained under EU's GSP by other countries. The benefits are modest because (a) the commodity coverage under the GSP is limited; (b) competing countries enjoy deeper margins of preference—for example, the average EU tariff on ethyl alcohol is 30 percentage points lower than what exporters from Russia and Ukraine face; and (c) utilization is limited, in part because of lack of information in the countries themselves and also because adhering to the GSP provisions regarding rules of origin is quite difficult, especially for small and medium enterprises (World Bank 2004i; World Bank 2004q).

It should be underscored that, as most of CIS exports to Organisation for Economic Co-operation and Development (OECD) markets consist of energy and raw materials, which are not significantly protected, market access conditions have not resulted in major constraints to overall export performance. There are significant problems, however, in specific export sectors, for example, metals, textiles, chemicals, and processed food, many of which have been the targets of antidumping and other protection in EU and other OECD markets.

A number of CIS members, notably Moldova, Ukraine, and some of the Caucasus countries, aspire to some type of closer association with the EU. Moldova, for example, has stated that it would wish to be included in the SAA process; Ukraine is considering how to associate itself with the EU. It is unclear at this stage how far the EU is willing to go in strengthening its economic links with these countries. It appears that the future economic relationships of these countries with the EU will depend a great deal on political and human rights issues, and less on strictly economic questions.

EU Enlargement

The EU enlargement will have profound effects not only on the economies in the Region who already have become EU members but also on countries in the Region who are not in the EU, especially those in the CIS who have no preferential arrangements with the EU. The effects are likely to be different in manufacturing from those in agriculture.

In manufacturing, EU enlargement is likely to have positive short-term effects on CIS countries. They will have relatively little change in access to the EU-15 markets, as the enlargement countries already have duty-free access in these markets. On the other hand, market access in the enlargement countries themselves will improve, as these countries (for example, Poland and Hungary), have tariffs that are much higher than the EU common external tariff (World Bank 2004f; World Bank 2004q). For countries in SEE, the situation regarding exports of manufactures is also likely to change little. These countries already enjoy very free access to the EU-15 markets. Access to the enlargement country markets has also been relatively free as a result of the membership of some of the SEE countries in the Central Europe Free Trade Agreement (CEFTA). For the Western Balkan countries that were not members of CEFTA (Albania, Bosnia and Herzegovina, FYR Macedonia, and Serbia and Montenegro), the enlargement will mean definitive improvement in market access.

The situation in agriculture will be very different. To begin with, existing EU agricultural policies under the Common Agricultural Policy (CAP) cause significant difficulties to both CIS and SEE agricultural development. These policies involve substantial production supports and export subsidies of products by other countries in the Region that these countries cannot match. Enlargement will have two negative short-term effects on these economies' agriculture: first, countries like Poland and Hungary, which are competitors to the SEE and CIS economies, will enjoy far better access to the markets of the EU-15 for agricultural products; second, the enlargement countries will benefit from EU supports and subsidies, thus making them stronger competitors in the SEE and CIS countries' own markets.

Against these negative effects, it is possible that market access in some enlargement countries, and for some products, will improve because protection in their own markets had been greater than EU protection. However, the net overall short-term effect in agriculture is likely to be negative.

In the longer term, however, EU enlargement is likely to have a net positive effect on the CIS and SEE countries. The short-term positive effect on manufacturing exports will be augmented by the dynamic effects that EU accession will likely have on the enlargement countries. In agriculture, EU supports could well decline as a result of internal budgetary constraints; at the same time, international pressure arising in the context of the Doha multilateral trade negotiations also may have salutary effects.

"Market" or "Nonmarket" Economies?

One of the most serious market-access problems the SEE and CIS countries face in virtually all markets globally is that their exports are frequently the target of antidumping actions by both developed and developing countries. In part, this is because many are not members of the WTO. In part, however, it also is because so many of these countries have been designated as "nonmarket economies" (NMEs) for purposes of antidumping cases by developed countries, such as the EU and the United States. It also arises in the case of the EU for the imposition of safeguards against SEE and CIS exports. The NME designation involves the use of different, less-demanding, and less-transparent procedures for the complainant countries in the determination of dumping and, in the case of the EU, also in the use of safeguards against imports from the NME. It results in more easy "findings" of dumping or the establishment of "price undertakings" that involve the cartelization of markets.

Since the establishment of the WTO in 1995, the Region's countries have been the target of 325 antidumping actions, or 13.5 percent of total antidumping actions worldwide.[14] This is much higher than their share in world trade. The bulk of the actions have been taken against Russia and Ukraine (86 and 51 antidumping investigations, respectively [see annex table 3.3]). Actions against the EU-8 have been less frequent relative to their share in world trade (see table 3.6) than have actions against countries in SEE, many of whom are not WTO members. Ukraine has the distinction of having a higher share of antidumping actions relative to its exports than any other country worldwide, including China. Russia's share is also large, especially if one considers that a large share of Russian

TABLE 3.6

Antidumping: Share of Affected Economies in Total Cases Relative to Share in World Exports in Percentages and Ratios

Affected economies	World exports 1995–2003		Total antidumping investigations 1995–2003			Definitive measures 1995–2003	
	Exports ($ billions)	Wld. export share (%)	No. of cases	Share (%)	AD share/ Wld. exp. share	DM share (%)	DM share/ Wld. exp. share
World	53,322	100.0	2,416	100.0	1.0	100.0	1.0
Industrial countries	34,541	64.8	683	28.3	0.4	25.4	0.4
Developing countries	16,354	30.7	1,408	58.3	1.9	58.0	1.9
All transition countries	2,427	4.6	325	13.5	3.0	16.6	3.6
Non-WTO members (10)	1,160	2.2	177	7.3	3.4	9.7	4.5
Nonmarket countries (7)	141	0.3	15	0.6	2.3	0.7	2.5
Nonmarket countries (18)	3,299	6.2	481	19.9	3.2	27.0	4.4
All Region	2,427	4.6	325	13.5	3.0	16.6	3.6
EU-8	1,058	2.0	90	3.7	1.9	3.0	1.5
CIS	1,161	2.2	175	7.2	3.3	9.9	4.6
SEE	214	0.4	63	2.6	6.5	3.1	7.8
Russian Fed.	815	1.5	86	3.6	2.3	4.7	3.1
Ukraine	141	0.3	51	2.1	8.0	3.1	11.8
China	2,142	4.0	356	14.7	3.7	16.8	4.2

Sources: WTO antidumping files and IMF Direction of Trade Statistics.

Note:
Non-WTO members include Azerbaijan, Belarus, Bosnia and Herzegovina, Kazakhstan, Russia, Serbia and Montenegro, Tajikistan, Turkmenistan, Ukraine, and Uzbekistan.
Nonmarket (7) includes Azerbaijan, Belarus, Cuba, Democratic People's Republic of Korea, Tajikistan, Turkmenistan, and Uzbekistan.
Nonmarket (18) includes above nonmarket 7 countries plus Albania, Armenia, China, Georgia, Kazakhstan, the Kyrgyz Republic, Moldova, Mongolia, Russia, Ukraine, and Vietnam. Moldova is included both in the CIS and in the SEE.

trade is in raw materials and fuels, which are not the subject of antidumping actions. Actions against these economies are more likely, as a general rule, to move beyond investigations and lead to the actual undertaking of definitive antidumping measures or price undertakings.[15]

The main sectors targeted have been ferrous and nonferrous metals and chemicals, including fertilizers. It is difficult to assess the impact of the antidumping actions on particular sectors of the economies affected. In Ukraine, at present, there are 25 tariff lines affected by EU AD restraints (World Bank 2004q). Although the overall volume of these exports is small relative to total Ukrainian exports to the EU, this is not to suggest that these measures have not had a significant restraining effect on Ukrainian exports: in some cases, Ukrainian exports simply ceased after the AD actions had been introduced; in others, they grew, but it is unclear by how much more they would have grown without the restraining effect of antidumping.

Designation of a country as a nonmarket economy makes it easier to obtain a finding of dumping because the procedures used are more arbitrary and less transparent. Such designations were started in the 1980s in order to take into account the price distortions inherent in central planning. They are still used today by the United States and the EU and other OECD countries, even in cases where central planning practices have long disappeared in the targeted economies.

When an antidumping investigation is initiated against an NME, the costs and exchange rates of a "surrogate" or "analogue" country are used for the determination of a "normal" value, against which the actual price is measured; this is because it is assumed that prices and exchange rates in centrally planned economies did not reflect true opportunity costs. This introduces the possibility for arbitrariness and nontransparency. Equally, these procedures make it easier to induce exporters to agree to minimum price undertakings such as those concluded with Russia on uranium and aluminum (Michalopoulos and Winters 1997), which involve the cartelization of the market in specific products.

With regard to antidumping, the WTO provides legal justification for such practices through the reference of Article 2.7 of the Antidumping Agreement to the second Supplementary Provision to paragraph 1 of Article VI in Annex I to GATT 1994, which permits such different treatment "in the case of imports from a country which has complete or substantially complete monopoly of its trade and where all domestic prices are fixed by the State" (Palmeter 1998). These practices perhaps were fully justified when virtually all trade was controlled by state trading enterprises or ministries under central planning, and prices were fixed by the state and hence could not be taken to reflect "normal value." Many—but not all—of the Region's countries have made great progress in introducing market forces and eliminating state trading in recent years. It would very difficult to argue that, for example, Ukraine or even Tajikistan at present has "a substantially complete monopoly on trade" or that all domestic prices are fixed by the state.

The EU distinguishes among three groups of countries for antidumping and safeguard purposes: (a) "nonmarket economies," which currently includes Azerbaijan, Belarus, Tajikistan, Turkmenistan, and Uzbekistan in the Region (as well as Cuba and the Democratic People's Republic of Korea outside the Region), none of whom are WTO members; (b) a second group of "transition economies," which includes Albania, Armenia, Georgia, Kazakhstan, the Kyrgyz Republic, Moldova, and Ukraine in the Region (as well as China, Mongolia, and Vietnam outside the Region); and (c) all other countries that are considered "market economies."

For the EU's nonmarket economies (group [a] above), a single antidumping margin is calculated for the whole country, using data from a third country that is a market economy. In the context of the second group, companies in these countries can be granted "Market Economy Treatment" (MET) on a case-by-case basis. However, the onus is on the countries to demonstrate that they operate under normal market conditions. Otherwise, such companies are treated as operating in NMEs and are subjected to the more arbitrary and less transparent "analogue" country treatment. A country listed in the first group can move to the second group if it becomes a member of the WTO. However, Russia is treated as a market economy, although it is not a member of the WTO; equally Kazakhstan, Ukraine, and Vietnam are in group (b) although they are not WTO members. In the context of safeguards, the EU standards for taking action against nonmarket economies are lower than they are for other countries that are WTO members. In the case of nonmarket economies, merely the coexistence of higher imports and injury to domestic producers—as opposed to a causal link—needs to be demonstrated, and there is no limit on the duration of the action, as required by GATT article XIX (Michalopoulos and Winters 1997).

In the United States, there is no formal NME list, and decisions are made on a case-by-case basis, usually involving the same taxonomy as utilized by the EU.

The continued designation of countries that are members of the WTO as NMEs is a serious problem that results in arbitrary, nontransparent, and discriminatory treatment of their exports relative to other countries with similar economic management. It is unclear, for example, under what standards EU classifies Bosnia and Herzegovina and Russia as "market economies," while it classifies Albania and Ukraine as "economies in transition." Similarly, it would appear that "economies in transition" includes both countries like Ukraine and Vietnam, who are not WTO members, and others, such as Albania, whose economies have been vetted extensively in terms of the degree of privatization they have achieved.

WTO membership would address the problem that nonmarket economies have regarding the different standards imposed by the EU on safeguards. WTO membership, however, would not automatically terminate the designation of countries as nonmarket economies nor completely terminate the problems they have with antidumping; however, it might help. Membership could inhibit the most egregious excesses in antidumping practices against which a nonmember has no recourse, as the WTO dispute settlement mechanism—albeit with some limitations—can be utilized for this purpose. More generally, the standards of accession have evolved in such a way as to provide members with assurances that a newly acceding country is fundamentally run on market principles, making current antidumping practices, if not illegal, demonstrably unfair. It can be reasonably assumed that countries in the Region would not secure WTO membership unless they could demonstrate that their trade was fundamentally based on market transactions. Thus, in principle, WTO membership undoubtedly would tend to create pressure to terminate the nonmarket designation in national practices of antidumping and permit all WTO members to be treated the same in major markets.

Unfortunately, this has not happened so far, and some WTO members continue to be subjected to NME designation on a case-by-case basis. Others are designated as NMEs even though there is no evidence that their economies are subject to central planning controls in any major way. Rationalizing the treatment of economies in the Region, especially WTO members, in the context of antidumping actions, would appear to be an important priority for the international community and would help improve the Region's economies' access to major developed-country markets.

Regional Trading Arrangements

All of the countries in the Region participate in one or more regional trade agreements (RTAs). The multiplicity of these RTAs has been likened to a "spaghetti bowl" (see figure 3.1). Among the Region's countries, those in Southeastern Europe and the CIS members are particularly active in a large number of regional cooperation agreements having potential impact on trade. While some of the challenges of regional integration in these two groups of countries are similar, many are not, and there is one country—Moldova—which straddles both groups; this itself poses unique problems (see box 3.7).

In SEE, the regional cooperation effort is underpinned by the development of an institutional framework formed by the countries of the region within the Stability Pact for Southeast Europe. This has led to the signing of a Memorandum of Understanding (MOU) on Trade Liberalization and Facilitation in 2001, which is playing a major role in promoting regional cooperation efforts among all eight countries and Kosovo.[16] Under the terms of the MOU, the countries have established a network of 28 bilateral free trade agreements. The main challenge they face is how to move forward and establish a single free trade area, as well as how to move beyond regional trade liberaliza-

FIGURE 3.1

The Myriad of Regional Trade Agreements Resembles Spaghetti Bowls

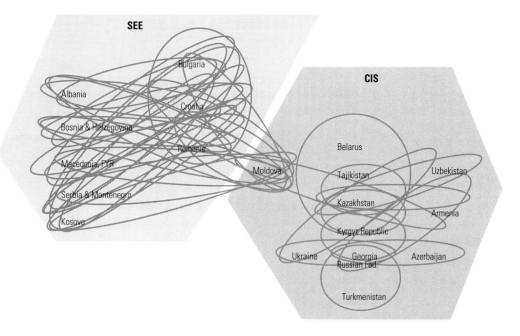

Southeastern European and CIS Spaghetti

tion to cooperation in other areas, such as liberalizing services and aligning trade-related policies and institutions to those of the EU.

In the CIS, the main problem is that implementation lags far behind the ambitious formal commitments on trade cooperation made at the highest level by participating governments. Both the CIS-wide Free Trade area, and the Eurasian Economic Community (Evrazes), which involves Belarus, Kazakhstan, the Kyrgyz Republic, Russia, and Tajikistan,

---

BOX 3.7

Moldova's Free Trade Arrangements

Moldova deserves separate mention in the context of regional integration because it has its foot in two subregions: it has bilateral preferential arrangements with Russia and Ukraine and has been granted "observer" status in Evrazes, whose aim is to establish a customs union among its members. At the same time, it has negotiated or signed seven bilateral FTAs with countries in SEE under Memoranda of Understanding on Trade Liberalization of the Stability Pact. Moldova can continue its FTAs with other CIS members, but it clearly cannot be a member of a customs union with Russia and others in the CIS (meaning it cannot have the same external tariff) while entering into FTAs with the Balkan countries.

amount in practice to far less than their names would lead one to believe. An issue that is common to both SEE and CIS is the form of regional trade liberalization: should it involve the establishment of free trade areas or is the establishment of one or more customs unions preferable?

Regional Integration in Southeastern Europe

Efforts at regional economic integration in SEE have been strongly promoted by the OECD countries and multilateral financial institutions, initially as a means of promoting regional political stability and later because regional trade came increasingly to be seen as one of the many elements needed to stimulate growth in some of the war-torn economies of the region. The EU also promoted regional trade through the SAA process, which explicitly links liberalization of trade with Europe to regional cooperation and liberalization among the countries in the region.[17] The regional cooperation effort in turn was underpinned by the development of an institutional framework in the form of a Working Group on Trade Liberalization and Facilitation established by the Stability Pact, in which all countries in the region and Kosovo, as well as developed countries and multilateral institutions, participate. The Working Group has been quite active, both in providing a setting within which agreements on regional cooperation such as the MOU can be negotiated and in monitoring their subsequent implementation.

The MOU contains commitments in a large number of areas:

- It commits countries to reach agreements to establish FTAs with each other, and it lays down standards for product coverage both for existing and future FTAs among the participating countries as well for the rules of origin they use in the FTAs.

- It commits the countries to a standstill on any measures that would adversely affect trade and to monitoring nontariff measures that impede trade.

- It recognizes the importance of liberalizing trade toward third countries.

- It invites countries to deepen their trade liberalization with each other through further opening up of their trade in services.

- Finally, it commits countries to take steps to harmonize their legislation and regulations on a number of trade-related topics, such as competition, investment, and standards and to bring them more in line with those of the EU.

Progress in implementing the MOU provisions concerning the conclusion of FTAs among the countries in the Region has been impressive. All of the bilateral free trade agreements envisaged by the MOU have been signed and are under implementation (annex table 3.4). Also, most agreements have met the "quality" standards regarding product coverage measured both in terms of trade volume and liberalized tariff lines agreed to under the MOU. The exceptions have been the result of limited liberalization in agriculture. Even here, however, the countries have committed themselves to take actions in the near term to ensure that the "quality standards" of the FTAs are met.[18]

There is no evidence of increased trade restrictions of a nontariff nature in SEE. However, there is increasing realization that, despite efforts at improving border crossings, simplifying procedures, and customs reform, serious problems in trade facilitation continue to plague regional and global trade.[19]

At the same time, one should not exaggerate the importance of the FTAs as a stimulus for trade and overall growth in SEE. Trade links among several of the countries in SEE are very small. Even if substantial growth in regional trade among them occurs, as is already happening, present trade volumes are so small that little overall effect on growth is likely to materialize.

Looking to the future, there are two key issues faced by the countries of SEE in regional integration. First is how to move forward in cooperation in other areas beyond regional trade in goods. The MOU covers much more than FTAs, but progress in such areas as services has proved slow, in part because of limited institutional development at the national level in the services sectors themselves.

The other issue has to do with the form of future trade relationships among these countries. Having a large number of bilateral FTAs—each with a different set of bilateral exemptions, even though they cover a small component of trade in each agreement—undermines the notion that a "virtual" unified FTA has been achieved throughout the Balkan economic space. The bilateral FTAs should be seen as an important step in the integration process, but not as an end in themselves. Implementing these agreements is important, but maintaining these agreements as they are may not be in the long-term interests of the countries that have signed them: the benefits in terms of trade creation are likely to be small and the dangers of distortions and corruption are high (Kaminski and de la Rocha 2003a). The more complex the system, the less transparent it is and the greater the opportunity for trade deflection, corruption, and distortions, especially when the trade-related institutions that have to implement the policies, such as customs and border crossings police, are as weak as they are in the countries of the Region. Thus, there is little doubt that the countries should start thinking about moving on to deepen their integration (see box 3.8).

BOX 3.8

Harmonization of FTAs in Southeastern Europe: The Options Ahead

Over a period of three years, the countries of SEE, plus Moldova, have finalized a network of 28 bilateral FTAs, a remarkable achievement. In November 2003, at the Rome Ministerial Meeting, the Stability Pact Working Group on Trade, within which the agreements were negotiated, was asked to come up with options for the next step, that is, "how best to harmonize the bilateral free trade agreements with each other in order to improve the transparency of the network of bilateral free trade agreements and its efficient administration" (2003 Rome Ministerial Statement). Harmonization makes sense only if it brings net benefits to firms—minimizing their operating costs and enlarging the market size covered by a unique FTA. Five options or suboptions have been identified and are discussed below.

Option 1. A Trade Working Group (TWG) with an Expanded Mandate

The first option would be to keep unchanged the current FTA texts and to minimize the costs of operating a web of 28 FTAs by expanding the role of the TWG. An expanded TWG could tackle the implementing rules by being conceived as the "Joint Committee" of all the FTAs. This role does not require eliminating the bilateral Joint Committees, which could remain the "first instance" bodies, with the TWG playing the role of an "appeal" body. In this context, the TWG could have two important roles. First, it could be in charge of the monitoring exercise following the implementation of the liberalization process specified by the FTAs, providing the necessary interpretations of the treaties in case of doubt, and possibly even playing the role of a dispute settlement mechanism for the signatories. Second, the TWG could ensure the consistency of the implementation of the various FTAs once the liberalization is achieved. If one wants the web of 28 FTAs to work smoothly, instruments of contingent protection defined in the FTAs (sometimes in quite different terms) require relatively similar domestic regulations, and—more important—a relatively similar way to enforce these regulations by the domestic institutions. An expanded TWG could play a useful role in this context.

Viewed from a technical point of view, this first (minimal) option would provide small benefits, but it would also entail small costs, which arises from the fact that an expanded TWG would require very limited institution building, and it could be quickly implemented and progressively expanded, as the demand for its services grew. An expanded TWG would simply need to meet more frequently and would probably need to include representatives from the FTA-related domestic institutions, such as offices in charge of implementing contingent protection. However, its expected benefits are also likely to be limited because, ultimately, an expanded TWG would be constrained by the existing FTA texts.

Option 2. An Expanded CEFTA

The second option to consider would be to expand the geographical coverage of the CEFTA text to the whole Region. However, most—but not all—of the FTAs have most—but not all—of the CEFTA provisions. This feature has two implications.

(Box continues on the following page.)

BOX 3.8 (*continued*)

First, the CEFTA solution would not be very costly for the three countries that have already used the CEFTA text between themselves (Bulgaria, Croatia, and Romania) and the fourth, FYR Macedonia, which is discussion about membership. And some of these countries would join the EC in a few years. As a result, the CEFTA solution would result in small costs. However, it also would provide small benefits to these countries: they would shift to another type of trade agreement between them and with the rest of the Region—the one imposed by the *acquis communitaire.*

Second, the CEFTA solution would undoubtedly be more costly for the other countries of the Region. They would have to shift from their existing FTAs to a new treaty (CEFTA) that does not really exist in their legal trade regime. The benefits of such a shift are limited because CEFTA is a treaty with deficient provisions on some traditional trade issues and no provisions on the new trade issues, such as services or public procurement, essential for the growth of the Region's economies.

In sum, the cost-benefit balance of a shift to CEFTA is probably positive, but only in a small and transitory way. It may be slightly positive only if one also makes the assumption that there would be small political costs for shifting to a new text—for the current signatories, because the economic soundness of key CEFTA provisions is doubtful.

Option 3. A SEEFTA

The third option is to fully face the challenge generated by the tensions between a complex web of 28 FTAs and the potential outcome within reach—a potentially effective regional FTA. If there are political costs to harmonizing the existing FTAs, then they should be counterbalanced by the largest possible economic gains. This option does not require that all countries in the Region choose it. It is possible that countries that are well advanced in the EC accession process would find it more suitable to keep their existing agreements, while the others go ahead. The decision in this respect would presumably depend on how quick and how deep are the changes being introduced. There are three suboptions in this respect, none of which require a unique "consolidated" text, as each could be provided by separate but harmonized texts, though obviously this second possibility might add unnecessary and undesirable complexity to an endeavor aiming at simplification.

A free trade area for SEE is one such option. How to do it is one of the key challenges for the countries concerned. The trade architecture in Southeastern Europe is changing. Many CEFTA members became members of the EU, while FYR Macedonia has been accepted for CEFTA membership by the remaining three countries (Bulgaria, Croatia, and Romania). In terms of the future, one could visualize either an expansion of CEFTA or a new integrated FTA that includes all of the countries that signed the MOU. What will be done in that regard is in large part a political issue. On the economic side, CEFTA

Suboption 3a. The first suboption can be characterized as a "minimal classical SEEFTA": classical because it deals only with trade in goods, and minimal because it does not go further than mere harmonization, aligning on the best available text. This limited objective confines the harmonization exercise to two crucial, from a business perspective, aspects of the existing FTAs' "General Provisions": competition rules and disciplines on contingent protection.

Suboption 3b. The second suboption can be characterized as a "maximal classical SEEFTA": classical because, again, it deals only with trade in goods, but maximal because it deals not only with the inconsistencies, but also with many of the serious concerns arising from the weaknesses of the existing agreements. It would do so by putting the intra-SEEFTA trade under more economically sound rules, like the ones governing intra-EC trade, on issues such as competition and state aid. Rules on contingent protection would also be harmonized in a more economically sound way—again, to the extent that they involve intra-SEEFTA trade. For instance, the provision on structural adjustment could be harmonized and improved by the creation of a plurilateral mechanism for monitoring the measures taken, as in the case of Article 115 of the Treaty of Rome. Similarly, one should consider the elimination of the provisions on reexports and balance of payment difficulties that refer to approaches well regarded in a faraway past, but which have proven their inefficiency since then.

Suboption 3c. The third suboption can be characterized as a "modern SEEFTA": modern because would shift the focus of the FTAs to the emerging core of trade relations (that is, services, public procurement, intellectual property rights, and so forth). Here, the scope of harmonization and thus the improvement are immense. As a result, the SEEFTA text could simply announce a few principles. The two most important principles, particularly in the EC context, are the mutual recognition principle and the country of origin principle. By adopting these two principles, a modern SEEFTA would put the Region on the same track as the EC, hence facilitating countries' progressive integration into the EC services, technology, and public procurement markets.

Source: Messerlin and Miroudout 2004

covers a wider area of commitments than the MOU, but the quality standards for the free trade area under CEFTA are less demanding than those of the MOU. However, in both respects the differences are not great. The other question is whether a future SEE-wide preferential arrangement should be in the form of an FTA or a customs union.

Regional Integration in the CIS

Soon after the breakup of the Soviet Union, the CIS members established a CIS-wide FTA. A plurilateral agreement to establish a Free

Trade Area was signed by all CIS members except Turkmenistan in 1994. However, the original framework agreement was never ratified by the Russian parliament and therefore remains inoperative. Over the last decade, however, a patchwork of bilateral free trade agreements linking most CIS members has been signed. Subsequently, Belarus, Kazakhstan, the Kyrgyz Republic, and Russia agreed to establish a customs union. Tajikistan joined the agreement in 1999.[20] The latest development is the agreement among all of these countries as well as Ukraine to establish an Economic Union. There are also other agreements with a regional focus (for example, the Central Asian Cooperation Organization, consisting of Kazakhstan, the Kyrgyz Republic, Tajikistan, and Uzbekistan), and there is one agreement—TRACECA—that is a project to develop a transit corridor between Central Asia and the Caucasus.

The bilateral FTAs stipulate free trade in all goods between participating countries, but each has different product coverage and exemptions, as well as rules of implementation, such as the use of safeguards and quantitative restraints. As a consequence, at present there is a complex network of bilateral agreements among various countries whose coverage and rules change frequently and whose impact is very difficult to evaluate. A few products (for example, alcohol and tobacco) are excluded from all agreements. Efforts to establish a standardized list of exemptions have so far failed, however. Exemptions can be imposed unilaterally and are supposed to be accompanied by a schedule for their termination. However, these schedules are often not followed, and there appear to be no penalties for slippages. While the exemptions are concentrated on a few products, their trade restrictiveness appears to be high (World Bank 2004p).

The web of agreements hampers transparency and consistent implementation. For example, Armenia, the Kyrgyz Republic, and Moldova do not levy tariffs on goods imported from most of the other CIS countries on a reciprocal basis. On the other hand, Tajikistan gives preferential treatment only to the members of the Eurasian Economic Community and applies tariffs on goods imported from the others. Uzbekistan has bilateral free trade agreements with Azerbaijan and the Kyrgyz Republic. Georgia has bilateral FTAs with Azerbaijan and Armenia (but does not report having one with Uzbekistan, which the latter says it signed in 1996). In Azerbaijan, imports from Russia are subject to tariffs and the VAT; imports from Georgia and Ukraine to VAT only; and imports from Moldova to import tariffs only.

Contingent protection measures are a feature in all agreements and have been used extensively in Russia's relationship with Ukraine, based on procedures that have little transparency and appear to be inconsistent with WTO provisions. The reciprocal retaliatory measures introduced by both countries against each other's trade have resulted in damage to both economies.

To operate an effective FTA, it is necessary to implement rules of origin, which is the responsibility of customs authorities. Given the extreme weakness in the customs institutions in all of the countries in the CIS, the porous borders, and the complex character of the agreements, the actual tariffs paid on any product to any authority on intra-CIS trade is a very chancy thing that has little to do with the formal agreements signed by the countries between which trade is occurring. Moreover, in the absence of a plurilateral dispute settlement mechanism, all disputes have to be resolved politically at the bilateral level. This is especially disadvantageous for small countries participating in these agreements.

The Eurasian Economic Community is supposed to be a customs union. Its main driving force has been the traditional exporters in Russia, who have wanted to maintain their preferences and links to the traditional industrial structures in the other countries.[21] At present, there is free trade among the participating countries, but their external tariffs diverge substantially, which means they have in place a free trade area, not a customs union.

The plans are to set up a customs union with a common external tariff by 2006. Russia expects the other countries to move to the Russian tariff. It is reported that progress on "harmonization" of the external tariff (which means convergence to the Russian tariff) is as follows. Between Russia and Belarus, approximately 95 percent of tariff lines have been harmonized; between Russia and Kazakhstan, approximately 85 percent; Russia and the Kyrgyz Republic, 14 percent; and Russia and Tajikistan, 60 percent. While these figures clearly reflect the dominance of Russia in this grouping, there is no information on the degree of divergence among the tariffs of the other countries.

FTA or Customs Union

Both in the CIS and in SEE, a major policy issue for future regional integration is whether the countries should aim to establish a customs union or aim to create or a maintain a free trade area. In the SEE, this issue has been raised primarily in academic circles (Kaminski and de la Rocha 2003a). In the CIS, it is of very important current policy interest because of Russia's continued efforts to forge such an arrangement with a number of CIS members. The basic difference between a customs union and a free trade area is that in a customs union all participating countries adopt a common external tariff, while eliminating all trade barriers among themselves. In a free trade area, countries retain their individual tariffs toward third countries, while liberalizing toward each other.

A customs union has some obvious advantages from an economic standpoint: it does away with the problem of determining rules of origin for each of the participating countries, and it reduces the chances of corruption in customs, a problem in many transition economies. It also involves a deeper form of integration requiring further coordination of policies, for example, in allocating the proceeds from collecting the common tariff. It is likely to involve fewer product exemptions than an FTA, hence increasing the opportunities for trade creation through competition with more efficient firms in the participating countries. And, depending on where the common external tariff of the customs union is set, it may lead to both less trade diversion and to higher short-term costs because of the need for domestic firms to adjust to increased competition.

A free trade area makes it easier to tailor the pace of regional integration to the needs of individual countries by not requiring the adoption of a common external tariff, which may result in increased competition both from within the union (which the FTA would also create) and the rest of the world. At the same time, operating FTAs with a large number of different countries increases the complexity of the tariff regime and makes implementation difficult because of the need to implement rules of origin. Advocates of customs unions favor them precisely because they are likely to result in greater competition and tend to downplay the adjustment costs such competition could engender.

Establishing a customs union among SEE countries whose external tariff approximates that of the EU would introduce more wide-ranging liberalization, especially in manufactures, and aim at preparing these countries toward rapid integration (and adjustment) to world prices and competition, as well EU accession. On the other hand, an FTA with the EU, which, as envisaged in the SAAs, could take as long as 10 years to complete, would expose countries slowly but surely to very substantial competition from EU firms that are frequently already their main suppliers. This has a twofold implication: first, the FTA with the EU is not likely to result in significant trade diversion costs for SEE countries, as the EU may already be the low-cost supplier. Second, establishing a customs union among the SEE whose external tariff moves over the same period to approximate the EU external tariff is not likely to lead to significant increases in competition from firms in the rest of the world (and hence more adjustment costs), but it would tend to reduce the rents (excess profits) that would be obtained by EU firms in SEE markets by reducing the margin of preferences that EU firms enjoy.

Some of the same economic arguments apply to the question of whether the SEE should seek to conclude a customs union with the EU: an FTA tends to permit greater flexibility and a slower and more narrow integration, with exemptions (that is, greater protection) and competition tailored to individual country circumstances. In the case of a customs union with the EU, there is one additional consideration: the EU is a major international market where entry is frequently on a preferential basis. If the SEE countries were to establish a customs union with the EU, they would have to provide all of the preferences the EU extends to a very large number of developing countries under the Cotonou agreement, the Mediterranean agreements, and others. These preferences could result in even greater competition and adjustment costs in the SEE countries' own domestic markets. It is for these reasons, as well as the fact that FTAs such as CEFTA have also worked well for member countries as a stepping stone toward integration with the EU, that the European Commission tends to favor FTAs rather than customs union agreements as vehicles for future integration in the European Union. Their argument can be summarized as follows: a customs union for the SEE with the EU would tend to result in the SEE countries incurring the bulk of the economic costs of adjustment but few of the benefits of integration with the EU.

On the political side, countries will face difficulties in making the more far-reaching commitments required by a customs union than a free trade area. Their governments showed remarkable commitment to Regional goals by reaching speedy agreement on the bilateral FTAs. However, the differences in the level of development among them are substantial and have resulted, for example, in Bosnia and Herzegovina obtaining asymmetrical treatment in the bilateral FTAs it has concluded, which suggests serious difficulties in negotiating a common external tariff. The Region also continues to be characterized by internal political uncertainties (for examply, with regard to the future of Kosovo, the future of Serbia and Montenegro, and the workability of the Dayton arrangements in Bosnia and Herzegovina), which would tend to make a customs union difficult to design as well as implement.

Finally, the SEE countries see little value in a customs union with the EU for several political reasons: first, they fear that it may become a substitute for full EU accession, which is their primary and foremost long-term goal; second, they see that they can achieve this long-term goal just as well through an FTA, as many countries in Central and Eastern Europe did, as through a customs union. Indeed, the customs union that Turkey has concluded with the EU, combined with the difficulties the latter has encountered in getting a political commitment to even starting negotiations for accession, is seen as further proof that a customs union may result in sidetracking the efforts for accession.

On balance, and while there may be some potential theoretical merit in urging the early establishment of a customs union among the SEE countries and between them and the EU, there is more merit to giving high priority to the practical and politically far more acceptable steps to establishing a free trade area among all the SEE countries and to using this area as an eventual springboard for accession to the EU. Once an FTA is agreed on, then individual countries would be well advised to start moving their external tariff toward that of the EU, but each should do so at its own pace. For each country to proceed at its own pace would both ease its future adjustment as well as reduce rents and increase competition and efficiency, but at a pace that would be dictated by its own economic situation.

In the CIS, the economic arguments in favor of a customs union are far weaker. Indeed, there is good reason to believe that a customs union with Russia, on the basis of the Russian tariff, is not in the economic interests of small open economies such as those of the Kyrgyz Republic and Tajikistan or, for that matter, Moldova, which has shown some interest in joining the arrangement. These countries would be better off keeping their existing free trade arrangements with Russia. There is strong evidence that moving to the much higher Russian tariff, which reflects the interests of protected Russian industry, will result in decreases in their welfare as a result of substantial trade diversion and will tend to tie their economies to the old technology of the Russian industrial structures. The only country that can expect welfare gains from a customs union as currently proposed would be Russia.[22] On the other hand, if these countries maintain a free trade agreement with Russia (and with each other), they would enjoy the benefits of access to the Russian market without having to incur the high costs of trade diversion that would result from a customs union with Russia that adopts the higher Russian tariff.

Just as it is for the SEE countries, however, the present web of bilateral, partial FTAs with nontransparent rules and arbitrary changes is not the answer. Instead, CIS members should seek to establish a single FTA or perhaps FTAs that cover a few contiguous countries, such as the countries in Central Asia, with comprehensive coverage, clear rules consistently enforced, and an institutional structure that permits review of implementation as well as help in adjudicating disputes.

Regional Integration and WTO Membership

Participation in the Eurasian agreement and regional preferential trade arrangements in general has led to some confusion regarding the implications of these agreements for WTO membership. A few years back, countries in Central Asia were discussing the two as alternatives: either become a WTO member or join the Eurasian Economic Community. Nothing could be further from the truth. When a country applies for WTO membership, it can be a member of any number of regional preferential arrangements, which however should be compatible with the WTO provisions regarding such arrangements. However, these provisions (Article XXIV of the GATT) are couched in such broad terms that they are typically relatively easy to fulfill. The problem with the preferential arrangements in the Former Soviet Union was a lack of clarity regarding what was covered by the agreements, the rules of origin, exemptions, and so forth.

With regard to the Eurasian Economic Community in particular, its members agreed to apply to join the WTO individually. This means that they recognized the fact that there was no common external tariff in place, as is required by a customs union, but only a free trade area with each of the members having a different tariff structure with regard to imports from the rest of the world. This was clearly understood during the accession negotiations of the Kyrgyz Republic, the first member of the Eurasian agreement to become a member of the WTO. The Kyrgyz Republic accepted legal commitments to bind its tariffs in the WTO at levels significantly lower than the levels applied by Russia, which are supposed to be the levels to be applied by the yet-to-be-formed Eurasian customs union. After the Kyrgyz Republic became a member of the WTO, it notified the WTO of its intention to participate in a customs union with the other countries of the Eurasian agreement (WTO 1999a). Now the Kyrgyz Republic has a problem, however: if it is to join the Eurasian customs union before Russia and the other members of the Eurasian community enter the WTO, it will have to seek a WTO waiver to permit it to raise its tariffs to the level of the Eurasian Community common external tariff. The alternative, and much more desirable, option is for the Kyrgyz Republic to keep its overall tariffs at their present low levels and maintain only an FTA arrangement with its partners in the Eurasian agreement.

At present, Kazakhstan and Belarus are tailoring their bilateral tariff negotiations to those of Russia so that the tariff bindings of the three countries will be at identical levels once they join the WTO. The three countries have stated their desire to enter the WTO as a customs union. It is hard to see how this can happen, given their separate accession processes.

At the same time, the approach has tended to delay Kazakhstan's WTO accession, in addition, as noted earlier, to being of questionable economic value. Given the present status of Kazakhstan's WTO negotiations, however, it is likely that Kazakhstan will be able to accede to the WTO soon after Russia does. Belarus' WTO accession is problematic, primarily because of the lack of progress on market reform; it has less to do with that country's tariff offers. Ukraine's accession has moved parallel to that of Russia, but the two economies are very different in many respects, as is their tariff structure, so that the notion of a "joint" accession is even more problematic. Thus, the question of whether to form a customs union before or after WTO accession appears to be largely academic. Should some or all of these countries decide to form a customs union after they have become WTO members, then they would have to abide by the WTO rules guiding the formation of customs unions. These include, among other things, the rule that the common external tariff of the customs union not be higher than the weighted average of the countries' individual tariffs.

Conclusions

This analysis of trade policies and institutions of the countries in the Region—primarily in SEE and the CIS—reveals many steps that need to be taken in order to improve these economies' relatively lackluster performance over the last 15 years.

While most of these countries have adopted liberal trade regimes, in a few cases (for example, Uzbekistan), there is still scope for import liberalization so as to eliminate barriers that introduce inefficiencies and hamper growth. Export restraints are present in many of the countries and need to be eliminated in order to ensure effective integration into the world economy. High priority should be given to establishing efficient and prompt rebates of VAT and import duties and eliminating taxes on labor.

Trade-related institutions, and especially customs, inhibit rather than facilitate trade and are in need of major reform; further, domestic regulations and procedures impede rather than facilitate trade. There are major problems in behind-the-border measures that inhibit trade expansion. Services sectors such as banking and finance and transportation, which provide important inputs to trade, are underdeveloped or inefficient. There are important transit issues that inhibit trade for several countries that are both remote and landlocked. There are also important problems of lack of interenterprise competition and weak governance, which adversely affect trade. (All these issues are addressed in the remaining chapters of this study).

By comparison to these domestic restraints to international trade, market access is not a serious general problem affecting these countries' exports. There are, however, problems in particular sectors stemming in part from extensive use of antidumping actions against the countries, as well as developed-country agricultural policies. Some of the market-access problems will be addressed by accession to the WTO. While substantial progress has been made in this area, there are still many countries in the Region that have a long way to go before they can accede. WTO accession is important to improve and secure market access; but it is even more important because it forces countries to strengthen their institutional capacity to trade, as well as introducing stability in the trade regime and locking in trade reforms.

Trade relations with the EU, the major market for many of these countries, are important and have been secured through various types of preferential agreements, which provide especially liberal access to countries of Southeastern Europe. Countries of SEE that have been promised eventual entry to the EU need to undertake major reforms in order to meet the EU requirements. One of the early reforms that would be beneficial for them to undertake is the realignment of their external tariffs to those of the EU.

All of the economies have endeavored to organize regional trade agreements among themselves. The agreements in the SEE appear to involve greater mutual trade liberalization than do those of the CIS. Both, however, are subject to enormous complexity and are focused primarily on the exchange of trade preferences. The main challenges faced by both groups of countries are: (a) how to rationalize the large number of bilateral FTAs into Region-wide agreements; and (b) how to extend regional cooperation beyond preferences in merchandise trade and include such matters as transit facilitation and liberalization of services.

Most of the burden of reform in improving trade performance will unavoidably fall on the countries themselves. The international community, however, has important responsibilities to assist them in a variety of ways. Technical and financial assistance are needed to strengthen national capacity in various trade-related sectors. High priority has been given in this respect to customs reform and related trade-facilitation measures. These efforts need to continue and to expand in more of the countries in the Region.

ANNEX

ANNEX TABLE 3.1

Average MFN Applied Tariffs and Bound Rate by Country in the Region in Recent Years

| Reporter | Year | Average MFN applied tariff rate (%) | | | | | | | | Binding coverage (%) |
| | | Total goods | | Agricultural goods | | Industrial goods | | Bound rate of all goods | | |
		Simple avg.	Weighted avg.	Simple avg.	Weighted avg.	Simple avg.	Weighted avg.	Simple avg.	Weighted avg.	
Albania	2001	8.5	8.5	9.9	9.5	8.4	8.2	7.0	7.9	100.0
Armenia	2001	3.3	2.2	8.3	6.6	2.9	1.1	8.5	9.6	100.0
Azerbaijan*	2002	10.1	6.2	13.4	10.3	9.8	5.6	n.a.	n.a.	n.a.
Belarus*	2001	10.6	8.1	9.8	8.7	10.7	8.0	n.a.	n.a.	n.a.
Bosnia & Herzegovina*	2001	5.4	5.1	4.2	6.8	5.4	4.6	n.a.	n.a.	n.a.
Bulgaria	2003	5.4	4.2	16.4	19.0	4.7	3.3	24.2	20.0	100.0
Croatia	2002	6.0	4.7	10.9	11.3	5.6	4.2	5.8	4.8	100.0
Czech Rep.	2003	5.0	4.3	8.2	10.9	4.7	4.0	5.0	4.5	100.0
Estonia	2003	0.2	0.1	2.4	0.9	0.0	0.0	8.6	6.3	100.0
Georgia	2002	10.0	10.6	14.2	15.1	9.5	9.6	7.2	8.3	100.0
Hungary	2002	3.2	2.2	17.4	15.7	2.2	1.7	9.7	8.3	96.2
Kazakhstan*	1996	9.5	n.a.	8.8	n.a.	9.6	n.a.	n.a.	n.a.	n.a.
Kyrgyz Rep.	2001	4.5	3.2	7.1	6.6	4.3	2.7	7.4	6.4	99.9
Latvia	2000	1.2	0.6	5.6	3.4	0.8	0.2	12.7	9.3	100.0
Lithuania	2002	3.5	2.2	8.9	9.4	3.1	1.5	9.2	9.4	100.0
Macedonia, FYR	2001	14.3	11.1	22.5	17.0	13.8	10.2	n.a.	n.a.	n.a.
Moldova	2001	5.1	2.8	11.2	9.2	4.5	2.0	0.0	0.0	100.0
Poland	2003	11.9	11.9	44.3	34.3	9.6	10.6	11.3	8.2	96.3
Romania	1999	24.7	22.8	123.1	126.2	16.3	13.9	40.4	40.3	100.0
Russian Fed.*	2001	10.8	8.9	9.8	8.9	10.9	8.9	n.a.	n.a.	n.a.
Serbia & Montenegro*	2001	9.0	5.8	13.1	11.9	8.7	5.0	n.a.	n.a.	n.a.
Slovak Rep.	2003	4.8	4.6	8.2	14.0	4.6	4.1	5.0	4.7	100.0
Slovenia	2003	11.1	10.0	13.0	14.0	10.9	9.7	23.3	21.3	100.0
Tajikistan*	2002	8.0	7.1	9.8	6.3	7.8	7.3	n.a.	n.a.	n.a.
Turkmenistan*	2002	5.3	2.9	18.9	15.5	3.8	1.1	n.a.	n.a.	n.a.
Ukraine*	2002	7.9	3.9	11.2	15.1	7.8	3.4	n.a.	n.a.	n.a.
Uzbekistan*	2001	10.6	5.9	11.7	3.5	10.6	6.2	n.a.	n.a.	n.a.
Memo:										
European Union (15)	2003	4.4	3.1	6.2	5.2	4.2	3.0	3.9	3.0	100.0

Sources: Based on UNCTAD TRAINS and WTO IDB databases.

Note: Agricultural goods are based on WTO classification of HS 01-24, and industrial goods are HS 25-96.
* Indicates non-WTO member.
Where countries are in bold, all bound tariffs are based on WTO IDB data; others are based on UNCTAD TRAINS data.

ANNEX TABLE 3.2

Antidumping Initiations of Countries in the Region by Product, 1995–2003

Perpetrators	Number of cases	Year of initiation	Target country	Sector	Products
Bulgaria	1	2002	Turkey	Agric	Active baker's yeast
Czech Republic	1	1999	Germany	Manuf	Salt suitable for human consumption (4 products)
	1	1998	Denmark	Agric	Infant milk formula
	1	1998	Netherlands	Agric	Infant milk formula
Latvia	1	2002	Lithuania	Agric	Butter
	1	2002	Lithuania	Agric	Milk
	1	2002	Estonia	Manuf	Portland cement
	1	2002	Hungary	Agric	Honey
	1	2002	Russian Fed.	Agric	Honey
	1	2002	Ukraine	Agric	Honey
	1	2001	Belarus (*)	Manuf	Portland cement
Lithuania	1	2000	Belarus (*)	Manuf	Grey portland-cement
	1	2000	Russian Fed.	Manuf	Grey portland-cement
	1	2000	Ukraine	Manuf	Grey portland-cement
	1	2000	Latvia (*)	Agric	Nondried baking yeast
	1	2000	Belarus	Manuf	Burnt lime
	1	2000	Russian Fed.	Manuf	Burnt lime
	1	1999	Latvia (*)	Manuf	Safety matches
Poland	1	2003	India	Manuf	Graphite electrodes
	1	2002	Czech Rep.	Manuf	Styrene-butadiene rubber (SBR)
	1	2002	Romania	Manuf	Styrene-butadiene rubber (SBR)
	1	2002	Russian Fed.	Manuf	Styrene-butadiene rubber (SBR)
	1	1999	China	Manuf	Pocket lighters, gas fuelled, refillable
	1	1999	Taiwan (China)	Manuf	Pocket lighters, gas fuelled, nonrefillable, refillable
	1	1999	Indonesia	Manuf	Pocket lighters, gas fuelled, nonrefillable, refillable
	1	1999	Vietnam	Manuf	Pocket lighters, gas fuelled, nonrefillable, refillable
	1	1999	Belarus	Manuf	Synthetic filament tow of polyesters
	1	1999	Belarus	Manuf	Synthetic staple fibers, not carded, combed
	1	1999	Germany (*)	Manuf	X-ray films – type Retina XBM
	1	1997	China	Manuf	Pocket lighters, gas-filled, nonrefillable
Slovenia	1	1999	Hungary	Agric	Fresh or frozen turkey breast, skinless, boneless
All above (6)	31 cases		18 countries		18 products

Source: Based on semiannual notifications by individual members to the WTO Antidumping Committee.

Note: (*) resulted in price undertakings.

ANNEX TABLE 3.3
Numbers and Share of Antidumping in Countries of the Region by Exporting Economy, 1995–2003

Exporting country	1995	1996	1997	1998	1999	2000	2001	2002	2003	Total
All countries	157	224	243	256	355	294	366	311	210	2,416
Industrial countries[a]	51	69	92	83	88	72	95	68	65	683
Developing countries[b]	86	133	124	129	207	174	231	189	135	1,408
of which: China[c]	20	43	33	28	40	43	53	51	45	356
Countries in the Region[d]										
of which:	20	22	27	44	60	48	40	54	10	325
Belarus	0	0	0	0	3	4	1	1	1	10
Bosnia & Herzegovina	1	0	0	0	0	0	0	0	0	1
Bulgaria	0	3	2	1	1	1	2	0	1	11
Croatia	1	0	0	1	1	1	0	0	0	4
Czech Rep.	1	1	0	2	7	3	2	1	1	18
Estonia	0	0	1	0	0	1	1	1	0	4
Georgia	0	0	0	0	0	0	0	1	0	1
Hungary	2	0	2	2	4	0	3	1	0	14
Kazakstan	3	1	2	4	0	3	3	6	0	22
Latvia	0	0	2	1	1	3	0	0	0	7
Lithuania	0	0	1	0	4	1	1	3	0	10
Macedonia, FYR	1	0	1	1	1	0	2	1	0	7
Moldova	0	0	0	0	0	2	1	0	0	3
Poland	2	3	3	4	3	5	1	4	0	25
Romania	1	2	1	5	4	4	5	8	2	32
Russian Fed.	2	7	7	12	17	12	9	18	2	86
Serbia & Montenegro	0	0	0	0	0	0	1	0	0	1
Slovak Rep.	0	1	1	1	3	1	2	1	0	10
Slovenia	1	0	0	1	0	0	0	0	0	2
Ukraine	2	3	4	9	9	7	6	8	3	51
Uzbekistan	2	0	0	0	0	0	0	0	0	2
Yugoslavia	1	1	0	0	2	0	0	0	0	4
Share of total (%):										
Industrial countries	32.5	30.8	37.9	32.4	24.8	24.5	26.0	21.9	31.0	28.3
Developing countries	54.8	59.4	51.0	50.4	58.3	59.2	63.1	60.8	64.3	58.3
of which: China	12.7	19.2	13.6	10.9	11.3	14.6	14.5	16.4	21.4	14.7
Region's countries	12.7	9.8	11.1	17.2	16.9	16.3	10.9	17.4	4.8	13.5

Source: WTO Antidumping Committee.

Note:
a. Includes Australia, Canada, 15 European Union members, Iceland, Japan, New Zealand, Norway, Switzerland, and the United States.
b. Includes all other countries and China, excluding industrial and transition countries.
c. Excludes Hong Kong (China), Macao, and Taiwan (China).
d. Includes 27 transition countries in the Region, excluding Turkey with 34 initiations.

ANNEX TABLE 3.4
Trade Coverage of SEE FTAs in the Agricultural and Manufacturing Sectors

FTA 1	Country 2	Share of harmonized system (HS) tariff lines freed (%)			Share of bilateral imports lliberalized (%)			Criteria t = tariff line i = import-based
		All products 3	Agriculture 4	Manufacturing 5	All products 6	Agriculture 7	Manufacturing 8	
GROUP III								
24. MAC-ROM	Macedonia, FYR	84.9	0.3	98.6	86.0	0.0	100.0	
23. MAC-MOL	Macedonia, FYR	85.0	0.3	98.8	19.5	0.0	100.0	
15. BUL-MAC	Macedonia, FYR	86.3	0.3	100.0	87.2	0.0	100.0	t<88%
24. MAC-ROM	Romania	86.3	10.3	98.6	59.8	0.0	100.0	i<88%
6. ALB-ROM	Romania	86.5	10.3	98.9	82.0	0.0	100.0	
2. ALB-BUL	Bulgaria	87.0	11.0	99.4	83.8	0.0	100.0	
3. ALB-CRO	Croatia	87.4	14.2	99.0	53.2	0.0	100.0	
20. CRO-MOL	Croatia	87.4	14.5	99.2	81.0	0.0	100.0	
21. CRO-ROM	Romania	87.6	11.2	99.8	71.4	0.5	100.0	
23. MAC-MOL	Moldova	87.3	13.7	99.2	97.9	0.0	100.0	
20. CRO-MOL	Moldova	87.4	15.0	99.2	100.0	—	100.0	t<88%
18. BUL-S&M	Serbia & Montenegro	87.6	15.0	99.4	94.0	2.5	99.9	i>88%
15. BUL-MAC	Bulgaria	87.7	10.9	100.0	89.1	0.8	100.0	
GROUP II								
21. CRO-ROM	Croatia	88.1	14.2	99.9	47.8	0.4	100.0	
18. BUL-S&M	Bulgaria	88.4	19.3	99.6	87.4	45.1	99.7	t>88%
16. BUL-MOL	Bulgaria	88.7	22.8	99.4	43.9	29.1	100.0	i<88%
2. ALB-BUL	Albania	88.9	23.7	99.5	75.5	18.3	100.0	
16. BUL-MOL	Moldova	89.9	30.7	99.5	84.0	11.9	100.0	
3. ALB-CRO	Albania	88.2	23.3	98.6	95.8	0.0	100.0	
6. ALB-ROM	Albania	88.4	23.7	99.0	99.6	80.4	100.0	
28. ROM-S&M	Serbia & Montenegro	88.5	20.3	99.5	96.9	1.0	99.9	t>88%
12. BIH-ROM	Romania	88.7	28.4	98.5	89.9	0.0	100.0	i>88%
28. ROM-S&M	Romania	88.8	22.4	99.6	89.9	3.4	100.0	
8. BIH-BUL	Bulgaria	88.9	24.6	99.3	95.6	0.0	97.6	
7. ALB-S&M	Serbia & Montenegro	89.3	27.0	99.4	99.6	31.1	100.0	
8. BIH-BUL	Bosnia & Herzegovina	91.5	42.0	99.5	75.9	7.9	97.1	
12. BIH-ROM	Bosnia & Herzegovina	91.8	43.3	99.6	83.7	61.3	100.0	
7. ALB-S&M	Albania	92.0	45.8	99.5	39.1	16.8	100.0	t>90%
5. ALB-MOL	Albania	92.5	49.2	99.5	36.4	0.0	100.0	i<88%
4. ALB-MAC	Albania	93.8	57.8	99.5	79.9	20.9	99.9	
22. CRO-S&M	Serbia & Montenegro	94.2	61.9	99.4	80.0	23.1	99.9	
19. CRO-MAC	Croatia	99.1	93.3	100.0	87.8	26.6	100.0	

(Table continues on the following page.)

ANNEX TABLE 3.4 (*continued*)

FTA 1	Country 2	Share of harmonized system (HS) tariff lines freed (%)			Share of bilateral imports lliberalized (%)			Criteria t = tariff line i = import-based
		All products 3	Agriculture 4	Manufacturing 5	All products 6	Agriculture 7	Manufacturing 8	
GROUP I								
1. ALB-BIH	Bosnia & Herzegovina	93.0	51.4	99.7	88.6	0.0	100.0	t>90%
4. ALB-MAC	Macedonia, FYR	93.1	52.0	99.6	89.6	65.0	100.0	i>88%
19. CRO-MAC	Macedonia, FYR	99.3	94.9	100.0	88.8	58.7	100.0	
5. ALB-MOL	Moldova	91.7	43.9	99.4	100.0	—	100.0	
1. ALB-BIH	Albania	92.6	49.9	99.6	91.7	59.5	100.0	
14. BUL-CRO	Bulgaria	93.9	59.8	99.3	95.6	17.8	100.0	
14. BUL-CRO	Croatia	94.5	62.1	99.7	91.7	79.1	100.0	
17. BUL-ROM	Romania	94.6	62.1	99.8	94.4	58.6	100.0	
17. BUL-ROM	Bulgaria	94.6	61.5	100.0	98.0	48.1	100.0	
22. CRO-S&M	Croatia	94.7	62.1	100.0	90.3	54.3	100.0	
27. MOL-S&M	Moldova	99.5	96.6	100.0	97.4	24.9	100.0	t>90%
27. MOL-S&M	Serbia & Montenegro	99.5	96.6	100.0	99.2	99.0	100.0	i>90%
25. MAC-S&M	Macedonia, FYR	100.0	100.0	100.0	99.9	100.0	99.8	
25. MAC-S&M	Serbia & Montenegro	100.0	100.0	100.0	99.9	100.0	99.9	
10. BIH-MAC	Bosnia & Herzegovina	100.0	100.0	100.0	100.0	100.0	100.0	
10. BIH-MAC	Macedonia	100.0	100.0	100.0	100.0	100.0	100.0	
11. BIH-MOL	Bosnia & Herzegovina	100.0	100.0	100.0	100.0	100.0	100.0	
11. BIH-MOL	Moldova	100.0	100.0	100.0	100.0	—	100.0	
13. BIH-S&M	Bosnia & Herzegovina	100.0	100.0	100.0	100.0	100.0	100.0	
13. BIH-S&M	Serbia & Montenegro	100.0	100.0	100.0	100.0	100.0	100.0	
26. MOL-ROM	Moldova	100.0	100.0	100.0	100.0	100.0	100.0	
26. MOL-ROM	Romania	100.0	100.0	100.0	100.0	100.0	100.0	
9. BIH-CRO	Bosnia & Herzegovina	100.0	100.0	100.0	100.0	100.0	100.0	
9. BIH-CRO	Croatia	100.0	100.0	100.0	100.0	100.0	100.0	

Source: National statistics, bilateral imports 2002 (2001 for Serbia and Montenegro). Imports for Bosnia and Herzegovina are replaced by partner country's exports. Agriculture: Harmonized System (HS) chapters 1 to 24; Manufacturing: HS chapters 25 to 97.

Endnotes

1. For a summary review of the same issues five years ago, at the end of a decade of transition, see Michalopoulos (2001); for a similar review of Russia and Ukraine, see Michalopoulos (1999).
2. The discussion in this section focuses primarily on trade policies in the transition economies that are not members of the EU.
3. There is little information such as, for example, a tariff schedule on formal trade restrictions in Turkmenistan. There is a general impression that the flow of imports is controlled through licensing and other NTBs.
4. This, however, does not mean that the agricultural sector as a whole receives more support than industry. Border protection is only one of several elements in calculating aggregate measures of support (AMS) to the sector.
5. For example, agricultural tariffs in Ukraine average 30 percent if specific rates are taken into account, not 15 percent, as shown in annex table 3.1; some rates even exceed 100 percent.
6. Albania, Armenia, Bulgaria, Croatia, Georgia, the Kyrgyz Republic, FYR Macedonia, Moldova, and Romania.
7. "Bound" tariff levels are maximum levels of tariffs that WTO members have committed to maintain.
8. These standards pertain to the freedom of access to foreign exchange for transactions in the current account of the balance of payments.
9. These are 39 percent in the Kyrgyz Republic—although there were proposals for their reduction.
10. In what follows, we summarize the findings from various studies undertaken by the governments or donors. As the problems in Tajikistan and Uzbekistan have not been extensively studied, there are far fewer references to these countries. This should not be interpreted to mean that they face fewer problems.
11. It is unclear whether this practice has been continued post-WTO accession in Armenia.
12. This is not always their fault, as some foreign governments change requirements frequently and without notice. A Georgian wine exporter reported that Russia recently changed labeling standards three times in a 12-month period (World Bank 2003d).
13. Serbia and Montenegro have recently announced that they will pursue WTO accession separately.
14. The totals include transition economies who are currently members of the EU.
15. There is no evidence that export subsidies by the transition countries are the reason for the frequency of antidumping measures against them. In any case, if there were export subsidization, the proper remedy would be countervailing tariffs, not antidumping.
16. The MOU was negotiated and signed by Albania, Bosnia and Herzegovina, Bulgaria, Croatia, FYR Macedonia, Romania, and the Federal Republic of Yugoslavia (as of 2003, Serbia and Montenegro). Moldova signed on to the MOU although it did not participate in its negotiation. In 2004 the United Nations Mission in Kosovo (UNMIK), on behalf of

Kosovo, formally declared its intention to abide by the MOU provisions and sign FTAs with countries in the Region.

17. As the Council Regulation (No. 2007/2000), September 2000, stated, "the entitlement to benefit from the preferential arrangement shall equally be subject to their readiness to engage in regional cooperation with other countries concerned by the European Union's Stabilization and Association process, in particular through the establishment of free trade areas in conformity with Article XXIV of the GATT 1994 and other relevant WTO provisions." This provision has also mitigated the "Hub and Spokes" problem that sometimes tends to characterize preferential trade arrangements between developed and developing countries (Kaminski and de la Rocha 2003a).

18. See Messerlin and Miroudot (2004).

19. Collaboration among the countries in a variety of trade-related facilitation measures has been assisted by many donors, including the World Bank-led TTFSE (Trade and Transport Facilitation in South Eastern Europe) multicountry project. Nevertheless, recent surveys suggest that many problems continue to persist (European Commission 2004).

20. Moldova was given observer status in the agreement in 2002.

21. Russia dominates the council, which provides operational direction to the agreement: it has four votes, compared to two each for Kazakhstan and Belarus and one each for the Kyrgyz Republic and Tajikistan.

22. For a detailed discussion, see Tumbarello (2004); Michalopoulos and Tarr (1997); and Olcott, Ashlund, and Garnett (1999).

PART III

The Influence of "Behind-the-Border" Policies and Institutions

Roles of Domestic Competition and Governance in the Region's International Integration: A "Two-Way" Street

Introduction

Institutions and incentives that engender competition among enterprises and sound governance practices, including the protection of property rights, are the sine qua non of a market economy. There is much empirical evidence that these are among the most critical factors accounting for differences in the progress of development among the countries of Eastern Europe and the Former Soviet Union since the start of the transition. Among other studies, recent cross-country research that focused on the seven Southeastern European economies and Moldova marshaled firm-level statistical analysis and numerous case studies on individual businesses that provide strong support for such linkages.[1] One of the ways in which the prospects for growth in the Region have been enhanced as a result of stronger competition and governance is through the effects these institutions and incentives have had on the countries' trade performance and other dimensions of international competitiveness.

This chapter assesses the extent to which vigorous interenterprise competition and sound governance are important behind-the-border elements that deepen the international integration of the countries in the Region and leverage the salutary effects that increased trade has on growth in the area—independent of the direct effects of trade policy.

While these linkages have been examined in the literature, they have been analyzed largely on the basis of anecdotal evidence or with respect to a relatively small number of countries. Our approach is to assess these relationships systematically among all of the countries in the Region, bringing to bear the most recent empirical evidence available.[2]

To be sure, there is actually a multifaceted set of behind-the-border institutions that are central to boosting the growth-enhancing effects of increased trade flows beyond the fundamental ones of competition and governance. These include (i) development of a modern national infrastructure and related institutions for trade facilitation; (ii) liberalization of trade and private investment in, and regulatory reform of, backbone and network services sectors; and (iii) reform of the FDI policy regime to exploit opportunities for global production-sharing network trade. These latter three topics are analyzed in detail in subsequent chapters of this book.[3]

There are two principal findings from this chapter. First, the notion that two "trade blocs" have been emerging in the Region over the course of the transition—a "Euro-centric" bloc, mainly comprising the EU-8, and a "Russia-centric" bloc, largely comprising the CIS countries—is increasingly apparent in the relationship between the extent of a country's international integration and the state of its domestic competition and governance regimes. The SEE countries lie somewhere between these two blocs, but many of them are increasingly gravitating to the Euro-centric bloc. Among other findings in this regard, there is clear evidence that a larger number of firms in the EU-8 and SEE countries have managed to gain much greater international exposure and reach new markets for their products and services through exports than have firms in the CIS countries. At the same time, although import competition has induced the efficiency of enterprises throughout much of the Region, its effects have been much stronger among businesses in the EU-8 and SEE countries than among those in the CIS. Moreover, the EU-8 (and, to a lesser extent, SEE) countries have been more successful than the CIS countries in fostering competitively structured markets, and these stark differentials appear to be closely correlated with the success of businesses in these locales in integrating internationally. Finally, where corruption and weak governance are more pronounced, the propensity of firms to integrate internationally is generally weaker.

Second, complementing trade liberalization and other "border" reforms that have been expanding trade flows in the Region, the behind-the-border strengthening of competition and governance appears to be important in both achieving *and* maintaining the economywide gains from these greater trade flows. Without competitive conditions at home, trade in the Region has become impeded. Indeed, without strong, competitive domestic markets, a country's firms would not be successful traders. Stated differently, the evidence suggests that "success at home breeds success abroad." At the same time, greater exposure to foreign commerce and adherence to commitments under international trade agreements that embody rules-based disciplines appear to engender pressure on domestic firms to become more competitive and efficient; they also appear to curb incentives and opportunities for government officials (as well as businesses) to engage in discretionary behavior and corruption. In essence, then, there is an important two-way, mutually reinforcing relationship between trade policy reforms and strengthening behind-the-border competition and governance.

The chapter is structured as follows. It opens with an analysis of the various channels of international integration that the Region's firms pursue and their effects on the competitiveness of domestic market structure. Next, the patterns of the international integration of the Region's firms are assessed. The roles that barriers to entry and barriers to exit, respectively, play in conditioning the extent of the Region's trade flows are then examined. The Region's firms' relationships with the state and how these affect competition and international integration are also explored. Property rights protection and contract enforcement, as well as the effects of corruption and weak governance on the Region's international integration, are also addressed. Next, we integrate these various dimensions of the domestic business environment and investigate empirically their effects on the performance of a sample of firms in the Region. Finally, we provide an assessment of the institutions that have been developed in these policy areas and highlight where the Region's governments can work to strengthen this capacity. We close the chapter with some policy recommendations.

Interrelationships between Competition, Market Structure, and International Integration

The importance of domestic competition in influencing the international integration of businesses located in the "home" market—controlling for other factors—has long been recognized in the literature in a variety of locales worldwide.[4] In Eastern Europe and the Former Soviet Union, for countries where domestic competition has been relatively stronger, international integration has been greater; conversely, where competition has been weaker, international integration has been more limited. New cross-country econometric analysis—covering all of the 27 countries in the Region over the period 1995–2003—suggests that the observed differentials in trade openness (measured as the ratio of the sum of exports and imports to GDP), controlling for tariff levels, are strongly statistically correlated with an index of the effectiveness of a country's competition policy regime and the extent of the country's FDI inflows as a percentage of GDP (a measure of the extent of business entry).[5]

One of the primary means through which international integration can improve the competitiveness and productive efficiency of domestic firms and, in turn, the allocative efficiency of the national economy, is by the entry (indeed even the threat of entry) of new foreign competitors. Entry can occur through several channels (see table 4.1). Initially it is usually through imports—that is, sales—and, if successful, subsequently through investment.[6] Conceptually, the competitive effects depend to a large extent on the ex ante and ex post structure of the market. Entry can affect market structure not only by altering the relative market shares of sales, but also the number of producers; thus, the effects of foreign business entry on domestic market structure and competition may vary.

When entry occurs through foreign firms *importing* into the market, seller concentration in the domestic market unambiguously decreases as more goods and services become available domestically. All other things being equal, market shares of incumbent firms decrease as a result of competition from imports or falling prices. It is this pressure from imports that creates incentives for domestic firms to become more efficient. Over the course of the Region's transition, especially in the EU-8 countries, this has been the rule rather than the exception. Foreign firms have introduced new or higher-quality products and services into the domestic market, which created incentives for local firms to restructure and improve their own performance. By contrast, in the CIS countries, import competition has been stifled through protectionist policies, and these salutary impacts have been far more muted.

TABLE 4.1

Channels of Entry and Effect on Domestic Market Structure (Concentration)

	Effect on market concentration			
Channels of entry	Import	Greenfield investment	Domestic takeover	Merger
Entrant sells output in host market	Decrease	Decrease	Neutral	Increase
Entrant sells output abroad	n.a.	Neutral	Increase[a]	Increase[a]

Note: a. Assumes that, prior to entry, existing firm(s) sold output in domestic market.
n.a. = not available.

Entry through foreign *greenfield investment* in new production facilities can increase the number of sellers and increase competition in the "host market," depending on where the output is sold. If sold in the host market, the competitive effects will be analogous to import competition. In countries in the Region where entry by foreign firms has been through such investments, this has helped the breakdown of former state-owned monopolies and increased competition. However, the domestic competitive effects of a new greenfield entrant might be neutral if the firm sells all its output abroad.

Entry through *mergers or takeovers* by foreign firms can have variable effects on domestic competition. If entry occurs through the takeover of an existing firm, the domestic effects on market structure can be neutral if there is simply a change in ownership. However, if the takeover results in sales of output being reoriented to a foreign (for example, a third-country) market, domestic concentration can increase. If entry occurs by a merger with one or more existing firms operating in the host market, the number of producers and sellers will be necessarily reduced and market concentration will increase. Horizontal mergers that consolidate the number of otherwise independent competitors can therefore lead to concerted efforts to raise prices artificially above (and reduce output below) competitive levels.

To be sure, there are also effects on the domestic economy from "outward" international integration by national firms. Through exporting (that is, outward international integration by sales) or making direct investments abroad, domestically based businesses can be exposed to competitive pressures in the host country that may result in corporatewide efficiencies that affect the competitiveness of operations in the "home market." This can be manifested in a variety of factors, including adoption of new production or processing techniques that lower costs; use of advances in technology transferred from abroad; and utilization of innovative marketing techniques, among others.

In the sections that follow, our empirical assessment of the interaction between domestic competition and international integration of firms in the Region focuses primarily on the sales channel—importing and exporting. We touch only relatively briefly on the investment channel, because FDI is discussed in detail in chapter 7.

Variation in International Integration among the Firms of the Region

Import penetration. In countries in the Region where import penetration has been greater, there is new empirical evidence from firm-level surveys that businesses are more prone to reduce production costs and innovate. Not surprisingly, this finding is strongest for firms of smaller scale and those with greater private ownership, often operating in less concentrated markets. Particularly telling is that private *foreign-invested* firms operating in host markets have been more likely to react to import competition than have their domestically owned counterparts (see table 4.2). This suggests that, on average, a foreign firm operating in a country in the Region may well be more "fleet-footed" than domestic incumbents; this finding is consistent with others in the literature analyzing import competition in other regions of the world.

More important, in the countries where there has been less progress in fostering a competitive market environment—especially in the CIS—the effects of imports on business decisions have been more muted than in countries, such as those in the EU-8 and, to a lesser extent, SEE, where markets are more competitively structured as a result of more advanced reforms. Thus, while import competition is inducing efficiencies, its effect appears to be weaker in the CIS countries than in the rest of the Region.

Export propensity. There is a trend of higher export intensity at the firm level in the EU-8 and SEE countries than in those of the CIS (see figure 4.1). Export receipts are the smallest among surveyed firms in Uzbekistan and Kazakhstan, where the average firm exports below 5 percent of annual sales, and largest in Slovenia, where the average firm exports more than 20 percent of total annual sales.[7] In the Region's countries where there has been greater introduction of private sector participation in the economy—whether through privatization of existing firms or through de novo investment—the export intensity by businesses (that is, the percentage of export revenues as a share of total sales revenues) tends to be higher.

TABLE 4.2

Importance to the Region's Businesses of Competition from Imports

Percentage of surveyed firms in 2002 indicating that competition from imports is very or extremely important

Ownership	CIS	SEE	EU-8
Domestic	27.1	37.6	30.5
Foreign	27.3	48.5	40.0

Source: BEEPS2.

Note: Preliminary results from the new BEEPS of 2005 are broadly consistent with those reported in this table. However, some changes may have occurred for individual countries or subgroups of countries in the Region.

FIGURE 4.1
Export Intensity of Businesses Is Greater in the More Advanced Countries
Average export revenues as a share of total annual sales, 2002

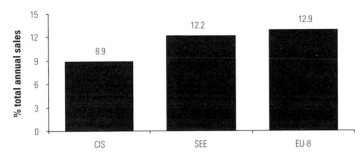

Source: BEEPS2.

Note: Preliminary results from the new BEEPS of 2005 are broadly consistent with those reported in this table. However, some changes may have occurred for individual countries or subgroups of countries in the Region.

Moreover, export intensity tends to be greatest for foreign-invested firms than for domestically owned businesses (see table 4.3). This is further evidence of the two-way relationship between international integration and behind-the-border competition: foreign firms investing in countries in the Region are more prone to react to import competition than are their domestic counterparts, and at the same time they are more likely to further their host countries' integration into world markets than are domestic businesses.

Consistent with the notion that less competition exists in the typical CIS domestic market than in other markets in the Region are data indicating that over the past decade, firms located in the EU-8 countries have exported to more numerous "new" markets than have firms in Central Asia and the Caucasus (see table 4.4). Similarly, a larger share of surveyed firms in the EU-8, closely followed by the firms in SEE, have been engaged in export compared with the relative share of exporting firms in the CIS.

TABLE 4.3
Export Intensity
Average export as a share of total annual sales, 2002

By ownership	Average exports in sales
Domestic, of which:	
State	11.8
Privatized	14.9
De novo	8.9
Foreign	20.2

Source: BEEPS2.

Note: Preliminary results from the new BEEPS of 2005 are broadly consistent with those reported in this table. However, some changes may have occurred for individual countries or subgroups of countries in the Region. Countries included are the Region and Turkey.

TABLE 4.4
Export Propensity by Sub-Region

Sub-Region	Exporter (% of all firms)	Exported to a new country between 1998 and 2002 (% of all firms)
CIS	22.1	10.9
SEE	32.3	18.6
EU-8	36.3	16.9

Source: BEEPS2.

Note: Preliminary results from the new BEEPS of 2005 are broadly consistent with those reported in this table. However, some changes may have occurred for individual countries or subgroups of countries in the Region.

Outward international integration via FDI abroad. By the same token, countries in the Region whose markets are more competitively structured—as measured by the number of competitors in various markets—tend to have more firms integrating into global markets through outward direct investment than do countries where markets are less competitively structured. On average, among recently surveyed firms in the Region, domestic state-owned enterprises tend to have less extensive direct investments abroad than do counterparts with other ownership forms—whether privatized, de novo private, or foreign-invested firms (see figure 4.2). To the extent that there are likely to be more infrastructure and utility businesses in the state-owned category

FIGURE 4.2
Number of Competitors and Operations Abroad

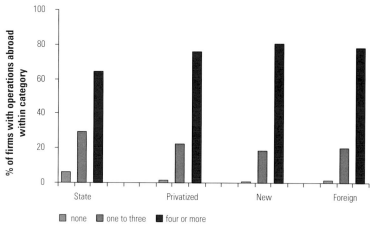

Source: BEEPS2.

Note: Preliminary results from the new BEEPS of 2005 are broadly consistent with those reported in this table. However, some changes may have occurred for individual countries or subgroups of countries in the Region. Countries included are the Region and Turkey.

than in the others, this result is to be expected. More important, regardless of firm ownership structure, as the number of competitors in the local market increases, there is a greater propensity for businesses to integrate abroad. Consistent with the broader literature, this suggests that as prospects for profits "at home" become more constrained, the drive for market opportunities abroad increases.

Impacts of Entry and Exit Barriers on International Integration

How do the underlying elements of market structure that determine the intensity of domestic competition relate to the extent of international integration by businesses in the Region? There is fairly clear evidence that countries in the Region that have high barriers to entry for business start-ups or high barriers to exit for money-losing firms are less integrated internationally and less able to capitalize on reallocation of capital and human resources stemming from exposure to trade so as to promote growth.

In-Country Barriers to Entry

Several worldwide studies in the literature have advanced the idea that high entry costs and cumbersome regulations not only make imports and inward foreign direct investment difficult, they also deter exports from enterprises operating in a country's domestic economy.[8] For Eastern Europe and the Former Soviet Union, the empirical evidence suggests that in the countries where the cost of entry is highest—measured, for example, by the time and resources required to get a new business license and registration—international integration is being hindered. The data suggest that the easier the new business entry into the Region's countries, the higher the export volumes (see figure 4.3).[9]

Worldwide, overcoming barriers to entry in a market by foreign firms requires that such firms have some form of competitive advantage because, by definition, domestic firms are more familiar with local market conditions. Such an advantage is usually in the form of firm-specific or proprietary assets: technological, organizational, or marketing knowledge; goodwill; or brand naming.[10] In fact, these factors appear to play a significant role in determining the profitability of firms operating in the Region. Of course, local firms also face barriers to entry in domestic markets, and it is important to distinguish between those and the barriers that firms engaged in international integration into the Region face to see whether and how they differ. New data collected through business surveys offer an opportunity to

FIGURE 4.3

Export Levels (2003) and Cost of Entry in the Region

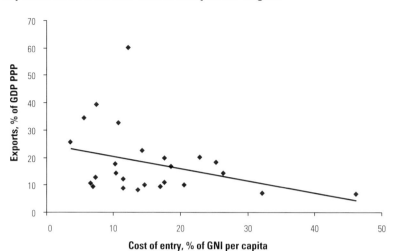

Sources: Export data based on UN COMTRADE Statistics and IMF DOT Statistics; cost-of-entry data from Doing Business (2004).

Note: GNI = gross national income. Each diamond represents one country in the Region; Turkey is also included.

assess which barriers are more important for each set of firms, thereby shedding light on the roles of various entry barriers in international integration.

For domestic firms, the data suggest that economic policy uncertainty, macroeconomic instability, and high tax rates are seen as the most severe entry barriers (see figure 4.4). More than 30 percent of the domestic businesses surveyed in the Region see these three policy-related factors as "major obstacles" to business development and operations. Interestingly, so-called administrative barriers are not perceived as the most critical impediments for starting businesses by domestic firms in the Region. This finding, at odds with the conventional wisdom of the 1990s and as recently as a few years ago, is also supported by recent empirical evidence at the sub-Regional level.[11]

For foreign firms, however, different entry barriers appear to be more impinging on business start-ups. Local anticompetitive business behavior and contract violations are seen as "major obstacles" by more surveyed foreign firms than other potential barriers to entry in the Region (see figure 4.5). Anticompetitive behavior and contract violations are perceived by roughly 40 percent of the surveyed foreign businesses as major obstacles. Thus, the most severe barriers to entry facing firms engaged in international integration in the Region are more of an institutional nature—and more specific—than those facing domestic firms. These findings suggest important policy impli-

FIGURE 4.4

Severity of Entry Barriers in the Region, Domestic Firms, 2002

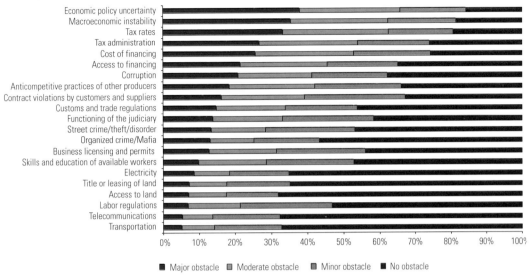

Source: BEEPS2.

Note: Preliminary results from the new BEEPS of 2005 are broadly consistent with those reported in this table. However, some changes may have occurred for individual countries or subgroups of countries in the Region. Countries included are the Region and Turkey.

FIGURE 4.5

Severity of Entry Barriers in the Region, Foreign Firms, 2002

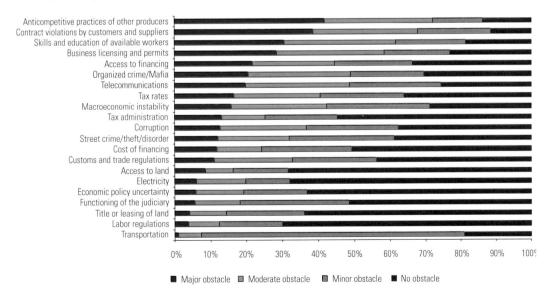

Source: BEEPS2.

Note: Preliminary results from the new BEEPS of 2005 are broadly consistent with those reported in this table. However, some changes may have occurred for individual countries or subgroups of countries in the Region. Countries included are the Region and Turkey.

cations for deepening integration in the Region: an emphasis on different reforms to reduce barriers to entry may well be needed if countries are to be more successful in integrating into international commerce.

In-Country Barriers to Exit: "Soft Budget Constraints"

Worldwide, "soft budget constraints" are the main mechanism through which unviable firms remain in the market.[12] There is abundant evidence over the course of the Region's transition suggesting that soft budget constraints impede the exit of money-losing firms from the Region.[13] Through greater fiscal and financial discipline ("hardening" of budget constraints), failing or value-subtracting firms in the Region have faced incentives to restructure or exit the market. The more difficult it is for such firms to go out of business, the less likely it is that the domestic market structure is competitive or that resources are allocated efficiently. Value-subtracting firms tie up productive assets, and in this way their presence deters entry of new business start-ups, distorts resource allocation, and constrains firm performance, including integration into the international marketplace. Here, we investigate soft budgets arising from two factors: (i) arrears in taxes, wages and social payments, utility payments, and payables to input suppliers and (ii) subsidies.

Recent survey data indicate that the incidence of arrears is greatest among firms in Central Asia and other CIS countries, although firms elsewhere in the Region also face this problem. Box 4.1 illustrates such a case involving an SEE firm in Republika Srpska. Across firms of different ownership forms, arrears are lowest among firms with significant private ownership, including those that are integrated internationally—that is, foreign-invested businesses. Significantly, there is evidence for the Region that in the countries where arrears are larger, the export performance (measured by the share of exports in GDP) is lower (see figure 4.6). This reaffirms the direct linkage between behind-the-border conditions and success in international integration among the countries in the Region: where there is a lack of domestic competition, firms' abilities to penetrate foreign markets are dulled.

Regarding subsidies, available firm-level survey data suggest that the incidence of direct business subsidies is greater in the CIS than in the EU-8 and SEE. On average, direct subsidies received by firms for the Region as a whole amount to between 10 and 15 percent of their sales revenues (see figure 4.7). More important, these data also show that the majority of such subsidies come from regional or local, rather

BOX 4.1

Arrears as Constraints on Firm Performance in SEE

The case of a large furniture manufacturer in Republika Srpska provides an illustration of how a poor business climate can hinder exports. Labor regulations and unresolved ownership status are the key factors affecting the performance of the firm in question. The company carries on its books 550 employees, of whom only 150–250 actually work. The company has been in arrears with pension contributions since 2000, which makes its workers ineligible for retirement. Moreover, political constraints prevent the company from laying off employees. There is little hope that the company will be privatized, as its total debt exceeds the market value of its assets by more than 50 percent. The company is in debt to the state, the IFC, and a commercial bank. Moreover, it has wage arrears and owes money to its suppliers. Currently, a large portion of its transactions take the form of barter. The unresolved labor situation leads to a vicious cycle: keeping the waitlisted workers on the books raises the arrears vis-à-vis the state and thus decreases the chances of privatization taking place. While the company's experience and reputation would allow it to receive additional orders from large multinationals, such as IKEA, fulfilling such orders is not possible because of a lack of working capital. In the 1990s, the company used to sell one container of products to IKEA every day. Currently, only two containers are shipped per month.

Source: World Bank staff.

FIGURE 4.6

Arrears and International Integration in the Region

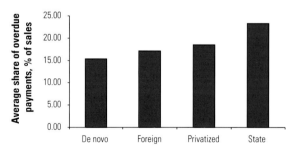
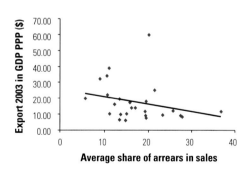

Sources: BEEPS2 and IMF DOT data.

Notes: Preliminary results from the new BEEPS of 2005 are broadly consistent with those reported in this table. However, some changes may have occurred for individual countries or subgroups of countries in the Region. Countries included are the Region and Turkey. The sample excludes firms with no overdue payments.

than central, governments. This makes the task of their reduction more challenging, in light of the difficulty of inducing change across multiple jurisdictional levels of government.

Taken together, the findings on arrears and subsidies corroborate the notion that the CIS countries have carried out less vigorous meas-

FIGURE 4.7
Size of Subsidies by Sub-Region, 2002

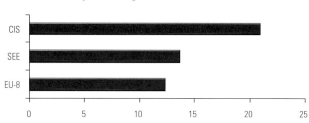

Source: BEEPS2.

Notes: Preliminary results from the new BEEPS of 2005 are broadly consistent with those reported in this table. However, some changes may have occurred for individual countries or subgroups of countries in the Region. The sample excludes firms with no subsidies.

ures to induce competitive restructuring and ownership change in the enterprise sector than have other parts of the Region. Given that the CIS countries on average have privatized fewer corporate assets than other countries in the Region, it is not surprising that the evidence indicates that the least competitively structured markets in the Region are those heavily populated by domestic, state-owned firms, whereas the most competitively structured markets are those in which a greater number of foreign private firms operate.

At the same time, the data show that from a sectoral perspective, the Region's markets in the energy and natural resource sectors, as well as in infrastructure, tend to have the fewest competitors and highest concentration, because in these sectors state ownership is most dominant. In contrast, the trade and retail sectors, where private ownership is the rule and state ownership the exception, are populated by the greatest number of competitors.

Market Dominance and International Integration

As elsewhere in the world, there is considerable diversity in the extent to which the Region's markets are populated by firms that have achieved dominant positions. This variance in the competitive structure of domestic markets can give rise to intra-Regional differences in the extent and consequences of international integration that take place.

How does domestic competitiveness affect the Region's firms' ability to integrate internationally? Recent survey data suggest that, throughout the Region, on average, firms with larger domestic market shares tend to have a higher propensity to export or import (see figure 4.8). Indeed, the data show this to be the case across all of the constituent parts of the Region. However, firms in the EU-8 that engage in export or import activity tend to have larger market shares on average than their counterpart firms in SEE, which in turn have larger market shares than exporting/importing firms in the CIS. This finding suggests that all other things being equal, firms that have been successful at home are those most likely to be successful abroad. This notion is consistent with the broader literature on the determinants of international business performance.[14] It also has important implications for national policies aimed at improving a country's international competitiveness: fostering a competitive business environment domestically can have payoffs globally.

However, market dominance can also cut the other way. The sustainability of new entrants able to penetrate markets already populated by dominant firms will be determined, in large part, by the extent to which anticompetitive conduct—in terms of price setting, production decisions, investment activities, and cozy relations with government, among other things—by the incumbent firms with large market shares is practiced. There is evidence that when there is a significant share of firms that possess market dominance and face relatively few competitors in the Region, there is a greater ability for incumbent businesses (whether domestic or foreign-owned) to exercise discretionary behavior—conduct that is generally at odds with the notion of competitive practice, where (in theory) firms are "price takers" and not "price makers." Available survey data on the price sensitivity for firms in the Region show that businesses with the

FIGURE 4.8
Market Share and International Integration

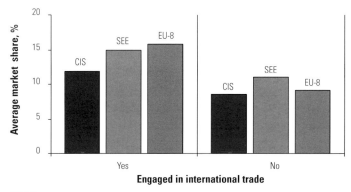

Source: BEEPS2.

Note: Preliminary results from the new BEEPS of 2005 are broadly consistent with those reported in this table. However, some changes may have occurred for individual countries or subgroups of countries in the Region.

largest market shares—generally the state-owned firms—indicate that they are the least sensitive to price changes (see figure 4.9).[15] On the other end of the spectrum, firms with the smallest market shares—generally de novo firms and foreign-invested firms—indicate that they are the most sensitive in their business decisions to changes in prices. Indeed, where there is a decrease in market dominance, we consistently observe a larger proportion of firms—across all ownership categories—that become increasingly sensitive to price changes.

Market dominance can arise as a result of extensive horizontal integration—the consolidation of multiple enterprises under one common corporate roof—within a market. Such integration is most pronounced in the CIS because of the legacy of central planning and agglomeration.[16] Although horizontal integration can exploit economies of scale and scope in certain sectors, such as utility services or other infrastructure sectors, an excessive level of such integration in most manufacturing sectors is likely to have little economic or technological justification. In such cases, in markets

FIGURE 4.9

Market Share and Price Sensitivity in the Region, by Ownership Category, 2002

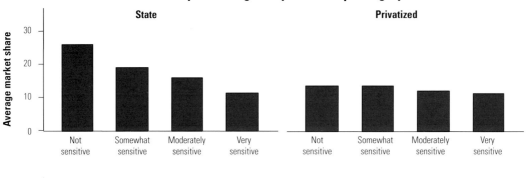

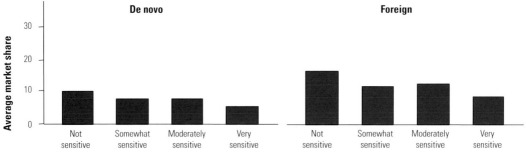

Degree of price sensitivity

Source: BEEPS2.

Note: Preliminary results from the new BEEPS of 2005 are broadly consistent with those reported in this table. However, some changes may have occurred for individual countries or subgroups of countries in the Region. Countries included are the Region and Turkey.

where a concentrated number of sellers already exist, dominant incumbents engaging in extensive horizontal integration can create opportunities to exercise market power and anticompetitive behavior. Firm-level data for the Region suggest that there is a clear negative association between the number of competitors firms face and the extent of horizontal integration. Among surveyed firms, those with no competitors have on average close to four business establishments within the boundaries of a national market, while firms with more than four competitors are less horizontally sprawled (see figure 4.10.)

Transactions with the State

Purchases of goods and services by national governments—through participation in "state orders" or other forms of public procurement—in a number of the Region's countries constitute a significant portion of business transactions for many firms and, as a result, can have a significant impact on competition in the market. In turn, this can have an influence on the extent and pattern of the Region's international integration. Not surprisingly, firms' commercial ties with the state are more extensive in CIS countries relative to other countries of the Region. For example, the average Uzbek firm surveyed earns about 34 percent of sales revenues through public procurement, while the average Belarusian, Kazakh, and Tajik firms surveyed earn between 22 and 24 percent of sales revenues from such transactions.

FIGURE 4.10

Competition and Horizontal Integration in the Region

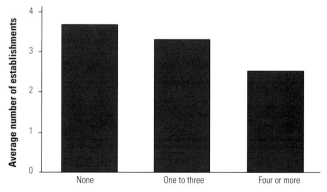

Source: BEEPS2.

Note: Preliminary results from the new BEEPS of 2005 are broadly consistent with those reported in this table. However, some changes may have occurred for individual countries or subgroups of countries in the Region. Countries included are the Region and Turkey.

These profiles contrast significantly with EU-8 and SEE businesses. For example, the average surveyed firm operating in FYR Macedonia or the Czech Republic earns 3 percent or less of sales revenues from government purchases. On average, about 10 percent of combined sales revenues of all of the surveyed firms in the Region are earned from purchases by government entities.[17]

While there is a relatively clear trend across the Region of a heavy reliance on sales to governments by domestically owned enterprises—especially state-owned and privatized enterprises—relative to foreign-owned firms operating in the market, this is most strikingly evident in the countries of the CIS (see figure 4.11). In contrast, in the EU-8 countries, although state-owned enterprises still dominate government purchases, there is much more balance across firm ownership categories. This suggests a more competitive public procurement market in that part of the Region.

Still, as elsewhere in the world—including in the OECD countries—the Region's governments discriminate against foreign players, often for political reasons. In varying degrees, the Region's governments follow rules and procedures for awarding contracts and making purchases that favor only selected—and often only domestic—market participants (see box 4.2). Adherence to WTO-based rules regarding government procurement that provide for open competition, transparent procedures, and nondiscriminatory treatment to domestic and foreign firms alike can be an important reform in minimizing existing distortions in international trade and investment in the Region and in fostering international integration.

FIGURE 4.11

Commercial Ties with the State of the Region's Firms

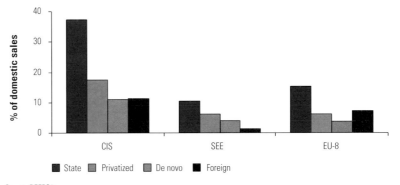

Source: BEEPS2.

Note: Preliminary results from the new BEEPS of 2005 are broadly consistent with those reported in this table. However, some changes may have occurred for individual countries or subgroups of countries in the Region. Average sales to governmental entities by ownership type and by sub-Region, 2002.

BOX 4.2

The "Home-Grown" Construction Sector in SEE: Evidence from Business Case Studies

Most of the sales of construction firms in SEE are concentrated in the domestic market and, in some cases, in the municipal market in which they are located. Bidding on government and (to a lesser extent) private contracts with neighboring or more distant countries is increasingly attempted but is not always successful. Neighboring country firms complain that they are subject to discrimination as foreign enterprises and that preference is shown to local companies, especially in the case of public procurement contracts. Consequently, home governments have sought to help their domestic firms win public contracts abroad through political persuasion.

In general, SEE construction firms find home government contracts quite attractive—some companies do more than 70 percent of their business with the government. However, the "competitive" selection process is not always transparent, and often the government agencies do not pay promptly, necessitating litigation. Some firms note that to be successful in the domestic public procurement construction business, they must be politically well connected. In some cases, ministries ask for pro bono construction, design, or engineering advice, which the firms readily give in order to build goodwill.

A few construction firms concentrate on winning construction contracts from domestic private companies or foreign private multinational subsidiaries located in the local market. Interestingly, complaints about the lack of transparency in the contracting process are voiced here as well, but these complaints are much more muted than they are in the case of domestic public procurement contracts. Some of these firms are interested in pursuing government contracts, but without a public procurement law in place, they are reluctant to do so.

Source: Broadman et al. 2004.

Property Rights Protection and Contract Enforcement

As has been well documented in research over the course of the transition, there is in many parts of the Region a lack of security in the commercial contracting process. Faced with this obstacle, many enterprises—not only foreign, but also domestic—have had to face the resulting higher cost of doing business (and in some cases have voted "with their feet" and taken their business elsewhere). In so doing, however, efficiency is lost in the transaction process, and resources are diverted from more productive activities. There is evidence that where there is relatively weak contract enforcement in the Region, international integration is relatively muted. Data from case studies of individual businesses in the Region reveal that foreign firms lose confidence in the durability of their transactions when property rights in the country they export to or invest in are not adequately protected.[18] On the other hand, domestic firms that want to engage in international trade through imports or attract foreign investors are constrained in doing so when the institutional and legal systems in their home countries cannot adequately protect and guarantee their contractual rights. International transactions become more risky and increase the likelihood of commercial disputes.[19]

Given the sizable commercial risks in many parts of the Region engendered by nascent legal institutions, what methods do firms operating in these countries use to reduce such risks? Firm-level survey data show an appreciable incidence of transacting on the spot or of using prepayment. Not surprisingly, the use of these mechanisms varies significantly within the Region. For example, surveyed firms in much of the CIS, especially Azerbaijan, Belarus, Tajikistan, Ukraine, and Uzbekistan, require prepayment for at least 40 percent of their sales. In contrast, surveyed firms in Armenia, Bulgaria, Hungary, and Slovenia, on average, use prepayment in less than 10 percent of sales. Box 4.3 illustrates how advance payments are used to diminish the risk of reneging on a contract in Bosnia and Herzegovina.

While genuine progress has been made in some of the Region's countries—most notably the EU-8—regarding the establishment of relatively well-functioning, market-based legal institutions that facilitate resolution of commercial disputes, in many other countries—largely the CIS but also a significant portion of SEE—such problems are either resolved through extra-legal means, are not resolved, or go unrecorded. For these countries, establishing credible legal institutions for commercial dispute resolution is a major unfinished agenda item.[20]

Governance and Corruption

Worldwide, weak governance and corruption impede international integration and the realization of the benefits of open trade. At the end of the day, consumers pay higher prices as the (tangible and intangible) costs of corruption are internalized into the final cost of internationally traded products or services. Product or service quality can also suffer. The real costs associated with corruption may well diminish the ability of domestic firms to export abroad and deter foreign firms' decisions to export to (or invest in) the domestic market. On the other hand, greater international integration, especially when governed by legally binding rules-based trade agreements, such as WTO membership, can *improve* the quality of domestic governance institutions and

---

BOX 4.3

Using Prepayment to Reduce Contractual Risks in Bosnia and Herzegovina

Companies interviewed as case studies often mention prepayment as a means of forestalling business disputes. Asking clients to pay a considerable proportion of the price in advance seems to be the norm in many SEE firms, regardless of sector, size, or ownership characteristics. A state-owned steel foundry in Bosnia and Herzegovina described three recent cases of business disputes and how it went about resolving them. In two of the cases, the firm was the creditor, and in one case, it was the debtor. One of the former cases is quite telling. The company produced goods to order for a Serbian metalworking company and delivered half of the order in 1995, but the company did not receive payment at the time. Several years ensued, and the Serbian firm closed down production. Even though the Bosnian company attempted to negotiate with the Serbian firm's administration on several occasions, the debt was still due seven years later. The Bosnian company's management is planning to pursue this case through the Bosnian court system. Even though a written contract exists, the management still faces uncertainty as to the duration and costs of the court procedure.

The risk associated with contracts for goods made to order is well illustrated in this case. The other half of the goods made to order are still stocked in the steel foundry's warehouse, but they have no alternative commercial use. Given this situation, it is hardly surprising that the same steel company now requires a 50 percent advance payment on its orders, with the remaining 50 percent falling due within five days after delivery. Furthermore, new clients must pay the full price of the model good in transactions for which the good is made to the client's order. Subsequent deliveries and payments are scheduled in five installments. In this manner, transactions and payments are structured to avoid the occurrence of payment disputes.

Source: Broadman et al. 2004.

---

help reduce opportunities for discretionary behavior and corruption. Evidence in the literature supports these propositions: countries that engage in freer trade tend to have better-quality institutions, and, conversely, countries with better-quality institutions tend to engage in freer trade.[21] Such findings suggest that there is a two-way, mutually beneficial interaction between increased international integration and improved governance and reduced corruption.

How consistent are these global findings with evidence from the Region? The incidence of corruption among countries in the Region is quite varied. More important, new data suggest that these differences appear to be associated with the extent of international integration—independent of the level of a country's development—among the countries in the Region (see figure 4.12). In particular, countries where corruption is more prominent tend to be those with the least amount

FIGURE 4.12

**Greater Trade Openness and Reduced Corruption in the Region:
A Two-Way Relationship**

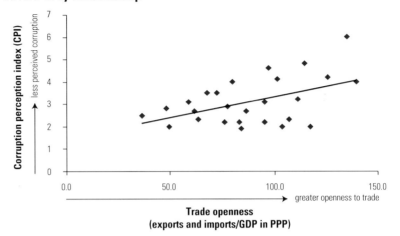

Sources: CPI from Transparency International; export and import in output (PPP) data from World Bank World Development Indicators.

Note: CPI ranks countries in terms of the degree to which corruption is perceived to exist among public officials and politicians. It is a composite index, drawing on corruption-related data in expert surveys carried out by a variety of reputable institutions. It reflects the views of business people and analysts from around the world, including experts. The higher the CPI, the lower the level of perceived corruption.

of integration into the world economy. The scatter plot indicates a positive association between greater international integration and less (perceived) corruption. These results are bolstered by multivariate regressions that indicate this positive association remains statistically significant even when the level of a country's development (measured by GDP per capita) is taken into account.[22]

One widely used measure of the quality of governance institutions is the use of irregular payments by businesses with the aim of "greasing the system." Firm-level analysis shows that there is an appreciable expectation among businesses operating in the Region that in order to effectively get things done in dealing with public officials, bribes need to be paid, with the frequency of such activity varying across the countries of the Region and the type of firm ownership. The incidence of bribes tends to be the highest in the CIS, followed by SEE countries; it is lowest in the EU-8 (see figure 4.13). More than 72 percent of surveyed firms in Albania, more than 63 percent of surveyed firms in Tajikistan, and more than 62 percent of surveyed firms in Georgia and Russia indicate that they pay bribes to ease their business transactions. More important, the data reveal that a greater proportion of the Region's foreign-owned firms—that is, those businesses that have integrated internationally—indicate that they pay bribes with greater frequency than do domestically owned privatized or

FIGURE 4.13
Frequency of Bribes by Sub-Region, 2002

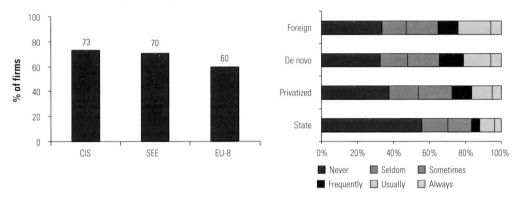

Source: BEEPS2.

Note: Preliminary results from the new BEEPS of 2005 are broadly consistent with those reported in this table. However, some changes may have occurred for individual countries or subgroups of countries in the Region.

state-owned firms. Indeed, more than one-half of the domestic state-owned firms surveyed indicate that they never resort to bribes. While this may suggest that domestic firms do not engage heavily in explicit payments to facilitate dealings with the state, it does not imply that such firms do not use other, perhaps less explicit, means to accomplish the same objective.

Impact of Competition and Governance on Firm Performance in the Region

The analysis in the foregoing sections suggests a variety of ways in which the extent of interenterprise competition and the soundness of governance affect (or are affected by) the degree of international integration of firms operating in the Region. To what extent do competition and governance systematically influence the business performance of such firms, which, in turn, affects the degree to which greater international integration and open trade can be leveraged to have salutary effects on job creation, income, and growth in the Region? In other words, all other things being equal, is there a systemic difference in the performance of the Region's firms that have participated in international integration to a greater degree than those who have not?

In order to test these hypotheses, a regression model of firm-level determinants of business profitability was estimated on approximately 6,000 firms operating in the Region. (The data used were from the 2002 BEEPS2 survey; see the annex for a description of the dataset). The specification of the model is consistent with mainstream models of firm profitability widely found in the industrial organization literature.[23]

Two variables were constructed to assess how international integration affects firm profitability: one that specifies whether the firm engages in export or import activity—*international trader*; the other, whether the firm is a foreign-owned business (operating in a "host market" in the Region) and thus has necessarily integrated internationally—*foreign ownership*.[24] Drawing on the arguments advanced in the preceding analysis, a series of variables chosen to capture the impact that certain dimensions of competition and governance are likely to have on firm performance was included. The variables depicting a firm's competitive position include the extent of the firm's *market dominance*, the degree to which it faces *low entry barriers*, the extent of the firm's *horizontal integration* and *vertical integration*, and two measures of the *softness of budget constraints* faced by the firm. The measures for governance are the extent to which the firm has *transactions with the state* and the degree to which the firm's commercial conduct reflects *contractual risk aversion*. Finally, firm-specific control variables that are also likely to impact profitability were included in the model: the extent to which the firm engages in *product differentiation*, the firm's *technological prowess*, and the firm's *size*. (The regression results are reported in table 4.5.)

The empirical results offer a number of insights. First, the estimated coefficients on the two variables depicting international integration are positive and statistically significant. This suggests that, all other things being equal, international integration enhances the performance of firms in the Region.

Second, firms in the Region that have achieved larger market shares tend to have higher profitability than those with smaller market shares, after controlling for firm size and other characteristics, such as vertical and horizontal integration, a finding consistent with the larger empirical literature.[25] In addition, the regression results suggest that relatively high entry and exit barriers have a significant and negative impact on firm performance.[26]

Finally, the estimated coefficient on intensity of business-state transactions is positive and statistically significant, suggesting that closeness with government—a measure of governance—"pays off." However, the estimated coefficient on the measure of property rights protection—utilization of prepaid sales, to depict degree of confidence in contractual relationships—does not differ statistically from zero.

Overall, the estimated model gives credence to the notion that the Region's firms that engage in international integration tend to out-

TABLE 4.5
Determinants of Business Profitability in the Region, 2002

Explanatory variables	Dependent variable Profit-to-sales ratio		
	Estimated coefficient	t test	Level of significance
Market dominance (market share)	0.002	2.44	**
Low entry barriers (price sensitivity)	−0.098	−7.36	***
Horizontal integration (number of establishments)	0.003	1.48	
Vertical integration (share of sales to a parent company or affiliated subsidiary)	0.001	1.27	
Softness of budget constraints (share of arrears in total sales)	−0.006	−4.41	***
Softness of budget constraints (share of subsidies in total sales)	−0.004	−1.73	*
Transactions with state (share of sales to government agencies)	0.001	2.15	**
Contractual risk aversion (share of prepaid sales in total sales)	0.000	0.76	
International trader (exporter or importer)	0.052	1.73	*
Foreign ownership (foreign firm)[a]	0.546	7.10	***
Domestic ownership (de novo firm)[a]	0.563	12.13	***
Domestic ownership (privatized firm)[a]	0.304	5.58	***
Product differentiation (share of advertising in total sales)	0.009	2.95	***
Technological prowess (share of R&D in total sales)	0.008	3.10	***
Size (number of employees)	0.000	0.01	
Constant	3.670	31.74	***
Number of observations	5,786		
R-squared	0.09		

Source: Author's calculations using BEEPS2 data.

Note: Preliminary results from the new BEEPS of 2005 are broadly consistent with those reported in this table. However, some changes may have occurred for individual countries or subgroups of countries in the Region. Countries included are the Region and Turkey.
a. The estimated coefficients on these variables indicate the performance of the firms in these ownership categories relative to that of domestic state-owned firms.
* = Statistically significant at the 10% level. ** = Statistically significant at the 5% level. *** = Statistically significant at the 1% level.

perform those that do not, all other things being equal. Moreover, where the business environment allows firms to compete with one another and provides for effective incentives for sound governance, there is better firm performance, all other things being equal.

Institutional Capacity for Competition and Governance

The evidence presented above indicates that enhancing both domestic competition and governance in the Region's economies is likely to be an important objective not only for deepening international integration but also for capitalizing on and leveraging the economywide benefits that such integration can engender for the countries. If this conclusion is correct, one implication for domestic policy makers is clear: in an increasingly globalized and competitive international economy, steps to enhance growth and improve national welfare should focus squarely on developing and strengthening the behind-the-border institutional capacity for competition and governance. Strengthening these two areas will help domestic policy reforms be implemented effectively, help businesses compete more efficiently for international market share, and help countries garner greater foreign investment. To that end, what is the state of such institutions in the Region today, how do countries in the Region compare along these lines, and what are the priority areas for institutional capacity building in the Region?

Competition Policy Institutions

A country's competition policy regime comprises laws, rules, regulations, standards, and instruments to prevent and reduce or eliminate the exercise of market power by firms who possess dominant market positions or engage in restrictive business conduct so as to deter entry by new rivals or drive from the market firms that otherwise are profitable. Such conduct includes monopoly pricing, abusive or predatory practices, anticompetitive mergers, and price fixing, among other actions.[27] As indicated by the firm-level survey data presented earlier, foreign firms operating in the Region perceive such conduct as especially pernicious to cross-border integration and entry. Box 4.4 illustrates the use of anticompetitive practices from a business case study in Serbia and Montenegro. Taken together, the evidence suggests that greater attention should be paid to strengthening domestic competition policy institutions in the Region.

Despite the increasing number of countries in the Region with sound competition laws, there is almost universally weak enforcement of these instruments and substantial variation in implementation across the Region. Figure 4.14 provides a cross-country comparison along this score using a rating index. Not surprisingly, the most advanced reformers in the Region—the EU-8—are ranked highest. Indeed, all of the countries in that group have competition policy ratings that exceed those of all the countries in the two other sub-Regions, where the rankings are fairly similar. The high scores attained by the Czech Republic, Hungary, Lithuania, Poland, and the Slovak Republic reflect relatively sound competition laws and enforcement actions on the part of these countries' governments to reduce or eliminate abuse of market power (including the divestiture of some dominant firms) and to promote competitive business environments. In addition, these countries have made much progress in reducing policy-driven barriers to entry. In contrast, either no or significantly subpar competition legislation and institutions are present in Bosnia and Herzegovina, Serbia and Montenegro, Turkmenistan,

BOX 4.4

Market Dominance and Anticompetitive Pricing in Serbia and Montenegro

The market structure in this sector is best characterized as a core of a few large, dominant firms and a competitive fringe of more numerous small- and medium-size firms. The combined market share of the three dominant firms—which are either privatized or de novo private enterprises—is approximately 45 percent. About seven other firms—all of medium size, mostly state-owned enterprises, but also some private businesses—have a combined market share of 15 to 20 percent. The remaining share of the market comprises many small private firms.

One of the private medium-size firms, which is affiliated with a major local bank, has been an aggressive marketer and has tried to break into the dominant core. Its market share in 2001 was 2.6 percent, but a year later its share had increased to 4.5 percent. The senior manager of this firm voiced great concern that his company was suffering from "unfair competition." In particular, pricing behavior in this market is often predatory, with the dominant firms lowering prices to try to drive out competitors. The result has been frequent price wars.

One of the price wars was so destructive to the bottom lines of the involved firms that this senior manager invited the two other chief executive officers over for lunch. In a discussion that lasted almost five hours, they agreed to fix prices on certain key products. One of the participants agreed to stop selling at a lower price for two months, another for four months, and the third for one month. Because they had the same or similar suppliers, they also agreed on markup margins. The margins were fixed at 25 to 30 percent for one firm, 22 to 23 percent for another, and 13 to 18 percent for the third. It is likely that the participants accepted the pricing deal in part because they were seeking credits from the firm affiliated with the bank. After four months, the predatory pricing resumed.

Source: Broadman et al. 2004.

Tajikistan, and Uzbekistan.[28] Overall, these data suggest that the emphasis on strengthening institutional capacity in competition policy regimes should be in SEE and in the CIS countries.

Bankruptcy Regimes

One way of ensuring low barriers to exit is through the functioning of an effective bankruptcy framework and related institutions. The quality of a country's bankruptcy policy regime can be measured in terms of the length and cost of insolvency procedures and by the efficiency with which the share of funds is recovered by creditors. Nearly all of the Region's countries have implemented new bankruptcy legislation or amended existing laws at least once since the early 1990s. How-

FIGURE 4.14

Index of Competition Policy Development and Implementation in the Region

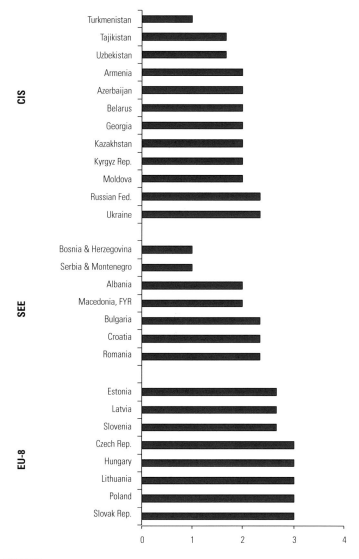

Source: EBRD 2004a.

Note: The index is defined as follows: 1 – no competition legislation and institutions; 2 – competition policy legislation and institutions set up; some reduction of entry restrictions or enforcement action on dominant firms; 3 – some enforcement actions to reduce abuse of market power and to promote a competitive environment, including breakups of dominant conglomerates; substantial reduction of entry restrictions; 4 – significant enforcement actions to reduce abuse of market power and to promote a competitive environment; 4+ – standards and performance typical of advanced industrial economies; effective enforcement of competition policy; unrestricted entry to most markets.

ever, throughout much of the Region—even in many of the EU-8 and EU accession and candidate countries—the insolvency process is comparatively lengthy and costly; further, investors do not recover a sizable share of their investments (see figure 4.15). Indeed, in most

FIGURE 4.15

Comparative Efficiency of the Bankruptcy Process

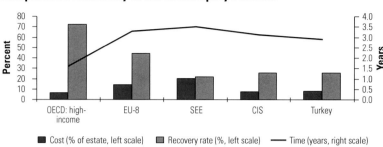

Cost (% of estate, left scale) ■ Recovery rate (%, left scale) — Time (years, right scale)

Source: World Bank (2004b) Doing Business database.

countries in the Region, the overall governing institutional framework for bankruptcy is still quite weak. In terms of progress in individual countries, only the Baltics, and to some extent Poland, match high-income OECD standards.

To be sure, only in part are the inefficiencies evident in the Region's bankruptcy regimes the result of poor legislation. Weak enforcement of creditor rights also results from the facts that basic property rights in many of the Region's countries are ill-defined and that powerful vested political economy interests would stand to lose from a reallocation of existing assets (and liabilities). At the same time, social pressures may constrain the reorganization or liquidation of failing businesses. Finally, as in other parts of the world, the notion of bankruptcy itself has negative connotations.

Developing effective bankruptcy institutions—whether in-court or out-of-court—is critical to improving the competitiveness of viable firms and to closing down, liquidating, or reorganizing firms that are value subtracting. Mechanisms that help in the reallocation of such resources—human as well as financial—will engender greater flexibility in the Region, which is key to ensuring growth and poverty reduction as the process of international integration continues.

Industrial Policy

Through a variety of fiscal and other instruments, such as export incentives, duty-free schemes, tax concessions, and accelerated depreciation allowances, some governments in the Region—like those elsewhere in the world—extend preferential treatment to select market participants as part of an overall industrial policy. Such treatment, however, can (though not necessarily) undermine the competitive nature of markets and ultimately distort the pattern and extent of a country's international integration. Box 4.5 illustrates the experience of Turkey and its use of economic incentives to incumbent firms.

Perhaps the most important linkages between industrial policy schemes and international integration arise through policy actions by the Region's governments to extend preferential treatment not only to incumbent domestic enterprises but also to foreign firms operating in the national economies. Export-processing zones (EPZs)— intended to attract FDI—are such examples.[29] These instruments typically offer special incentives for export-oriented investment and take the form of free-trade zones, duty-free zones, free-investment zones, and offshore zones, among other schemes. The ownership composition of EPZ firms can be domestic, foreign, or mixed.

In many respects, EPZs can be thought of as attempts to apply trade policy instruments in limited locations to compensate for broader failures in a country's investment climate. In this way, EPZs can lead to the formation of "enclaves" from the national economy, where export-oriented firms may operate without undue interference from the state. This may well put EPZ firms at an advantageous behind-the-border position in comparison with non-EPZ firms. All other things being equal, this can impede non-EPZ firms' competitiveness in foreign markets. At the same time, it allows governments to avoid deeper or more extensive domestic liberalization and deregulation in the rest of the economy. Moreover, without proper safeguards, such policies can produce opportunities and incentives for discretionary behavior and corruption.

BOX 4.5

Economic Incentives in Turkey

Historically, Turkey has made frequent use of investment incentives and export incentives and has relied heavily on state-owned enterprises. The Turkish public enterprise sector is still large. State-owned enterprises have generally been poor economic performers as a result of soft-budget constraints—including direct transfers from the government, equity injections, and debt consolidation. In recent years, Turkey has eliminated most investment and export incentives. Similar progress could not be achieved in the case of public enterprises. Privatization gained momentum only after the 2001 crisis, when it was recognized that state-owned firms and the related structure of subsidies and soft budget constraints were a part of the problem underlying the large nonperforming assets of the banks. As Turkey moves forward with EU accession, it will have to align its state aid policies to those of the EU and apply the same competition policies to all firms, whether private or public.

Source: Hoekman and Togan 2005.

Although EPZs are not as widespread in the Region as they are in other parts of the world (including, among others, East Asia), they do exist in several countries. For example, they are currently utilized in Azerbaijan, the Kyrgyz Republic, and Uzbekistan, and used to be present in Hungary and Poland, among others. Other countries, such as Russia, are contemplating the establishment of EPZs. However, the experience of countries in the Region with EPZs has been mixed. On the one hand, some EPZs appear to have been effective in generating exports in the areas in which they were located (although it is difficult to truly ascertain this because there is no knowledge of the potential outcome from the opposite scenario [that is, the exports that would be generated in the absence of EPZs]). On the other hand, in some EPZs there have been only limited positive productivity or technological spillovers to the rest of the domestic economy. Box 4.6 illustrates this point based on the experience of the Kyrgyz Free Economic Zones.

The long-run net benefits to the Region's domestic economies from such preferential schemes—as elsewhere in the world—are of dubious size partly because such regimes can result in distorted enclave markets with limited positive spillovers to the rest of the economy and opportunities for corruption. Although political and vested interests will be strong, reform in the Region to phase out distortive special investment or export incentives—to domestic firms as well as foreign businesses—is recommended. Such reform could be conducted on a time-bound, sector-specific basis. It would likely be advantageous to countries' abilities to deepen international integration on an enduring basis and to exploit the benefits of increased international openness economywide.

Legal/Judicial Institutions for Governance

Effective legal and judicial institutions that provide the rules, procedures, and policies for sound governance are critical to enabling businesses in the Region to start, grow, and expand, including internationally. As noted earlier, in the discussion on bankruptcy, in many of the countries in the Region, although good legislation exists "on the books," there is a significant implementation gap resulting from either a lack of or poorly designed institutions that allow for discretionary conduct on the part of government officials. In such a governance environment, businesses face an uneven playing field and the extraction of rents.

Of course the development of such institutions varies within the Region, in part because of "initial conditions" and other country-specific factors rooted in culture and history. Moreover, this variation is

BOX 4.6

Free Economic Zones in the Kyrgyz Republic

Four Free Economic Zones (FEZs) were set up in the Kyrgyz Republic to attract FDI; investors in these areas were exempted from several taxes and duties, although, at present, only one of them (the Bishkek FEZ) operates effectively. Firms operating in the FEZs are exempt from prof-it taxes and most other taxes, including the VAT, emergency and road funds, and retail sales tax-es when they export their products. Individual income taxes are collected from the employees, and a fee equal to 2 percent of revenues is collected from the firms. The fee is used for opera-tion of the FEZ. The tax advantages of operating in the FEZ, combined with limited regulatory burdens, facilitate production efficiency for external markets, but create significant disadvan-tages for domestic producers, unless sales from the FEZ into the domestic market are subject to all required taxes. This results from firms operating in the FEZs maintaining their tax advan-tages when producing for local markets, both implicitly (that is, payment of some taxes may be delayed until goods are "imported into the Kyrgyz Republic") and explicitly (that is, some taxes [such as the profits tax] are not paid). Despite improvements over the last several years, leakage from FEZs into domestic markets continues to be a problem (see figure).

With their improved investment climates, the FEZs have in principle been an important inter-vention for increasing foreign investment and technology transfer. The analysis of the FEZ pro-duction data suggests that firms in the FEZ in Bishkek have five-to-seven times higher produc-tivity than the average Kyrgyz firm because of the improved business environment and because of the use of superior technology (for example, better machines, management practices, work-er training schemes, market information, and so on). What is difficult to assess, however, are the technology transfer "spillover" effects from these FEZ firms to the broader economy. For example, some of the FEZ workers could, over time, leave their jobs to work for non-FEZ com-panies or to start their own firms, taking new technological ideas with them. Increasing the links between FEZ firms and the local economy can help to increase such beneficial spillovers.

Production, Exports, and Domestic Sale of Goods Produced in the Kyrgyz FEZ (mil. $)

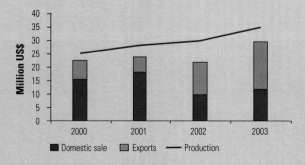

Source: World Bank staff.

also likely to be the result of cross-country differences, not only in judicial capacity (the "supply" side) but also in society's "demand" for well-functioning judiciaries. There is evidence that such demand and capacity are both positively associated with the progress of economic reform and a country's standard of living. This suggests that where demand for well-functioning judiciaries is weak, the institutional capacity to deliver high-caliber judicial services has been shallow, and vice versa (see figure 4.16).

Based on our earlier analysis, the demand for well-functioning judicial and legal institutions that protect and enforce property rights is likely to increase with the deepening of the Region's firms' international integration. In part, this will come from the firms' needs to reduce costs stemming from poor governance, and in part, it will be prodded by the need to comply with internationally binding standards embodied in trade agreements. In turn—if "the market" for legal/judicial services operates smoothly, largely a function of how well information flows—an increase in demand should facilitate a "supply response" for the creation of, or improvement in, sound legal and judicial institutions. Even more generally, however, as countries in the Region find it necessary to compete more vigorously for investment resources in the global market, this itself should produce such demand.

In the main, the need for establishing these basic institutions pertains to the CIS countries, but also to some extent in SEE. In the countries where some institutional capacity already exists—largely the EU-8 and some SEE countries—reforms should focus on refining cur-

FIGURE 4.16

Capacity and Demand for Judicial Reforms in the Region

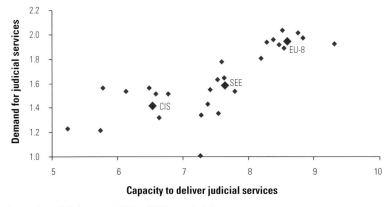

Sources: James H. Anderson et al. 2005 and EBRD transition indicators.

Note: Capacity is the log of GDP per capita; demand is based on court usage and EBRD transition indicators.

rent rules and procedures and on rectifying remaining areas of weakness. These include strengthening judicial independence and accountability; improving court efficiency, performance, and accessibility; and facilitating development of alternative dispute-resolution mechanisms.[30]

Conclusion

The fundamental conclusion from the analysis conducted in this chapter is that domestic, or behind-the-border, reforms that foster interenterprise competition and sound governance are important complements to policies that liberalize trade regimes to enhance the Region's countries' integration into the world economy and realize greater growth therefrom. At the same time, the analysis makes clear that governments of the Region should anchor these domestic reforms within international commitments that liberalize trade. These can take place at a variety of levels: globally through WTO accession; regionally through plurilateral RTAs, such as EU membership, or bilateral RTAs, such as those in SEE; or unilaterally through autonomous trade liberalization (see chapter 3). These legally binding commitments will not only help to lock in the behind-the-border reforms already achieved; the liberalization of trade engendered by such agreements and the associated disciplines embodied in them will themselves instill greater competition and stronger incentives for sound domestic governance. In short, there is a mutually beneficial two-way interaction between reforms that open trade and those that strengthen competition and governance, and this interaction should be fully exploited to enhance growth in the countries of the Region.

The chapter also has found broad empirical support for the notion that two "trade blocs" in the Region have been emerging over the course of the transition—a "Euro-centric" bloc, essentially comprising the EU-8, and a "Russia-centric" bloc, essentially comprising the CIS countries. The SEE countries lie somewhere between these two blocs, but many of them are increasingly gravitating to the Euro-centric bloc. There is evidence that firms in the EU-8 have managed to gain much greater international exposure and reach new markets for their products and services through exports compared with the firms in the CIS countries. In addition, export revenues as a percentage of sales have been weaker in CIS-based firms than in EU-8-based firms. Although import competition has induced efficiency throughout the Region, its effects have been much stronger among businesses in the EU-8 countries, compared with those in the CIS.

Moreover, the EU-8 (and to a lesser extent SEE) countries have been far more successful than the CIS countries in bringing about more competitively structured markets, and these stark differentials appear to be closely correlated with the success of businesses in these locales in integrating internationally. Governments in the CIS have been more reluctant in lowering barriers to entry, which has protected incumbent domestic firms with market power from competition from abroad. Successful competitive restructuring and ownership change of CIS firms also have been hindered by the presence of arrears and subsidies to incumbents, which have prevented the exit of value-subtracting businesses.

To be sure, checks on weak governance and corruption should be strengthened throughout the entire Region. But the incentives for sound governance are stronger in the EU-8 countries compared with the other countries in the Region. More important, where corruption and weak governance are most pronounced, the propensity of firms to integrate internationally is weakest.

The incidence of successfully resolving commercial disputes associated with international business transactions is highest in the Euro-centric bloc and weakest in the Russia-centric bloc, implying that there is likely an important relationship between the sophistication and availability of instruments for dispute resolution and the level of development of the relevant institutions. Not surprisingly, firms in the CIS have relied more heavily on bribes to resolve disputes associated with international trade transactions and to overcome related institutional hurdles than businesses in the rest of the Region.

Taken together, these findings indicate that policies that enhance the conditions for greater interenterprise competition in domestic markets should be a priority item on the reform agenda of most the Region's governments. Relatively few of the countries in the Region have either sufficiently established or strengthened the basic market institutions that protect firms and consumers from anticompetitive structures and conduct. In fact, promoting vigorous competition domestically is a critical prerequisite for developing a vibrant private sector populated by firms that can compete effectively in international markets. As has been suggested, firms that can compete at home are more likely to be able to do so abroad.

To this end, the Region's governments should work toward eliminating not only barriers to the establishment of new businesses and allowing for the continued entry of rivals but also barriers to the ongoing challenges that businesses face behind the border on a day-to-day basis. Reducing so-called administrative barriers for business start-ups and postestablishment operations were important "first generation" reforms. To a large extent, the most egregious of these barriers are being dealt with in many of the Region's countries. Some of them are now in need of "second-generation" reforms—ones that deal with the more underlying and complex challenges in the national economies of reducing barriers to entry and exit and of enhancing competition. Although an increasing number of the Region's countries have sound competition laws, widespread enforcement of these instruments is weak. Competition policy agencies in every country should have sufficient competencies to assess and penalize dominant firm structures and behavior, as well as other forms of restrictive business practices that harm competition. Of course, such agencies also must have the political "teeth" to make a difference; this means that strong political buy-in by the highest authorities is likely to be required.

On the exit side, the restructuring or liquidation of large loss-making enterprises that take up resources and economic space has not been facilitated sufficiently, in large part because vested interests stand to lose. Hardening budget constraints through the elimination of arrears and subsidies to businesses will go a long way toward ensuring that exit barriers are lowered. At the same time, developing an effective bankruptcy process and associated institutions, including courts staffed by competent judges and a pool of trained trustees, is essential. Taken together, such measures will improve the competitiveness of viable firms while exposing businesses that are no longer commercially viable and will provide mechanisms to reallocate resources—both capital and human—to higher values in use.

Only a relatively limited number of the Region's governments systemically extend preferential treatment to select market participants to help promote the growth of exports through special zones as part of an industrial policy. Nevertheless, where they exist, such schemes may undermine rather than enhance the competitive nature of these economies' markets, and they can distort the extent and pattern of a country's international integration. Indeed, on net, the positive benefits to the domestic economy from the establishment of export processing zones in the Region's countries are of dubious size. Existing schemes should either be phased out in accordance with a time-bound schedule or generalized to *all* sectors of the economy and to firms of *all* ownership forms.

Related to the issue of industrial policy is the way in which many of the Region's governments conduct their public procurement with, and grant contracts to, the "outside" business world. Adherence to WTO-based rules regarding government procurement—which provide for open competition, transparent procedures, and nondiscriminatory treatment to domestic and foreign firms alike—can be an important reform in minimizing existing distortions in trade in the Region and realizing the domestic benefits that can come from international integration.

Throughout much of the Region there is a lack of, or very weak, security in property rights. Businesses—not only domestic but also foreign—have resorted to extralegal methods to get around this obstacle, but in so doing lose efficiency in the transaction process and ultimately divert resources from more productive activities. While some progress has been made in some of the Region's countries regarding the establishment of relatively effective, market-based legal institutions that protect property rights and facilitate resolution of commercial disputes, in many countries these are major unfinished reform agenda items and the "Achilles heel" of the transition. Efficient settlement of commercial disputes is generally limited by lengthy procedures, lack of qualified and independent judges, and poor enforcement mechanisms. In addition, effective alternative out-of-court administrative channels for dispute resolution—such as the use of arbitration—do not effectively exist in many of the countries. Policies that provide for the simplification and cost reduction of formal legal procedures, as well as the establishment of out-of-court mechanisms for dispute resolution, will strengthen contract sanctity and improve the level of confidence that traders have in the business environment of the Region.

Finally, improving the quality of institutions to strengthen governance and reduce incentives for corruption is a critical component of the domestic reforms needed to deepen the international integration of the Region's countries. This will require greater transparency and accountability of public officials' conduct, a reorientation of the public sector incentive framework—for example, through civil service and public administration reform—and establishment of a stronger system of checks and balances.

Annex: BEEPS Dataset

The EBRD-World Bank BEEPS instrument was developed to study the environment in which businesses in 26 countries of Eastern Europe and the Former Soviet Union operate. Close to 6,700 firms from the Region took part in the survey in 2002. The firms operate in industrial sectors such as mining and quarrying, construction, and manufacturing or are active in services such as transportation, storage, communications, wholesale trade, retail trade, repairs, real estate, renting, business services, hotels, restaurants, or other. With regard to firm size, the survey instrument was designed so that there is an intended overrepresentation of smaller firms in all 26 countries. With regard to vintage and ownership, the respondents were chosen to match sample quotas, so that state-owned firms, privatized firms, and newly established firms are interviewed in each country. For a complete description of the BEEPS dataset and survey methodology, see http://info.worldbank.org/governance/beeps2002.

A major caveat of the survey is that the sample of firms interviewed across the 26 countries is not representative of each national economy. Instead, the samples are stratified to cover firms with different characteristics within a country. This allows us to make comparisons among different firm characteristics. Annex table 4.1 summarizes the sample structure of the survey.

ANNEX TABLE 4.1
BEEPS2 Sample Structure

BEEPS2 sample	Number of firms
Industry	
Mining and quarrying	78
Construction	808
Manufacturing	1,685
Services	
Transport, storage, communications	524
Wholesale, retail, repairs	2,027
Real estate and business service	675
Hotels and restaurants	457
Other services	413
Size (number of employees)	
Small (2–49)	4,499
Medium (50–249)	1,248
Large (250–9,999)	920
Ownership	
State-owned	998
Privatized SOE	1,074
De novo	4,174
Foreign	365
Other	56
Vintage	
Oldest	1,800
Youngest	1,999
Average age	1,987

Endnotes

1. The study on Southeastern Europe is Broadman et al. (2004). Among other studies on the importance of competition and governance in the Region's transition, see World Bank (2002e).

2. We use extensively (i) official data from the countries in the Region; (ii) data from the 2002 EBRD-World Bank BEEPS; and (iii) the findings from numerous recently completed case studies of individual businesses located in selected countries in the Region.

3. Enhancing flexibility in factor markets to increase mobility of labor and capital is also a critical ingredient to ensuring that liberalization of trade improves the prospects for growth and reduction of poverty. This issue was taken up in chapter 4.

4. The relevant literature is large. The seminal pieces are, among others, Vernon (1966), Horst (1972 and 1974), and Caves (1996).

5. These statistical findings are generally robust regardless of model specification. The FDI variable can also be interpreted as a measure of the quality of the governance environment for business investment.

6. The literature is large. See, among others, Caves (1996) and Dunning (1993). For an application to Russia, see Broadman and Recanatini (forthcoming).

7. While covering firms in the mining sector, the BEEPS survey does not cover firms in the petroleum sector. This is important in interpreting the results regarding Kazakhstan. See the annex to this chapter.

8. Evidence for the less developed countries in Tybout (1997, 2000).

9. Similar evidence exists with regard to import performance and FDI inflows, which we do not report here.

10. See Caves (1996) and Dunning (1993).

11. See, for example, Broadman et al. (2004), which focuses on barriers to entry in SEE.

12. See Kornai et al. (2003).

13. See World Bank (2002e).

14. See Vernon (1966), Horst (1972 and 1974), and Caves (1996).

15. The BEEPS survey asks all firms a hypothetical question about the effects on their business decisions of a 10 percent increase in the market price of their principal product, which we use as a proxy for measuring price sensitivity.

16. See, in the case of Russia, Broadman et al. (2002). For other transition countries, see Kornai et al. (2003).

17. Based on the BEEPS2 data.

18. For case studies of firms in SEE, see Broadman et al. (2004).

19. See La Porta et al. (2000), Ramasastry (2000), and Schwartz (1998).

20. For evidence on Russia, see Hendley and Murrell (2002); for evidence in SEE, see Broadman et al. (2004).

21. There is a growing literature on this point. Jansen and Nordas (2004), for example, find a statistically significant positive association between government effectiveness, and quality of institutions and trade openness.

22. A typical regression result obtained was CPI = −3.076 + .014 Trade Openness + .565 GDP per Capita PPP, with the estimated coefficients on the

two explanatory variables statistically significant at the 95% level and an R2 = 0.63.

23. See, among others, Scherer and Ross (1990).

24. To be complete, the model necessarily also includes the possible *domestic* ownership categories of firms. See the notes to table 4.5.

25. There is a strong bivariate correlation between vertical and horizontal integration in the dataset. This suggests that multicolinearity is present, which can diminish any independent effects that vertical and horizontal integration may have on firm performance.

26. We use price sensitivity as a proxy for entry barriers: as suggested earlier, price-sensitive firms operate in a more competitive environment, where new rivals face de facto lower barriers to entry. To depict barriers to exit, we utilize measures of arrears and subsidies as proxies for softness of budget constraints faced by firms in the sample. Consistent with the literature, technological prowess and product differentiation are also included to measure firms' competitive advantage in keeping rivals in check.

27. See, for example, Kwoka and White (2003).

28. For analysis of Uzbekistan's competition policy framework, see Broadman (2000).

29. For more, see, for example, Madani (1999) and Jayanthakumaran (2003).

30. For a detailed policy reform agenda, see Anderson et al. (2005).

CHAPTER 5

Trade Facilitation: Challenges and Opportunities in Eastern Europe and the Former Soviet Union

Introduction

The traditional definition of "trade facilitation" centered on ways to achieve lower international transport costs. In modern commerce, however, a broader definition is required. In addition to lowered transport costs, facilitating trade today also involves improved efficiency in logistics at ports and customs through greater transparency; through ensuring that operational decisions are rules-based (rather than discretionary); and through the use of advances in technology (including, but not limited to, information technology), among other things. In addition, modern trade facilitation also includes streamlined regulatory environments, deeper harmonization of standards, and conformance to international norms so that overall transactions costs are lowered (Wilson, Luo, and Broadman 2004; Wilson, Mann, and Otsuki 2004).

Security protocols are also at the forefront of today's policy discussions on trade facilitation, given the growing international security focus in the post–September 11 era. Trade-facilitation rules, especially those applied to transport and border clearance regulations, are also being negotiated at the WTO, as part of the Doha Development Agenda. It is in this broad context that trade facilitation in the countries of the Region should be viewed.

While *transport* costs remain a core element driving trade logistics costs, there are also broader, interrelated elements that must be considered in strategic reform and development-assistance initiatives for trade facilitation for the Region. Indeed, reducing the behind-the-border barriers associated with achieving the goal of lowering overall *transactions* costs through domestic reforms is increasingly at the center of the Region's policy deliberations on trade facilitation. Thus, many of the Region's countries are faced with the wider challenge of facilitating trade through moving goods through ports more efficiently, streamlining the movement of documentation, enhancing the professionalism of customs officials, harmonizing product and technical standards with international or regional regulations, and strengthening the integration of new technologies into the transport and communications infrastructure.

Meeting this set of challenges systematically places enormous importance on the need for well-designed capacity-building initiatives and informed choices on priorities. Accordingly, as countries in the Region and in the international donor community decide on how to best deploy resources, a critical policy question arises: what are the impacts of various improvements in trade facilitation on trade flows and, in turn, on economic development? This drives the need for empirical analysis of the linkages between reforms in trade facilitation and greater trade flows and international integration. To this end, this chapter assesses the constraints in modern trade logistics and facilitation in the Region and presents empirical estimates of how strengthening capacity in these areas could enhance the Region's international trade flows.

The next section describes in detail the heterogeneous conditions of the Region's trade-facilitation infrastructure and institutions, highlighting four dimensions—customs, ports and transport, technical standards and regulation, and information technology. The assessment is organized around five country groupings of the Region—the EU-8, Southeastern Europe, Central Asia, the Caucasus, and Russia and the remaining CIS members—Belarus, Moldova, and Ukraine. The section concludes by summarizing how each country grouping is impacted by weak capacity in each of the dimensions of trade facilitation examined, indicating the particular challenges to reform.

This assessment sets the stage for the empirical analysis presented in the subsequent section. The analysis estimates—through a simulation exercise—the gains to trade that could come about if particular improvements were made in the four dimensions of trade-facilitation infrastructure and institutions, providing a means for assessing where the largest payoffs among various reforms are likely to be found. It also compares how such gains in the Region stack up against gains that would be realized elsewhere in the world if similar improvements were made.

The chapter concludes with recommendations for reform by policy makers.

A number of central themes are reflected throughout the chapter. In particular, the analysis suggests that understanding the prospects for improving trade facilitation in the Region requires a reorientation of perspectives that more fully considers the specifics of widely differing country and sub-Regional characteristics. In addition, the evidence suggests that trade facilitation and modern commerce driving economic integration at the sub-Regional level should indeed be viewed in a broader context than has been the case in the past. Initiatives to lower transactions costs through improved transportation systems and deregulation of transport remain critical. However, policy reform and infrastructure upgrades in standards, ports, customs, and information technology must also be included. Taken together, the analysis suggests that a more comprehensive approach for capacity building in trade facilitation than has been used to date will be needed.

Trade-Facilitation Conditions across the Region

The variation in current economic conditions and poverty levels across the Region's countries—along with different benchmarks of performance and readiness for reform in trade-related areas—most certainly constitutes the major factors affecting the current conditions of, and priorities for reform of, trade facilitation. While sub-Regional cooperation is one important element of economic integration and trade competitiveness, the Region is shaped by different economic, geographical, and political factors. The result is that each country in the Region has different levels of capacity in trade facilitation. While some countries, especially those in the EU-8, are moving toward genuine global integration, others, such as the countries in SEE and the Caucasus, still confront long-lasting conflicts and political tensions that clearly hinder trade and economic integration. The landlocked Central Asian countries, in contrast, are affected in a significant manner by the continued constraints of geography and a lack of harmonized border and customs clearance regimes. Thus, in analyzing how important trade-facilitation barriers are to the Region's economic prospects, it is important to capture their variation at the sub-Regional level. In assessing these barriers across the sub-Regions, we concentrate on four factors:

- Customs and border crossings

- Key challenges for the port and transport sector

- Challenges related to standards, technical barriers, and regulatory policy

- Development of information technology infrastructure.

Central Asia

Geography constitutes a major obstacle to the trade and export competitiveness of Central Asia. The Karakum Desert alone, for example, occupies about 70 percent of the land area of Turkmenistan. Moreover, most of the land in western Kazakhstan and Uzbekistan is also covered with deserts. This feature clearly makes the development of transport networks in these countries difficult. In addition, most of the sub-Region's border areas are extremely mountainous. The Tian Shan Mountain, with a peak of 7,439 meters, is part of the border between Kazakhstan and the Kyrgyz Republic. There are a limited number of transport corridors, which drives up the cost of transporting goods to export markets. All of the Central Asian countries are landlocked and far from seaports that would connect their economies to major global markets. The shortest route to the sea from much of Central Asia is the Afghanistan route to Karachi, via Quetta (World Bank 2004n). Table 5.1 shows the distance to seaports by roads in Central Asia.

Long distances to export markets and transit routes translate into high trade transactions costs in Central Asia (see figure 5.1 for a sam-

TABLE 5.1

Central Asian Republics: Sea Access by Road
Kilometers

Route	From Bandar Abbas Turkmenistan*	Afghanistan			Quetta	To Karachi Afghanistan Peshawar
		I[a]	II[b]	III[c]		
Almaty	3,600	4,610	4,020	3,810	3,380	4,010
Tashkent	2,730	3,730	3,175	2,930	2,720	3,345
Dushanbe	2,940	3,370	2,790	2,680	2,040	2,660
Bishkek	3,270	4,330	3,750	3,530	3,100	3,730

Source: World Bank 2004n.

Note: a. Route I via Kabul, Kandahar, Herat.
b. Route II via Kabul, Kandahar, Delaram, Zaranj.
c. Route III via Meymaneh, Herat, Delaram, Zaranj.

ple of land transit costs in Central Asia). Landlocked countries are highly dependent upon the state of transport infrastructure and border clearance regulations in transit neighbors. Political relations with transit neighbors are also critical to facilitate the movement of goods. The most striking example of obstacles to trade in the region is Uzbekistan. This is a double-landlocked country: it shares a border with Afghanistan, where infrastructure is extremely poor. It also faces political tension with neighbors in Kazakhstan, the Kyrgyz Republic, Tajikistan, and Turkmenistan (Faye et al. 2004). A lack of safe access to transit routes and poorly developed infrastructure significantly constrain trade activities.

Historical factors also help to explain the low levels of trade and transport facilitation in Central Asia. For example, the collapse of the Former Soviet Union (FSU) continues to affect security in border regions. When the former republics became independent, their national borders were not based on ethnic or political groups, but rather on administrative boundaries. Regulations were not harmonized, and nontariff barriers were raised across the region. This has resulted in a number of border disputes. Moreover, the former republics protect border areas with landmines and physical barricades. This imposes high risks on traders crossing borders and discourages trade. Furthermore, under the Soviet regime, the purpose of the railway networks was to link the former republics to Russia, which lies north of the region. Railway networks in Central Asia are, therefore, extended in a north-south direction that leaves links among the Central Asian countries and other neighbors, including

FIGURE 5.1
Land Transit Costs in Central Asia
$/TEU

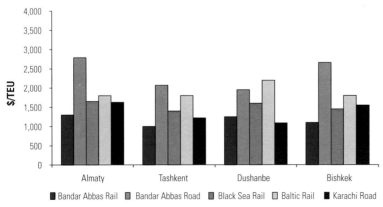

Source: World Bank 2004n.

Note: TEU = twenty feet equivalent unit.

Afghanistan, China, and Iran, largely underdeveloped. The legacy of the USSR, among other factors, has clearly contributed to Central Asia's lagging behind other subregions in accelerating trade and economic progress.

Central Asian customs and border crossings. New border and customs-clearance regimes were established in Central Asia after independence. Efforts have been made to improve customs administration in the region. The Transport Corridor Europe-Caucasus-Asia (TRACECA) project is focused on harmonization of border-crossing procedures and documents. New customs standards are being developed based on the Russian model and using international best practices, such as conformity with the Revised Kyoto Convention, compliance with WTO standards, and elements of risk management. The introduction of new standards has largely been completed in Kazakhstan, Turkmenistan, and Uzbekistan, and is in progress in the Kyrgyz Republic and Tajikistan (World Bank 2004o). Customs clearance in Central Asia is less efficient, however, than the Southeast European average, for example. While the SEE average is one-to-three hours to clear goods at inland terminals, it is estimated to take one day in Kazakhstan, three-to-four hours in the Kyrgyz Republic, and three hours in Tajikistan (see table 5.2).

Delays in customs clearance are mainly the result of the following problems:

TABLE 5.2

Time Taken to Clear Goods at Selected Inland Terminals

	Official estimated average	Indicator	Remarks	Southeastern Europe benchmark
Kazakhstan	1 day	85 percent cleared in under 1 day	Traders estimate 48 hours.	Average: 2 hours (maximum 3 hours, minimum 1 hour), based on total time for release
Uzbekistan	2–3 hours, can be as short as 20–30 minutes		Traders estimate between 24 and 48 hours, up to 1 week.	
Kyrgyz Republic	3–4 hours		Traders estimate between 4 and 5 days.	
Tajikistan	3 hours	Maximum 10 days	A legal provision limits clearance to less than 10 days. Traders estimate 2 hours for diplomatic consignments, and 1 day on average for normal shipments.	
Turkmenistan	n.a.		Traders estimate 1–2 hours for diplomatic consignments, and 1 day on average for normal shipments (depending on completeness of the documentation).	

Source: World Bank 2004o.

Note: n.a. = not available.

- Uncertainty remains about implementation of new customs codes and standards for measuring the value of imported goods.

- Customs clearance processes require an excessive number of documents (in Tajikistan, for example, customs procedures require up to 18 accompanying documents, forms, certificates, and applications, issued by different agencies [World Bank 2004o]).

- Border posts are often too far to be convenient for traders.

- There is lack of cooperation among border agencies, including customs, border policy, road traffic policy, and transport inspectorate agencies.

- There is a lack of capacity to fully utilize information technology in customs administration.

Key challenges for Central Asia's transport sector. Rail is the most dominant mode of transport in the sub-Region, accounting for more than 75 percent of all freight and a high percentage of intercity passenger transport (ADB 2004). The railway network in place in the FSU is relatively well developed (see table 5.3). Compared with road transport, moving goods—particularly products in bulk cargoes—via railway networks is more efficient. These goods include metals, coal, cotton, grain, oil, and oil products. Among the five Central Asian countries, Kazakhstan has the highest labor productivity per traffic unit.

The road sector provides a more extensive network than that provided by railways. The majority of roads in Central Asia are paved. Figure 5.2 shows that the percentage of paved roads in Central Asia is

TABLE 5.3
Central Asia Railways, 2002

Railways	Total route length (km)	Double-tracked (km)	Electrified (km)	Freight net ton-km (millions)	Total pass-km (millions)	No. of staff	Labor productivity traffic units (tkm+pkm/staff)
Kazakhstan	13,600	—	5,800	133,088	10,449	113,688	1,263
Kyrgyz Rep.	428	108	—	395	43	4,960	88
Tajikistan	547	—	—	1,085	41	6,013	187
Turkmenistan	2,554	34.5	—	7,476	1,127	15,932	540
Uzbekistan	3,645	—	609	18,428	2,018	41,913	488
Total	20,774			160,472	13,678	182,506	954

Source: World Bank 2004o, based on UN Economic Commission for Europe 2002.

Note: Turkmenistan data are for 2003.

FIGURE 5.2

Paved Roads

Percentage of total roads, 1999

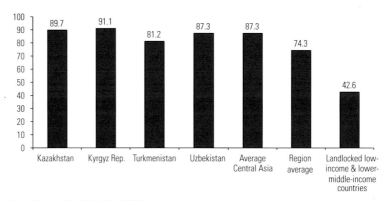

Source: Calculated from World Bank 2005i.

higher than the Region's average and higher than the average for the countries with the same income level.[1] The World Bank (2004o) reports that the current road network is largely sufficient to meet the needs of users.

Over the past decade, efforts to expand both road and rail networks in this sub-Region have met with demonstrated success and have had subsequent impact on lowering transactions costs for firms. For instance, a railway link between Turkmenistan and Iran was opened in 1996. In April 1997, China, the Kyrgyz Republic, and Uzbekistan agreed to reconstruct railways and road links from Ardijan-Osh-Kashgar. China and the Kyrgyz Republic have also agreed to open the Irkashtan Pass. Moreover, in 2001, the first consignment of cargo from Turkmenistan to Afghanistan was sent by rail that links Turkmenabat and Atamyrat. The Asian Development Bank has initiated the Almaty-Bishek Regional Road Rehabilitation project with Kazakhstan and the Kyrgyz Republic. The road is at a cross-link between the corridors that connect the Far East with Europe and Fergana Valley with Russia, and the completed project is expected to be of significant benefit to the region (ADB 2001).

Despite recent progress, major challenges for Central Asia still include extending transport networks to neighboring countries. Most goods shipped by rail and road travel between Central Asia, Russia, and Belarus. Figure 5.3 shows that 35 percent of imports carried by rail and roads are from Central Asian Republics (CARs) and 46 percent are from Russia and Belarus. Figure 5.4 indicates that exports carried by rail and roads in 2002 were mostly directed to Russia-Belarus (62 percent), following the Central Asian Republics (11 percent). Moreover, despite the sub-Region's borders with China, the

FIGURE 5.3
Origin of Imports Carried by Rail and Roads, 2002

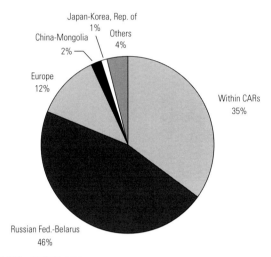

Sources: World Bank 2004o; TRACECA database.

share of foreign trade by rail and roads to rapidly expanding Chinese markets is extremely limited. This results in part from the fact that transport links to China are limited, particularly those involving rail. There is one rail corridor connecting the CARs with China, and all trade must pass through the Druzba-Ala Pass at the Kazakhstan-China border (ADB 2004). This highlights the need to invest in road and other transport infrastructure to extend east-west trade routes.

FIGURE 5.4
Destination of Exports Carried by Rail and Roads, 2002

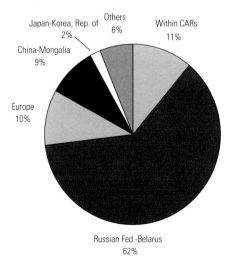

Sources: World Bank 2004o; TRACECA database.

There is a clear need to build new transport networks and upgrade roads and railways that link Central Asian countries to Russia. This is especially true given that Russia remains the top export partner for Central Asian countries (see chapter 2). The railway network has deteriorated, in part because of maintenance backlogs, an aging locomotive fleet consisting of units that lack many of the efficiencies of modern stock, and emerging shortages of freight wagons of various kinds. Furthermore, the road network in the region is poorly managed because of a limited maintenance budget. In addition, there is limited use of new technologies and new techniques—that could reduce costs—in road construction and maintenance.

With respect to transport services, the freight-forwarding business in Central Asia is not reliable, and transport regulations are not adequately developed to meet current business needs. Foreign traders do not trust the domestic freight-forwarding companies. This is true, in part, because domestic companies do not provide consignment-tracking services, among other reasons. Moreover, the technical standards for roads continue to be based on FSU specifications and therefore are not adequate for today's traffic volume. In Kazakhstan, problems with the legal and regulatory framework in the transport sector are either gaps or overlaps in regulations and inadequate allocation of responsibilities for enforcement (World Bank 2005h). Harmonization of existing regulations and rules in the region is an urgent agenda item. Harmonized rules with regard to axle-load, transit, and the introduction of IT, among others, would "considerably lower transport and transit cost and time" (UNESCO 2002). Private participation in infrastructure sectors, including ports, railways, and roads, is almost nonexistent in Central Asia, except for a small amount of private sector participation in the railway sector in Kazakhstan (EBRD 2004c).

The information technology infrastructure in Central Asia. Given that Central Asian countries are landlocked, the development of information technology infrastructure and expansion of e-commerce could help overcome geographic boundaries. Government regulation, among other factors, is clearly limiting expansion of Internet access. Figure 5.5 shows that private sector participation in fixed-line telephone service is almost nonexistent. Mobile telephone service has been privatized, yet it remains extremely costly, and access is limited because of the limited number of providers. In Turkmenistan, for example, there is only one mobile telephone service provider, and it has a poor mobile telephone network (U.K. Trade & Investment 2003). In Uzbekistan, Internet service providers are monitored and under strict government controls, which chills commercial activity. In addition,

FIGURE 5.5

Private Participation in the Telecommunications Sector, 2004

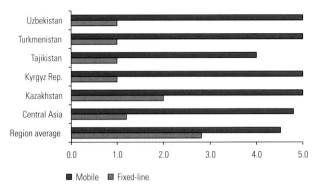

Source: EBRD 2004c.

Note: Scale: 1=no or negligible private sector participation; 5=sector fully privatized.
There are only small levels of activity in the mobile sector in Tajikistan and Turkmenistan.

unreliable infrastructure and high dial-up costs contribute to a low rate of Internet use in the country (EIU 2004).

Information infrastructure in Central Asia is in general not developed enough to support e-commerce. Figure 5.6 shows the numbers of telephone mainlines in each Central Asian country, in comparison with the overall Region and the countries with the same income level (for example, "L & LM," or low-income and lower-middle-income countries).[2] The number of telephone mainlines in Central Asia is greater than the average for the same income group. Compared with the average for the Region, however, the number is significantly lower. The number of Internet users in Central Asia is limited. Figure 5.7 shows that the number of Internet hosts is strikingly small. Phys-

FIGURE 5.6

Telephone Main Lines
Per 100 People, 2003

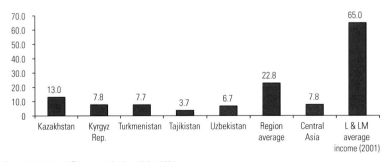

Source: International Telecommunications Union 2004.

Note: "L & LM" = low-income and lower-middle-income countries.

FIGURE 5.7
Internet Hosts
Per 10,000 People, 2003

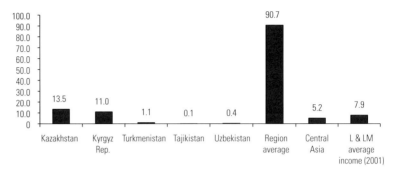

Source: International Telecommunications Union 2004.

Note: "L & LM" = low-income and lower-middle-income countries.

ical investment in information technology and communications infrastructure—along with the liberalizing of services—will be a crucial part of the overall objectives for trade facilitation and lowering transaction costs in the Region.[3]

The Caucasus

Customs and border crossings in the Caucasus. Continued conflict and tensions in the Caucasus are reflected in problems in customs regimes and clearance procedures in these countries. Because of the Nagorny-Karabakh conflict between Armenia and Azerbaijan, for example, there is no trade between these two countries, aside from informally traded energy, agriculture, and consumption goods. The border between Armenia and Turkey is officially closed because of the Turkish-Armenian conflict from the World War I period. These conflicts affect the confidence of shippers in using transport routes, and closed borders distort trade patterns by blocking the most efficient trading routes in the region. The Caucasus are more likely to trade with politically friendly neighbors, while they undertrade with hostile neighbors. In an effort to facilitate trade in the Caucasus, a peace settlement and a reopening of borders are priorities.

Recent analysis of the potential impact on trade costs of restoring borders and transport networks resulting from peace agreements in the Caucasus provides insight into the benefits that would derive from reform driven by regional cooperation and integration. For example, Polyakov (2001) finds that opening borders would result in significant savings in transport logistics costs. If peace agreements were concluded, transportation savings for Armenia would amount to $6.4 million–$8.4 million. For Azerbaijan, total savings would range between $0.7 million and 1.8 million. Georgia would have a total savings of $1.9 million, though it would lose transit revenues by $5.6 million–$7.4 million. Another study shows that if the Armenian-Turkish borders were opened, transport costs to ship one TEU ("twenty-foot equivalent unit," taken to mean a twenty-foot container) between Poti and Yereven would drop by 30–50 percent, or $450–$750 (World Bank 2000d). In sum, if conflicts were resolved and regional cooperation achieved, trade-facilitation measures would be a driving force for trade expansion in the Caucasus. This would also necessarily include reducing regulatory barriers, strengthening institutional frameworks, and improving infrastructure and transport networks.

Table 5.4 shows the basic productivity ratios of customs procedures in the Caucasus compared with those of Southeastern Europe. While the average number of declarations per staff in SEE is 250, it is 40–45 in the Caucasus. Compared with the SEE average, cost per declaration is twice as high in Georgia and Azerbaijan, and 1.8 times higher in Armenia. Among the Caucasus countries, Armenian customs lag behind those in Georgia and Azerbaijan in customs efficiency, especially in rail and road network.

The major problems common to all Caucasus countries include (1) a lack of regional harmonization of customs practices, (2) limited transparency in clearance regulations and procedures and problems with corruption, and (3) limited application of information technology in border clearance systems. Among these problems, corruption and the imposition of unofficial fees at the border are most frequently reported by the private sector as the most serious issues. For example, on the rail system from Armenia to Georgia, unofficial fees account for approximately 6–13 percent of the total cost of transport

TABLE 5.4

Customs Productivity in the Caucasus Compared with Southeastern Europe

	Armenia	Georgia	Azerbaijan	Southeastern Europe		
				Average	Minimum	Maximum
Revenue collected/customs staff ($)	188,047	94,650	113,019	308,668	85,597	745,548
Total customs cost/ revenue collected	1.1%	2.9%	2.3%	1.5%	1.2%	5.8%
Salaries/revenue collected	0.6%	1.2%	0.8%	0.9%	0.5%	2.6%
Trade volume/staff ($ millions)	1.2	0.78	2.4	2.8	1.1	7.2
Declarations/staff	40	45	44	250	80	422
Cost per declaration ($)	50	61	59	28	11	49
Average monthly staff cost ($)	81	91	73	362	194	757

Sources: National customs administrations and World Bank calculations cited in World Bank 2003f.

(Molnar and Ojala 2003). A typical container shipment by truck from Tbilisi to Rotterdam is subject to unofficial payment costs totaling 7–40 percent of the total logistics cost, with customs clearance being the most significant element.

In addition, information technology systems need to be adopted to raise the efficiency of customs administrations. In Georgia, the Automated System for Customs Data (ASYCUDA) has been used since June 1998, and now more than 60 percent of customs declarations are cleared through ASYCUDA. The system is available, however, only at the Lilo terminal. In Azerbaijan, there is no national computer network similar to ASYCUDA in operation. It is also reported that the country lacks sufficient computer facilities at border-crossing points. Armenia, however, has made progress relative to other countries in the region. ASYCUDA was deployed in 1996 and has been implemented at all border-crossing points in the country.

The Caucasus' port and transport infrastructure. Ports in the Caucasus provide the shortest routes between Europe and Central Asia. The major two Black Sea ports are Batumi and Poti in Georgia, and the two major Caspian Sea ports are Baku and Dyubendi in Azerbaijan. Traffic at the port of Poti has been growing rapidly. In the first six months of 2004, the port handled 39 more vessels than in the same period in 2003, and the total throughput increased by 42 percent (Port of Poti Web site). Links from Batumi and Poti are being developed with other Black Sea ports, including Ilyichevsk (Ukraine), Constanza (Romania), and Burgas and Varna (Bulgaria). Another important port is Baku in Azerbaijan, which handles ferry cargo, dry cargo, and oil. The ports are fully privatized in Armenia, while they are highly controlled by the government in Georgia and Azerbaijan.

Rail and road networks are also crucial in attaining the shortest route for moving goods across the Caucasus. This is especially important for Armenia, which is landlocked. The recent development of the new Silk Road and the Trans-Caucasian railway as a part of the TRACECA project will be important for the sub-Region. Once these projects are completed, a railway will link the ancient Silk Road from the Chinese port of Lianyungang on the Yellow Sea to the ports of Poti and Batumi—and then with Western Europe.

Despite the importance of inland transport, infrastructure systems in the entire Caucasus region require modernization. Most of the rail track and rolling stock in Azerbaijan are in need of repair or replacement. Rail and road links from Georgia to Armenia, which account for 70 percent of Armenian trade, are in poor condition as a result of major delays in maintenance. Despite financial support from the EU and other donors to rehabilitate infrastructure, because of limited funds and a lack of long-term budget planning, problems remain.

Another factor affecting the transport sector is the lack of harmonized and cost-effective transport regulations and duties. All Caucasus countries apply road transport quotas that, for example, limit the annual number of vehicles allowed to enter or pass through their territory. Armenia and Georgia impose high transit fees on foreign vehicles, while Azerbaijan does not. In October 2000, it cost the equivalent of $245 in local currency for a truck with a capacity of 10–20 tons to transit across Georgia, and the equivalent of $197 for a similar vehicle to transit across Azerbaijan (Polyakov 2001). With respect to railway tariffs, Georgia and Azerbaijan are under an agreement that allows a 50 percent tariff reduction for all goods traveling within member countries. Armenia, on the other hand, is not under this agreement. These differences in regulations reduce railway shipments across borders throughout the Caucasus region.

Development of information technology infrastructure in the Caucasus. Once borders are reopened and transport networks are restored, information technology would allow the Caucasus to expand markets in a significant way. This does not imply a compelling need in the short run for advanced information technology, but rather for basic infrastructure upgrades in telecommunications via expanded landline telephones. The number of telephone lines in the Caucasus is below the Region's average, as are the number of Internet hosts (see figures 5.8 and 5.9). The extent of private ownership in telecommunications services varies widely in the Caucasus. Armenia has fully privatized fixed-line and mobile telephone services. In Georgia and Azerbaijan, the governments have strong control over fixed-line telephone service.

The EU-8

From the first day of their membership in the EU—May 1, 2004—the EU-8 countries have been required to apply the common EU legal framework, the *acquis communitaire;* this includes, of course, the chapters concerning customs administration, port and transport policy, standards and technical regulations, and IT policy. As far back as 1998, the then-existing EU members initiated a program of policy advice, technical assistance, and investment in the EU-8 countries so as to facilitate prospective entry into the Union.

Customs and border crossings in the EU-8. In fulfilling the customs reform requirements of the *acquis,* the EU-8 countries' administration of cus-

FIGURE 5.8

Telephone Lines in the Caucasus

Per 100 People, 2003

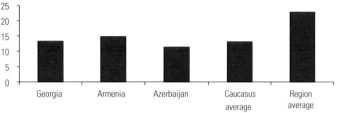

Source: Calculated from International Telecommunications Union 2004.

FIGURE 5.9

Internet Hosts in the Caucasus

Per 10,000 People, 2003

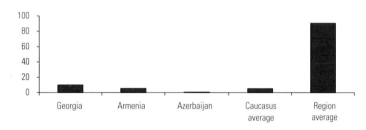

Source: Calculated from International Telecommunications Union 2004.

toms has been greatly simplified. Much of customs clearance work has "disappeared" in intra-EU trade (World Bank 2004o). Furthermore, the adoption of new information technology systems has increased efficiency in customs procedures. For example, Estonia, Latvia, Lithuania, and the Slovak Republic have adopted ASYCUDA.

However, although customs procedures in intra-EU trade have improved, problems remain at the EU's "new" external borders. The enlargement of the EU means that the EU-8 countries are now responsible for part of the external EU borders with Russia and Belarus. At the Russian border, there are administrative problems with goods inspections and border crossings, leading to excessive delays at the border-crossing points. At the border-crossing points between Belarus and Lithuania (at Medininku and Salcininku), corruption is a major, well-documented problem. Unofficial payments of up to $500 per transit are required, and shipments are sometimes stopped and even confiscated for undisclosed reasons (World Bank 2005g). Although the routes via border-crossing points through Belarus are the shortest for Lithuanian exports to Russia, the unofficial payments demanded discourage traders from using these routes.

The EU-8's port and transport infrastructure. The EU-8 have clearly improved their port management and efficiency over the past two decades. According to a Trade and Transport Facilitation Audit, ports in the Baltic states are generally considered to be very profitable. Ports operate 24 hours a day, 7 days a week, and docking and dwell times at ports do not normally hinder trade (World Bank 2005g). A number of ports in the EU-8 countries have improved service quality, as well. The Port of Koper is the only international cargo port in Slovenia; it provides the shortest link for traders to the Mediterranean, and via the Suez Canal, to the Middle and the Far East. The port has attained ISO 9001 certification.[4] Another example of reform is the Klaipeda Port in Lithuania. The port has become more competitive, with longer breakwaters, dredged and widened port waters, and an entrance channel that have allowed the port to accept larger vessels. This has increased the turnover of cargo handled and the number of new jobs.

Nevertheless, there remains a need to expand the adoption of information technology in EU-8 port management to build on progress achieved. In Estonia, for example, many port users complain that port authorities have not taken IT system development seriously enough (World Bank 2004o). Latvia's largest cargo port at Tiga is behind in adopting Electronic Data Interchange (EDI). Shippers and agents consider the use of EDI to be a top priority in port development.

Continued progress toward privatization of port operations is an important component of ongoing reform in the EU-8.[5] As figure 5.10 illustrates, private participation in ports and airports remains limited in many of these countries. Even in cases where there has been private participation in port management, the presence of domestic companies in management and service provision remains limited. In the Baltics, for example, even though transit of oil and oil products constitutes a significant portion of the business in ports, virtually none of this trade is carried by Baltic shipping companies (World Bank 2005g).

As in the case of ports, much remains in achieving liberalization of the transport sector. With respect to rail transport, privatization programs are under way in the Czech Republic, Hungary, Latvia, and Poland. Estonia has fully privatized its railway service (see figure 5.11). The EU-8 countries as a group, however, still lag behind the EU average. The Rail Liberalization Index 2004 classifies EU countries into three groups by the degree of market liberalization in the rail sector: (1) on schedule, (2) delayed, and (3) pending departure (see figure 5.12). None of the EU-8 countries are classified as "on schedule." The Czech Republic, Hungary, Latvia, Poland, the Slovak Republic,

FIGURE 5.10
Private Participation in Ports and Airports Sector, 2004

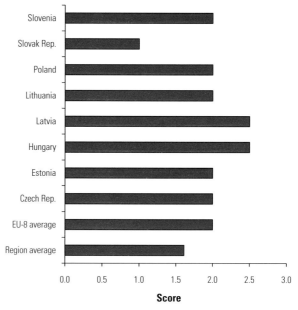

Source: EBRD 2004c.

Note: Scale: 1=no or negligible private sector participation; 5=sector fully privatized.

and Slovenia are classified as "delayed." The index categorizes Estonia and Lithuania as "pending departure." In these countries, the liberalization process, from an overall perspective, is practically nonexistent (IBM Business Consulting Services 2004).

EU-8 standards and technical regulations. Eliminating technical barriers to trade (TBT) is the key to further integrating the EU-8 into the EU market, where tariffs and nontariff barriers have already been substantially removed. Firms perceive that technical regulations are more important in exporting to the EU than in exporting to other industrial countries, including the United States, Canada, and Japan (see figure 5.13). For the purpose of harmonizing technical standards, the EU has developed a new approach that streamlines technical harmonization and the development of standards for certain product groups.[6] Where technical standards are not harmonized, the EU applies a mutual recognition principle. This provides for free movement of goods and services without the need to harmonize member countries' national legislation, by allowing goods that are lawfully produced in one member country to be sold in any other member countries where technical or quality specifications may be different from those of the exporting country. Most of the EU-8 countries have aligned their

FIGURE 5.11
Private Participation in Transport Sector, 2004

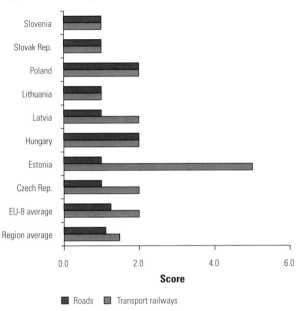

Score

■ Roads   ■ Transport railways

Source: EBRD 2004c.

Note: Scale: 1=no or negligible private sector participation; 5=sector fully privatized.

FIGURE 5.12
Rail Liberalization Index, 2004

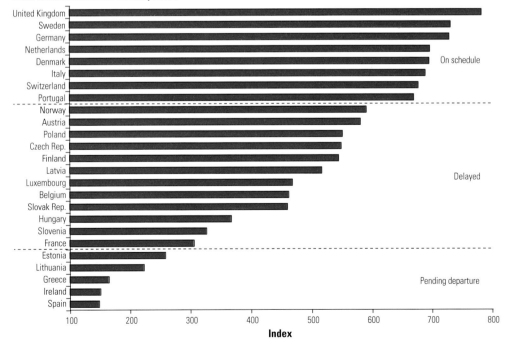

Index

Source: IBM Business Consulting Services 2004.

Note: Scale: 100 = little rail liberalization; 800 = much rail liberalization.

FIGURE 5.13

Importance of Technical Regulations in Exporting to the EU, the United States, Canada, and Japan

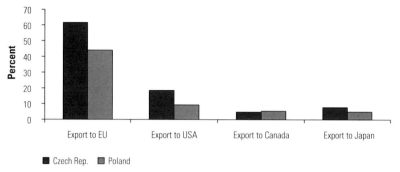

Source: Calculations based on the World Bank's Technical Barriers to Trade database.

national legislation with the *acquis*.[7] While this facilitates the access of the EU-8 products to the EU single market, it is important to note that the EU standards may differ from those of other countries. For instance, the EU standards are different from the U.S. standards. Firms in the EU-8 still have to pay costs arising from TBT that exist between the EU and the United States.

Development of information technology infrastructure in the EU-8. All of the EU-8 countries have more highly developed telecommunications infrastructures than the average for the Region (see figures 5.14 and 5.15). This is partly the result of the numerous investments from the EU community and other donor agencies. For instance, the Slovak Republic increased its number of installed telephone lines from 935,000 in 1992 to more than 2,070,000 in June 2000, and the number of working lines from 821,000 in 1992 to more than 1,730,000 as of June 2000. Figure 5.16 shows that Slovenia and the Czech Republic lag behind in liberalizing telecommunications service while other countries have fully privatized it.

Southeastern Europe

Longstanding and continued ethnic conflicts have severely affected trade and investment prospects in SEE (see Broadman et al. 2004). Over the course of the transition, the breakup of the Former Republic of Yugoslavia and war in Kosovo have contributed to significant destruction of trade-related infrastructure, which has critically affected trade flows within the sub-Region. Damaged transport routes also contributed to a rapid decline in the use of transit routes across SEE. Before the war, traders between Turkey and Europe used road

FIGURE 5.14

Telephone Lines in the EU-8

Per 100 people, 2003

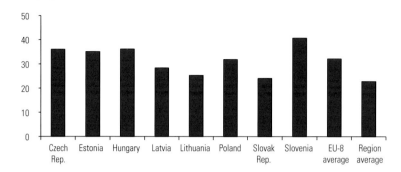

Source: Calculated from International Telecommunications Union 2004.

FIGURE 5.15

Internet Hosts in the EU-8

Per 10,000 people, 2003

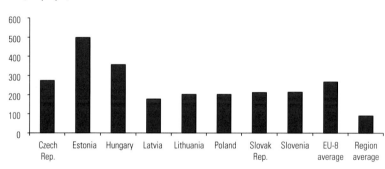

Source: Calculated from International Telecommunications Union 2004.

transport through the former Yugoslavia. More recently, an estimated 30 percent of Turkish trucks completely bypass the sub-Region, using Ro-Ro ferries between Turkey and Italy (World Bank 2002c).

The role of international donors' investment and capacity-building programs has been crucial in reconstructing SEE (see box 5.1). The EU development programs and assistance have been dominant, because the EU is the major trading partner for most of SEE and long-term plans for EU accession by the countries continue.[8] The EU's Phare Program provides preaccession support in areas including transport infrastructure; the EU's Stabilization Association Agreements help reduce the complexity of logistics systems and improve transparency in customs; and through the Stability Pact, the EU, along with other donors, has set in place a political-economic framework that seeks to enhance democracy, peace, and prosperity in the sub-

FIGURE 5.16
Private Sector Participation in the Telecommunications Sector

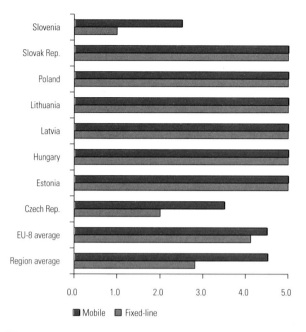

Source: EBRD 2004c.

Note: Scale: 1=no or negligible private sector participation; 5=sector fully privatized.

Region. SEE countries are also major beneficiaries of the World Bank's Trade and Transport Facilitation in Southeast Europe (TTSFE) program.[9] Since 2001, the TTFSE has been working on institutional development of customs and implementation of IT systems by providing computer equipment and telecommunications infrastructure.

SEE customs and border crossings. Conflict has been a major factor driving inefficient and nontransparent customs regimes in SEE. Croatia, for example, now has international borders with four countries, compared with just one before the war. The problem is that customs systems were "temporarily" designed after independence and still remain underdeveloped. There are 420 roads connecting Bosnia and Herzegovina with neighboring countries. There were only 32 official border-crossing points, however, at the beginning of 2001. There are many unofficial border crossings with no rules governing trade transactions. Customs procedures are complicated and differ among countries. Given the tension that exists at the borders, regional border cooperation is far below what is needed to facilitate trade. Nonetheless, reforms in customs have been proceeding. In some SEE countries, the results have been substantial (see table 5.5).

BOX 5.1

Examples of Development Assistance in Trade Facilitation in the Region

In 1991, the EU launched the TACIS program, which provides technical assistance in trade and transport to 12 of the Region's countries, including the Southern Caucasus; it also enhances cross-border cooperation among the countries involved. Since 1993, the EU also has funded the Transport Corridor Europe-Caucasus Asia (TRACECA) program, which delivers technical assistance for development of a transport corridor on a west-east axis from Europe, across the Black Sea, through the Caucasus and the Caspian Sea, to Central Asia.

The importance of trade-facilitation reform in the Region over the past decade, in both unilateral action to remove barriers and efforts at sub-Regional cooperation, is demonstrated by increased focus on cooperative programs. For example, the Trade and Transport Facilitation in Southeast Europe (TTFSE) program is led by the World Bank and the United States, with collaboration of the EU and eight national governments: Albania, Bosnia and Herzegovina, Bulgaria, Croatia, FYR Macedonia, Moldova, Romania, and Serbia and Montenegro. The TTFSE aims at reducing nontariff costs to trade and transport, eliminating smuggling and corruption at border crossings, and improving customs administrations and other border-control agencies. To achieve these goals, the project's components include customs services procedures reform, support to integrated customs information systems, and improvement of roads and border-crossing facilities. The estimated total program cost is $101.9 million.

An important example of reform and modernization anchored in a cross-regional platform is the Silk Road Rehabilitation project. On October 26–18, 2004, the Third Silk Road Conference was held in Xi'An, where representatives from Azerbaijan, China, Georgia, Iran, Korea, the Kyrgyz Republic, Pakistan, Tajikistan, Turkey, Turkmenistan, and Uzbekistan agreed to: commit to further regional cooperation, increase investment in transport infrastructure, improve cross-border conditions along the routes, establish international transport regulations for the region, and exploit ways to seek financial assistance from international organizations. If strong regional commitment is realized, the project is expected to be completed in 2014; this will not only extend the trade route to eastern China through Central Asian and European countries to the Atlantic Ocean but it will also modernize the ancient trading route.

Sources: TRACECA Web site at http://www.traceca-org.org/, TTFSE Web site at http://www.seerecon.org/ttfse/, and World Bank 2004g.

There are a number of obstacles to continued reform of customs and border-crossing rules, including (1) corruption; (2) a lack of regional coordination and cooperation in customs; (3) border delays; (4) outdated customs and border facilities; (5) a lack of cooperation among agencies in border clearance, including agencies with mandates for imposing technical standards and regulations on imports; (6)

TABLE 5.5

Reduction of Waiting Time at the Borders' Crossing Points and Inland Clearance Terminals

	Pilot site	WT 2001	WT 2002	Reduction (%)	Final target
Albania	Tirana	4.5 hours	1.7 hours	62	1 hour
Bulgaria	Plovdiv	3.7 hours	1.5 hours	60	< 1 hour
Croatia	Jankomir	5.3 hours	3.0 hours	43	< 1 hour
Croatia	Stara Gradiska	3.3 hours	0.4 hour	88	< 1 hour
Romania	Bacau	3.0 hours	1.4 hours	53	1 hour
Romania	Constanta	4.3 hours	3.0 hours	31	2 hours

Source: Trade and Transport Facilitation in Southeast Europe (TTFSE) program.

Note: "WT" stands for waiting time.

the need to upgrade technology applied in customs; (7) variations in interpreting legislation and procedures; and (8) the overall complexity of procedures.

Not all of these problems are universally evident in every country: some are more pronounced than others. For example, sizable nontariff barriers to trade and transport are evident in Bosnia and Herzegovina. Large-scale inefficiencies in customs administration and border-clearance systems (opening hours and organization) remain in Croatia. The lack of effective interactions with the government is a problem in Albania, Croatia, and FYR Macedonia. There is a need to clarify the responsibilities between the customs and border police in FYR Macedonia and Albania. Even in the more advanced SEE countries, there remain significant barriers to effective customs administration. For example, the EU accession and candidate countries—Bulgaria and Romania, and Croatia, respectively—have introduced the EU's Community Customs codes. Still, these countries face the challenges of bringing customs legislation and administrative structure into alignment with EU standards, modernizing customs procedures with IT systems, and eliminating corruption.[10] Tables 5.6 and 5.7 depict the challenges that remain in select SEE countries in reforming customs so as to reduce corruption.

The transport sector in SEE. Several major challenges remain in reforming the transport sector in SEE. Better maintenance and improvements in the quality of the transport infrastructure are required, as is the need to upgrade destroyed or damaged transport infrastructure. The levels of investment in new transport infrastructure need to be substantially increased. Reform of the regulatory regime governing pricing and access to transport services is also a priority. Reducing overregulation is especially important for the EU accession and candidate countries. After accession to the EU, their transport sectors will

TABLE 5.6
Recipients of Bribes
As a percentage of all surveyed trucks crossing borders, 2003

	Customs service staff (%)	Ministry of Interior staff (%)	Staff of other agencies (%)
Albania	100	74	39
Croatia	76	41	29
Macedonia. FYR	78	27	14
Romania	90	53	41
Serbia and Montenegro	71	33	21

Source: PlanConsult, Interim Report III, cited in TTFSE Progress Report 2003.

Note: These data are not confined to TTFSE pilot sites.

TABLE 5.7
Average Amount of Bribes
Per truck at one border crossing (EURO)

	2001	2002	2003
Albania	386.9	324.4	160.3
Bosnia and Herzegovina	52.8	53.4	n.a
Croatia	102.3	112.4	146.6
Macedonia, FYR	42.8	43.6	77.0
Romania	27.1	23.7	44.4
Serbia and Montenegro	110.8	120.8	153.6

Source: Plan Consult, Interim Report III, cited in TTFSE Progress Report 2003.

Note: These data are not confined to TTFSE pilot sites.

be exposed to a significantly higher level of competition, and efficiency will thus need to increase.

SEE's challenges related to standardization. Implementation of EU-harmonized technical standards has become increasingly important in SEE—especially for Bulgaria, Croatia, and Romania—as EU accession approaches. The 2004 Regular Report of the EU concludes that the alignment with the EU *acquis* in these countries is incomplete. While the Regular Report mentions that Bulgaria has made "good progress" in aligning standards with the EU, it points out that the country still needs work in certain fields. Bulgaria is, for example, still working on harmonizing its national legislation with the EU veterinary standards, and the country is also trying to catch up in areas of the phytosanitary standards. The report points out that enforcement of legislation in Romania is hampered by limited management and administrative capacity, particularly in the areas of veterinary and phytosanitary standards. Progress in standardization in the other SEE countries has been more limited.

Development of IT infrastructure in SEE. The average number of telephone lines in SEE as a whole is higher than the Region's average, while the number of Internet hosts in the sub-Region overall is far below the Region's average (see figures 5.17 and 5.18). Of course, there is significant variation among the countries in the number of telephone lines and Internet hosts. For example, basic connectivity is especially weak in Serbia and Montenegro, and the level of Internet and e-commerce development is rated as "fair" in FYR Macedonia, "medium" in Bosnia and Herzegovina, "low" in Albania, and "very low" in Kosovo (World Bank 2001). The most important obstacles to vibrant e-commerce in SEE are the lack of vigorous competition, an incomplete legal framework (and fuzzy private property rights as a result), and the limited awareness of Internet and e-commerce oppor-

FIGURE 5.17

Telephone Lines in SEE

Per 100 people, 2003

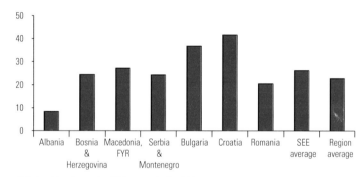

Source: Calculated from International Telecommunications Union 2004.

FIGURE 5.18

Internet Hosts in SEE

Per 10,000 people, 2003

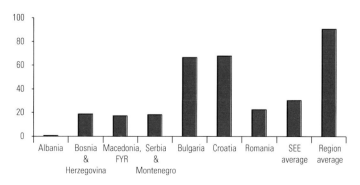

Source: Calculated from International Telecommunications Union 2004.

tunities—among both government agencies and the private sector. A relatively underdeveloped banking sector that could efficiently enable routine electronic payments is also a barrier to e-commerce in the sub-Region. (Larive International 2000).

Russia, Belarus, Moldova, and Ukraine

The physical location of these CIS countries makes them an increasingly critical fulcrum for trade flows between Europe and Asia. Moldova, for example, will become important as the future border between Europe and countries to Moldova's east once Romania joins the EU. Ukraine and Belarus both provide Russia with important transport links that connect Russia's oil and gas pipeline networks to countries in Central and Eastern Europe. As in the Caucasus, however, political tensions, conflicts, and hostilities complicate cooperation among these countries. The Trans-Nystria conflict for independence from Moldova, for example, has seriously impeded Moldova's road and rail links with Ukraine. Other hostilities, such as the Chechnya conflict within Russia, have also disrupted the transport links between these countries. Ukraine limits Moldovan transit to Russia and Kazakhstan, and Armenian transit to the ports on the Black Sea. Although there are several agreements on transit among these (and other) CIS countries, they have been relatively ineffective in practice (Freinkman, Polyakov, and Revenco 2004).[11]

Customs and border crossings. The issues affecting performance of customs in these CIS countries center around (1) customs clearances, (2) goods inspections, and (c) border crossings. In Russia, the size of the country is a critical factor. Currently, there are seven regional customs directorates and 141 customs offices that process goods and vehicles. Although customs procedures are based on the same legislation, regulation, and instruction, interpretation and implementation of these instruments vary widely, depending on customs officers throughout the territory (World Bank 2003e). The opportunities for discretionary behavior give rise to corruption, which is a serious problem at customs. For example, at the border-crossing points to Russia from Yerevan, truck drivers are asked for $1,800–$2,000 for the "02 guard service" provided by the Ministry of National Security. If they refuse, drivers meet difficulties with the road policy or organized local gangs (Molnar and Ojala 2003). New preshipment inspection rules proposed by the Russian Trade Ministry affecting certain imports would add 1 percent charges of the customs value to certain goods, such as furniture, shoes, clothing, and household appliances, among others.

Additional costs are expected, with associated transit delays and higher logistics costs.[12]

In Ukraine and also Belarus, many of the nontariff barriers in trade logistics and facilitation are related to customs administration. Domestic exporters make informal payments to facilitate dealing with complex rules and burdensome customs clearance procedures (World Bank 2004q).

In Moldova, customs regulations constitute a major constraint for business operations. A new customs code was passed in 2000, but legislation is subject to frequent changes that create costly uncertainty in trade transactions and logistics. Another problematic trend is the increasing fiscal role of the customs services. The state budget receives about 50 percent of government revenue from customs activity. In addition, the time required to obtain export permits increased by 40 percent in 2002, delaying and complicating export transactions, although the cost of these procedures declined (World Bank 2004e).

Key challenges for the transport sector. The quality of transport across the various modes differs widely among these CIS countries. Although Moldova has about 85 percent of its roads paved—almost the same level as the Region's average—only 30 percent of the country's road network is considered to be in good shape. In addition to roads, similar problems are evident in Moldova's railway and air transportation. The country's railway rolling stock is antiquated, and most engines run on diesel, which hampers operations and causes delay during winter months. Wagons are often of poor quality, and thefts during transit are common. Air services in Moldova are largely limited to passenger traffic (World Bank 2004m).

In contrast, the percentage of paved roads in Russia is the lowest among all CIS countries. The major corridors, such as those between Moscow and the European border and the Black and Caspian Sea regions, are now so heavily congested that they have become barriers to further economic and social development of the regions they serve. Some major roads that have a design capacity of about 5,000 vehicles per day are now trying to accommodate demand in excess of 15,000 vehicles per day. However, Russia has one of the largest and most intensively operated rail systems in the world. Nearly half of the Russian rail lines are electrified, and the share of passengers (as opposed to freight) in Russian rail traffic is low (World Bank 2004j). While Russia's ports, especially St. Petersburg and Novorossiysk, are some of the most important transportation hubs, their basic infrastructure facilities are in need of improvement because of busy urban traffic associated with port activities.

Key challenges related to standardization. Belarus, Moldova, Russia, and Ukraine confront major challenges and opportunities for market expansion in meeting standards and technical regulations. Since the Soviet era, the Committee of the Russian Federation for Standardization, Metrology, and Certification (GOST) has been the main agency responsible for monitoring the production of Russia's enterprises to ensure conformity to existing standards. In fact, GOST was initially adopted throughout much of the Former Soviet Union. While GOST has undergone significant operational and policy reforms during the transition, its role remains too narrowly defined. For example, industries are responsible for the development and adoption of their own voluntary standards for product or process specifications.

In all these countries, as a result of the process of international integration that has been part and parcel of the transition to market economies, there has been an increasing need to introduce more internationally recognized standards aligned with the ISO and EU Norms. The Interstate Council on Standards, Metrology, and Certification has been working to align national standards with international practice; nevertheless, the process has been slow. Only 20 percent of standard positions are in line with international standards, while the rest remain aligned with GOST standards (Freinkman, Polyakov, and Revenco 2004).

Ukraine's standardization system is a case in point. The country's system of technical standards has insufficiently integrated its norms and practices with international ones, relies too heavily on mandatory standards, and fails to sufficiently involve private industry in setting and enforcing standards. The system is oriented toward standards as product specifications, as opposed to performance specifications. This is largely the result of the fact that, under central planning, standards acquired many functions and a degree of detail that in free markets are taken care of by competition and company standardization. Foreign producers' and importers' perceptions of Ukraine's standardization system is that it is unpredictable in its results, in regard both to time and to cost (Reihlen 2000).

Development of infrastructure. In all of these CIS countries, there are tangible impacts of the relatively low levels of investment in infrastructure that have been taking place in terms of relatively high logistics costs; these, in turn, hinder trade flows and international integration. Moldova's investment in telecommunications and transport infrastructure, for example, is less than 3 percent of GDP. In the more developed countries in the Region, the level ranges between 8 and 10 percent of GDP (World Bank 2004m).

The development of telephone lines in Belarus, Russia, and Ukraine is close to or even above the Region's average; telephone lines in Moldova, however, are significantly less developed than the average for the Region (see figure 5.19). On the other hand, across the board for the four countries, Internet hosts are far below the Region's average (see figure 5.20). For example, in Moldova, only 38 percent of companies report using e-mail regularly, and fewer than 30 percent regularly use the Internet to deal with customers and suppliers. This is the lowest of any comparator country.

Summary Comparison of Trade-Facilitation Capacity across the Region

Customs and border crossings. Among the most serious problems across the CIS and much of SEE is the frequent incidence of unofficial pay-

FIGURE 5.19

Telephone Lines in the Russian Federation, Belarus, Moldova, and Ukraine

Per 100 people, 2003

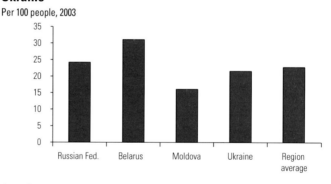

Source: Calculated from International Telecommunications Union 2004.

FIGURE 5.20

Internet Hosts in the Russian Federation, Belarus, Moldova, and Ukraine

Per 10,000 people, 2003

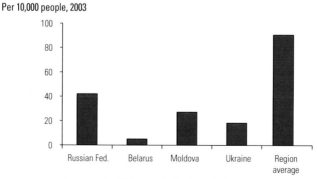

Source: Calculated from International Telecommunications Union 2004.

ments needed to move goods across national borders. This compounds other impediments in customs administration, including (1) a lack of coordination among border-related agencies, (2) complex customs procedures, (3) unclear customs codes and regulations, and (4) low utilization of information technology. Most important, perhaps, some countries are still experiencing political tensions with neighbors, and therefore the level of intra-Regional cooperation in facilitating trade remains low.

For most of the EU-8 and EU accession and candidate countries (Bulgaria and Romania, and Croatia and Turkey, respectively), in contrast, customs administrations have been significantly improved, at least in part because of the reforms necessary to accede to the EU. Figure 5.21 compares customs efficiency, as measured by the average number of days required to obtain customs clearance by sea, in four such countries—the Czech Republic, Estonia, Poland, and Turkey—to that found in select South Asian, East Asian, and developed countries. The data show that these four countries have more efficient customs than do the countries in the other regions of the world.

Key challenges for the port and transport sector. With regard to port and transport systems, most countries in the Region confront similar problems: (1) poor transport services, (2) low infrastructure maintenance, and (3) high transportation and handling costs. Central Asian countries are landlocked, making it important to extend their transport infrastructure to transit neighbors. For the Caucasus and SEE, restoring war-damaged infrastructure and reopening links arising from the transport network inherited from the Former Soviet Union are an ongoing critical priority.

FIGURE 5.21
Average Days Required for Customs Clearance by Sea

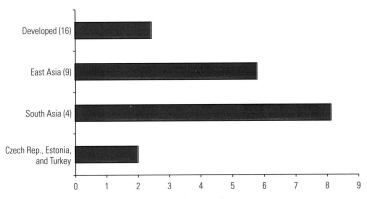

Source: Calculated from International Exhibition Logistics Associates data.

Continued privatization and deregulation of transport services across the entire Region remain critical. Private sector participation is often called upon to improve operational efficiency in the infrastructure sector. Yet private sector involvement in the countries of the Region has been limited. The degree of private sector involvement in port, rail, and road sectors in each sub-Region is provided in figure 5.22. Privatization is especially important for the EU-8, where physical infrastructure is relatively well developed and the transport sector has been liberalized among the original EU membership. Not surprisingly, then, the EU-8 countries are the most advanced in terms of privatization. However, the level of private sector participation in the EU-8 countries is still considered low by global standards. Estonia is the only country that has privatized its railway sector (EBRD 2004c).

Challenges related to standards, technical barriers, and regulatory policy. Standards and technical and regulatory barriers represent an important factor in trade logistics costs, in particular as they relate to border-crossing procedures and administrative rules. Many of the countries in the Region, particularly those in Central Asia, the Caucasus, and SEE, are still at an early stage of reform in standardization. In September 2004, the World Trade Organization held a workshop in Istanbul, Turkey, where officials from the Region's countries discussed the issues of standards in the context of trade facilitation. The objective of the workshop

FIGURE 5.22
Degree of Private Sector Participation in Infrastructure, 2004

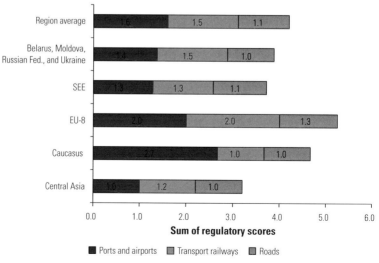

Sum of regulatory scores

■ Ports and airports   ▨ Transport railways   ▨ Roads

Source: EBRD 2004c.

Note: Scale: 1=no or negligible private sector participation; 5=sector fully privatized.

was to assist participating countries in their understanding of the main principles and provisions of the TBT agreement and to raise awareness of the importance of the implementation and administration of the agreement (WTO 2004b). Although some countries, like Kazakhstan and Ukraine, have been making efforts to harmonize their standards with international standards, their progress has been slow.

Figure 5.23 depicts the importance of standards to exports as reported by surveyed firms—including firms in the EU-8—in various regions around the world,. A high percentage of firms in the EU-8 indicate that standards, testing, certification, and other regulatory requirements play a key role in export performance.

Development of information technology infrastructure. For the Region as a whole, the development of e-commerce in trade transactions and adoption of information technology are low relative to other regions of the world—although this varies widely among sub-Regions. While advances have been made in the EU-8, SEE and Central Asian countries are far behind, and their Internet infrastructure is not sufficient to support the use of e-commerce in trade. The United Nations Conference on Trade and Development (2002a) suggests:

> Fast growth in both B2B and B2C e-commerce is expected in the Central and Eastern European countries with economies in

FIGURE 5.23
Technical Regulations and Standards

Percentage of surveyed firms ranking regulations important to export expansion

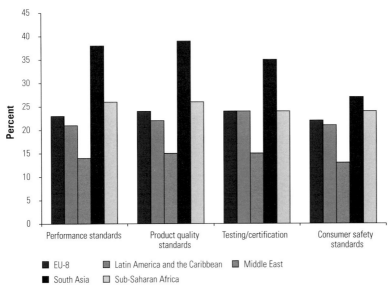

Source: Wilson, Mann, and Otsuki (2004), based on the World Bank Technical Barriers to Trade database.

transition. However, e-commerce in transition economies is not likely to reach 1 percent of global e-commerce before 2005. While the more technologically advanced nations in Central Europe and the Baltic have relatively high rates of digital literacy and are laying the foundations for the development of e-commerce activity, others (particularly in the Balkans, the Caucasus, and Central Asia) remain far behind.

By way of comparison, box 5.2 illustrates the advances in "paperless trading" in East Asia.

Mobile telephone services have been privatized in the entire Region; however, fixed-line telephone service remains largely under government control, particularly in Central Asia (figure 5.24). This limits the development of telecommunications services. Figure 5.25 shows the contrast among the sub-Regions in level of Internet hosts, which are particularly important to developing business in the services sector (as discussed in chapter 6).

BOX 5.2

E-Commerce: Promoting Paperless Trading in East Asia

The expansion of electronic commerce is advancing in East Asia, where regional initiatives are playing an increasingly important role. Experience in this region provides one indication of what countries in Eastern Europe and the Former Soviet Union could achieve through cooperative programs. The Asia-Pacific Economic Cooperation (APEC) has adopted a goal of achieving paperless trading among all member economies by 2010. This is being implemented through computerizing customs procedures aligned with the United Nations Directories for Electronic Data Interchange for Administration, Commerce, and Transport (UN/EDIFACT) program. APEC is also supporting programs to reduce the number of documents required for sea, air, and land transport. Under this initiative, each member must include a strategy for achieving paperless trading in its Individual Action Plans in APEC.

Benefits from a paperless trading regime could be significant. In intraregional manufacturing trade, "three per cent average reduction in the cost of imported items would involve gross savings of the order of US$60 billion annually when extended to total intra-APEC merchandise trade" (Commonwealth of Australia Ministry of Foreign Trade and Economic Cooperation 2001). The introduction of a single-window system for customs clearance could produce benefits for the Thai business community of approximately $700 million per year, and the Korean business community around $1.6 million per year. Singapore already benefits more than $1 billion each year from such a system (APEC 2004).

Sources: APEC 2004; Commonwealth of Australia Ministry of Foreign Trade and Economic Cooperation 2001.

FIGURE 5.24

Private Participation in the Telecommunications Sector, 2004

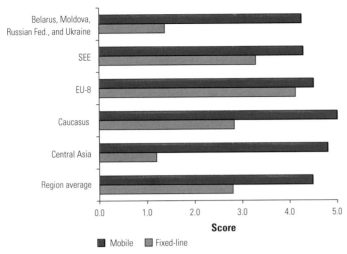

Source: EBRD 2004c.

Note: Scale: 1=no or negligible private sector participation; 5=sector fully privatized.

FIGURE 5.25

Internet Hosts in the Region

Per 10,000 people, 2003

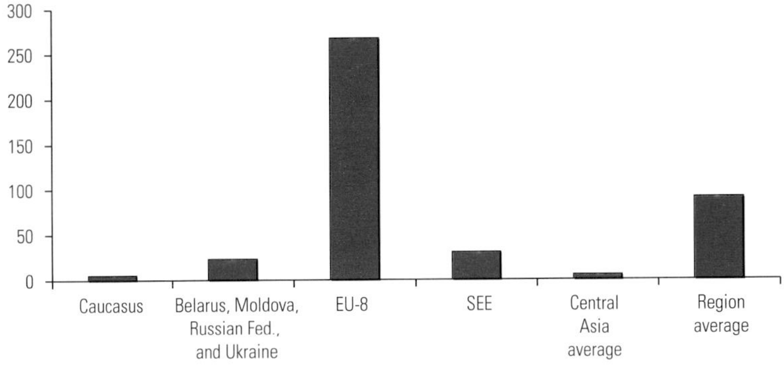

Source: Calculated from International Telecommunications Union 2004.

Based on the preceding case-by-case assessment that shows the diversity of obstacles to trade facilitation throughout the Region, table 5.8 summarizes the key challenges by sub-Region.

Assessing Trade Gains for the Region from Domestic Capacity Building

Understanding the relationship between economic development and transport-related costs in international trade is relatively straightfor-

TABLE 5.8

Summary of Major Constraints and Challenges in the Sub-Regions

	Border crossings and customs	Transport sector	Standards	IT infrastructure and services
Central Asia	• Political tension at borders • Uncertainty about implementation of new customs codes and standards • Excessive number of documents required • Inconvenient location of border posts • Lack of cooperation among border agencies • Limited application of information technology in border clearance systems	• Limited access to seaports (critical for landlocked countries) • Limited rail and road networks to neighboring countries (for example, China) other than Russia • Deteriorating railway network inherited from the FSU • A lack of reliable transport service and regulation	• Limited information on initiatives that involve standards and conformity assessment requirements at the border	• Lack of basic information technology infrastructure to support e-commerce, especially in Turkmenistan and Tajikistan
Caucasus	• Closed borders resulting from conflicts and wars (for example, Armenia and Azerbaijan) • A lack of regional harmonization of customs practices • Limited transparency in clearance regulation and procedures • Corruption/unofficial payments • Limited application of information technology in border clearance systems	• Limited utilization of port capacity • Rail and road networks in need of repair or replacement • Lack of harmonized transport regulations and duties • Low level of private sector participation in infrastructure	• Limited information on initiatives that deal with standards and conformity assessment	• Low level of information technology infrastructure to support e-commerce, especially Internet hosts
EU-8	• Continued problems with unofficial payments at the new EU external border with Russia and Belarus	• The growing need to adopt information technology in port management • A lack of participation of domestic companies in port operation • Liberalization of transport sectors (for example, railway) lagging behind original EU members	• A need to address technical barriers between the EU-8 and non-EU member countries	• Relatively well-developed information technology infrastructure, yet a need to work on privatization in some countries (Strictly regulated fixed-line telephone service in Slovenia and Czech Republic)
SEE	• "Temporary" customs systems still in place after independence • Unofficial border crossings • Corruption/unofficial payments • Lack of regional coordination and cooperation • Outdated customs and border facilities • Lack of interagency cooperation in border clearance • A need to update technology applied in customs • Variations in interpreting legislation and procedures • The overall complexity of procedures	• Decreasing demand for transport services in some areas • Transport infrastructure damaged by conflicts • Low maintenance and poor quality of transport infrastructure • A need to further reconstruct transport infrastructure • Low levels of investment funding to upgrade transport infrastructure • A need to liberalize transport services	• The increasing need to align standards with the EU *acquis* • EU accession candidate countries lacking administrative capacity to enforce EU legislation	• The low level of information technology infrastructure to support e-commerce in some countries (for example, Albania) • A lack of fair competition in Albania, Bosnia and Herzegovina, and Serbia and Montenegro resulting from low degree of privatization of telecommunication services
Russian Federation, Belarus, Moldova, Ukraine	• Informal payments • Variation in interpreting legislation and procedures among customs agencies (for example, Russia) • Frequent changes in customs legislation (for example, Moldova)	• Transport links disrupted by conflicts (for example, the Trans-Nystria conflict affected transport links between Moldova and Ukraine) • Low levels of investment in transport sector • Antiquated railway rolling stock (for example, Moldova) • Low percentage of paved roads in Russia	• Insufficiently integrated standardization system in Ukraine • Lack of private sector involvement in setting and enforcing standards (for example, Ukraine)	• A low number of Internet hosts

Source: World Bank staff.

ward—in theory. Economic development and poverty alleviation are both achieved through income growth. As discussed in earlier chapters, economic growth expands with world trade. Lower transport and other trade-related transactions costs, in turn, provide the engine through which trade expands to achieve advances in development. Analysis of how—in practice—modern trade logistics influence the facilitation of international commerce, however, is more challenging in empirical design and estimation: the linkages between the two are multifaceted, subtle, and complex.

Over time, with advances in technology, *transport costs* have become less subject to distance. Hummels (1999) suggests that in 1974, shipping commodities over a distance of 9,000 kilometers by sea was approximately 60 percent more expensive than shipping over a distance of 1,000 kilometers by land. By 1998, this cost differential was estimated to have been reduced by one-half, that is, to 30 percent. Given that a number of the Region's countries—including the new EU members and those in line for EU accession—are relatively far from the central markets of Europe, reductions in transport costs would certainly facilitate trade, all other factors held constant.

The reduction in "effective distance" that comes with lowered transport costs reduces the overall *transactions costs* of trade. Conventional gravity model analysis suggests that transactions costs impede the exchange and the transfer of goods and services between different countries or regions in a variety of ways. The wedge between export and import prices reduces profit margins. In particular, trade barriers—both tangible and intangible—limit trade and slow prospects for regional development. According to Overman et al. (2001), access to foreign markets alone could explain some 35 percent of the cross-country variation in per capita income. Regions with higher transactions costs exhibit slower growth (Diamond 1997; Limao and Venables 2001; Redding and Venables 2003).

Trade Facilitation: Performance Benchmarks in the Region

At the global level, empirical analysis provides one indication of the potential benefits of reduced transactions costs engendered by reform in trade facilitation. Wilson, Mann, and Otsuki (2004) suggest that improvements in the four dimensions of trade facilitation that are the focus of this chapter—transport and port efficiency, customs regimes, standards and regulatory policy, and information technology infrastructure—could lead to significant trade gains. Their estimates indicate that, for the 75 sample countries examined, raising capacity halfway to the worldwide average would yield a $377 billion gain to world trade.

The empirical estimates of the benefits of improving trade facilitation in the Region take as their starting point the same analytical framework as the one underpinning the global assessment. It also draws on new work by Wilson, Luo, and Broadman (2004) that focuses on trade-facilitation capacity affecting trade between the EU-8 and countries in line for accession to the EU. The analytical framework moves beyond simulating the benefits from improvements in trade facilitation based on a single parameter, such as the price of imports, the productivity of the transport sector, or the costs of transportation; rather, it examines all four dimensions of trade facilitation noted above. The scenarios examined do not assume that all countries in the sample improve capacity by the same amount. Some countries in the Region have further to go to reach best practice in regulatory reform or in port efficiency, for example, than do others. Moreover, to keep the simulated scenarios more realistic, it is assumed that the countries initially less developed in trade facilitation are able to achieve only a relatively low level of trade-facilitation improvements. The empirical estimates derived are based on a gravity model of bilateral trade flows, rather than on a computable general equilibrium (CGE) approach.

The four indicators of trade-facilitation capacity used in the empirical estimation are "port efficiency," which measures the quality of infrastructure of maritime and air ports; "customs environment," which measures direct customs costs, as well as administrative transparency of customs and border crossings; "regulatory environment," which measures the economy's approach to regulations; and "IT infrastructure," which measures the extent to which an economy has the necessary domestic infrastructure (such as telecommunications, financial intermediaries, and logistics firms) and is using networked information to improve efficiency and to transform activities to enhance economic activity.[13]

The available data for the estimation cover 15 countries in the Region, as well as Turkey: the EU-8; the four EU accession and candidate countries (Bulgaria and Romania, and Croatia and Turkey, respectively); and FYR Macedonia, Russia, Serbia, and Ukraine.

Figure 5.26 benchmarks the trade-facilitation capacity of these 16 countries compared with that of the EU-15 countries. The sample countries exhibit a relatively low level of performance in all areas of trade facilitation: development levels in port efficiency, customs regimes, regulatory policy, and IT infrastructure are approximately 68 percent, 73 percent, 79 percent, and 80 percent, respectively, of the EU-15. The EU-8 countries on average exhibit a higher level of development than do the EU accession/candidate countries. While Ukraine

FIGURE 5.26
Benchmark Comparisons of Trade-Facilitation Indicators

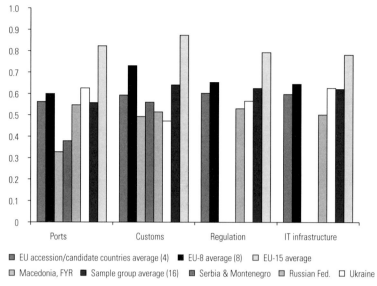

Source: Wilson, Luo, and Broadman 2004.

Note: 0 = least developed and 1.0 = most developed.

performs at a relatively high level in port efficiency, FYR Macedonia and Serbia are the least developed in port efficiency. Ukraine also performs well in IT infrastructure. Yet its level of customs efficiency scores the lowest. Ukraine performs better than Russia except in customs regimes. Russia lags behind the average of the sample group, the EU-15, and the EU-8 in all areas.

Figure 5.27 compares the various areas of trade facilitation between the four EU accession/candidate countries and the EU-8. The EU-8 are all relatively strong performers in customs regimes and regulatory policy. Estonia is the best performer among the group, with benchmarks from 0.75 to 0.85 in three trade-facilitation indicators—port efficiency, regulatory policy, and IT infrastructure—compared with the other new EU member countries. While Hungary has the highest level in customs efficiency, Latvia is the least developed in customs among the new EU members. IT infrastructure in Lithuania is the least developed, and Poland's development level is low in all areas of trade facilitation. On the other hand, Romania is well developed in port efficiency, regulatory policy, and IT infrastructure among the four EU accession/candidate countries. In addition, Bulgaria exhibits the highest level in regulatory policy—0.67—in the same country group.

Even though they do not have direct access to seaports, landlocked countries are included in the analysis. This is because land-

FIGURE 5.27

Benchmarking EU Accession and Candidate Countries against the EU-8

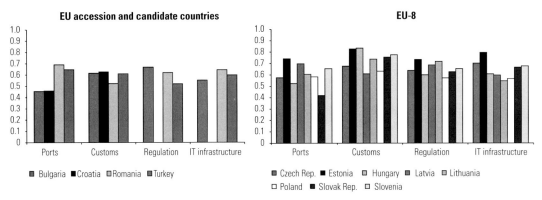

Source: Wilson, Luo, and Broadman 2004.

Note: 0 = least developed and 1.0 = most developed.

locked countries, such as the Czech Republic, Hungary, FYR Macedonia, and the Slovak Republic, can use inland waterways as alternative transportation. The Danube River flows through 17 countries,
including Hungary and the Slovak Republic, and is the major transportation route connecting large cities in the Region and Europe,
including Belgrade, Bratislava, Budapest, and Vienna. The River Elbe
plays a role in moving freight from the Czech Republic to the seaport
of Hamburg in Germany. Moreover, landlocked countries can use
seaports in neighboring countries. Gdansk, Gdynia, and Szczecin in
Poland are major transshipment seaports for the Czech Republic and
the Slovak Republic. Hamburg is used as a transshipment seaport for
the Czech Republic and Hungary. For landlocked countries, accessibility to seaports in neighboring countries is more important than it
is for countries that are not landlocked. Therefore, the indicator of
port efficiency in landlocked countries reflects the degree of development of inland waterways, as well as that of airport facilities. As
Figure 5.28 indicates, landlocked countries are ranked between 26th
and 94th, and some of them score higher than countries with coast-
lines. For instance, the Czech Republic is ranked 66th, while the
Philippines, an island, is ranked 83rd.

Benchmarking the Relationship between Economic Development and Trade Facilitation

Taking into account GDP per capita permits an assessment of how the
relationship between trade facilitation and economic development
for each of the 16 countries under examination compares with that of

FIGURE 5.28

Benchmarking Port Infrastructure, Port Facilities, and Inland Waterways

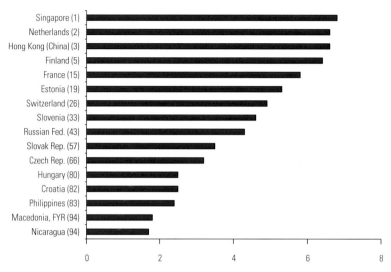

Source: World Economic Forum 2003.

Note: Note: 0 = least developed and 8.0 = most developed.
The number in brackets indicates ranking.

other countries around the world (see figures 5.29–5.32). For the group as a whole, given their economic development, trade-facilitation performance is relatively low compared with the benchmark levels. The only exception is Estonia, which performs stronger than the benchmark level in all four areas of trade facilitation. Compared with Hungary, a country of similar development level, Estonia is 40 percent more developed in port efficiency, 30 percent more developed in IT infrastructure, and 20 percent more developed in regulatory policy.[14] The trade-facilitation level of Estonia is even more developed than the average of EU-15 countries in IT infrastructure.

In port efficiency, besides Estonia, four countries—Latvia, Romania, Turkey, and Ukraine—perform above their benchmark levels. The other countries are lagging behind: in particular, the Czech Republic, Croatia, Hungary, and the Slovak Republic perform at lower levels, despite their relatively high levels of economic development. FYR Macedonia's port efficiency indicator shows the lowest value among the 16 sample countries. In customs, again, aside from Estonia, three countries—Hungary, Lithuania, and the Slovak Republic—perform above their benchmark levels. The other countries cluster close to their benchmarks, except FYR Macedonia, Romania, Russia, and Ukraine, which have relatively poor customs performance for their economic levels. Many countries—apart from Estonia—perform poorly in regula-

FIGURE 5.29

Benchmarking Port Efficiency to the Value of GDP per capita

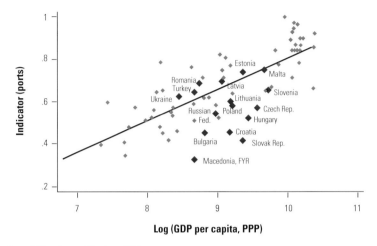

Source: Wilson, Luo, and Broadman 2004.

FIGURE 5.30

Benchmarking Customs Regimes to the Value of GDP per capita

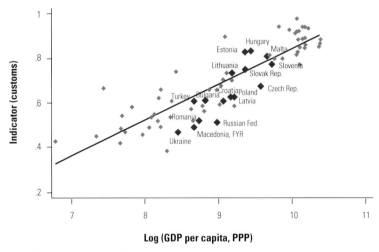

Source: Wilson, Luo, and Broadman 2004.

tory policy, after taking their economic development levels into account. In IT infrastructure, while Russia performs far below its benchmark, Romania and Ukraine score higher than their benchmarks.

Estimating Trade Gains from Reform and Capacity Building

Trade gains are estimated in two situations: (i) how would trade flows among the 16 countries change if they all improved capacity in trade

FIGURE 5.31

Benchmarking Regulatory Policy to the Value of GDP per capita

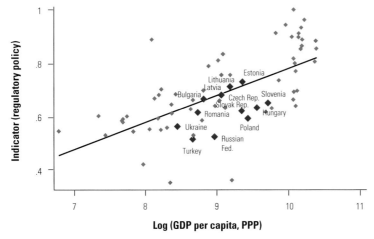

Source: Wilson, Luo, and Broadman 2004.

FIGURE 5.32

Benchmarking IT Infrastructure to the Value of GDP per capita

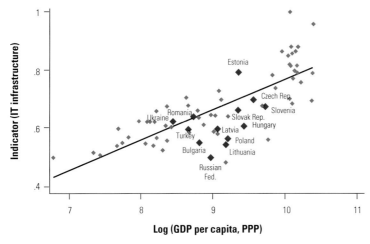

Source: Wilson, Luo, and Broadman 2004.

facilitation at the same time? and (ii) how would these countries' trade flows with the rest of the world change if the same improvements were made? In other words, trade gains from regional integration are estimated first, followed by an estimate of the trade gains stemming from global integration. The simulation framework follows the analysis in Wilson, Mann, and Otsuki (2004) and Wilson, Luo, and Broadman (2004). "Improvement in trade facilitation" is defined as attaining one-half the level of the trade-facilitation capacity of the EU-15 countries.

Regional gains in trade from collective reform. As table 5.9 indicates, trade flows among the 16 countries would increase substantially if, collectively, the countries were to improve their trade-facilitation capacity to one-half the level of the EU-15 countries. In particular, the total estimated gain from capacity building in all four categories of trade facilitation would be approximately $94 billion for the countries as a whole. The country with the largest projected gains is Russia. Trade flows for Russia would be expected to increase by $19 billion. Capacity building in IT infrastructure would contribute the most to those gains.

The estimated trade gains in percentage terms are depicted in figure 5.33. Trade volumes in Lithuania, Poland, Russia, and Ukraine would rise more than 100 percent if trade-facilitation levels in the four areas reached 50 percent of the EU-15 level. Improvements in port efficiency would raise trade volumes significantly in Croatia, the Czech Republic, FYR Macedonia, the Slovak Republic, Slovenia, and Serbia and Montenegro. In contrast, improvements in IT infrastruc-

TABLE 5.9
Regional Trade Gains from Collective Capacity Building
$ millions

	Ports efficiency	Customs regimes	Regulatory policy	IT infrastructure	Total
EU-8					
Czech Rep.	3,539	1,509	1,362	2,708	9,118
Estonia	293	255	180	529	1,256
Hungary	2,433	879	1,079	2,749	7,140
Latvia	425	457	252	1,002	2,137
Lithuania	721	487	336	1,610	3,154
Poland	2,895	1,903	1,643	4,477	10,918
Slovak Rep.	3,319	902	980	1,999	7,200
Slovenia	948	441	377	859	2,625
Subtotal	*14,573*	*6,832*	*6,209*	*15,933*	*43,547*
EU accession/candidates					
Bulgaria	936	551	307	1,124	2,918
Croatia	808	341	214	479	1,843
Romania	794	823	506	1,191	3,315
Turkey	1,510	1,597	1,305	2,996	7,408
Subtotal	*4,048*	*3,312*	*2,332*	*5,790*	*15,483*
Others					
Russian Fed.	3,939	4,244	2,785	7,990	18,958
Ukraine	2,682	3,621	2,038	4,900	13,242
Macedonia, FYR	624	275	97	247	1,244
Serbia & Montenegro	1,024	455	141	383	2,003
Subtotal	*8,269*	*8,595*	*5,061*	*13,520*	*35,447*
Total	26,890	18,739	13,603	35,244	94,476

Source: Based on calculations in Wilson, Luo, and Broadman 2004.

FIGURE 5.33

Shares of Regional Trade Gains from Collective Action

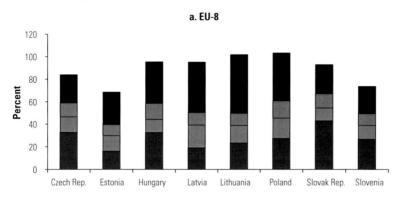

a. EU-8

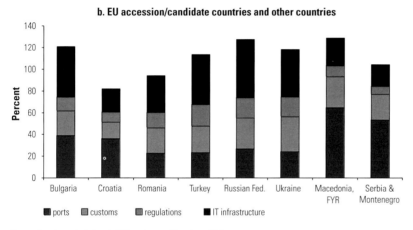

b. EU accession/candidate countries and other countries

■ ports ▨ customs ▦ regulations ■ IT infrastructure

Source: Based on calculations in Wilson, Luo, and Broadman 2004.

ture would yield trade gains in Bulgaria, Hungary, Latvia, Lithuania, Poland, Russia, Turkey, and Ukraine. Reform in customs regimes would result in the second-largest trade gains, based on improvements in Latvia, FYR Macedonia, Romania, Russia, Turkey, Ukraine, and Serbia and Montenegro.

Global gains in trade from collective reform. Sixty-three countries are taken to represent the rest of the world. Two scenarios are simulated: (i) gains from trade with the rest of the world even if the rest of the world does not reform or invest in capacity-building measures and (ii) the trade gains that would be realized if the rest of the world upgraded capacity in trade facilitation simultaneously.

As shown in figure 5.34, the total gains to the 16 countries from unilateral capacity building are estimated at approximately $178 billion. This represents about 50 percent of these countries' trade with the rest of the world. More important, 87 percent of the total gains to the coun-

FIGURE 5.34

Trade Gains from Removing Barriers in Trade Facilitation

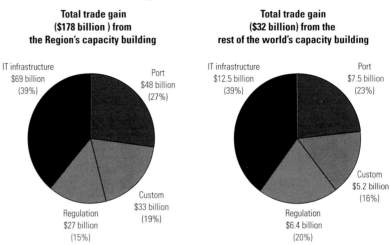

Total trade gain
($178 billion) from
the Region's capacity building

IT infrastructure
$69 billion
(39%)

Port
$48 billion
(27%)

Custom
$33 billion
(19%)

Regulation
$27 billion
(15%)

Total trade gain
($32 billion) from the
rest of the world's capacity building

IT infrastructure
$12.5 billion
(39%)

Port
$7.5 billion
(23%)

Custom
$5.2 billion
(16%)

Regulation
$6.4 billion
(20%)

Source: Based on calculations in Wilson, Luo, and Broadman 2004.

tries are generated from the countries' own actions to upgrade infrastructure in ports, develop information technology, harmonize regulations, and improve customs. This illustrates the significance of capacity building in trade facilitation as a means of strengthening these countries' global trade ties. The most promising area for improvement is in IT infrastructure, with trade gains estimated to be $69 billion. In fact, more than 60 percent of the trade gains are associated with IT infrastructure and port efficiency improvements. This is similar to the conclusions reached in the regional analysis.

Figure 5.35 indicates the importance of capacity building to the 16 countries relative to that of the rest of the world. Trading partners outside of these countries clearly gain from regional improvements. Therefore, raising capacity in the 16 countries could significantly contribute to trade expansion not only among these countries but also in the rest of the world. If the countries and the rest of the world improved capacity in trade facilitation at the same time, total trade gains would increase by 60 percent.

Table 5.10 details the country breakdowns in trade gains that would result from trade-facilitation improvement with the rest of the world. The results show that the largest trade gains are expected from IT infrastructure improvements. Russia and Poland would gain the most from improvements in IT efficiency—$19 billion and $14 billion, respectively.

Figure 5.36 shows that improving IT infrastructure is a priority for Bulgaria, Hungary, Latvia, Lithuania, Poland, Russia, Slovenia, and

FIGURE 5.35
Relative Trade Gains from Regional Action and the Rest of the World

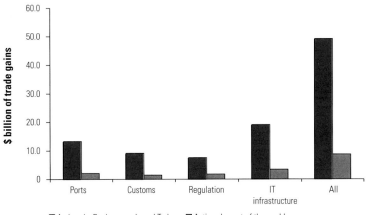

Source: Based on calculations in Wilson, Luo, and Broadman 2004.

TABLE 5.10
Global Trade Gains from Collective Capacity Building
$ millions

	Ports efficiency	Customs regimes	Regulatory policy	IT Infrastructure	Total
EU-8					
Czech Rep.	6,700	3,514	2,762	3,854	16,830
Estonia	192	78	103	—	373
Hungary	8,769	547	3,601	9,575	22,493
Latvia	182	397	121	690	1,389
Lithuania	535	237	116	1,393	2,282
Poland	7,295	5,593	5,078	14,689	32,656
Slovak Rep.	4,620	571	929	1,808	7,928
Slovenia	1,047	414	644	1,369	3,475
Subtotal	*29,341*	*11,350*	*13,354*	*33,379*	*87,424*
EU accession/candidates					
Bulgaria	1,690	718	288	1,889	4,586
Croatia	1,609	728	254	518	3,108
Turkey	3,852	4,856	5,465	9,463	23,636
Romania	1,083	3,040	1,168	2,642	7,933
Subtotal	*8,234*	*9,343*	*7,175*	*14,511*	*39,263*
Other					
Macedonia, FYR	719	304	92	212	1,327
Russian Fed.	7,931	9,553	5,910	19,322	42,717
Ukraine	1,110	2,266	1,030	1,893	6,299
Serbia & Montenegro	991	453	—	—	1,443
Subtotal	*10,752*	*12,576*	*7,033*	*21,427*	*51,787*
TOTAL	48,326	33,269	27,562	69,317	178,474

Source: Based on calculations in Wilson, Luo, and Broadman 2004.

Note: — = data unavailable.

FIGURE 5.36
Shares of Global Trade Gains from Collective Action
Percentage

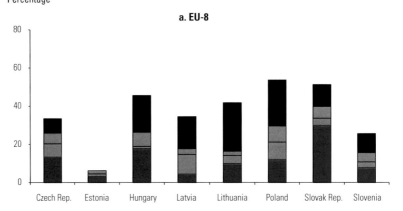

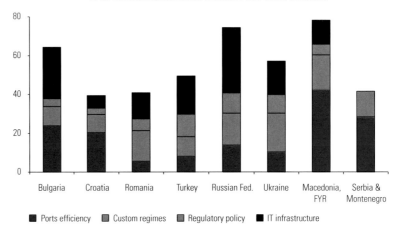

Source: Based on calculations in Wilson, Luo, and Broadman 2004.

Turkey. Improvement in ports efficiency would result in large trade gains for Bulgaria, Croatia, the Czech Republic, the Slovak Republic, and Serbia and Montenegro. Reform in customs is a priority for Romania and Ukraine in the context of global trade. Romania's trade gains from improvement of customs regimes would increase 16 percent, while Ukraine would increase trade by 20 percent from the same capacity building.

Global regional comparisons. To further shed light on the potential of trade gains through capacity building in Eastern Europe and the Former Soviet Union, comparisons with other regions of the world are instructive. Figure 5.37 compares the increase in trade flows from capacity building in trade facilitation among different regional

FIGURE 5.37

Global Comparison of Trade Flows from Trade-Facilitation Improvements

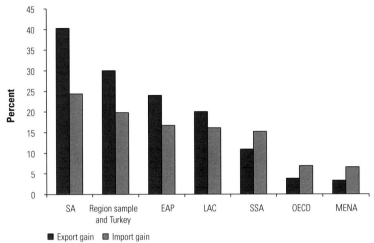

Source: Based on calculations in Wilson, Luo, and Broadman 2004.

groups: South Asia (SA), East Asia and the Pacific (EAP), Latin America and the Caribbean (LAC), Sub-Saharan Africa (SSA), OECD countries, and the Middle East and North Africa (MENA).[15] The figure shows that South Asia would gain the most both in exports and imports—40.3 percent and 24.4 percent, respectively. As a group, the 16 countries highlighted here would enjoy the second-greatest gains—a 30 percent increase in exports and an increase of 19.8 percent in imports.

Figure 5.38 shows which regions would gain the most across the four areas of trade facilitation. South Asia would gain the most in all areas. Following South Asia, the 16 countries under examination would gain the most from improving port efficiency, the regulatory environment, and IT infrastructure. In the area of customs, however, LAC would enjoy larger gains. Compared with other areas of trade facilitation, improvements in IT infrastructure would bring relatively large gains to all groups.

Moving Forward on the Trade-Facilitation Agenda in the Region

The Region is large and constitutes a heterogeneous group of countries. The analysis presented here suggests that understanding the challenges and opportunities for trade facilitation in the Region requires a reorientation of perspectives that more fully considers the

FIGURE 5.38

Global Comparison of Share of Gains from Improvements across Trade-Facilitation Areas
Percentage

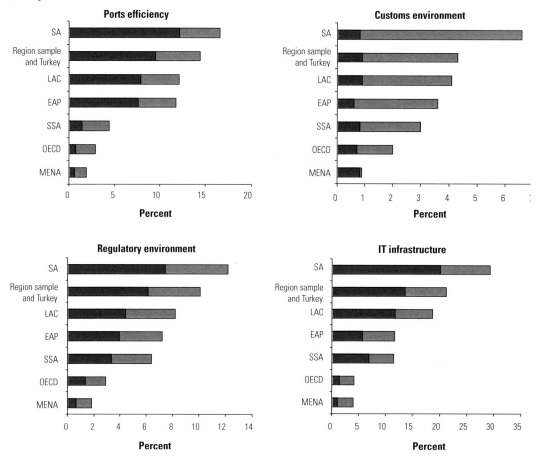

Source: Based on calculations in Wilson, Luo, and Broadman 2004.

specifics of widely differing country and subregional characteristics among these countries.

Supplementing that assessment, the new empirical evidence documented in this chapter suggests that the elements that constitute trade-facilitation activities that drive economic integration in the Region should be viewed in a broader context than has been done in the past. Initiatives to lower transactions costs through improved transportation systems and deregulation of transport services remain critical. Policy reform and infrastructure upgrades in standards, ports, customs, and information technology must also be considered, however, if the facilitation of trade is to be realized.

In particular, the empirical analysis demonstrates significant potential gains to trade from capacity building—both unilateral reform and reform at the sub-Regional level—in port efficiency, customs environment, regulatory environment, and IT infrastructures. From the perspective of intra-Regional trade, if countries in the Region improved capacity halfway to EU-15's average, trade flows are estimated to rise by $94 billion. The area that would produce the greatest gains is IT infrastructure improvement ($35 billion), followed by efficiency in air and maritime ports ($26 billion). The countries of Eastern Europe and the Former Soviet Union also have a stake in the success of efforts to promote trade-facilitation capacity building outside their borders. If the countries of the Region and the rest of the world both raised their levels of trade-facilitation capacity halfway to the EU-15's average, the gains to the Region are estimated at $210 billion. Again, the greatest gains would be found to be in improving IT infrastructure ($81.5 billion). Overall, the results indicate that the priority areas for reform in the Region center on port and IT infrastructure improvements; however, collective action to streamline regulations and improve customs would also produce significant gains to trade.

In sum, the key policy considerations for the Region are the following:

- Targeted programs of reform at the sub-Regional level are required across all areas of transport and trade facilitation. Priority areas for reform, however, clearly differ across the sub-Regions and at the national level.

- The potential gains to trade through domestic reform and unilateral action could be significant. If complemented with sub-Regional cooperation and programs of capacity building—including leveraging the demand-pull of EU accession and expanding opportunities for trade with China and East Asia—all of the countries in the Region would benefit. Trade-facilitation development-assistance strategies going forward will require taking into account these complementarities, as well as new analytical tools and data to inform sub-Regional and national priorities.

- There are significant potential gains to intra-Regional trade in the Region with the removal of nontariff barriers in trade facilitation. The largest trade gains would be associated with removing barriers to investment in IT infrastructure, including information technology, in the Region.

- There are differing priorities among new members of the EU and the candidates for accession to the EU. The new members of the European Union exhibit large potential gains to trade with investments in port efficiency (both air and maritime ports), which represent a third of total trade gains. The results for prospective members suggest more widely dispersed gains with investments in port efficiency, customs regimes, and regulatory policy. Improvements in each dimension would share around 20 percent of the total trade gains.

- Capacity building in trade facilitation and removal of behind-the-border barriers in large countries in the Region—such as Hungary, Poland, and Russia—could produce large gains to trade for these countries. It would also have a significant positive impact on other countries in the Region, because performance in trade-facilitation measures in these countries remains relatively low in comparison with others.

- Barriers to trade anchored in weak laws and regulatory and administrative procedures at the border—and behind the border—remain key obstacles to progress in a number of countries in the Region. This affects all countries, especially those landlocked countries that must move goods across multiple borders. Reform in these areas will not require significant levels of physical capital investment, but rather the political will to reform. The estimated gains to trade from reform outlined here suggest a large net national welfare benefit from such efforts.

- Physical infrastructure investment—in particular in rail and road networks—across the Region will remain important to progress in economic integration and trade expansion. This is true especially in regard to rapidly expanding trade opportunities with China and competition with countries in regional trading blocs outside of the Region that have more modern transport systems, such as those in East Asia.

- Informing the transport and trade-facilitation reform agenda in the Region requires understanding the increasingly important interrelationships between the Region and East Asia and South Asia. Geographic boundaries among these three regions are disappearing, and there is much to be learned from best-practice examples in each one. The potential for interregional cooperation and platforms for reform remain largely unexplored.

Data Annex

Data come from the World Economic Forum, *Global Competitiveness Report 2001–2002* (GCR); IMD, *World Competitiveness Yearbook* (2000) (WCY); and Kaufmann, Kraay, and Zoido-Lobaton (2002) (KKZ). All survey data in GCR come from the World Economic Forum's Executive Opinion Survey. A total of 4,022 firms were surveyed.

To provide the basis for a comparative assessment on a global basis, it is essential that we interview a sufficient number of senior business leaders in individual countries and that the sample in each country is not biased in favor of any particular business group. We have taken a number of steps to ensure this. First, we have asked each of our partner institutes, the organizations that administer the surveys in each country, to start with a comprehensive register of firms. From this, they were asked to choose a sample whose distribution across economic sectors was proportional to the distribution of the country's labor force across sectors, excluding agriculture. They were then asked to choose firms randomly within these broad sectors (for example, by choosing firms at regular intervals from an alphabetic list) and to pursue face-to-face interviews, following up for clarifications where necessary. The employment distribution was taken from data in the *1998 Yearbook of Labour Statistics* of the International Labour Office. The respondents to the survey are typically a company's CEO or a member of its senior management (World Economic Forum 2001).

The WCY uses a 115-question survey sent to executives in top and middle management of firms in all 49 countries of the WCY. The sample size of each country is proportional to GDP, and firms "normally have an international dimension" (IMD 2000). The firms are selected to be a cross-section of manufacturing, service, and primary industries. There were 3,532 responses to the survey.

KKZ (2002) updates the data on governance that were developed in Kaufmann, Kraay, and Zoido-Lobaton's "Governance Matters" (1999). The database contains more than 300 governance indicators for 175 countries compiled from a variety of sources in 2000–2001. Six aggregate indicators are constructed, corresponding to six basic governance concepts: voice and accountability, political stability, government effectiveness, regulatory quality, rule of law, and control of corruption.

The various raw data series were chosen because of their relevance to the four concepts of trade facilitation:

- "Port efficiency" is the average of two indexed inputs (all GCR):
  - Port facilities and inland waterways are 1=underdeveloped, 7=as developed as the world's best, GCR
  - Air transport is 1=infrequent and inefficient, 7=as extensive and efficient as the world's best, GCR

- "Customs environment" is the average of two indexed inputs (all GCR):
  - Hidden import barriers other than published tariffs and quotas
  - Irregular extra payments or bribes connected with import and export permits

- "Regulatory environment" is constructed as the average of two indexed inputs:
  - Transparency of government policy is satisfactory (WCY)
  - Control of corruption (KKZ)

- "IT infrastructures" is the average of two indexed inputs (all GCR):
  - Speed and cost of Internet access are: 1=slow and expensive, 7=fast and cheap
  - Internet contribution to reducing inventory costs is: 1=no improvement, 7=huge improvement

Source: Wilson, Mann, and Otsuki 2004.

Endnotes

1. Countries in the same income level include low-income and lower-middle-income countries. Except for Tajikistan in the low-income group, central Asian countries are in the lower-middle-income group.
2. The similar income group includes low-income and lower-middle-income countries. Except for Tajikistan, Central Asian countries are in the lower-middle-income group. Tajikistan is in the low-income group.
3. The World Bank has invested in the installation of 130,000 digital lines, while phasing out 60,000 analog lines in the Kyrgyz Republic. One component of the project also included building the institutional capacity of Kyrgyz Telecom.
4. Some single terminals in some European ports, which have attained the quality certificate, but no port as a whole has received the certificate. The Port of Koper is a unique example. For more details, see http://www.luka-kp.si/index.asp?lang=en.
5. The World Bank implemented the Port Access and Management Project, which upgraded the legal and administrative framework of the ports.
6. These groups are toys, machine, lifts, pressure vessels, nonautomatic weighing machines, and gas appliances.

7. For more details about the World Bank TBT database, see http://web.worldbank.org/WBSITE/EXTERNAL/TOPICS/TRADE/0,,contentMDK:20234189~menuPK:222955~pagePK:148956~piPK:216618~theSitePK:239071,00.html.

8. In 2007 (Bulgaria and Romania) and after 2007 (Croatia) and sometime in the future (other Balkan countries).

9. See more details at http://www.ttfse.org/default.aspx?p=12&c=84.

10. For a detailed discussion of the effects of governance problem in customs and other institutions in the Balkan economies, see Broadman et al. (2004).

11. These agreements include Agreement on Transit through Territories of CIS Members (1997), Agreement on Common Transport Policies in the CIS (1997), Agreement on Road Transport Union of EURASEC (1998), and Agreement on Common Railway Tariffs in EURASEC (2002).

12. Trade Facilitation Alliance, Russia/CIS Archives, November 10, 2004.

13. Wilson, Mann, and Otsuki (2004) indicators rely on three sources—*Global Competitiveness Report, World Competitiveness Yearbook*, and a dataset compiled in Kaufmann, Kraay, and Zoido-Lobaton (2002). Each indicator is constructed as a simple average of two inputs, as described in the annex.

14. Hungary and Estonia share a similar developmental level of customs regimes.

15. Note that the results for MENA and SSA should be regarded with caution, because the data from these two regions are limited.

CHAPTER 6

Services Trade and Investment in Eastern Europe and the Former Soviet Union

Introduction

Since 1990, the services sector has grown rapidly in all of the countries in the Region. The share of services in total employment and GDP in many of the countries is now close to that observed in OECD countries. Foreign investment, especially foreign direct investment (FDI), has played an important role in this process—much greater than the norm in many countries—reflecting the relatively limited experience and understanding of the need for market-based services among the inhabitants of the Region.

One of the stylized facts of economic development is that the share of services in GDP and employment rises as per capita incomes increase (Francois and Reinert 1996). The rise in the share of services reflects a number of factors, including increasing specialization and exchange of services through the market ("outsourcing"), with an associated increase in variety and quality that may raise the productivity of firms and the welfare of final consumers, in turn increasing demand for services. It also reflects the fact that the scope of (labor) productivity in services provision is less than in agriculture and manufacturing, implying that over time the (real) costs of services will rise relative to merchandise, as will the share of employment in services (Baumol 1967; Fuchs 1968).

281

Services also play a critical role in international trade. Transport services are a key input into trade in goods, and technological advances in transportation have had a major impact on the observed expansion of trade in goods. Services themselves are also becoming increasingly tradable as a result of the greater mobility of people and developments in information, computer, and telecommunications industries. This has resulted in the ever-increasing specialization in production of goods also extending to services. To a large extent, the process of globalization reflects the internationalization of production, consumption, and trade in services.

An implication of these technological developments is that the competitiveness of firms—both domestic enterprises operating on the local market and exporters on international markets—increasingly depends on the availability of low-cost and high-quality producer services in an array of areas. To illustrate with a few examples, *telecommunications and related services* are crucial for the international diffusion of information and knowledge. For some services, telecommunications technology serves as the means of export delivery. Ensuring access to modern networking technology is a vehicle that allows the economy to diversify by utilizing information technologies to export labor-intensive services. Well-known examples are call centers and back-office processing activities. Efficient *transport and distribution services* ensure that goods and people arrive in foreign countries in a timely manner. In places where it is expensive to ship goods abroad and service delays are frequent, transportation can become a prohibitive barrier to trade or can bias the geographic composition of exports and preclude countries from participating in the global production sharing that increasingly characterizes international trade. Access to *financial services*—working capital, export credit, insurance—is critical if firms are to obtain and fulfill orders from abroad; the existence of markets for foreign exchange, forward contracts, options, and other derivatives can reduce exporters' risk exposure. Efficient producer services and the proliferation of e-commerce (Internet) are of great importance in expanding export earnings and fostering economic growth. For some economies where the biggest export industry is *tourism*—a service export par excellence—good transportation and communications infrastructure are also key for growth.

Under central planning, services industries were generally neglected. Marxist thinking emphasized the importance of tangible (material) inputs as determinants of economic development, and classified employment in the services sector as unproductive. Bićanić and Škreb (1991) also note that the properties of modern producer services, namely marketability, tradability, and small scale of business, did not comply with features of Marxist economies and the bias in favor of large company scale. A result was excess demand for producer services under central planning. In market economies, producer services are among the fastest-growing services subsectors and have been subject to increasing externalization (outsourcing). A similar development was not feasible under central planning. The lack of producer services in the Region's countries was reflected in transport bottlenecks, lack of telephones and low quality of existing lines, an obsolete banking structure, and extremely low employment in services (for example, less than 1 percent of the labor force was employed in finance and insurance).

This situation severely hampered economic development in the Region before 1990. One example concerns the role of vertical integration of transport services. Because of the preference for large company size, transport services were often integrated into production firms— there was no market for such services. The lack of services also helps explain economic developments after 1990. Campos and Coricelli (2002) note that under central planning, countries had high savings rates, with the central bank allocating funds according to political priorities. This resulted in inefficient (often over-) investment, reflected in part in the low quality of the physical capital stock before 1990. After 1990, price liberalization was implemented, along with tight monetary policies. Given the absence of an effective private financial system, this led to a credit crunch in many transition economies.

Services also play an important role in coordination of economic activity in a market economy. Under central planning, economic relations were highly specific (that is, firms were locked in relationships with other firms). Input prices were administered, and firms did not accumulate information on other firms and markets. The decentralized bargaining process with many potential business partners and customers that characterizes a market economy requires flows of information and an efficient service infrastructure, which did not exist.

Thus, the former centrally planned economies of the Region inherited very weak services sectors. Many of the services that are critical to the efficient functioning of a market economy—not just a financial sector that could allocate investment funds efficiently but also the design, packaging, distribution, logistics, management, and after-sales services that are needed in order to establish, maintain, and expand market share, whether domestically or on international markets— simply did not exist. This chapter provides an overview of the status quo on services in the countries of the Region, with a more in-depth discussion of developments on trade in services. In terms of policy, the primary focus of the chapter is on policies toward trade and investment in services. There are large differences in the policy stances toward trade and investment in services across the Region. In part, these differences reflect the strategies that were chosen by governments in terms of liberalization and regulatory reform more generally. In part, they also are the result of differences in "access" to, and use of, trade agreements.

The EU-8 countries—the Baltic and the Central and Eastern European (CEE) states—have used the prospect of accession to the EU as a focal point for reform and reregulation of the services sector. Accession implies that the *acquis communitaire* become the template for legislative and regulatory changes. For those countries where accession is not on the agenda, this "EU convergence" strategy is in principle still available because the "template" is common knowledge. An important policy challenge confronting countries that are not in line for EU accession is to determine to what extent other multilateral instruments such as the WTO and regional cooperation can be used as a signaling device and a focal point for reforms. The ongoing Doha Round offers an opportunity for non-EU-accession candidates to substantially expand specific commitments on market access and national treatment for service sectors.

This chapter opens with a discussion of the changes that have occurred in the structure of the Region's economies in terms of the share of services in GDP and employment. Changes in trade and FDI in services, respectively, are then analyzed. This is followed by a review of the policy stances toward international transactions in services across the Region's countries, focusing in particular on so-called "backbone" service industries: finance, telecommunications, and infrastructure. The relationship between services policies and changes in services intensity of the Region's economies and aggregate growth performance are analyzed next. The chapter concludes with a summary of a number of policy conclusions.

Shifts in the Structure of Services in the Region

The share of services in GDP and employment has grown significantly in the last 15 years. Compared with the high-income OECD average in 1990—when the share of services in employment and GDP was around 63 percent—the Region's countries clearly lagged far behind: services accounted for 30–40 percent of GDP and employment. As of 2003, these services shares had increased substantially, with the greatest growth observed in the Baltic States, which have now almost converged on the OECD average of 68 percent in terms of GDP shares

FIGURE 6.1
Changes in the Share of Services in GDP and Employment

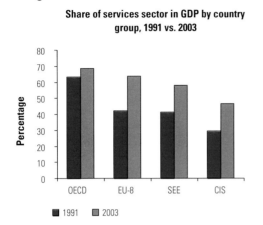

Share of services sector in GDP by country group, 1991 vs. 2003

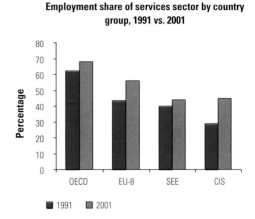

Employment share of services sector by country group, 1991 vs. 2001

Source: World Bank World development indicators.

(although employment shares remain lower). While the EU-8 states have come close to converging, much less progress has been made by the CIS, where natural-resource-based activities continue to constitute a major share of GDP (see figure 6.1). SEE countries lie in between, but are much closer to the level of the EU-8.

Labor productivity performance has demonstrated great increases in many of the Region's countries. As is the case with regard to the share of services in GDP and employment, there is a distinct pattern, with the EU-8, and to a lesser extent SEE, registering an increase in productivity, both overall and within services (broadly defined to include government); see figure 6.2.[1] Conversely, for those other sub-Regions for

FIGURE 6.2
Labor Productivity

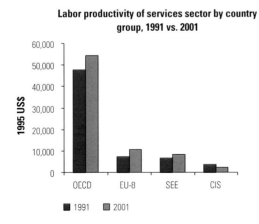

Labor productivity of services sector by country group, 1991 vs. 2001

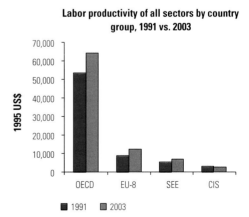

Labor productivity of all sectors by country group, 1991 vs. 2003

Source: World Bank World development indicators.

FIGURE 6.3
Change in Value Added per Worker

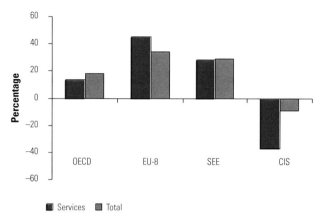

Total percentage change in value added per worker
in services and total 1991–2001 by country group

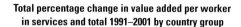

■ Services ■ Total

Source: World Bank World development indicators.

which data are available, there has been a decline in the value of services output per employee. Nor have these countries increased their
overall labor productivity performance in the last decade. The performance of the Baltic countries—where labor productivity in services outpaced the productivity increase in other sectors of the economy—is
noteworthy. The charts also show, however, that convergence with
respect to high-income OECD countries in terms of productivity levels
is still in the earlier stages for all of the Region's countries, regardless of
the total progress and deterioration shown in figure 6.3.

Trade in Services in the Region

Services differ from goods in that they are intangible and often cannot be stored—they must be consumed as they are produced. These
characteristics make them difficult to trade internationally at arm's
length in a manner analogous to goods. Although technological
developments are increasingly making it easier to exchange services
through telecommunications networks and the Internet, trade in services often requires the physical movement of either the supplier or
the consumer so that they can be in the same location. As a result of
this technological "constraint," the WTO has defined four so-called
"modes of supply" through which international trade in services may
occur (see box 6.1). Mode 1 is cross-border supply, which applies
when service suppliers resident in one country provide services in

another country without either supplier or buyer/consumer moving to the physical location of the other. Mode 2, consumption abroad, refers to a consumer who is the resident of one country moving to the supplier's country to consume a service. Mode 3, commercial presence, refers to legal persons (firms) moving to the consumer's location on a long-term basis to sell services locally through the establishment of a foreign affiliate or branch. Essentially, this comprises FDI. Mode 4 is the mode of supply through which services can be traded by the temporary movement of natural persons to the location of the consumer or demander of the service. Note that if the movement is long-term, this would constitute immigration. National accounting conventions do not regard immigration as trade insofar as the output produced by immigrants is part of the host country's GDP.[2]

The primary source of data on the magnitude of trade in services is the balance of payments (BOP). Unfortunately, this is only an imperfect source. Most countries do not collect detailed statistics on each of the four modes, which is also the case for the countries of the Region. The balance of payments generally has reasonably good coverage of Mode 2 (consumption abroad) because this tends to overlap to a large extent with the expenditures associated with tourism and business travel. Mode 3 (local sales of foreign affiliates) tends to be very badly covered, if at all—in almost all cases, data on this must be collected separately through surveys. The same is true of Mode 4. Insofar as this is recorded in the balance of payments, it will be conflated in the labor income and remittances categories. Finally, Mode 1 services are also imperfectly captured because such services trade may not give rise to a movement of foreign exchange, as is often the case with intrafirm cross-border transactions.

In short, there is a large discrepancy between the conceptual classification of trade in services and the available statistics. The latter capture trade in services only very imperfectly. As a result, it is necessary to use the existing BOP classifications—which distinguish trade in transport services; foreign exchange transactions associated with the travel of natural persons; and all other types of services exchanges, ranging from financial to educational services. In practice, any or all four of the modes of supply may be used—it is generally not possible to determine which mode has been used. In this chapter, use is made of BOP data and information on the services share of inward FDI flows. Unfortunately, no data are available on the sales of foreign affiliates—that is, the magnitude of the trade in services that is associated with FDI flows (stocks) in services.

Although all of the Region's countries have seen the share of services in GDP and employment expand in recent years, this does not

BOX 6.1

Modes of Trade in Services as Defined by WTO

- *Mode 1—Cross-border*: services supplied from the territory of one Member into the territory of another. An example is software services supplied by a supplier in one country through mail or electronic means to consumers in another country.

- *Mode 2—Consumption abroad*: services supplied in the territory of one Member to the consumers of another. An example is a consumer moving, for example, to consume tourism or education services in another country. Also covered are activities such as ship repair abroad, where only the property of the consumer moves.

- *Mode 3—Commercial presence*: services supplied through any type of business or professional establishment of one Member in the territory of another. An example is an insurance company owned by citizens of one country establishing a branch in another country.

- *Mode 4— Presence of natural persons*: services supplied by nationals of one Member in the territory of another. This mode includes both independent services suppliers, and employees of the services supplier of another Member. Examples are a doctor of one country supplying through his or her physical presence services in another country, or the foreign employees of a foreign bank.

Source: Broadman 1994.

necessarily translate into an expanding share of services in total trade (see table 6.1). Indeed, for many of the advanced countries in the Region, the opposite is observed—the relative importance of services has been declining, reflecting the expansion of trade manufactures or other tangible goods. Most countries in the Region are not heavily dependent on services as a source of foreign exchange—the two exceptions are Albania and Croatia. For both, services are more than 50 percent of total exports (goods plus services). In both cases, the activity that underlies the high dependence on services is travel (tourism), accounting for some 75 percent of total services receipts. Also noteworthy is that for both countries, the share of services in total receipts has grown very substantially since 1996, reflecting a recovery in tourism in the case of Croatia.

Three of the Region's countries see significant growth in their share of services exports: Bulgaria, FYR Macedonia, and Moldova. Tourism is again the explanation for the rise in Bulgaria; data constraints do not allow a determination for FYR Macedonia, while in the case of Moldova, the growth is the result of an expansion in services other than transport and travel. In contrast to these countries, the countries

TABLE 6.1

Share of Services in Foreign Exchange Receipts, 1996 and 2003 (%)

Country	Services (% of total exports)		Transport (% of all services)		Travel (% of all services)		Other services (% of all services)	
	1996	2003	1996	2003	1996	2003	1996	2003
Albania	35.0	61.7	23.4	9.6	59.4	72.5	17.2	17.9
Armenia	21.0	23.0	46.5	35.2	15.2	35.1	38.3	29.7
Azerbaijan	19.0	14.1	36.0	45.9	30.5	13.4	33.5	40.8
Belarus	14.0	12.9	52.6	57.0	6.1	17.8	41.3	25.2
Bosnia and Herzegovina	n.a.	24.6	n.a.	7.8	n.a.	48.1	n.a.	44.0
Bulgaria	22.0	29.8	32.2	29.7	28.4	52.4	39.4	17.9
Croatia	41.0	57.8	22.3	9.1	63.1	74.0	14.7	16.9
Czech Rep.	27.0	13.8	16.3	27.6	49.9	45.8	33.8	26.6
Estonia	38.0	32.7	39.8	44.1	43.7	30.2	16.5	25.7
Georgia	n.a.	34.7	n.a.	44.9	n.a.	33.3	n.a.	21.9
Hungary	27.0	15.6	6.4	12.7	60.7	43.1	32.9	44.1
Kazakhstan	10.0	11.4	64.0	48.4	29.5	33.2	6.4	18.4
Kyrgyz Rep.	6.0	n.a.	23.0	n.a.	13.4	n.a.	63.6	n.a.
Latvia	43.0	32.5	62.8	58.7	19.1	14.5	18.2	26.8
Lithuania	19.0	19.7	44.9	49.7	39.6	34.0	15.5	16.4
Macedonia, FYR	12.0	19.3	31.4	n.a.	13.4	n.a.	55.2	n.a.
Moldova	11.0	23.7	52.2	50.6	31.6	23.2	16.2	26.2
Poland	26.0	15.5	28.2	35.8	32.4	36.4	39.4	27.8
Romania	16.0	14.7	36.6	39.8	33.8	14.8	29.6	45.4
Russian Fed.	13.0	10.5	27.3	38.2	53.5	28.1	19.2	33.7
Serbia and Montenegro	n.a.	n.a.	n.a.	n.a.	n.a.	n.a.	n.a.	n.a.
Slovak Rep.	19.0	13.1	31.1	n.a.	32.6	n.a.	36.3	n.a.
Slovenia	20.0	17.8	22.5	27.6	58.1	47.9	19.4	24.5
Tajikistan	n.a.	8.9	n.a.	55.3	n.a.	1.7	n.a.	43.0
Turkmenistan	5.0	n.a.	76.1	n.a.	8.9	n.a.	15.0	n.a.
Ukraine	24.0	18.0	84.0	67.4	4.8	17.9	11.2	14.7
Uzbekistan	n.a.	n.a.	n.a.	n.a.	n.a.	n.a.	n.a.	n.a.
Turkey	30.0	27.2	13.1	11.4	42.1	69.2	44.9	19.4
World average	20.1	20.8	22.9	21.2	32.3	29.3	44.9	49.4

Source: IMF balance of payments.

Note: n.a. = not available.

that have recently acceded to the EU have experienced a decline in the share of services in total exports—often by 50 percent or more. Underlying this relative drop is a relatively stagnant level of services receipts combined with more dynamic exports of manufactures. Noteworthy is the fall in the relative importance of tourism receipts for the CEE and the Baltic countries, offset by a relative increase in transport and other services. The latter catchall category expands substantially as well in the cases of Romania and Russia. Croatia and Lithuania are the only countries where services export growth has outpaced merchandise exports since 1995.

These data reveal differences between subsets of the Region's countries. In the EU-8, exports of manufactures have dominated, with the exception of Estonia and Slovenia. In the case of the CIS and SEE, the share of services in total exports has grown significantly. Services exports as a share of GDP more than doubled for all of these countries on average since 1995. This development is not exceptional, in that the ratio of service exports to GDP has simply been converging toward those found in other parts of the world (table 6.2). Thus, this can be seen as one dimension of the transition to a more market-based economy. A similar pattern can be discerned on the import side—a process of convergence on the part of the Central Asian republics and SEE toward the pattern that already prevailed in the EU-8 and the EU-15 (table 6.3). However, this does not appear to be

TABLE 6.2
Exports of Services as a Share of GDP
Percentage

	1990	1995	1996	2002	2003
CIS (excluding Central Asia)		2	1	5	5
Central Asia		3	4	5	5
SEE	2	6	7	10	11
EU-8	4	10	10	8	8
The Region	1	5	5	6	6
The Region and Turkey	2	6	7	7	7
European Union (15)	5	6	6	8	8
Latin America and the Caribbean	3	3	2	3	3
Middle East and North Africa	4	5	5	4	n.a.
Africa	4	4	4	4	3
East Asia	2	3	3	4	3
South Asia	2	2	2	5	1

Source: IMF balance of payments.

TABLE 6.3
Imports of Services as a Share of GDP
Percentage

	1990	1995	1996	2002	2003
CIS (excluding Central Asia)		3	4	9	11
Central Asia		5	5	7	7
SEE	2	5	6	7	7
EU-8	3	7	7	7	7
The Region	1	4	5	6	6
The Region and Turkey	1	5	5	7	7
European Union (15)	5	6	6	8	8
Latin America and the Caribbean	3	3	3	4	4
Middle East and North Africa	8	8	8	6	n.a
Africa	7	8	8	6	4
East Asia	3	4	4	5	4
South Asia	2	3	3	4	1

Source: IMF balance of payments.

accompanied by any distinct pattern in the relative performance of services compared with goods imports.

Input-output tables for the year 2001, the latest available year for many of the Region's countries, provide information on differences in economic structure and the extent to which the countries have con-verged with comparable countries in the rest of world in regard to both intermediate services use and final demand, as well as on the service intensity of exports. Tables 6.4 and 6.5 report such informa-tion for a sample of the Region's countries for which input-output tables are available, drawn from the Global Trade Analysis Project (GTAP) database. Table 6.6 reports information on the sectoral inten-sity of exports: the direct contribution of agriculture, mining, manu-factures, and services to total exports, expressed as a share of total exports. (Note that this export revenue includes services as well as goods exports). The data confirm that Albania, Croatia, and the Baltic States are much more services-intensive in their export structure than are other countries in the Region.

Another measure of services intensity of exports that can be derived from input-output information is the sum of the direct and indirect contributions made by all sectors to a unit of foreign exchange earn-ings, taking into account the linkages between activities. This can be calculated by taking the direct contributions by sectors to total exports and using the input-output structure to determine how much activity a unit of exports generates. Any export, whether of a good or a service, will generate demand for inputs from all other sectors of the economy.

TABLE 6. 4
Sectoral Intensity of Exports
Sectors' share of total export revenue (percentage)

	Agriculture/Food/ Mining	Manufactures	Services
Albania	19	35	46
Croatia	9	49	42
Czech Rep.	5	80	15
Hungary	7	76	17
Poland	10	73	17
Romania	4	85	10
Slovak Rep.	4	86	10
Slovenia	4	81	15
Estonia	11	66	22
Latvia	13	64	24
Lithuania	13	63	24
Russian Fed.	40	52	8
Memo:			
Greece	12	29	58

Source: GTAP input-output data derived from Social Accounting Matrices for 2001.

TABLE 6.5
Total Export-related Activity
Direct plus indirect linkages, 2001

	Total "Multiplier" (index)	Shares (%)			
		Agriculture/Food	Mining	Manufactures	Services
Albania	4.8	20	4	24	52
Croatia	2.9	18	1	36	45
Czech Rep.	3.0	10	2	61	27
Hungary	2.8	10	2	51	37
Poland	4.2	17	3	43	38
Romania	6.6	27	3	39	30
Slovak Rep.	2.9	12	3	57	28
Slovenia	2.9	10	1	58	31
Estonia	2.5	15	2	49	35
Latvia	3.0	17	1	36	47
Lithuania	3.5	17	4	36	42
Russian Fed.	3.6	14	17	30	39
Memo:					
Turkey	3.7	17	2	40	41
China	3.7	18	3	62	17
Malaysia	2.1	8	3	64	25
Germany	3.3	7	1	49	43

Source: GTAP input-output data derived from Social Accounting Matrices for 2001.

TABLE 6.6
Inward FDI Stock by Sector, Selected Countries in the Region
End-2003 unless otherwise indicated; shares in total stock (%)

Sector	Czech Rep. 2002	Hungary 2002	Poland 2002	Slovak Rep.	Slovenia 2002	Estonia
Agriculture, forestry, fishing	0.1	1.3	0.4	0.2	0.0	0.4
Mining and quarrying	1.4	0.3	0.3	0.8	0.0	0.4
Manufacturing	35.5	45.8	35.8	37.5	43.3	18.2
Electricity, gas, water supply	6.9	4.6	2.6	11.7	1.0	2.4
Construction	1.9	1.1	2.6	0.7	0.1	2.5
Distribution and repair services	11.9	11.1	17.1	11.2	14.5	15.9
Hotels and restaurants	1.2	1.1	0.6	0.5	0.4	1.7
Transport, storage, and communications	13.6	10.1	10.4	10.0	4.4	17.7
Financial intermediation	15.9	10.3	21.3	23.5	18.8	28.1
Real estate, rental, and business act.	9.3	11.7	7.5	3.2	15.2	11.4
Education, health, social work	0.2	...	...	0.4	0.1	0.1
Other community and personal services	2.4	...	...	0.3	0.5	0.8
Other not classified activities	...	1.0	1.4	...	1.7	0.4
Purchase of real estate by foreigners	...	1.5	...	...	...	...
Total services share[a]	56.2	47.9	60.9	49.8	55.7	78.6
Value of services FDI stock ($ bn)	26.7	22.9	36.8	5.6	2.8	5.1
Services FDI stock as % of GDP	31.6	27.7	17.6	17.6	7.7	60.7

Source: wiiw-WIFO database on FDI, July 2004 edition.

Note: a. Includes finance and business services. b. Covers all industry, including mining/energy. c. Includes hotels and restaurants. d. Not including utilities.
... = not available.

The extent to which such demand is for service-related activities provides another measure of the relative service-intensity of an economy. The results of such a calculation are reported in table 6.5, where (for convenience) activities are aggregated into four broad categories.

The first column in table 6.5 is the sum of the direct and indirect linkage effects generated by a unit of export revenue—it indicates the total activity generated by (going into) one unit of foreign exchange (exports). The average "multiplier" is 3.6 for the countries of the Region covered in the sample (that is, every dollar of exports generates $3.6 in economic activity, both direct and indirect demand). Of greater interest from a services-intensity perspective is how much of this is the result of services. On average, a little over one-third of this total activity is services-related, ranging from a high of 52 percent (Albania) to a low of 27 percent for the Czech Republic. Even taking into account the indirect linkage effects, Albania, the Baltic states, and Croatia are relatively services-intensive. However, many the Region's countries are more services-oriented than many developing countries such as China or Malaysia, two comparators reported in table 6.5. On this measure, they are rather similar to EU countries.

Balance of payments data provide no information on the origin and destination of trade. Given the absence of customs statistics—the source of such data for goods trade—it is very difficult to determine

Latvia	Lithuiania	EU-8	Bulgaria	Croatia	Romania	Russian Fed. flow 2000–2002	Ukraine 2002
1.5	0.8	0.5	0.3	0.3	0.7	0.4	2.1
0.6	0.8	0.7	1.1	3.1	...	...	2.4
15.5	31.1	37.0	33.4	30.6	54.3	45.0[b]	46.4
3.4	4.4	4.8	1.0	1.1	...	...	1.6
1.0	1.2	1.8	2.7	0.9	2.4	2.2	2.9
18.0	17.9	14.0	18.0	6.9	16.4	22.0[c]	18.5
1.3	1.6	0.9	1.7	4.0	2.4	...	2.3
11.9	17.1	11.5	15.7	25.0	7.8	9.5	7.2
15.0	15.7	17.5	17.7	24.6	...	1.8	8.1
24.5	7.3	9.3	3.9	3.1	...	8.2	4.7
0.1	0.2.	0.1	0.3	...	...	...	2.3
1.1	1.5	0.8	0.8	0.5	...	0.2	1.5
6.0	0.3	0.9	3.2	...	16.0[a]	11.0	...
...	...	0.3	...	...	...	...	...
78.9	62.8	57.1	65.2	64.9	45.0	54.6	47.5
2.6	3.1	106.6	3.3	7.4	5.7	35.5	3.6
26.8	37.8	...	16.6	26.1	9.4	8.2	7.3

who are the partners for the observed foreign exchange flows associated with services. A sense can be obtained of the origin and destination of services exports and imports by using data that should be highly correlated with certain types of trade in services. For example, telecommunications traffic is collected by telecom firms on a bilateral basis, and this should be closely correlated with Mode 1 trade. Similarly, the origin of tourist arrivals may provide information on Mode 2 trade. Finally, FDI data and immigration flows will provide some information on the geographic pattern of Modes 3 and 4 trade.

The available data for the Region on the origin and destination of travelers are very weak—statistics provided by the World Tourism Organization are very incomplete and not comparable across destination countries. One source of data that can be used to assess the origin and destination of trade in services is merchandise trade statistics, because these will by necessity be accompanied by transport services. (These were discussed in chapter 2.) The other source on origin and destination is telecommunications flows. These are reported in figure 6.4, for various subgroups of the Region's countries, for the year 2002. These data give an indication not only of the current situation but also of the change that has taken place since 1990 because before that, the presumption is that virtually all international telecommunications traffic would have taken place between the Region's countries, reflecting the closed nature of the economic regime.

The telecom data reveal substantial differences in the origin and destination of "trade in services." For the Central and Eastern European (CEE), Southeastern European (SEE), and Baltic countries, the EU accounts for about 50 percent of all outgoing traffic, with the SEE share being slightly higher and the Baltic share slightly lower than this. The relative importance of the other countries of the Region, taken as a whole, varies greatly across these three groups: in the Baltics, other countries of the Region account for almost the same share in traffic as does the EU-15 (43 percent as opposed to 46 percent). In the SEE countries, other countries of the Region account for 20 percent of the total, as compared with 28 percent for CEE. Other (non-EU) OECD countries represent between 4 and 6 percent of outgoing traffic. Turkey is also an important destination (4.5 percent).

The pattern is quite different for the three other subgroups. Here, rather than CEE, SEE, or the Baltics, Russia in particular accounts for the lion's share of outgoing traffic, ranging from a low of 69 percent for the Caucasus to a high of 81 percent for the Central Asian countries. All of the Region's countries account for 77 percent of outgoing traffic on average for Russia, Ukraine, Belarus, and Moldova. The EU-15 represents 8 percent of total outgoing traffic for these four coun-

FIGURE 6.4
Bilateral Telecom Traffic, 2002

CEE, shares of destination areas in outgoing
telecom traffic, 2002

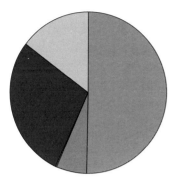

SEE, shares of destination areas in outgoing
telecom traffic, 2002

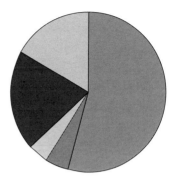

Baltics, shares of destination areas in
outgoing telecom traffic, 2002

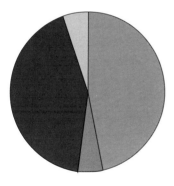

CIS (excl. CARs & Caucasus), shares of destination areas
in outgoing telecom traffic, 2002

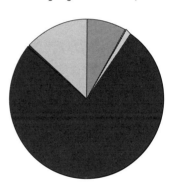

Caucasus, shares of destination
areas in outgoing telecom traffic, 2002

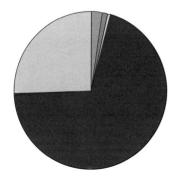

Central Asia Republics, shares of destination
areas in outgoing telecom traffic, 2002

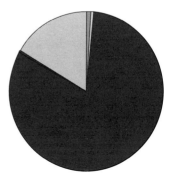

▨ EU-15 ▨ Non EU OECD ☐ Turkey ■ Region ■ Middle East/Asia ▨ Not specified

Source: International Telecommunications Union.

tries; the EU-15 accounts for only 1–2 percent for most of the other CIS countries. Similarly, other OECD countries account for only negligible shares. While it should be noted that some of these CIS countries report relatively large shares of outgoing traffic as "not specified," so that it is not clear whether the outgoing share toward OECD countries or Asia is actually as low as is reported, the data do show unambiguously that there has not been much diversification away from traditional partners in much of the CIS. In contrast, there has been a very marked shift away from other countries in the Region, in particular Russia, in the CEE and SEE countries.

FDI in Services in the Region

Given that services trades (sales) often require proximity between service provider and consumer, FDI is an important mode of international trade in services. For the countries of the Region, FDI is an important avenue through which to acquire access to best practices and new service varieties and technologies. There are substantial differences across the Region's countries in the pattern of services vs. nonservices FDI, as well as in terms of the magnitude of FDI inflows.

Table 6.6 reports data on the share of services in total inward FDI in the Region for countries for which these data are available.[3] Overall, services account for some 62 percent of the stock of FDI in the reporting countries—that is, services FDI tends to reflect closely the prevailing share of services in the GDP of OECD countries. Finance, transport, communications, and distribution services account for the largest share of this FDI. The intensity of FDI in services is highest in the Baltic states, presumably reflecting their relatively small size and limited manufacturing base, and lowest in Romania and Ukraine. In the case of Estonia, financial services are the number-one sector for FDI, including nonservices sectors, while for Latvia, business and real estate services are the largest sector.

In general, the EU-15 generate about 80 percent of inward FDI into the Region's countries, with Germany, the Netherlands, and Austria generally being among the top three foreign investors (see also chapter 7). Geographic proximity and historical links play an important role in some instances—for example, Sweden and Finland are major investors in the Baltics, France has large shares in FDI inflows into Romania and Poland, and Greece in Bulgaria. For Russia, Ukraine, and resource-rich Central Asian Republics, FDI from the United States is important—the United States is the major investor in both Russia and Ukraine. As can be seen from table 6.6, services FDI is also very high as a ratio of GDP in the Baltic states, is highest in the Czech Republic among the CEE states, and is lowest in Romania, Russia, and Ukraine. Croatia, the only SEE country for which such data are available, also has a very high share of services FDI, consistent with the high service intensity of its exports.

The pattern that emerges is similar to that suggested by the services trade data—there is a distinct difference between the EU-8 states and the Central Asian Republics. The former have attracted large flows of services FDI, whereas the latter have not. The magnitude of the associated capital inflow is significant in the former countries, with Estonia and Lithuania being the outliers. Given that FDI in services can be expected to be associated with new technologies, higher service standards, and more effective delivery—as illustrated by the indexes discussed below—these inflows help to explain both the observed higher labor productivity performance in services noted earlier and the aggregate growth performance of these countries.

Policy Stances and Reform Progress

Services sector reform involves a mix of deregulation (the dismantling of barriers to entry and promotion of competition) and improved regulation (putting in place an appropriate legal environment, strengthening regulatory agencies and increasing their independence and accountability, and ensuring universal access to key services). The policy challenge is to achieve a balance between traditional regulation and the introduction of competition (see chapter 4). Much has been done by countries in the Region to reform and adapt policies and regulatory regimes for services industries. Figure 6.5 plots three indicators of the extent of policy reform for banking, nonbank financial services, and infrastructure. In all three cases, the value of this index is set at zero for 1989. Thus, the 2004 value of the index provides a measure of the progress that has been made by countries in converging to "best-practice" standards—measured by a maximum value of 4.3. Box 6.2 discusses the construction of these indexes.

The EU-8 (the CEE and the Baltic countries) have made the most progress on all three fronts. For the other country groups, there is significant variation across the three indexes. SEE has advanced the most on reforms in banking and infrastructure, followed by the Caucasus. Belarus, Moldova, Russia, and Ukraine have done the most in the nonbank financial area, followed by SEE. The Central Asian Republics have made the least progress in all three areas, with one country—Turkmenistan—not advancing at all in any of the three areas.

FIGURE 6.5

Services Reform Index, 2004

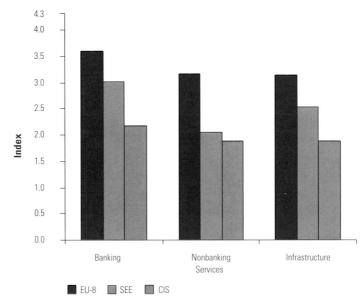

Source: EBRD 2004a.

BOX 6.2

The EBRD Reform Indexes

The index ranges from 1(little progress) to 4.3 (most advanced implementation of reform agenda).

Banking and interest rate liberalization: A 4.3 means full convergence of banking laws and regulations with Bank for International Settlement (BIS) standards, provision of full set of competitive
banking services.

Securities markets and nonbank financial institutions: 4.3 means full convergence of securities
laws and regulations with International Organization of Securities Commissions (IOSCO) standards, fully developed nonbank intermediation.

Infrastructure: average of the following five infrastructure reform indicators:

- *Electric power*: 4.3 means tariffs are cost-reflective and provide adequate incentive for efficiency improvements. Large-scale private sector involvement in the unbundled and well-
  regulated sector. Fully liberalized sector with well-functioning arrangements for network access and full competition in generation.

What follows provides an overview of the state of reform in services sector policy regimes, with a particular focus on banking, telecommunications, and other utilities and infrastructure services. A more detailed overview of the stance of policy reforms in banking and telecommunications and their evolution over time can be found in annex tables 6.1 and 6.2.

Banking

The banking sector in the EU-8 countries is characterized by small shares of credit allocated through state-owned banks, high foreign participation, and stronger regulatory regimes. Evidence from these countries indicates that foreign banks have been contributing to the modernization of the sector. Bottlenecks relevant to sustained financial development do, however, often persist within the legal framework (tax system, creditor rights, and the bankruptcy code). Central bank independence has also been strengthened in most of these countries. Cukierman, Miller, and Neyapti (2001) use a measure of

- *Railways*: 4.3 means separation of infrastructure from operations, and freight from passenger operations. Full divestment and transfer of asset ownership implemented or planned, including infrastructure and rolling stock. Rail regulator established and access pricing implemented.

- *Roads*: 4.3 means fully decentralized road administration. Commercialized road maintenance operations competitively awarded to private companies. Road user charges reflect the full costs of road use and associated factors, such as congestion, accidents, and pollution. Widespread private sector participation in all aspects of road provision. Full public consultation on new road projects.

- *Telecommunications*: 4.3 means effective regulation through an independent entity. Coherent regulatory and institutional framework to deal with tariffs, interconnection rules, licensing, concession fees, and spectrum allocation. Consumer ombudsman function.

- *Water and wastewater*: 4.3 means water utilities fully decentralized and commercialized. Fully autonomous regulator exists with complete authority to review and enforce tariff levels and quality standards. Widespread private sector participation via service/management/lease contracts. High-powered incentives, full concessions, and/or divestiture of water and wastewater services in major urban areas.

Source: EBRD 2004a.

independence called LVAW with 16 weighted components. As figure 6.6 shows, the degree of independence in the eight new EU member countries has converged toward the level achieved by the German Bundesbank during the 1980s. All of other countries in the Region, however, fall substantially short of the most advanced ones. Note that this indicator reflects only legal, not actual, independence. If the latter were to be taken into account, the picture would look even more pronounced. The Central Bank of Belarus, for instance, has a high degree of legal, but a low degree of actual, independence.

Banking markets in the vast majority of CIS countries, as well as in some SEE countries, tend to be relatively closed in both a formal and an informal sense. Nevertheless, Armenia's financial sector is rather open and sound, underlining that this country is the reform engine of the Region in financial services. Belarus, in spite of its relative proximity to the EU, is one of the least advanced countries in that sense, as are some Central Asian countries. While actual or potential limits on foreign participation (globally or in an individual bank) do play a role in some countries, bureaucratic impediments seem to play a more prominent role in inhibiting foreign participation. Among the factors reported are limitations on bringing in foreign staff, lengthy licensing procedures, financial repression, public ownership of major banks, and inadequate regulatory practices. In general, the banking sector in these countries suffers from weak capital bases and lack of confidence. These impediments to financial development are reflected in figure 6.7, which illustrates that the depth of the banking sector has developed accordingly. Again, the EU-8 countries fare best. Box 6.3 discusses in somewhat greater depth the impacts of policies that restrict

FIGURE 6.6
Central Bank Independence

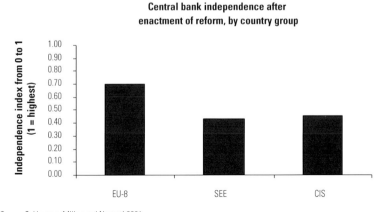

Source: Cukierman, Miller, and Neyapti 2001.

FIGURE 6.7
Financial Sector Performance

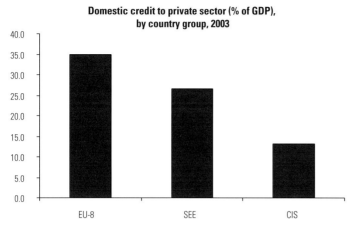

Domestic credit to private sector (% of GDP),
by country group, 2003

Source: WDI 2004.

foreign providers' access to the financial sector, based on the experience of Russia.

Regulated Utilities

Regulated utility and infrastructure services such as telecommunications can play an important role in fostering (or deterring) international integration because they can greatly affect the transactions costs of international exchanges. Their cost, quality, and accessibility become central to international integration. Although much reform progress has been made in some of the Region's countries, significant challenges to the efficient provision of utility and infrastructure services to firms and consumers in the Region remain. In part, current problems have their roots in the obsolescence of equipment resulting from perverse investment incentives that linger from the era of central planning and the concomitant disrepair after the fall of Communism. The key challenges include tackling regulatory problems in the provision of utility and infrastructure services, which have been subject to extensive cross-subsidization, inefficient pricing, poor revenue collection, insufficient separation of industry branches, and overall poorly designed regulatory frameworks. These problems led to distortions in the development and operation of utility and infrastructure services markets and stifled needed investment in the Region.[4]

The lack of competition in specific segments of these markets in most of the national economies of the Region signals an urgent need for institutional and structural reform. The rules and institutions established in each country that govern these services are important

BOX 6.3

Foreign Participation in Russia's Banking System— Experiences and Perspectives

Since the late 1980s, the Russian banking system has undergone fundamental changes. So far, these changes do not include a sustained opening of the sector to foreign participation. The prospect of WTO accession, however, puts the topic back on the agenda. It is therefore worth taking a brief look at respective past and future policy changes, as well as their impact on the sector and the entire economy. As a first step, however, a look at the general financial-sector background against which market opening occurs seems useful. Reforms in the banking sector go back to 1987, when first attempts at establishing a two-tier banking system were made with the registration of special state and commercial banks. In the early 1990s, this process continued under the auspices of the Russian Central Bank and a large number of commercial banks emerged in a short time. Growing private demand for credit and low-cost liabilities attracted new market entrants. Most banks, however, were inefficient and managed to survive only because of low returns on deposits. The financial crisis that took off in August 1998 disrupted the process of financial deepening. The government failed to service its debt, the ruble devalued, and creditors panicked. As a result, households and nonresident creditors suffered substantial losses, whereas the real economy was hardly affected. As a matter of fact, banks' assets were not too heavily involved in the production side of the economy. Postcrisis market consolidation was weak and primarily affected banks with a high share of foreign liabilities. Instead, insiders often stripped and recycled assets. After the crisis, financial services again became more concentrated in state-owned banks, which were most heavily involved in funding production activity. In 2000, for instance, state banks were given special privileges such as implicit guarantees, capital injections, and preferential funding sources.

Positive economywide fundamentals, as well as risk-averse strategies adopted by banks, subsequently improved financial health in general. Improvements in the legal and regulatory framework are under way. Deficiencies in depositor protection, however, have remained in place. This

because they affect service delivery and the size and nature of the market in which they are supplied. The regulatory framework needs not only to reflect the cost of, and demand for, these infrastructure services, as well as the rate of technical progress in the field, but also to ensure equal access and prevent domination by incumbents in many portions of the market. Regulatory institutions affect the scope for competition by opening segments of these markets to privatization and liberalization (see World Bank 2004h).

Introducing competition into these sectors has brought about increased efficiency in the provision of regulated utility and infrastruc-

fact helped trigger a minor run on deposits following the closure of a bank in mid-2004. This, along with a weak capital base and the prevalence of short-term liabilities, poses important policy challenges. Foreign banks increased their market share in the wake of the financial crisis. They became a haven for both domestic and international depositors. In spite of these favorable conditions, their market share never significantly exceeded 10 percent. Even though the policy regime is formally liberal, market access is not easy. Licensing discrimination, practices and subnational regulations violating federal law, abuse of power, and other problems have been noted in the entire services sector. In financial services in particular, the federal law on "Banks and Banking Activity of 1996" allows the Central Bank to impose a ceiling on the total amount of foreign capital as a share of total bank capital in Russia. In addition, since 1997, the Central Bank has required of foreign banks that at least 75 percent of their employees and 50 percent of their management board be of Russian nationality. Heads of foreign banks' Russian offices are required to be proficient in Russian. There are other restrictions requiring work experience in the country. These issues are currently subject to WTO negotiations.

Potential benefits of liberalizing the sector are manifold: more foreign presence provides enterprises with easier access to cheaper, long-term financial resources. The net return to capital increases, which fosters capital accumulation and improves the investment climate. Both quality and quantity of financial services may improve. The financial sector's capital base increases and deposits become safer and more long-term. More efficient credit allocation may imply the adoption of better production technologies, which may spill over into the whole economy. This has a positive effect on total factor productivity. Jensen and Tarr (2004) estimate the welfare gains from Russian WTO accession to amount to between 3.3 and 11 percent of GDP in the medium and long run, respectively. They assert that most of these gains would result from the liberalization of barriers against FDI in the services sectors. A negative implication is the likely squeeze of Russian commercial banks by foreigners and state-owned banks, which receive high international credit ratings. The commercial banks may be taken over by foreigners, leaving the rest of the sector in the hands of the state.

Sources: Vedev 2004; Jensen and Tarr 2004; Mikhailov et al. 2001.

ture services in the Region. Two main reforms have been responsible for this: (i) allowing entry of new domestic (or foreign) infrastructure providers; and (ii) opening the domestic market to imports of such services. Complementary to the issue of entry into these industries is the process of change of ownership. Privatization of utilities and infrastructure service providers is, however, not a necessary condition for improved efficiency in the provision of these services. The incumbent provider might remain state-owned, but as long as the regulator allows for the entry of new providers into the market, such competition can yield efficiency gains in the industry overall (see EBRD 2004a).

The experience to date of countries in the Region in developing modern regulated utilities and infrastructure services providers has been quite mixed. The EBRD index for these sectors reveals the heterogeneity found in the Region (figure 6.8).[5] The index shows little or no progress in utility and infrastructure reform in Belarus, the Kyrgyz Republic, Tajikistan, Turkmenistan, and Uzbekistan as opposed to the advancements made in the Czech Republic, Estonia, Hungary, Poland, and Romania. The relatively high rankings of Bulgaria, Croatia, the Kyrgyz Republic, Romania, and Russia reflect the growing recognition and actions by the governments in these countries to invest efforts in crafting better regulation, commercialization, and tariff reform for the effective provision of utility and infrastructure services. Figure 6.9 disaggregates the infrastructure index along five sectoral dimensions—electric power, roads, railways, telecommunications, and water and wastewater—and assesses the cumulative reform progress in each of the Region's countries. On average for the Region, progress has been most pronounced in the sectors of telecommunications and electric power. These higher rankings are likely a result of commercialization, including deregulation and the successful privatization of the national telecom companies (see below).

In the telecommunications sector, fixed-line services are still quite underdeveloped in most of the Region's economies. This has given rise to a faster growth of, and stronger competition in, the mobile services sectors. As can be seen in figure 6.10, however, this holds pri-

FIGURE 6.8
Index of Infrastructure Reform, 2004

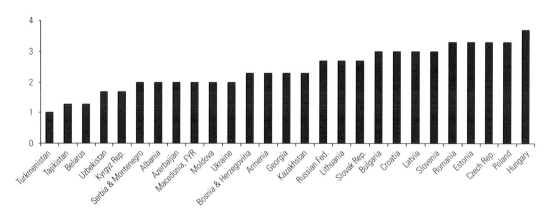

Source: EBRD 2004a.

Note: The ratings are calculated as the average of five infrastructure reform indicators covering electric power, roads, railways, telecommunications, and water and wastewater. See box 6.2.

FIGURE 6.9

Infrastructure Reform, by Country and Sector, 2004

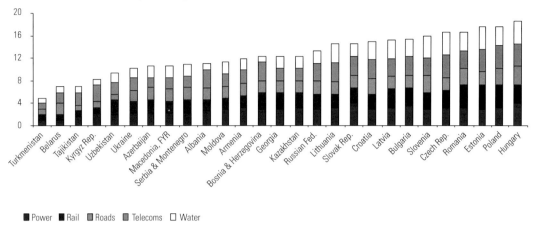

■ Power ■ Rail ▨ Roads ▨ Telecoms □ Water

Source: EBRD 2004a.

Note: Each indicator ranges from 1 to 4.3, with 1 representing little or no change from a rigid centrally planned economy, and 4.3 representing the standards of an industrialized market economy. The scale ranges from 0 to 20, representing the cumulative progress for each country. For a detailed classification system for the five indicators, refer to the EBRD Transition Report 2004, p. 200.

marily for the EU-8, and to some extent for SEE. In the rest of the Region, mobile penetration rates fall short of even fixed-line services.

In many countries in the Former Soviet Union, independent telecom regulators have yet to be established. Although regulatory independence is also compromised in some EU-8 countries, this adversely affects fixed-line services, where competition requires network access. Interconnections between different operators should be pro-

FIGURE 6.10

Telephone Services

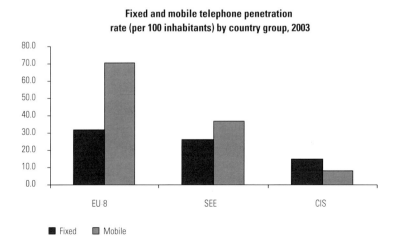

Fixed and mobile telephone penetration rate (per 100 inhabitants) by country group, 2003

■ Fixed ▨ Mobile

Source: EBRD 2004a.

moted. The incumbent fixed-line operator often impedes the conclusion of interconnection agreements with other providers. Tariffs are low and distorted in many countries. There are cross-subsidies between different types of calls and customers. These issues will have to be tackled in the future, taking into account social concerns about low-income groups.

On average, the least progress has been made across the Region in the rail, road, and water sectors. Reforms in road transport appear to be lagging behind the railway sector in many countries. Private sector participation remains limited. Only some EU-8 and SEE countries, such as Croatia, Hungary, and Poland, have introduced private sector participation through toll roads. Success, however, has been mixed so far because of traffic diversion to alternative roads and high risks associated with private investment. Toll-based concessions in Hungary have been converted into payments to the private investors via the public budget. This transfers traffic risk back to the state while maintaining the character of the public-private partnership. Reforms in the railway sector are also at an early stage in terms of private sector participation, although the separation of infrastructure from operations is either planned or has been put in practice in many countries.[6] The EU-8 countries have in theory adopted EU standards of open access, although implementation has been lagging. The challenges to reform of the water sector are illustrated in box 6.4 for the case of Albania, but the messages are pertinent for many other of the Region's countries.

Regulatory Reform, Privatization, and International Integration

Case-study research in various countries in the Region documents that improvements in transport have been crucial for enhancing the movement of goods from one country to another; that progress in reform of telecommunications and the role of the Internet have provided a low-cost channel for supplier and customer searching internationally and the conduct of related transactions; and that financial-service reforms have facilitated cross-border payments for goods and services (for case-study work on Russia, see Broadman [2002] and for Southeastern Europe, see Broadman et al. [2004]).

The modest (or small) size of some the Region's countries can create a challenge to exploit the economies of scale and scope—and hence reduced costs—that often are generic to the provision of utility and infrastructure services. Cross-border supply of such services—that is, through imports—can provide opportunities to realize such economies. For example, a firm operating in one of the Region's

---

BOX 6.4

Challenges in Water Reform in Albania

Albania faces acute challenges in watershed and flood management; water sanitation; irrigation and drainage; and management of lakes, wetlands, and coastal areas. The country also lags in institutionalizing a framework with broad stakeholder ownership and water services delivery institutions. The government did not liberalize the national uniform water supply tariffs until July 1998, when it established the Utility Regulatory Commission, with tariff-methodology and tariff-setting powers. However, even then the allowed tariff for many local water utilities was well below the requested one. The country continues to experience water problems resulting from outdated supply and sanitation systems and from sluggish progress with reforms. In Tirana, more than 50 percent of the water is lost because of leakages and illegal connections. In the urban areas, some 40 percent of the population has a sewerage connection, and around 80 percent has access to piped water. Although the privatization of the water sector has started, major efforts are needed in modernizing and maintaining the sector.

Sources: World Bank 2003i, "Water Resource Management in Southeast Europe," and EU Stabilization and Association Report Albania 2003.

---

countries might find it cheaper to purchase electricity through wheeling from a provider based in a neighboring country (or even farther away) rather than from a utility based in the home country. With the heterogeneous resource endowments and variation in market sizes across the countries in the Region, the potential benefits of creating a regional market for the provision—and hence regulation—of infrastructure services might well be substantial. Box 6.5 discusses the experience of the SEE countries and Turkey in establishing a regional energy market.

Privatization of utility firms is another channel through which deregulation and infrastructure reform and international integration are linked. While there are some (in fact, quite few) cases where FDI in these sectors has taken the form of greenfield investment, the vast majority of FDI inflows associated with these sectors in the Region has been through the privatization process.[7] Not surprisingly, the extent of privatization activities varies tremendously by country and sector, as presented in figures 6.11 and 6.12. The EU-8 countries are the leaders in attracting FDI in the utilities sectors, with more than $30 billion in cumulative FDI inflow for the period 1992–2003. The SEE countries as a sub-Region have attracted the least. From a sectoral perspective, the highest revenues have come from the privatization of telecommunications companies in the Region, followed by

BOX 6.5

Benefits and Challenges to a Regional Energy Market in SEE and Turkey

The international community's support for Southeastern Europe (SEE) within the energy sector has gradually shifted from emergency support and efforts to address reconstruction needs to a more coordinated regional long-term approach. With the SEE Electricity Regulatory Forum initiative, the European Commission has proposed a coherent vision with respect to the development of a competitive regional energy market. It has set the basis for the Region's electricity standards to catch up, in the medium to long term, with the standards of the European Union. This initiative proposes that countries open their national electricity markets by 2006. This regional market will be based on the principles of the European Commission's Electricity Directive (96/92) and the relevant secondary legislation. The intended result will be that the electricity systems and companies of the Region will participate fully in the internal electricity market of the European Union.

The benefits of the process potentially include increased reliability in electricity supply; lower operating costs; reduced needs for additional-capacity investments, especially in generation; improved opportunities for intra- and interregional trade, including peak load by hydroproducers in the Region; and lower prices for the end customers. However, the challenges entailed in the transition to the new systems are considerable. They include adopting numerous new laws and regulations; setting up independent regulatory agencies; training personnel; and introducing new business concepts and practices, stranded assets, and protection of the poorest customers.

Under a memorandum of understanding, which was signed in Athens in 2002, all SEE countries, together with Turkey, have committed to undertaking steps toward opening their energy markets. These steps include adopting energy strategies; setting up independent regulators; unbundling industry; and developing grid codes, cross-border transmission pricing, congestion management principles, and trading and commercial codes. Markets for eligible customers are expected to be open by 2007.

Source: Adapted from Broadman et al. 2004.

proceeds from gas and power transmission privatizations. Transport and water services privatization has generated the smallest revenues for the Region in comparison with the other utilities sectors.

Further liberalization of access in telecom markets by foreign providers of telecommunications services—especially through FDI—would generate substantial gains for the countries concerned. Recent analysis for Russia, for example, concludes that this could increase Russian real consumption by 1.6 percent (see box 6.6). While private sector participation is relatively developed in telecommunications in

FIGURE 6.11

Utility Privatization Proceeds in the Region, by Sub-Region, 1992–2003

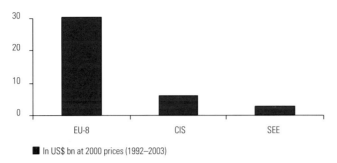

■ In US$ bn at 2000 prices (1992–2003)

Source: EBRD 2004a.

Note: Includes telecom, gas, power, water, and transport proceeds from privatization.

FIGURE 6.12

Utility Privatization Proceeds by Sector for the Region, 1992–2003

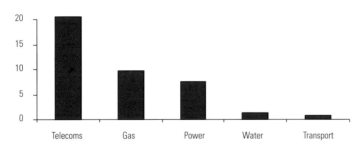

■ In US$ bn at 2000 prices (1992–2003)

Source: EBRD 2004a.

many transition economies, in the CIS, there is less progress in opening the sector to private investors and in reforming the sector's policy framework. State control and monopolies still prevail in fixed-line services in many of the countries in question. Where privatization of incumbents has occurred, its objective has often been the maximization of revenue. As a result, private investors were granted monopoly status for significant periods of time. Armenia, for instance, provided its Greek investor with a 15-year exclusivity clause.

International experience suggests that countries that have had the objective of maximizing privatization revenues or a desire not to be accused of getting a price that is "too low" have tended to grant whole or partial monopoly privileges to new private incumbents. This can come at the expense of future improvements in the network, as well as high prices that over time will generate high profits for the owners of the firms.[8] Empirical evidence indicates that what matters most is

BOX 6.6

The Gains from Foreign Direct Investment in Service Sectors

A growing body of evidence and economic theory suggests that the close availability of a diverse set of business services (like telecommunications services) is important for economic growth. Liberalization of barriers to foreign direct investment in services plays an important role in this regard, especially in sectors such as financial services and telecommunications. The key idea is that a diverse set (or a higher-quality set) of business services allows users to purchase a quality-adjusted unit of business services at lower cost. As services markets are opened to foreign entry (FDI), domestic businesses and consumers will have improved access to services—whether they are telecommunications, banking, insurance, transportation, or other business services. This will lower the cost of doing business and increase the productivity of the economy.

Research suggests that liberalization of barriers to FDI in services may generate gains that substantially exceed those that come from merchandise trade liberalization undertaken in isolation. In the case of Russia, for example, recent analysis concludes that opening access to services FDI in the context of accession to the WTO will generate about three-quarters of the total gains to Russia from WTO accession in the medium term—an increase in consumption of some 6 percent —because the ad valorem equivalent of barriers to FDI is a multiple of the average tariff on imports of goods. Estimates for Russia of the tariff equivalent of barriers to FDI in services average around 33 percent for nontransport services and some 80–90 percent for air and maritime transport (Jensen and Tarr 2004).

Among the key restrictions against foreign telecom suppliers in Russia are that (i) Rostelekom maintains a monopoly on long-distance fixed-line telephone services, (ii) affiliate branches of foreign banks are prohibited, and (iii) there is a quota on the multinational share of the insurance market. The protocol on Russian accession signed between the European Union and Russia on May 21, 2004, calls for the termination of the Rostelekom monopoly by 2007 and allows for an increase in the upper limit of the multinational share of the Russian insurance market. Jensen and Tarr (2004) conclude that elimination of barriers to FDI in telecommunications alone will result in a gain in Russian consumption of 1.6 percent (conversely, if Russia were not to lower barriers to FDI in telecommunications, the gains to Russia would be reduced by 1.6 percent of Russian consumption). Thus, reduction of barriers to FDI in telecommunications is one of the more important actions Russia could take in order to improve Russian real income.

Source: World Bank staff.

competition in markets and the incentives confronting management of monopoly providers, not ownership. Indeed, countries that first privatized network service providers (such as telecoms) and then gradually opened up the market to competition saw worse performance of the sector in terms of service delivery—for example, the number of fixed lines added to the telecom network—than that of countries that introduced competition immediately (Fink, Mattoo, and Rathindran 2003).[9] The penetration rates in most of the CIS countries, as opposed to the EU-8, where privatization and market opening were more synchronized, confirm this. In Latvia, the partial privatization with exclusivity clause lasting till 2013 was therefore converted into a faster market opening (2003 instead of 2013).

Regulatory Effectiveness and Rate Structures

The effectiveness of the regulatory process is critical when establishing competitive markets. Another key aspect is the structure of rates and other elements of the pricing schemes for the provision of the services. Enhancing regulatory efficiency is uneven in the Region, not only across the countries, but also among the sectors within a country. The literature increasingly focuses on several dimensions of an effective regulatory system: coherence, predictability, capacity, independence, accountability, and transparency (see EBRD 2004a). Table 6.7 summarizes achievements in regulatory effectiveness in each country of the Region[10] across four sectors (electricity, railways, telecommunications, and water) along one of the dimensions of regulatory efficiency: establishment of an independent regulator. These data suggest that the Czech Republic, Estonia, Latvia, Poland, and the Slovak Republic have made the most progress in this area, whereas many of the CIS countries have made very poor progress. The SEE economies are somewhere in between.

Nevertheless, even with an independent regulator, the difficult challenge facing a national government is to endow that entity with technically competent people and give those people the authority and budget needed to effectively implement the entity's mandate—a problem common in many of the countries in the Region. In this regard, some case studies are telling: there are only five employees in the recently established electricity regulator in FYR Macedonia, compared with several hundred in some of the EU-8 countries. Less than $100,000 was budgeted for the creation of an independent electricity regulator in the Kyrgyz Republic, in comparison with several million dollars in the EU-8.[11] Thus, assessing overall regulatory effectiveness needs to take into account the interrelationships among the various dimensions. The EBRD (2004a) provides an assessment of the five other dimensions of regulatory efficiency for these countries and sectors.

The effective provision of regulated utility services also requires the establishment of tariffs that both reflect costs and take into account differences in value of service across customer classes (Vis-

TABLE 6.7

Indicators of Regulatory Effectiveness in the Region, by Country, 2004

Country	Electricity (year autonomous regulator established)	Railways (autonomous regulator)	Telecommunications (year autonomous regulator established)	Water (decentralized)
Albania	1996	No	1998	No
Armenia	1997	No	Planned	Planned
Azerbaijan	—	No	Planned	Planned
Belarus	—	No	—	No
Bosnia	2004	No	2001	No
Bulgaria	1999	No	2002	Planned
Croatia	2002	Planned	2002	Full
Czech Rep.	2001	Yes	2000	Full
Estonia	1998	Yes	1998	Full
Serbia and Montenegro	Planned	No	—	Partial
Macedonia, FYR	2003	No	—	Partial
Georgia	1997	No	2000	Partial
Hungary	1994	Planned	1993	Full
Kazakhstan	2002	Yes	2002	Partial
Kyrgyz Rep.	1996	No	2001	No
Latvia	1996	Yes	2001	Full
Lithuania	1997	No	2001	Full
Moldova	1998	No	2000	Partial
Poland	1998	Yes	2002	Full
Romania	1999	No	2002	Full
Russian Fed.	2004	Planned	2004	Partial
Slovak Rep.	2001	Yes	2000	Full
Slovenia	2001	No	2001	Partial
Tajikistan	—	No	Planned	No
Turkmenistan	—	No	—	No
Ukraine	2000	No	—	Partial
Uzbekistan	2000	No	—	Partial

Source: EBRD 2004a.

Note: — = not available.

cusi, Vernon, and Harrington 2000). There are two main regulatory mechanisms—rate-of-return regulation and price-cap regulation—for establishing pricing rules.[12] The choice depends on a variety of country and sector characteristics, including the quality of cost accounting and auditing systems, the availability of economic and technical expertise, the institutional checks and balances, and the investment requirements of the regulated sectors.

In light of the scarce technical expertise and severe informational problems in many of the Region's countries, utilities must set up clear regulatory goals and simplify administrative procedures as much as possible. The role of the regulator can be limited to imposing floors on prices to protect against predation and imposing ceilings on prices to protect against monopolistic behavior. These floors and ceilings should be based on an economic analysis of costs or on appropriate international benchmarks. In the final analysis, in order to ensure that real sector businesses behind the border face "hard budget constraints" to foster efficiency, productivity, and international competitiveness, in accordance with the discussion in chapter 4 and above, prices charged to them for utility and infrastructure services generally should be subsidy-free; at the same time, payments should be made to the utility and infrastructure services providers in full and on time.

In many of the Region's countries, cross-subsidization is evident in the rates charged for various utility services. For example, local calls are essentially free, while international calls are very expensive (by international standards) in many CIS countries. Cross-subsidization is also practiced among customer groups. For example, railway companies in Russia cover their losses from passenger traffic by using revenues collected from freight customers. Figure 6.13 illustrates that cross-subsidization in the electricity sector, for example, prevails in about one-half of the countries in the Region. Generally, industrial consumers, many of whom have the ability to switch fuels or operate with interruptible service, should be charged lower tariffs in comparison with their residential customer counterparts.[13] This is not the case in 13 of the Region's countries.

Finally, there is the issue of rate setting for cross-border sales of utility services. If the market structure for such utilities services is competitive, then, ultimately, the utilities' international and domestic prices would have a tendency to converge on a regional level, should the necessary economic investments in transmission or transportation networks be undertaken and if prices are subsidy-free. In the case of

FIGURE 6.13

Cross-Subsidization in the Electricity Sector in the Region and Turkey

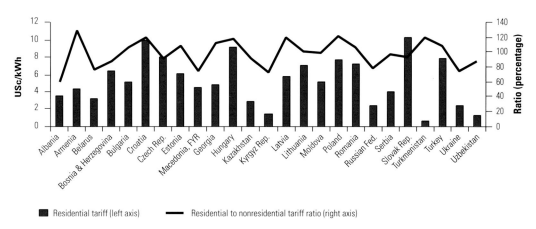

Sources: EBRD 2004a. Data for Bosnia and Herzegovina and Turkey are World Bank staff estimates.

Russia, however, dual pricing of natural gas might prove to be the most beneficial option for the country as long as the internal domestic price of natural gas is close to the long-run marginal costs and subsidy-free. This has meant a doubling of the domestic price of natural gas in Russia. However, the export price of the country's natural gas to Europe was, up until recently, about five times the Russian domestic price, and price convergence would not have been beneficial to the world's largest gas exporter. Taking advantage of its natural economic power on the international gas market, Russia should be able to benefit from charging export prices on European markets that are different from its domestic ones. Box 6.7 discusses the economics of gas pricing in Russia.

BOX 6.7

Dual Pricing of Russian Natural Gas

Within the context of Russia's WTO accession, some WTO members had sought a commitment by Russia to unify gas pricing—in other words, to align the prices charged for gas in the domestic market and the prices charged to customers outside Russia. The World Bank undertook an examination of the economic effects of gas pricing on Russia and on its major consumers and concluded that it is not in Russia's interest to introduce unified pricing of natural gas.

Russia is endowed with very significant natural gas resources. Its proved reserves of 47 trillion cubic meters represent about 27 percent of the world's proved reserves. Its 2003 production of 579 billion cubic meters (BCM) constituted 22 percent of world production and its reserves-to-production ratio is in excess of 80 years, higher than any other major producer. Russia is also by far the world's largest exporter of natural gas. In 2003, it exported about 134 BCM to Europe and Turkey and about 40 BCM to CIS countries.

It is in Russia's interest to try to maximize the overall revenues associated with export volumes. Russia can achieve this through a combination of prices and volumes. Two factors, however, constrain the volumes that can be delivered to export markets. In the medium term, the primary constraint is the availability of transportation facilities. This constraint provides a current incentive for Russia to maximize the sales price to export markets. The transportation constraint can be overcome, which would create increased capacity to deliver gas. However, Russia would then run up against the second constraint, which is the absorptive capacity of the markets. Russia's proven reserves are sufficient to support a doubling, or even tripling, of its production capacity. In order to absorb this volume of gas, markets in Europe would have to increase dramatically. As a result, Russia would not be able to sell significantly more natural gas in Europe without applying substantial downward pressure on the price there. Russia would thus face a trade-off between the added revenues from additional sales of gas and the lost revenue resulting from lower prices.

Trade Agreements: EU Accession, Regional Cooperation, and the WTO

The overall picture emerging from the preceding analysis is one of a clear clustering of countries and sectoral reform progress, as well as number of outliers. While sectoral policies are roughly equally advanced in all EU-8 countries, the Baltics fare somewhat better in horizontal policies relevant to foreign activity such as the bankruptcy code (see annex tables 6.1 and 6.2); in some CEE countries, these horizontal impediments contain the progress made in sectoral policies. In much of SEE, there has been less, but still substantial progress,

These two factors will effectively constrain for the foreseeable future the volumes of gas that Russia can sell to export markets below the levels that Russia could potentially supply. The economic value of gas in the domestic market therefore is dictated by the long-run marginal cost (LRᴍC), not by export parity price levels. In Russia, Gazprom is likely to retain its monopoly power for some time. If the domestic price of natural gas is set above LRMC, there will be inefficiency from monopoly constriction of output. If the price is below LRMC, the product will not be efficiently used, and production levels will decline from lack of investment.

The World Bank has estimated that the LRMC for natural gas is in the range of $35 to $40 per thousand cubic meters (MCM). Domestic prices have been increasing and approaching the LRMC levels. The average domestic price in 2004 was on the order of $28/MCM. In December 2004, the Federal Tariff Service approved increases of 35 percent and 21 percent respectively for gas sales to households and to industrial customers starting on January 1, 2005. This will increase the price to households to about $27.95 per thousand cubic meters and the price to industrial customers to about $37.15 per thousand cubic meters, and the average price will increase to about $34 per thousand cubic meters, just below the LRMC range. At present rates of consumption (about 400 BCM), increasing domestic prices by about $20/MCM would increase the overall cost to consumers by about $8 billion per year. Consumption of natural gas, however, would be reduced and more efficiently allocated, generating a welfare gain to the economy. Based on the assumption of a market elasticity of –0.5, this would generate a welfare gain on the order of $1.25 billion per year.

The alternative of reducing export prices to LRMC parity levels would require a significant reduction in prices. In the first half of 2004, the export parity price averaged about $130/MCM; thus a reduction on the order of $90/MCM would have been required, which would have translated into an annual loss of revenue on the order of $12 billion.

The WTO negotiators ultimately accepted that a dual pricing system makes economic sense in Russia's case and would not constitute an export subsidy for Russian exporters, provided that domestic prices are increased to LRMC levels.

Source: Tarr and Thomson 2004.

despite political tensions and military conflict. In the CIS, the picture is far more mixed, if not sober. Belarus is an outlier in the sense that its proximity to the EU has had no effect on speed of reform. In the Caucasus and Central Asia, Armenia has made the most progress in reform, while Turkmenistan and Uzbekistan have achieved the least.

Much of the enduring services policy reform that has taken place in the Region during the transition has been and continues to be implemented in the context of efforts to integrate into the EU—this is the case for more than one-third of the countries in the Region. The prospect and process of preparing for accession to the EU provide a ready-made template for services liberalization. The EU is a common market, and free trade and investment in services constitute a major objective pursued by incumbent and aspiring EU member states.

Over time, a large number of directives and regulations and case law that define the "rules of the game" for intra-EU competition in services have emerged: these are contained in the *acquis communitaire*. The *acquis* spans a large number of service sectors—that is, it contains specific directives that must be implemented by a member state. These cover sectors such as financial services and telecommunications, as well as transport and energy, to mention two important backbone services industries (box 6.8). The *acquis* also involves a set of general obligations and disciplines that are aimed at ensuring that markets are contestable for other EU (as well as non-EU) providers. These include the competition policy provisions of the EU Treaty: provisions that discipline horizontal anti-competitive practices such as market sharing and price fixing (cartels) and that restrict the ability of governments to provide subsidies to national incumbents and the ability of monopoly providers to engage in cross-subsidization and abuse of a dominant position in a market.

The EU *acquis* "template" is largely nonnegotiable for accession countries—there is some flexibility in regard to timing and sequencing of reforms, but there is a body of law with which all members must conform. This clearly facilitates the design of policy reforms—accession governments have simply to implement measures that will satisfy the conditions laid down by the *acquis*. This is not to say that the prospect/process of accession is a panacea. In the case of Turkey, for example, accession was already being discussed in the 1960s. Very little progress was made to converge toward EU norms until the early 1990s, and thus accession talks did not proceed very far (see box 6.9).

Countries that do not have any prospect of accession to the EU—most of the CIS—do not have to adhere to the policy reforms set implied by the EU template. This has potential benefits—there is no need to undertake actions that may have little immediate payoff, and the EU *acquis* extends far beyond economic policy narrowly defined.

BOX 6.8

The EU *Acquis* Spans All Services

EU directives and regulations go well beyond the financial and telecommunications sectors, the two industries on which most policy attention often focuses. For example, the *acquis* for the transportation sector revolves around the EU's common transport policy, which aims to develop integrated transport systems based on advanced technologies that contribute to environmental and safety objectives, improving the functioning of the single market and strengthening transport links between the EU and third countries. A major emphasis is put on the strict application of competition rules and state aid disciplines, with a recent focus on increased liberalization of rail transport, landing rights/access to airports (allocation of slots), the abolition of the queuing system for inland waterway markets, and enforcement of rules on work practices in the road haulage sector. Public monopoly providers of port, rail, and other transport services must separate out and report on the results of each of their activities (to identify cross-subsidies) and end cross-subsidies from ports to rail or from freight to passenger traffic by shifting to a system of direct subsidies to achieve social objectives such as universal service.

EU energy policy objectives include the improvement of competitiveness, security of energy supplies, and protection of the environment. The energy *acquis* consists of rules and policies, notably regarding competition and state aid (including in the coal sector); the internal energy market (for example, opening up of the electricity and gas markets, promotion of renewable energy sources, crisis management, and oil stock security obligations); energy efficiency; and nuclear energy. There are five main challenges associated with adoption of EU norms in this area: market opening, unbundling, third-party access, public service obligations, and regulation.

These two policy areas illustrate the primary objective of EU rules: to create a single market for services. This is pursued through measures requiring member states to ensure that their markets are contestable for foreign service providers (the competition aspect) and requiring that measures be taken to harmonize regulatory provisions so as to further integrate the market. Part of the latter agenda revolves around setting standards to achieve easier interconnection—whether of roads, rail, electricity grids and networks, or gas pipelines.

Source: World Bank staff.

In the environmental area, for example, there are numerous requirements, many of which necessitate large-scale investment, which may not be a priority for some countries. However, it also has costs: the burden of identifying policy reforms, sequencing them, and ensuring their implementation and enforcement must be determined and carried out by national governments. As a result, and because of politically strong vested interests that will oppose reform, there may be less of a focus on taking actions to liberalize access to services markets.

BOX 6.9

The Incentive for Services Reform in Turkey in the Context of EU Accession

In 1999, the European Council officially recognized Turkey as a candidate state for accession. Under an Accession Partnership, the EU works with Turkey on adoption of the *acquis communautaire*. A Department for EU Affairs was set up in 2000 to coordinate Turkey's policies related to accession. A Reform Monitoring Group chaired by the deputy prime minister supervises the reforms. Major regulatory reforms in the post-1999 period have covered several sectors, including the energy and banking sectors.

In the area of energy, Turkey confronts five main challenges: market opening, unbundling, third-party access, public service obligations, and regulation. The Turkish electricity sector has historically been dominated by state-owned enterprises that provide distribution, generation, trading, and transmission services. Privately owned electricity firms have entered the industry through build-operate-transfer (BOT) or auto-generator schemes. They account for about 21 percent of electricity generation. In addition, competitive bidding for build-operate-own (BOO) contracts for electricity generation has been occurring, and transfer-of-operating-rights contracts have been awarded in a number of regions. Privatization of generation assets is envisaged to start in 2006 and be completed in 2011. All assets in the distribution sector will be divested by mid-2006. A new Electricity Law, passed in 2001, provides for the establishment of an independent Energy Market Regulatory Authority and the introduction of a market model that will transfer most of the task of supplying and distributing electricity to the private sector, eliminate the need for additional state-guaranteed power-purchase agreements, and minimize costs through competitive pressures on producers and distributors. The government will largely withdraw from the electricity-generation and -distribution businesses; and electricity-generation companies will negotiate directly with distribution companies, without government guarantees. The government's role will be largely confined to determining sector policy, owning the transmission system, and ensuring that the rules are respected and that prices are competitively determined. Once the law is fully implemented, the regulatory and supervisory regime for the electricity sector will have been brought up to the level of international practice in line with EU standards. The various

The distinct differences in depth of reform and service sector performance suggest that the EU accession process played an important role in promoting liberalization of services trade and investment and in the subsequent trade and FDI inflow response. However, "initial conditions" also have an important bearing on performance—the CEE countries were almost all GATT (General Agreement on Tariffs and Trade) members during central planning and were founding members of the WTO. This implies that they had already made some international commitments on services trade and investment policies.

BOT and BOO contracts signed in the past imply that the establishment of a competitive environment will take time, however.

A weak banking sector has been a cause of recurrent macroeconomic crises in Turkey. Governments have used state banks for noncommercial objectives such as agricultural support; income redistribution; and industrial, urban, and physical infrastructural development. As a result, banks came to confront unrecoverable costs from mandates carried out on behalf of the government (so-called "duty losses"). Since 1999, Turkey has reformed the regulatory and institutional framework of the banking sector and restructured both state and private banks. In 1999, the Parliament passed a new banking law, which called for the creation of an independent Banking Regulatory and Supervisory Agency (BRSA) to take over bank regulation and supervision responsibilities from the Treasury and central bank. In the case of state banks, the Treasury issued bonds (floating rate notes) to securitize their duty losses and strengthen their capital base. A law was introduced that prohibited state banks from running more duty losses: that is, any support provided to the state banks will henceforth have to be budgeted. The regulation of all banks was greatly strengthened. As of 2004, Turkish prudential requirements were in general in conformity with those in the EU regarding capital adequacy standards, loan classification and provisioning requirements, limits on large exposures, limits on connected lending, and requirements for liquidity and market-risk management. A major remaining issue concerns the privatization of state banks. In 2001, private domestic banks accounted for 53.6 percent of total assets of the banking sector, with foreign banks' shares amounting to only 2.6 percent. This compares with 77 percent in Greece, 31 percent in Spain, 61 percent in Hungary, and 51 percent in the Czech Republic.

Arguably, everything that has been and is being done by Turkey could be done unilaterally. Many of the benefits from reforms undertaken to date were undertaken autonomously—for example, measures to strengthen the banking system. How much the templates provided by the EU model helped is not possible to determine. Clearly, however, the *prospect* of accession helped in the pursuit of many of these reforms.

Source: Hoekman and Togan 2005.

While in principle the EU accession process forced these countries to do more as far as trade policy is concerned, much if not all of what is required by the EU *acquis* can also be pursued unilaterally.

Moreover, even when EU accession is not a realistic prospect, international cooperation on services can be pursued through the WTO and bilateral/regional trade agreements, both with the EU and with neighboring countries (see chapter 3). Indeed, in many areas, regional cooperation has the potential for supporting national reforms by increasing the payoffs and reducing costs. The trade and transport facilitation program that has been put in place by the countries of SEE is an example of such intraregional cooperation on services. As discussed in chapter 5, here the focus is specifically on international facilitation. Similar initiatives could be pursued in other areas of the Region and in other sectors. As mentioned earlier, regional cooperation in the area of energy is already being pursued (see box 6.5).

A number of countries in the Region acceded to the WTO after 1995 (that is, they were not GATT contracting parties). These include Albania (which acceded to the WTO in 2000), Armenia (2003), Croatia (2000), Georgia (2000), the Kyrgyz Republic (1998), and Moldova (2001). Others are in the process of negotiating accession to the WTO. In either case, this requires that commitments be made to liberalize access to foreign providers of services, both cross-border and through FDI under the General Agreement on Trade in Services (GATS) (see chapter 3). There is, however, a major difference between the WTO and the EU accession processes: the former does not require complete liberalization of services trade and investment. Rather, the extent of liberalization is the outcome of a negotiating process that depends in part on how attractive the market is to potential foreign entrants and on the preferences of the acceding government. A feature of the WTO's GATS disciplines on services is that governments can decide how much they want to open up—a so-called "positive list" approach is taken to the sectoral coverage of commitments made by members; see Broadman 1994.

One potential advantage of the WTO's GATS approach is that the process of expanding the access of foreign suppliers to services markets can be managed so as to increase competition gradually. This can allow incumbents to improve their competitiveness and may create alternative employment opportunities in the sectors concerned and thus help mobilize support for trade liberalization more generally. The mechanism that can be used in this connection is to precommit to reforms over a period of time. Given the advantages of incumbency in industries characterized by high fixed costs and with substantial network externalities, the process of gradual introduction of competition can allow management of the public companies concerned to improve productivity over a period of time, attenuating the social impact in terms of the magnitude of possible layoffs, and increasing the value of the firm as a prelude to privatization.

The countries in the Region that acceded to the WTO between 1998 and 2003 all made significant commitments on services. For example, the Kyrgyz Republic made commitments in 11 out of 13 services sectors, compared with 5.7 on average for all WTO members. The same is true for the other countries—specific commitments were made in all of the major services categories that are distinguished in the GATS classification list. As a group, the Region's countries stand out as having made more commitments than either OECD or developing countries (figure 6.14).

However, these countries' WTO GATS commitments have not, for the most part, translated into increases in services trade comparable to those registered by the EU-8 countries. In part this may simply be a reflection of time—all of these countries, with the exception of the Kyrgyz Republic, have acceded to the WTO only recently. Geography and other fundamental institutional factors play a major role as well. But as can also be seen from figure 6.14, although the Region's countries as a whole have made significant commitments under the GATS, there is still much to be done with regard to making full liberalization commitments and in the sense of locking in open market access and national treatment, including for Modes 1 and 3—cross-border trade and FDI, respectively.

The ongoing Doha Round negotiations—which span services— offer an important opportunity to further enhance commitments in those sectors and modes of supply that are most important for improving the performance of the economy. They also offer an oppor-

FIGURE 6.14
WTO Market Access Commitments in Services Trade Liberalization, by Mode
Percentage of bindings

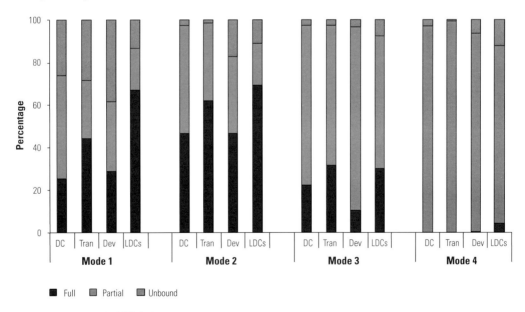

Source. Marchetti 2004, based on WTO database.

Note: Calculated on the basis of a sample of 37 sectors deemed representative for various services areas (actualizes WTO document S/C/W99).
DC (Developed Countries); Tran (the Region's Transition Economies); Dev (Developing Countries); LDCs (Least-Developed Countries).

tunity to seek better access to export markets, including through the temporary movement of natural persons supplying services. Indeed, for those countries that are not on track to join the EU, the WTO is an important instrument through which to seek to offset some of the preferential access that has been granted to the new member states of the EU from the Region. There will be a quid pro quo demanded for such improved access, however. But as the experience of the Baltic and CEE countries reveals, this quid pro quo—the opening up of services sectors to foreign participation—can have significant payoffs that are in the national interest.

The big difference between the EU accession process and the WTO is that, while the latter is much less specific about how liberalization will be achieved, the EU is much more prescriptive. This raises the question of whether it makes sense for countries that have little prospect of acceding to the EU to unilaterally adopt the "EU model" (the *acquis*). A good case can be made for considering the implementation of specific aspects of the *acquis*, especially those parts that revolve around the introduction of market disciplines, controlling state aids, and encouraging competition from foreign service providers on the domestic market. Integrating transport and energy markets with those in neighboring countries also makes good economic sense, as do measures aimed at increasing the contestability of these markets and removing competition-distorting cross-subsidies.

This is not to say that the EU model in these areas is optimal. The point is, however, that it is better than the status quo ante that once prevailed in all of the Region's countries, and that continues to prevail in the CIS and some SEE countries. The EU *acquis* is a public good in the sense that any country can avail itself of that body of legislation and regulation. What matters is implementation, which in turn requires commitment and that the relevant institutions apply the standards. In the case of countries that have acceded or are in the queue, the regular monitoring and interaction between the European Commission and the partner government, facilitated by the provision of technical and financial assistance, can do much to help maintain progress. However, accession does not have to be part of the equation for countries to obtain such assistance—a very similar structure is available in the form of the EU's Association and Partnership Agreements that numerous countries have signed with the EU. They also offer a model for implementation of commitments under the GATS. That said, and as stressed in the analysis of behind-the-border reforms in chapter 4, while trade-agreement-based commitments of the type made in the WTO can be helpful, they are not sufficient to achieve and cement far-reaching policy reforms and liberalization. What matters more is the overall investment climate that prevails.

Services Reforms and Growth Performance

It is clear that many countries in the Region have implemented significant services sector policy reforms. What matters of course is whether these reforms are subsequently associated with better economic performance. One method that can help determine whether there is a positive relationship between reforms and performance is the use of econometric evidence to assess the links between service sector development and economic growth. Will cross-country growth regressions, where the share of domestic investment in GDP is used as the main explanatory variable for per capita GDP growth, reveal a linear, positive relationship between various measures of service sector policy reform and per capita GDP growth?

To test this proposition, it is more appropriate to use the investment share in GDP as an explanatory variable in such regressions than the usual set of control variables that measure initial income because, even after controlling for policy variables determining different steady states (such as inflation, political stability, size of government, and so forth), it is likely that in transition economies, the macroeconomic shocks incurred in the early 1990s were greater in countries where initial income was lower because of the absence of market institutions. Thus, use of initial income may bias results because there is likely to be a correlation between income levels and services sector development. Cross-country evidence generally suggests that per capita income growth is strongly related to the (past) investment share of GDP (for example, Levine and Renelt 1992). This is not the case for many transition economies, reflecting the fact that investment in centrally planned economies was often of poor quality. To measure the quality of the service sector framework in the estimated regressions, the three sectoral EBRD reform indexes for banking, nonbanking financial services, and infrastructure are used. (Recall that the latter is a composite indicator of progress in five areas of infrastructure policy reform: power, railways, roads, telecom, and water services.) The variables are all averaged over the 1990s.

The regression analysis reported in table 6.8 (column 4) is consistent with the literature in finding a positive relationship between growth in per capita income and investment (statistically significant at the 5 percent level). However, when the services policy reform indexes are added as explanatory variables, this positive association

TABLE 6.8

Results of Some Simple Growth Regressions

Dependent variable	Adj. R^2	Constant	Gross domestic fixed investment (% of GDP)	EBRD infrastructure reform index	EBRD nonbanking financial sector reform index	EBRD banking sector reform index
Per capita GDP growth	0.13	−11.3 (−2.7)**	0.41 (2.1)**			
Per capita GDP growth	0.28	−16.1 (−3.8)***	0.32 (1.73)*	4.23 (2.3)**		
Per capita GDP growth	0.32	−14.4 (−3.8)***	0.1 (0.46)		5.65 (2.65)**	
Per capita GDP growth	0.42	−16.8 (−4.5)***	0.22 (1.3)			4.74 (3.37)***

Note: Coefficients and t-values in brackets; *** = significant at the 1percent level; ** = significant at the 5 percent level; * = significant at the 10 percent level. Number of observations: 23 for all equations.

gradually disappears. All three reform indexes are highly significant determinants of per capita income growth, but most striking is the performance of the banking sector variable. The model fit increases from 0.13 to 0.42 in terms of adjusted R^2 as one moves from the first to the last equation. These econometric results therefore suggest a clear positive association between the adoption of policies that promote the efficient functioning of the service sector and economywide economic growth performance.

The prominent role of the banking sector in this regard is noteworthy. In those transition economies where financial intermediation existed during the 1990s, the output collapse was much less pronounced, and the subsequent recovery occurred at a faster pace. Creating confidence in the private commercial banking sector by means of generating an adequate policy framework therefore is of great importance. Indeed, in many of the countries in question, potential depositors still shy away from banks, and credit remains influenced by, or subject to, direct or indirect government control. Full compliance with banking and securities markets best practices (as defined by the IMF, Bank for International Settlements [BIS], and the International Organization of Securities Commissions [IOSCO] and other standards-setting bodies) and credible and effective implementation-cum-enforcement are important dimensions of creating an independent and competitive financial sector. As discussed above, the policy reform agenda in infrastructure spans many dimensions, including procompetitive regulation of public providers (for example, tariffs that reflect costs and provide incentives for efficiency improvements); actions to increase the scope for private provision (including privatization of monopolies, ensuring access to networks, and interconnection on reasonable terms); and the development of effective, independent regulatory bodies to establish and implement a coherent regulatory and institutional framework.

Conclusions

Firms in the Region's services sectors, such as finance, telecommunications, and transport, are major inputs into the production of goods (and other services)—including agriculture as well as manufacturing. The costs of these inputs can account for a major share of the total cost of production and are thus an important factor affecting the competitiveness of firms. Services are also important determinants of the productivity of workers in all sectors—education, training, and health services are key "inputs" into the formation and maintenance of human capital. Thus, service sector reforms can help reduce the costs of trade liberalization by assisting industry and agriculture in confronting competition from imports through lower input costs and higher-quality inputs. They can also play an important role in creating the employment opportunities that are required to allow structural adjustment to occur (and absorb new entrants into the labor force).

While trade and structural reforms must be tailored to national circumstances, efficient services—both public and private—are a vital element of any successful strategy for attaining and sustaining high rates of growth. A comprehensive behind-the-border policy reform agenda focusing on services can help attract much-needed investment, both domestic and foreign, and in the process enhance the benefits of merchandise trade liberalization. Inefficient and high-cost intermediate "backbone" services are a burden on the economy because they reduce the competitiveness of firms, thus impeding trade expansion and investment.

Openness to foreign competition—through policies that permit foreign participation in domestic markets—is a key element of good services sector policy. No good measure of the "multiplier" effect of services openness is available. The experience of the EU-8 reveals clearly that an open merchandise trade policy is important; the evidence from these countries shows that liberalization of trade with the EU and the rest of the world led to significant improvements in productivity and trade performance. But merchandise trade liberalization is not enough—services trade and investment policy are also important. The limited stock of inward FDI in countries such as Turkey and Central Asian economies is in striking contrast to the EU-8 countries.

So is the overall economic performance of these different countries, measured in terms of both average performance and its volatility. The stark differences in the levels and sectoral distribution of FDI in services indicate that foreign investors perceive the attractiveness of locating in many countries in the Region to be limited or that prevailing barriers to FDI are prohibitive. Simulation analyses for countries such as Russia also reveal the potential of liberalization of trade and investment in services—for example, Jensen and Tarr (2004) conclude that services liberalization that allows FDI in all sectors would generate a multiple of the gains that could be achieved through merchandise trade liberalization.

Liberalization—greater participation by foreign services firms in domestic markets—is of course not sufficient. Given the characteristics of services and services markets—often characterized by asymmetric information or high fixed costs and associated barriers to entry—there is a need for effective regulatory supervision of both domestic and foreign operators. In an environment characterized by limited (if any) competition in key network services industries (energy, telecoms, transport), a weak financial sector, and limited fiscal discipline (and thus extensive cross-subsidization and transfers), trade liberalization is not enough. As discussed in chapter 4, it needs to be complemented by measures to harden budget constraints and to ensure that markets are contestable. Actions also will be needed to ensure that social (equity) objectives such as universal service obligations are realized. Taken together, this calls for a regime of *procompetitive* regulation.

To be sure, this is a significant reform challenge for many countries in the Region. Given that the EU-8, and increasingly some SEE countries, offer relatively attractive policy environments for FDI and have done much to converge on OECD (EU) regulatory standards in services, the policy reform thresholds for the CIS countries are becoming much more competitive. Institutional barriers to FDI, monopoly provision of services by state-owned enterprises, and slow privatization all reflect political decisions. In the case of the countries that have already acceded to the EU or are in the process of doing so, there is a template for reform that all must satisfy. Although the experience of Turkey and a number of the "second wave" of EU accession candidates illustrates that progress can be slow, the fact remains that, by necessity, much of the behind-the-border reform agenda must be implemented for EU accession to become feasible.

In the case of countries that do not have a near-term prospect of accession to the EU, the burden of liberalization, regulatory reform, and strengthening of enforcement capacity falls squarely on national governments. The prospect and process of accession cannot be used as mechanisms to push forward reforms by governments that desire to deepen services liberalization and reforms. Other instruments do exist, however: in particular the WTO, regional cooperation, and association agreements with the EU. Trade agreements may help by allowing gradual commitments to be made in a more credible manner, but much depends on the substance of the reforms. For any international agreements (multilateral or regional) to be effective in supporting reforms, there must be extensive coverage of services and investment policies.

The ongoing Doha Round negotiations—which span services—offer an immediate and important opportunity to further enhance market access and national treatment commitments for all service sectors, especially for those modes of supply that are most important—cross-border trade and FDI. They also offer an opportunity to seek better access to major export markets, including through the temporary movement of natural persons supplying services. The implication of this is that for those countries that are not on track to join the EU, the WTO is an important instrument through which to seek to offset some of the preferential access that has been granted to the new member states of the EU from the Region. Signaling greater openness through enhanced GATS commitments is not a panacea, given that the new EU member states have already effectively made commitments for complete openness vis-à-vis the EU and the need for complementary efforts to improve domestic regulation. However, making such commitments can not only have a powerful signaling effect, it will also help ensure that the domestic policy efforts to put into place the complementary regulatory framework are made.

ANNEX TABLE 6.1A

Restrictiveness of Service Sector Policies in Transition Economies: Banktruptcy Regime and Telecom

Criterion of restrictiveness	No.	Czech Republic	Hungary	Poland	
Bankruptcy regime	1				
Major post-1990 changes in bankruptcy law	1a	1993/1998	1991/1993	1998/2003	
Length of process (years), high-income OECD=1.6	1b	9.2	2	1.4	
Cost (% of estate), high-income OECD= 6.8	1c	18	23	18	
Recovery rate, high-income OECD= 72.2	1d	16.8	30.8	68.2	
Telecom sector general assessment	2				
Infrastructure reform index 1995/2004 (see EBRD Annual Report, 1 to 4.3=best)	2a	3.3/4.0	3.3/4.0	2.7/4.0	
Fixed-line (mobile) penetration rate 2003	2b	36.0 (96.5)	33.4 (78.3)	31.9 (45.1)	
Market access/national treatment	3				
MA Trade: restrictions in (a) domestic and international leased-line/networks, (b) third-party resale, c) connections of leased-lines/private networks to PSTN	3a	n.a.	n.a.	n.a.	
MA invest (fixed and mobile):					
Fixed:	3b	In 2001, fixed-line market was officially opened; some competition in local services before 2001	In 2002 fixed-line market was officially opened	In 2003 fixed-line market was officially opened	
Number of firms in the market	3c	n.a.	n.a.	n.a.	
Competition in sector (local, domestic long-distance, international, data, leased lines) (a) monopoly, (b) partial, (c) full competition	3d	n.a.	n.a.	n.a.	
Percentage of incumbent privatized investors	3e	49, mainly to Telsource (Ned) Swisscom, AT&T, currently 51% for sale	100, German Telecom and Ameritech, rest publicly traded state: 1 share	47.57 France Telecom, also Polish investors	
Mobile: Number of firms in the market	3f	3	4	3	
Competition in sector: (a) monopoly, (b) partial, (c) full competition	3g	(b) partial	n.a.	n.a.	
Percentage of incumbent privatized investors	3h	49 (1996), now 100 % owned by Cesky Telecom	49 Deutsche Telecom, 51 fixed incumbent	34 France Telecom, rest fixed incumbent	
NT trade: Call-back services allowed ?	3i	n.a.	n.a.	n.a.	
NT invest: % of foreign ownership allowed in competitive carriers (a) fixed, (b) mobile	3j	n.a.	n.a.	n.a.	
Licensing discrimination (mobile)	3k	n.a.	n.a.	n.a.	
Regulation	4				
Regulator independent (since) ?	4a	yes (2000)	yes (1993)	yes (2002)	
Quality of independence	4b		1997 extended		

Sources: EBRD; OECD; World Bank; Contessi, Cukierman, Miller, and Neyapti 2001.

Note: n.a. = not available.

	Slovak Republic	Slovenia	Albania	Bosnia & Herzegovina	Bulgaria	Croatia
	1998/2000	1994	1995/2002	2003	1994/96	1997/99/2003
	4.7	3.6	4	3.3	3.3	3.1
	18	18	38	8	8	18
	39.6	23.6	24.6	32.1	34.2	26.1
	2.3/3.3	1.0/3.0	1.0/3.3	1.0/3.3	2.3/3.3	1.0/3.3
	24.1 (68.4)	40.7 (87.1)	8.3 (35.8)	22.5 (27.4)	37.2 (50.0)	43.3 (58.4)
	n.a.	n.a.	restrictions in (a) and (b)	restrictions in (a) and (b)	restrictions in (a) and (b)	n.a.
	In 2003 fixed-line market was officially opened	End of monopoly in 2001	Monopoly in 2004	There are three operators, but each is a monopoly in a region	End of monopoly in 2003	In 2003 fixed-line services were opened to foreign competition. Croatian Telecom had transition period until end of 2004
	n.a.	n.a.	1, 2 for local	3	1	
	n.a.	n.a.	(a) Monopoly (b) Partial in local services	Sprske (a) Fed. (c), but (a) for intern.	(a) Monopoly	
	n.a.	By 2001 33.5% had been sold to Slovenian private investors	0	n.a.	65 (2004) Viva Ventures (Austria)	51, 35 (1999), 16 (2001), German Telec., remaining 7% to be sold
	n.a.	3	2, 3 as of 2005	2	3	2, third to be tendered 2004
	n.a.	n.a.	(b) partial	(b) partial	(b) partial	(b) partial
	n.a.	100% owned by fixed-line incumbent	85 (2000), Norw./Greek consortium	n.a.	100, 60 of them Austrian, rest international	35 (1999) 16 (2001)
	n.a.	n.a.	no	no	no	n.a.
	n.a.	n.a.	(a) 100 (since 2003), (b) 100 FDI is 49%	(a)100, but no FDI, (b) n.a.,	(a) 0 before 2003 (b) 100	n.a.
	n.a.	n.a.	no	no	no	n.a.
	yes (2000)	yes (2001)	yes (1998)	yes (2001)	yes (2002)	yes (2002)
			Limited			

ANNEX TABLE 6.1B

Restrictiveness of Service Sector Policies in Transition Economies: Bankruptcy Regime and Telecom

Criterion of restrictiveness	No.	Estonia	Latvia	Lithuania	Belarus	Moldova	Russian Fed.	
Bankruptcy regime	1							
Major post-1990 changes in bankruptcy law	1a	1996	1996	1997/2001	1991	2001	1998/2002	
Length of process (years), high-income OECD=1.6	1b	3	1.1	1.2	5.8	2.8	1.5	
Cost (% of estate), high-income OECD= 6.8	1c	8	4	8	4	8	4	
Recovery rate, high-income OECD= 72.2	1d	40	85	52.4	11.9	29.3	48.4	
Telecom sector general assessment	2							
Infrastructure reform index 1995/2004 (see EBRD Annual Report, 1 to 4.3=best)	2a	3.0/4.0	2.7/3.0	1.0/3.3	1.0/2.0	2.0/2.3	2.3/3.0	
Fixed-line (mobile) penetration rate 2003	2b	33.9 (72.3)	28.3 (52.9)	25.3 (66.6)	31.1 (11.3)	16.3 (8.2)	26.0 (25.0)	
Market access/national treatment	3							
MA Trade: restrictions in (a) domestic and international leased-line/networks, (b) third party resale, (c) connections of leased-lines/private networks to PSTN	3a	(b) n.a. (a) and (c) no restrictions	(b) n.a. (a) and (c) no restrictions	Restrictions in (b) likely	n.a.	Restrictions in (a) and (b)	Restrictions in (b) and (c)	
MA invest (fixed and mobile):								
Fixed:	3b	Market was opened to competition in 2001	Fixed-line monopoly established in 1994 as joint venture, to last until 2013	Market was opened to competition in 2003	Fixed-line services still operated by national monopoly	Privatization of national monopoly not successful so far; bids have been rejected	De facto monopoly in international and long-distance calls, also local	
Number of firms in the market	3c	3	1	1	1	1	n.a.	
Competition in sector (local, domestic long-distance, international, data, leased lines) (a) monopoly, (b) partial, (c) full competition	3d	(c) full competition	(c), monopoly expired 2003, not 2013	(c) full competition	n.a. lines, (a) rest	(a) monopoly	(c) for data and leased	
Percentage of incumbent privatized investors	3e	73, 49 of them sold to Baltic Tele AB (Sweden, Fin.)	49 (1994), sold to consortium of European operators	90	0	0	62	
Mobile:								
Number of firms in the market	3f	3	2	4	2	2	More than 3	
Competition in sector: (a) monopoly, (b) partial, (c) full competition	3g	(c) full competition	(c) full competition	(c) full competition	(c) full competition	(b) partial	(b) partial	
Percentage of incumbent privatized investors	3h	n.a.	100	100	n.a.	90	100	
NT trade: Call-back services allowed ?	3i	Yes	No	No	n.a.	No	Yes	
NT invest: % of foreign ownership allowed in competitive carriers (a) fixed, (b) mobile	3j	(a) and (b) 100	(a) and (b) 100	(a) and (b) 100	n.a.	(a) and (b) 100	(a) and (b) 49	
Licensing discrimination (mobile)	3k	n.a.	n.a.	n.a.	n.a.	No	n.a.	
Regulation	4							
Regulator independent (since) ?	4a	Yes (1998)	Yes (2001)	Yes (2001)	No	Yes (2000)	Yes (2004)	
Quality of independence	4b							

Sources: EBRD; OECD; World Bank; Heritage Foundation.

Note: n.a. = not available.

	Ukraine	Armenia	Azerbaijan	Georgia	Kazakhstan	Kyrgyz Rep.	Tajikistan	Turkmenistan	Uzbekistan
	2000	1995/1997	1994/1997	1997	1997	1997	n.a.	1992	1994/1996
	2.6	1.9	2.7	3.2	3.3	3.5	n.a.	n.a.	4
	18	4	8	4	18	4	n.a.	n.a.	4
	25.5	39.6	33.2	20.4	13.4	24.4	n.a.	n.a.	12.5
	1.0/2.3	2.0/2.3	1.0/1.7	1.0/2.3	1.0/2.3	2.0/3.0	1.0/2.3	1.0/1.0	1.0/2.0
	22.4 (13.4)	14.8 (3.0)	11.8 (13.0)	13.3 (10.7)	14.7 (9.4)	7.9 (1.2)	3.7 (0.7)	7.7 (0.2)	6.7 (1.3)
	n.a.	n.a.	n.a.	n.a.	n.a.	n.a.	n.a.	n.a.	n.a.
	National monopoly long considered as strategically important, now privatization is on the agenda	National monopoly sold to foreign investor with exclusive rights	Fixed-line services still largely under state control, entry only through joint venture, many small state-owned companies, one major public fixed-line network	n.a.	State monopoly in long-distance and international fixed-line calls to expire 2005	State monopoly in long-distance and international fixed-line calls to expire 2003	n.a.	n.a.	National monopolist has exclusivity rights for international fixed-line services till 2006
	n.a.	1		n.a.	n.a.	n.a.			
	n.a.	(a) monopoly until 2013		n.a.	(a) domestic long-distance	(a) domestic long-distance			
	n.a.	90 (1997) OTE (Greece)		n.a.	n.a.	n.a.	n.a.	n.a.	n.a.
	More than 3	1	2 joint ventures with ministry	n.a.	n.a.	n.a.	n.a.	2, exclusivity rights till 2004	n.a.
	n.a.	(a) monopoly until 2013	Further privatization is under way	n.a.	n.a.	n.a.	n.a.	n.a.	n.a.
	n.a.	n.a.	64.3 (1996)	n.a.	n.a.	51% (2003)	n.a.	49	n.a.
	n.a.	n.a.	n.a.	n.a.	n.a.	n.a.	n.a.	n.a.	n.a.
	n.a.	n.a.	n.a.	n.a.	n.a.	n.a.	n.a.	n.a.	n.a.
	n.a.	n.a.	n.a.	n.a.	n.a.	n.a.	n.a.	n.a.	n.a.
	No	No, but planned	No, but planned	Yes (2000)	Yes (2002)	Ues (2001)	No, but planned	No	No
					Limited	Limited			

ANNEX TABLE 6.2A

Restrictiveness of Service Sector Policies in Transition Economies: Banking

Criterion of restrictiveness	No.	Czech Rep.	Hungary	Poland	Slovak Rep.	Slovenia	
Banking sector general assessment	**1**						
Banking sector reform index 1995/2004 (See EBRD Annual Report, from 1 to 4.3=best)	1a	3.0/3.7	3.0/4.0	3.0/3.3	2.7/3.7	3.0/3.3	
Financial sector restrictiveness index 1995/2005 (from 1 to 5, 1=free, see Heritage Foundation)	1b	1.0/1.0	3.0/2.0	3.0/2.0	3.0/1.0	n.a./3.0	
Credit to private sector (% of GDP) 2003	1c	34.0	43.0	29.0	33.2	43.8	
Policy framework and outcome in a nutshell	1d	High degree of openness and privatization	High degree of openness and privatization	High degree of openness and privatization	High degree of openness and privatization	Concentration and restrictions persist	
Restrictions on commercial presence	**2**						
Allocations of new banking licenses? (a) no, (b) up to 6, (c) yes	2a	Sector is liberal. Largest banks	Foreign participation is	Sector is liberal.	n.a.	Sector is very concentrated,	
Licensing discrimination	2b	are owned by	very high, total	Penetration of		and state still	
Maximum equity share in domestic bank (%)	2c	foreign inves-	foreign owner-	foreign invest-		holds a large	
Market entry through joint venture required? J.V. (a) not allowed, (b) required, (c) possible	2d	tors, range of financial	ship is about 60% of total	ment very high, especially in		stake in some important banks	
Possible forms of establishment? (a) Subsid, (b) branches, (c) represent. offices	2e	products has increased to	capital, foreign know-how	large banks		Foreign share	
Foreign staff entry possible? (a) no entry, (b) entry up to 3 or (c) 5 years or more Staff: exec., senior managers, and/or specialists	2f	standards of other market economies	helped modern- ization of many banks			is not as high as in some other countries	
Other restrictions	**3**						
Can banks raise funds domestically? (a) no, (b) restricted, (c) yes	3a	n.a.	Regulation was brought roughly	Regulation was brought roughly	n.a.	Regulation is almost fully in	
Restrictions on lending? (a) no, (b) some services, (c) no domestic clients	3b		in line with EU standards	in line with EU standards		line with EU standards	
Can banks provide non-banking services? (a) no, (b) restricted, (c) yes	3c						
Restrictions on number of banking outlets? (a) yes (1), (b) no	3d						
Temporary entry of foreign staff allowed ? up to (a) 30, (b) 60, (c) 90 days or more Staff: exec., senior managers, and/or specialists	3e						
Foreign/private market share	**4**						
Number of banks (foreign-owned): 1995 2003	4a	55(23) 35(26)	43(21) 38(29)	81(18) 58(46)	33(18) 21(16)	39(6) 22(6)	
Asset share of state-owned banks: 1995 2003	4b	17.6 3	49 7.4	71.7 25.7	61.2 1.5	41.7 12.8	
Regulation	**5**						
Enactment of central bank reform	5a	1991	1991	1997	1992	1991	
Subesequent degree of legal independence (0 to 1=highest, Germany 1980s=0.69)	5b	0.73	0.67	0.89	0.62	0.63	
Capital adequacy ratio	5c	8%	8%	8%	8%	8%	
Deposit insurance system	5d	Yes	Yes	Yes	Yes	Yes	
Secured transaction law	5e	Yes	Yes	Yes	Yes	Restricted	
Securities commission	5f	Yes	Yes	Yes	Yes	Yes	

Sources: EBRD; OECD; World Bank; Heritage Foundation.

Note: n.a. = not available.

	Albania	Bosnia & Herzegovina	Bulgaria	Croatia	Macedonia, FYR	Romania	Serbia & Montenegro
	2.0/2.7	1.0/2.7	2.0/3.7	2.7/4.0	3.0/2.7	3.0/3.0	1.0/2.3
	3.0/3.0	n.a./2.0	3.0/2.0	n.a./2.0	n.a./2.0	3.0/3.0	n.a./n.a.
	7.8	42.1	25.8	55.2	19.4	9.0	n.a.
	Open, but still rudimentary, cash economy	Confidence is increasing, weak capital base	High degree of openness and privatization	High degree of openness and privatization	Weak sector, many bad loans, but improving	Weak sector, but openness is improving	Inefficient with weak capital base, closed
	(c) Yes, new licenses issued	(c) Yes, new licenses issued	(c) Yes, new licenses issued	(c) Yes, new licenses issued	(c) Yes, new licenses issued	(c) Yes, new licenses issued	No foreign entry
	No	No	No	No	No	No	n.a.
	100	0	100	100	100	100	100
	(c) Joint venture possible	(c) Joint venture possible	(c) Joint venture possible	(c) Joint venture possible	(c) Joint venture possible	(c) Joint venture possible	Privatization is more advanced
	(a), (b), (c) are all allowed	(a), (b), (c) are all allowed	(a), (b), (c) are all allowed	(a), (b), (c) are all allowed	only (a) and (c) are allowed	(a), (b), (c) are all allowed	in Montenegro than in Serbia
	(c) Foreign staff entry allowed up to 5 years	(b) Foreign staff entry allowed up to 1 year	(b) Foreign staff entry allowed up to 3 years	(c) No time limit on foreign staff entry	(c) Foreign staff entry allowed up to 5 years	(b) Foreign staff entry allowed up to 1 year	Foreign share smaller than in other countries
	(c) Yes	(c) Yes	(c) Yes	(c) Yes	(c) Yes	(c) Yes	n.a.
	(a) No	(a) No	(a) No	(a) No	(a) No	(b) In some services, yes	n.a.
	(b) Restricted	(b) Restricted	(b) Restricted	(b) Restricted	(b) Restricted	(b) Restricted	n.a.
	(b) No restrictions	(b) No restrictions	(b) No restrictions	(b) No restrictions	(b) No restrictions	(b) No restrictions	n.a.
	(c) More than 90 days	(c) More than 90 days	(c) 90 days	(c) 90 days	(c) 90 days	(c) More than 90 days	n.a.
	6(3)	n.a.	41(3)	54(1)	6(3)	24(8)	112(3)
	15(13)	37(19)	35(25)	41(19)	21(8)	30(21)	47(16)
	94.5	n.a.	n.a.	51.9	n.a.	84.3	94.7
	51.9	5.2	0.4	3.4	1.8	40.6	34.1
	1992	n.a.	1991	1992	1995	1991	n.a.
	0.51	n.a.	0.55	0.44	0.41	0.34	n.a.
	12%	12%	12%	10%	8%	12%	8%
	Yes	Yes	Yes	Yes	Yes	Yes	No
	Yes	No	Yes	Yes	Yes	Yes	Yes
	Yes	Yes	Yes	Yes	Yes	Yes	Yes

ANNEX TABLE 6.2B
Restrictiveness of Service Sector Policies in Transition Economies: Banking

Criterion of restrictiveness	No.	Estonia	Latvia	Lithuania	Belarus	Moldova	Russian Fed.	
Banking sector general assessment	1							
Banking sector reform index 1995/2004 (See EBRD Annual Report, from 1 to 4.3=best)	1a	3.0/4.0	3.0/3.7	3.0/3.0	2.0/1.7	2.0/2.7	2.0/2.0	
Financial sector restrictiveness index 1995/2005 (from 1 to 5, 1=free, see Heritage Foundation)	1b	2.0/1.0	n.a./2.0	n.a./1.0	3.0/4.0	5.0/3.0	3.0/4.0	
Credit to private sector (% of GDP) 2003	1c	36.0	39.6	20.6	12.0	20.4	20.9	
Policy framework and outcome in a nutshell	1d	System sound, open, efficient. No. 1 in Baltics	High degree of openness and privatization	High degree of openness and privatization	Inefficient and largely state-owned sector	Moderately restricted, officially open	Capital base is weak, sector is rather closed	
Restrictions on commercial presence	2							
Allocations of new banking licenses ? (a) no, (b) up to 6, (c) yes	2a	(c) Yes, new licenses issued	(c) Yes, new licenses issued	(c) Yes, new licenses issued	Sector is highly distorted:	(c) Yes, new licenses issued	(c) Yes, new licenses issued	
Licensing discrimination	2b	No	No	No	four of the main	No	No	
Maximum equity share in domestic bank (%)	2c	100	80	100	banks remain in	100	100	
Market entry through joint venture required? J.V. (a) not allowed, (b) required, (c) possible	2d	(c) Joint venture possible	(b) Joint venture required	(c) Joint venture possible	public hands until 2010;	(c) Joint venture possible	(c) Joint venture possible	
Possible forms of establishment? (a) Subsid, (b) branches, (c) represent. offices	2e	(a), (b), (c) are all allowed	(a), (b), (c) are all allowed	(a), (b), (c) are all allowed	directed credit programs	only (a) and (b) allowed	(a), (b), (c) are all allowed	
Foreign staff entry possible? (a) no entry, (b) entry up to 3 or (c) 5 years or more Staff: exec., senior managers, and/or specialists	2f	(c) Foreign staff entry allowed up to 5 years	(c) Foreign staff entry allowed up to 5 years	(b) Foreign staff entry allowed up to 3 years	and interest rate ceilings still in place	(c) Foreign staff entry allowed up to 5 years	Substantial limitations on foreign staff	
Other restrictions	3							
Can banks raise funds domestically? (a) no, (b) restricted, (c) yes	3a	(c) Yes	(c) Yes	(c) Yes	Central bank contiues to	(c) Yes	(b) Restricted	
Restrictions on lending? (a) no, (b) some services, (c) no domestic clients	3b	(a) No	(a) No	(a) No	strengthen its supervisory	(a) No	(a) No	
Can banks provide non-banking services? (a) no, (b) restricted, (c) yes	3c	(b) Restricted	(b) Restricted	(b) Restricted	policies	(b) Restricted	(b) Restricted	
Restrictions on number of banking outlets? (a) yes (1), (b) no	3d	(b) No restrictions	(b) No restrictions	(b) No restrictions		(b) No restrictions	(b) No restrictions	
Temporary entry of foreign staff allowed? up to (a) 30, (b) 60, (c) 90 days or more Staff: exec., senior managers, and/or specialists	3e	(c) 90 days per 6 months	(c) 90 days	(c) 90 days		(c) 90 days	Substantial limitations on foreign staff	
Foreign/private market share	4							
Number of banks (foreign owned) 1995 2003	4a	19(5) 7(4)	42(11) 23(10)	15(0) 13(7)	42(1) 30(17)	25(n.a.) 16(9)	2297(21) 1329(41)	
Asset share of state-owned banks 1995 2003	4b	9.7 0	9.9 4.1	61.8 0	62.3 63.7	n.a. 15.5	n.a. n.a.	
Regulation	5							
Enactment of central bank reform	5a	1993	1992	1991/96	1992	1991	1995	
Subesequent degree of legal independence (0 to 1=highest, Germany 1980s=0.69)	5b	0.78	0.49	0.28/0.78	0.73	0.38	0.49	
Capital adequacy ratio	5c	10%	10%	10%	10%	12%	8%	
Deposit insurance system	5d	Yes	Yes	Yes	Yes	Yes	Restricted	
Secured transaction law	5e	Yes	Restricted	Yes	Restricted	Restricted	Yes	
Securities commission	5f	Yes	Yes	Yes	No	Yes	Yes	

Sources: EBRD; OECD; World Bank; Heritage Foundation.

Note: n.a. = not available.

Ukraine	Armenia	Azerbaijan	Georgia	Kazakhstan	Kyrgyz Rep.	Tajikistan	Turkmenistan	Uzbekistan
2.0/2.3	2.0/2.3	2.0/2.3	2.0/2.7	2.0/3.0	2.0/2.3	1.0/2.0	1.0/1.0	1.7/1.7
3.0/3.0	n.a./1.0	n.a./4.0	n.a./3.0	n.a./4.0	n.a./3.0	n.a./5.0	n.a./5.0	n.a./5.0
24.6	6.0	6.7	8.8	22.8	4.9	16.4	n.a.	n.a.
Capital base is weak; strong state influence	High degree of openness and privatization	Sector is weak, cash economy, state prevails	Some progress, but still weak, cash economy	Strong state influence, but sector is stable	Sector is weak though open, cash economy	Inefficient and largely state-owned sector	Inefficient and largely state-owned sector	Inefficient and largely state-owned sector
Ukraine has one of the most liberal regimes of the CIS; foreign penetration is slow, however	No retrictions on establish-ment of foreign-owned resident banks as long as licenscing and prudential requirements are met; high foreign share in the system	Establishing a foreign bank involves lengthy procedures, restrictions on obtaining licenses persist, limit on foreign bank ownership increased from 30 to 50%	Foreign investment in amounts to about one-third of total assets, but consists essentially of minority share-holdings	High degree of concentration in the sector; no private/ foreign equity limits; only (a) and (c) allowed	Sector open to foreigners since 1993; no private/ foreign equity limits, but sector remains small and underdeveloped; weak capital base	n.a.	No formal restrictions	Foreign entry free since 1996
						n.a.	n.a.	Most assets are concentrated in a single state-owned bank
						Below 50 %	35%	
						System is very underdeveloped and capital base is weak	Government influence still prevails; little private and foreign participation	Only c) allowed
								n.a.
n.a.	Central bank contiues to strengthen its supervisory policies	Capital base is weak; super-visory policies need further strengthening; privatization still in early stages	Capital base is weak, super-visory policies need further strengthening	Regulatory framework has improved; substantial amount of consolidation	Regulatory framework is still insufficient; legal situation, political interference and lack of deposit insurance undermine confidence	Regulatory framework is still insufficient	Regulatory framework is still insufficient	Regulatory framework is still insufficient
230(1) 158(19)	35(3) 19(8)	180(5) 46(4)	101(3) 24(6)	130(8) 36(16)	18(3) 21(7)	18(n.a.) 11(1)	67(3) 13(4) (in 2002)	31(1) 28(5)
n.a. 9.8	2.4 0	80.5 55.3	48.6 0	24.3 5.1	69.7 7.2	n.a. 6.1	26.1 95.7 (in 2002)	38.4 91.0
1991	1993	1992/96	1995	1993/95	1992	1993	1992	1991/95
0.42	0.3	0.22/0.25	0.73	0.32/0.44	0.52	0.36	0.26	0.41/0.56
10%	12%	12%	12%	12%	12%	12%	10%	8%
Yes	in 2005	No	No	Yes	No	No	No	Yes
Yes	Yes	Restricted	Restricted	Yes	Yes	Yes	Restricted	Yes
Yes	Yes	Yes	Yes (not indep.)	Yes	Yes	Yes	No	Yes

Endnotes

1. Output data are measured in constant 1995 U.S. dollars, as reported in the World Bank development indicators.
2. This is also the case for FDI. However, because of the increasing prevalence of FDI in services, the convention has emerged that the sales of foreign affiliates in a host country are regarded as trade in services for the purposes of trade agreements.
3. Aggregate data on FDI inflows are available for a wider set of countries, but these are not broken down across services sectors. The missing countries account for about 90 percent of the total stock of inward FDI in the Region.
4. For an overview of the problems, see EBRD (2004a).
5. The index comprises the following components: electric power, railways, roads, telecommunications, water and wastewater (EBRD estimates).
6. In terms of actual reform measures, a few examples are worth mentioning. Estonia, for instance, has fully privatized its railway system. Network maintenance is carried out privately in the Czech Republic, Kazakhstan, Poland, and Romania. Passenger services are not profitable in many transition economies and are in general subsidized. In the Czech Republic, Latvia, and Romania, the operation of some passenger services has been handed over to private companies. In Kazakhstan, Poland, Romania, and Russia, private rail freight services have developed following gradual liberalization in this area.
7. See chapter 7 for more details on FDI.
8. Granting monopolies to new private owners (restricting competition) generally does not stimulate investment. A monopolist's market power makes it less, not more, likely to undertake a given investment, because monopoly profits are typically obtained by providing lower quantities of the good or service at higher prices. A firm with a guaranteed monopoly is also likely to invest less because it does not have to worry about more efficient competitors stealing market share. The mere threat of entry—which is typically the situation when reforms are introduced—can be enough to induce the incumbent to invest (see chapter 4).
9. In a sample of about 20 countries that privatized their telecommunications firms, Wallsten (2000) found that private investors were willing to pay more for an exclusivity period, but that telecom investment was substantially lower in countries that granted such exclusivity periods.
10. These data exclude Turkey.
11. For more specific details, see EBRD (2004a), chapter 3.
12. Fixed-rate-of-return or cost-plus contracts offer no incentives to firms to reduce costs because any variation in cost is appropriated by the regulator (and through the regulator, by the government). A fixed-price contract induces the right amount of effort because the regulated firm appropriates any reduction in cost. The enterprise is the residual claimant for cost savings.
13. See World Bank 2004h.

CHAPTER 7

Linkages between Foreign Direct Investment and Trade Flows

Introduction

The increasing globalization of the world economy and the fragmentation of production processes have changed the economic landscape facing the nations, industries, and individual firms in Europe and Central Asia, as they have in the rest of the world. Multinational corporations have been key agents in this transformation by creating international production and distribution networks spanning the globe and actively interacting with each other. The result has been the growth of intraindustry or increasingly intraproduct trade at the expense of traditional interindustry trade.

This chapter analyzes the participation of the countries of Eastern Europe and the Former Soviet Union in this process. After a brief review of characteristics of "buyer-driven" and "producer-driven" networks, the chapter first discusses the degree to which countries in the Region have been involved in network trade. The buyer-driven supply chains examined encompass the apparel, furniture, and diamond sectors. The analysis of producer-driven supply chains focuses on the automotive and information technology sectors.

Several stylized facts emerge from this discussion:

- While the eight countries of the Region that joined the EU in 2004 (EU-8) and Turkey have been heavily involved in network trade,

337

many—but not all—of the other successor countries of the Former Soviet Union—the CIS—have been left out of this process. The extent of participation in network trade by the countries of Southeastern Europe (SEE) lies in between.

- Seven countries of the Region, namely, the Czech Republic, Estonia, Hungary, Poland, the Slovak Republic, and Slovenia, and Turkey (referred to as "High Performers" or the HP-7, hereafter) have become very successful in network trade.

- In the initial phase of the transition process, the HP-7 had relied on unskilled-labor-intensive exports associated with buyer-driven production chains in clothing and furniture. However, rising wages prompted these countries to shift toward skilled-labor- and capital-intensive exports conducted through producer-driven networks encompassing automotive and information technology industries.

- Foreign direct investment has been instrumental in the shift to producer-driven networks. Countries that experienced the largest FDI inflows have also seen the largest increase in exports of network products and parts.

- Several of the SEE economies, as well as some CIS countries, have been active in buyer-driven production chains, but have not managed to make a transition toward producer-driven supply chains. The CIS members of this group include Armenia (which is engaged in the diamond supply chain), Belarus (which participates in the furniture network), and the Kyrgyz Republic, Moldova, and Turkmenistan (all of which are still heavily involved in the clothing network).

- The remaining CIS countries have largely remained outside network trade.

The second part of the chapter examines how the differing performance of the countries of the Region in terms of network trade can be attributed to the large variation in the amount of FDI they have attracted. The heterogeneity of FDI inflows observed across the countries is largely determined by the quality of the domestic business climate and related "behind-the-border" institutional conditions discussed in chapter 4. Building on that analysis, the discussion here focuses specifically on investment climate characteristics vital to attracting FDI and facilitating a country's participation in international production and distribution networks.

The chapter closes with lessons drawn from the experience of the HP-7 that can be useful for other countries in the Region, particularly those left outside the international fragmentation of production.

International Production and Distribution Networks

Links between Trade and FDI

While the theoretical literature examining the determinants of multinational corporate investment often assumes that firms choose between supplying a foreign market through exports or establishing production facilities in a host country, the empirical evidence is less clear-cut. A few cases of "tariff-jumping" FDI aside, empirical studies find that affiliate sales are positively correlated with exports at the aggregate country or industry level. Similarly, firm-level studies point to the complementarity between FDI and exports.[1] An exception is the product-level analysis performed by Blonigen (2001), who finds evidence of both substitution and complementarity effects between affiliate production and exports of Japanese auto parts for the U.S. market.

The increasing complementarity between FDI and trade has been the result of the growing fragmentation of production combined with the creation of distribution networks spanning across continents. The information revolution and new technologies have made it possible to divide an industry's value chain into smaller functions that are performed by foreign subsidiaries or are contracted out to independent suppliers. While producers from developing and transition economies may not possess intangible assets or services infrastructure developed at a level sufficient to have a comparative advantage in the manufacturing of final goods, thanks to production fragmentation, they are able to join the production chain by specializing in the labor-intensive fragment of the manufacturing process.[2] Production fragmentation not only enables firms from less developed and transition countries to access foreign markets without large outlays on advertising and market research, it also may lead to an additional benefit in the form of knowledge spillovers, which is discussed later in the chapter.

Global diffusion of productive activity leads to an increased international trade in both final goods, and parts and components. Thus it comes as no surprise that about one-third of world trade consists of intrafirm trade, that is trade among various parts of a single corporation, and that the importance of intrafirm trade has been growing over time. Estimates also suggest that about two-thirds of world trade in the latter half of the 1990s involved multinational corporations, including both intrafirm trade and arms-length transactions (UNCTAD 2002b).

As observed in the *World Investment Report,* "the issue is no longer whether trade leads to FDI or FDI to trade; whether FDI substitutes for trade or trade substitutes for FDI; or whether they complement each other. Rather it is: how do firms access resources—wherever they are located—in the interest of organizing production as profitably as possible for the national, regional or global markets they wish to serve? In other words, the issue becomes: where do firms locate their value added activities? . . . Increasingly, what matters are the factors that make particular locations advantageous for particular activities, for both domestic and foreign investors" (UNCTAD 1996).

Fragmentation of production offers a unique opportunity for producers in less developed and transition countries to move from servicing small local markets to supplying large multinational firms and, indirectly, their customers all over the world. This phenomenon is accompanied by an evolution in the nature of competition, with its growing emphasis on customization of products, rapid innovation, flexibility, and fast response to changes in demand. In many cases, managerial and technological skills required to successfully compete in global markets make it impossible to rely on the resources of one country. Under these circumstances, integration into the production and marketing arrangements of the multinational corporations, rather than the pursuit of an autarchic national development strategy, has become the most efficient way of taking advantage of growth opportunities offered by the global economy.

Fragmentation of production, however, also means that the multinational corporations have become more sensitive to changes in investment climate. They can relatively easily shift their production from one geographic location to another in response to changes in the cost of production, market access, regulatory conditions, or perceived risks. Relocation is easier to accomplish in labor-intensive industries, where low capital investments are required, and thus disinvestment does not represent a large loss for the investor, but the ability to shift production tends to diminish with the technological intensity of exports. This difference in the ability to be footloose is clearly visible in a comparison of buyer-driven and producer-driven value chains, which is the issue to which we turn next.

Buyer-Driven vs. Supplier-Driven Value Chains

The term *international production and distribution network*, also known as a *global commodity chain*, refers to the whole range of activities involved in the design, production, and marketing of a product. For the purpose of our analysis, it is useful to utilize the typology proposed by Gereffi (1999), which distinguishes between *buyer-driven* and *producer-driven* commodity chains. The former denotes the case of global buyers creating a supply base upon which production and distribution systems are built without direct ownership. The latter refers to vertically integrated arrangements (that is, common ownership of successive stages of production under one corporate entity). While the differences in terms of foreign ownership are less clear-cut in reality, the two network types exhibit different geographic and temporal patterns in the Region.

Buyer-driven commodity chains tend to exist in industries in which large retailers, branded marketers, and branded manufacturers play the key role in setting up decentralized production networks, usually in developing or transition economies. Such networks are prevalent in labor-intensive, consumer goods sectors, such as apparel, footwear, and furniture. Production is generally carried out by tiered networks of contractors in developing countries, which export finished goods made to the specifications of a foreign buyer. Many countries in the Region have been actively participating in such networks, particularly in the apparel and furniture sectors. The diamond-cutting network—Armenia's specialty among countries in the Region — also falls into this category. However, in contrast to a "typical" buyer-driven commodity chain, it is associated with foreign direct investment and, unlike apparel outward processing, requires relatively skilled labor.

In producer-driven supply chains, the production process tends to be coordinated by large multinational corporations. Such networks are mainly present in capital- and skilled-labor-intensive industries such as automobiles, computers, semiconductors, and heavy machinery. A classic example of a producer-driven supply chain is the automobile industry, which encompasses multilayered production systems involving thousands of firms, including parent companies, subsidiaries, and subcontractors.[3] Automobile production networks centered around multinational corporations have played a prominent role in shaping trade of the HP-7 economies.

According to Gereffi (1999), while the multinationals in producer-driven chains often belong to global oligopolies, where there is only a handful of competitors, buyer-driven commodity chains are characterized by highly competitive, locally owned, and globally dispersed production systems. Their profits derive not from scale, volume, and technological advantage, as in producer-driven chains, but rather from a combination of high-value research, design, sales, marketing, and financial services. This combination allows the retailers, branded marketers, and branded manufacturers to act as strategic brokers in linking factories abroad with evolving product niches in the main consumer markets. Developing and transition countries initially start participating in buyer-driven networks as subcontractors, involved solely in simple assembly operations for which they receive all of the necessary inputs from the buyer. However, with time, some of them manage to move up in the value chain by taking on the responsibility for sourcing materials and some design activities.

Network trade has been the driving force of several of the Region's economies' integration into global markets, as evidenced below. The HP-7—the most developed of the Region's economies, as well as Turkey—have moved through two stages. In the first stage, buyer-driven network exports served as a major vehicle linking them to external markets. The second stage has been participation in producer-driven networks. Not all countries, however, have embarked on this path, and it remains to be seen whether all will follow the same pattern. Only a few countries among CIS economies have become part of network trade. The exceptions are Armenia (diamonds), Belarus (furniture), and the Kyrgyz Republic, Moldova, and Turkmenistan (apparel). On the other hand, all EU-8 economies appear to be moving along the same path, albeit at different speeds.

In fact, the link between FDI and network trade seems to be ubiquitous for producer-driven networks. The entry into producer-driven networks is rather inconceivable without FDI. Two of the Region's countries who are the largest recipients of FDI—the Czech Republic and Hungary—have also been the best performers in producer-driven network exports. On the other hand, although participation in furniture or clothing global chains does not necessarily require foreign investment, it is often associated with FDI. A good example is Romania's clothing sector, characterized by relatively high foreign penetration (Hunya 2002). A large number of small Italian firms appear to dominate both clothing and leather industries in Romania (Kaminski and Ng 2004).

Participation in Buyer-Driven Value Chains: Clothing, Diamonds, and Furniture

Clothing (and to a lesser extent) furniture have been the quintessential engines of export growth for many EU-8 countries during the initial stages of the transition. They accounted for a considerable share of value added and manufacturing employment, with significant implications for poverty reduction. With increasing wages in the more successful reformers, many outward-processing operations in the clothing sector have been shifting to economies less advanced in the transformation process, to take advantage of lower labor costs.

The pace of transition to competitive markets, which is correlated with success in attracting FDI inflows (see chapter 4), has shaped developments in buyer-driven value chains. For countries that moved fast in both stabilization and structural reforms, clothing ceased to be a major engine of export growth by the mid-1990s. This observation applies to five EU-8 countries, including the Czech Republic, Estonia, Hungary, Poland, and Slovenia (see table 7.1). In Poland, the first country to implement a radical stabilization-cum-transformation program, the share of clothing in manufactured exports peaked in 1993, or four years into the transition. In the Slovak Republic, clothing exports did not reach their peak until 1997, but the Slovak Republic lagged on structural economic reforms and privatization until 1999 (Kaminski and Smarzynska 2001). While not a transition economy,

TABLE 7.1

Share of Clothing in Exports of Manufactured Goods, Excluding Chemicals, 1992–2002 (%)

	Peak year	Share in peak year	Share in 2003 or latest available	Index, 2003 Peak=100	Average annual growth rate 1996–2003
Countries that shifted out of the clothing network					
Hungary	1992	21.2	4.1	20	3.8
Slovenia	1993	13.8	3.5	25	−7.5
Poland	1993	18.9	5.2	27	−1.9
Czech Rep.	1994	3.8	1.8	46	2.2
Estonia	1995	14.1	7.3	52	8.4
Slovak Rep.	1997	7.3	3.9	54	14.7
Countries heavily involved in clothing network trade					
Croatia	1997	25.8	15.5	60	−0.9
Serbia & Montenegro	1998	18.7	14.5	78	−4.4[a]
Albania	1998	48.5	41.1	85	17.2
Latvia	1999	20.4	16.0	78	9.7
Lithuania	1999	27.7	16.6	60	12.0
Romania	1999	32.8	29.8	91	18.5
Turkmenistan	2000	24.4	24.4	100	n.a.
Bulgaria	2002	34.8	34.0	98	27.0[a]
Macedonia, FYR	2002	46.4	44.9	97	7.3
Moldova	2002	52.4	49.1	94	27.3
Kyrgyz Rep.	2003	12.6	12.6	100	8.6
Countries outside clothing network trade					
Kazakhstan	1996	0.8	0.1	15	−20.0
Georgia	1996	4.6	2.8	60	1.9
Azerbaijan	1997	7.3	0.2	3	−37.7
Armenia	1999	9.4	0.5	5	−22.7[a]
Belarus	1999	7.0	6.0	86	−1.3
Russian Fed.	1999	2.3	0.9	41	14.7
Ukraine	1999	5.4	4.8	89	10.9[a]
Bosnia & Herzegovina	n.a.	n.a.	n.a.	n.a.	n.a.
Tajikistan	n.a.	n.a.	n.a.	n.a.	n.a.
Uzbekistan	n.a.	n.a.	n.a.	n.a.	n.a.
Turkey	1995	40.3	26.3	65	7.3

Source: Authors' calculations based on national trade statistics reported to the UN COMTRADE database.

Note: n.a. = not available.

a. Armenia: data available for 1997–2003; Bulgaria, Serbia and Montenegro, and Ukraine have not yet submitted 2003 trade data to the UN COMTRADE database. Their respective data are for 2002.

Turkey has shared a similar experience, with the export share of clothing peaking at 40 percent in 1995 and then falling to 26 percent by 2003. These seven countries (the HP-7) have managed to make a transition from clothing to producer-driven networks in automotive and IT sectors, as discussed below.

The SEE countries, the remaining two Baltic states, and the Kyrgyz Republic, Moldova, and Turkmenistan became involved in the apparel network later than the HP-7. Clothing and textile exports are still an important foreign exchange earner in that group. Their share of manufactured exports ranged from 13 percent in the Kyrgyz Republic to 34 percent in Bulgaria and 49 percent in Moldova in 2003 (see table 7.1). While SEE and Baltic firms have been involved in outward processing for EU customers, this probably is not the case—given their remote location—for Kyrgyz or Turkmen firms, which serve mostly CIS markets; see chapter 2.

The demise of clothing has been taking place in both groups—on average, the share of clothing in manufactured exports in 2003 was 5.8 percentage points below its respective peak level. This, however, should not suggest that the clothing sector is going to disappear completely, because some of these countries have moved or probably will move to higher value added operations, where higher labor productivity and flexible production arrangements could offset higher wages. Contrast, for instance, Bosnia and Herzegovina and Slovenia, the latter having one of the highest wage rates in the Region. The unit value of Slovenian exports of clothing was on average three times higher than that of clothing exports from Bosnia and Herzegovina (World Bank 2004a).

Increasing labor costs in the EU-8 have prompted relocation of the clothing value chains farther East. However, the performance of CIS countries in this activity, other than those mentioned above, has been neither spectacular nor uniform. During 1996–2003, exports of apparel networks were on the rise in absolute terms in Russia and Ukraine, although they declined in relative terms in both countries. During the same period, clothing exports almost completely disappeared in Armenia, Azerbaijan, and Kazakhstan. The performance of Belarus and Georgia has been modest. Thus, by and large, CIS countries have failed to take advantage of the clothing network as a potential engine of export growth.

Their proximity to Western Europe places the EU-8 at a great advantage and makes them primary candidates for becoming rapid-response suppliers to apparel retailers throughout Europe. Moving up this route requires investment in both physical and human capital, yet it is certainly not beyond the reach of local companies. This is, however, a less viable option for most CIS countries, given their geographic location. The only way to overcome the geographic disadvantage is to compensate with improvements in business climate and transport infrastructure.

One of the CIS countries has, however, found a unique specialization niche. The combination of unequaled skills and commercial contacts that had been developed before the demise of the Soviet Union has been responsible for Armenia's participation in the diamond value chain. As a result of FDI inflows, Armenian diamond-polishing factories are firmly entrenched in a global diamond value chain, not only in commercial links but also in equity (box 7.1).

In contrast to the apparel value chain, which often involves only simple cut-make-trim operations applied to fabrics supplied by buyers and thus boils down to the use of only local unskilled labor, the furniture network is more diversified and complex, requiring a larger local input of skills and investment in capital assets. Similar to cloth-

---

BOX 7.1

The Diamond Global Value Chain

Exports of diamonds have shaped Armenia's overall export performance to an even greater extent than clothing has in some other transition economies. They accounted for more than 40 percent of total exports and almost two-thirds of all manufactured exports (excluding chemicals) in 2002.

Armenian diamond-cutting firms are tied to value chains ending in Belgium and Israel. One of the largest factories, "Lori," is owned by Belgian investors, whereas the Israeli-based Lev Leviev Group, which—in contrast to the Antwerp-centered link—specializes in all stages of diamond production, owns "Shoxakn," the largest company in Armenia. Belgium remains a major supplier and recipient of diamonds, accounting for 55 percent of Armenian exports and 51 percent of imports of diamonds in 2002. However, there was a major shift toward Israel in 2001–2002, with its share on the import side rising from 1 percent in 2000 to 30 percent and 48 percent in 2001 and 2002, respectively. The share in exports grew from 10 percent to 28 percent and 43 percent over the same time.

While a high dependence of the Armenian export performance on cut diamonds is beyond doubt, this does not appear to be a major threat to Armenia's external position. In fact, diamonds seem to be less vulnerable than other "single crops" to international supply or demand volatility for two reasons. First, Armenian firms are foreign-owned and deeply embedded in diamond global value chains. Second, despite the 42 percent fall in the value of diamond exports in 2001, the value of total exports contracted 10 percent, indicating that other exports expanded.

Source: Kaminski 2004b.

ing, furniture producers operating in a global value chain supply products according to specifications provided by large multinational retailers. They also tend to be locally owned. However, the relationship between supplier and multinational retailer frequently reflects a complexity of tasks involved. In consequence, the relationship between buyers and suppliers is based on a more long-term mutual commitment, with multinationals often providing assistance in technology development, production management, and personnel training (box 7.2). Skills acquired in this way can be used to develop a specialization in activities going beyond mere assembly operations to, for instance, production of specialized parts or higher value added

BOX 7.2

Case Study from the Furniture Network

As the case of Vilniaus Baldu Kombinatas (VBK) demonstrates, establishing commercial ties with a multinational corporation may be a successful strategy for integrating into a global distribution network.

VBK had been established as a small workshop in 1883, and since then it has become one of the largest furniture producers in Lithuania. The company produces both home and office furniture. Because the Lithuanian furniture market is too small to support a company the size of VBK, the firm has to rely on exports. About 95 percent of VBK production is exported to Belgium, Canada, France, Great Britain, Italy, Japan, the Netherlands, Sweden, the United States, and other countries. About 90 percent of output is sold to the Swedish company IKEA, which in 1999 named VBK as its best supplier in the Baltics.

The relationship between VBK and IKEA began in 1998, and the cooperation between the two companies has remained very close. IKEA has provided support to VBK in terms of technology, production organization, and personnel training. VBK is connected to IKEA's computer system, through which invoices and payment and delivery information are processed. VBK has upgraded its computer system so it is able to receive information on sales of its products in IKEA stores abroad and new orders on daily basis. While relying so strongly on one customer may be perceived as a risky strategy, VBK is not very concerned, because it is one of the top 25 IKEA suppliers out of some 2,000 companies producing for the Swedish concern. Moreover, closer technological integration with IKEA will make VBK more competitive relative to other IKEA suppliers.

The strategy chosen by VBK appears to have been successful. The company increased its sales from 4.5 million euro in 1998 to 24.2 million Euro in 2002. During the same period, its employment almost doubled, and the value of its exports increased more than tenfold. In 2001, the company was awarded the ISO 9001 quality certification and currently it is working toward the ISO 14001.

Sources: World Bank staff; VBK Web site.

furniture. As a result, the furniture network is less sensitive to the rise in labor costs and creates more opportunities for knowledge transfer and productivity spillovers.

The furniture production chain has been an important driver of manufacturing exports in the Region, as well as in Turkey, but, again, not all countries have tapped into this network (see table 7.2). Eight CIS countries have not been engaged in the furniture value chain (and they are not listed in table 7.2). Among CIS countries, only Belarus, the Kyrgyz Republic, Moldova, Russia, and Ukraine have been involved. But in two of them—the Kyrgyz Republic and Moldova—the importance of network exports has significantly declined, and high import intensities (imports of parts as percentage of network exports of parts and final products) suggest that participation of local firms in the network has been limited. Exports within the furniture network, driven mainly by parts, from Russia and Ukraine recorded significant growth, especially in 2000–2003, albeit from a

TABLE 7.2
Evolving Significance of Furniture Network Trade: Share in Manufactured Exports
Excluding chemicals

	Exports ($ millions)	Share of network in exports of manufactured goods			Index, 2003[a]	Share of parts in network's exports			Index 2003[b]	Import intensity[c]	
	2003	1995	1999	2003	1995 = 100	1995	1999	2003	1995 = 100	1999	2003
Poland	3,902	9.2	10.1	9.7	292	12	17	31	805	9	10
Lithuania	366	3.9	5.8	9.2	792	10	36	27	2,080	9	6
Slovenia	881	6.9	9.1	9.0	194	46	64	67	284	11	13
Latvia	135	7.0	9.3	8.9	289	38	45	37	285	9	10
Estonia	308	6.7	7.4	8.1	448	23	37	45	883	8	5
Romania	789	9.7	6.9	5.8	153	3	10	16	840	3	5
Slovak Rep.	859	3.3	2.4	4.8	446	13	36	24	853	30	25
Belarus	218	n.a.	3.6	4.4	168	n.a.	5	12	431	3	5
Serbia & Montenegro	35	6.2	4.2	3.2	77	12	11	11	126	15	28
Czech Rep.	1,297	2.6	3.5	3.1	323	37	62	68	587	23	20
Bulgaria	131	1.7	2.7	3.0	368	14	20	22	578	18	11
Hungary	829	3.3	2.8	2.4	356	41	73	76	663	19	23
Albania	6	1.1	1.8	1.5	399	79	74	56	283	194	69
Macedonia, FYR	5	6.5	1.0	0.6	13	9	17	17	26	22	43
Russian Fed.	144	0.4	0.4	0.6	196	24	32	37	296	25	49
Moldova	1	4.2	1.5	0.5	12	2	50	37	376	58	112
Kyrgyz Rep.	1	0.7	0.2	0.5	62	34	49	21	115	886	128
Ukraine	56	0.3	0.4	0.5	210	9	18	19	456	30	21
Turkey	457	0.5	0.7	1.2	605	24	22	23	568	33	19

Source: Authors' calculations based on national trade statistics reported to the UN COMTRADE database.

Note: a. Index refers to the change in value of furniture network exports.
b. Index refers to the change in value of exports of furniture parts.
c. The ratio of parts imports to total network exports.
n.a. = not available.

low base. This, together with low network import intensities, suggests that Russian and Ukrainian firms have entered furniture supply chains. Considering Russia's endowment in wood, the current level of involvement in the furniture supply network (at 0.5 percent of manufactured exports) remains well below potential.

On the other hand, exports within the furniture network by other economies in the Region have largely kept up with the growth of exports of manufactured goods. Two exceptions are FYR Macedonia and Serbia and Montenegro, where furniture exports practically disappeared by 2002, suggesting the demise of production links inherited from the former Yugoslavia.

The shift toward specialization in furniture parts has been significant for most countries, indicating overall progress in industrial restructuring. While in 1995, only Slovenia—one of the most industrialized EU-8 country and an important supplier to EU-15 furniture producers—and (to a lesser extent) Hungary specialized in furniture parts, the situation changed by 1999. In fact, parts have become the driver of furniture network exports in Croatia, Estonia, FYR Macedonia, Poland, Romania, and the CIS countries included in the table. In Albania, on the other hand, the share of parts in network exports declined, probably resulting from the fall in import content of production by substituting domestically produced parts for previously imported items.

Producer-Driven Chains: Automotive and Information Technology Networks

Worldwide, the combination of advances in technology and creation of business-friendly environments has spurred a new global division of labor. Its trademark is dividing up the value chain into smaller components and moving them to countries where production costs could be lower. Production fragmentation in vertically integrated sectors is behind producer-driven network trade. It differs in several important respects from traditional, buyer-driven global value chains. It includes two-way flows of parts and components for further processing and development across firms located in various countries. Outside of the Region, a historical example of production fragmentation at a regional level is the Canada-United States Automotive Products Agreement of 1965, which, followed by the significant reduction in trade barriers, led to an expansion of trade in auto parts (Jones, Kierzkowski, and Lurong forthcoming). Production fragmentation has also been prevalent in East Asia (see box 7.3).

In both the IT and automotive sectors, the pressures on a global basis of technological change have led to a practical disappearance of

BOX 7.3

Production Sharing in East Asia

Production sharing in East Asia experienced remarkably high growth during the last decades, much higher than either in Europe or in North America. "Production sharing" refers to trade in parts and components and entails the development of specialized and frequently labor-intensive activities that take place within vertically integrated international manufacturing industries. A study by Ng and Yeats (2001) analyzed the evolution of international trade in parts and components in machinery, transport equipment, and miscellaneous manufactured articles in East Asia during 1984–96. The results of the analysis showed that:

- Exports of parts and components of Asian countries increased more than 500 percent during 1984–96, as compared with a 300 percent increase in total exports.

- Trade in parts and components recorded the fastest annual growth rate in both regional and global exports, exceeding by 5 to 6 percentage points the export growth of all other goods and significantly increasing in relative importance.

- Parts and components accounted for approximately 20 percent of the region's total exports and imports of manufactures in 1996.

Source: Ng and Yeats 2001.

"one-stop shop" industrial structures.[4] Miniaturization, as well as exponential growth in information processing and storage capacities, combined with integration of Internet and imaging technologies, have been the major driving forces behind transformation of both auto industry and IT sectors worldwide over the last two decades. Large multinationals, which have traditionally coordinated production and marketing activities across the globe and dominated both sectors, have undergone dramatic changes over the same time period. Their common denominator has been increasing geographic dispersion of the production process. Thanks to new technologies that make it possible to trace parts and components moving through chains of production spread over several countries and continents, vertically integrated firms have been replaced by structures connected through complex, borderless supply chains. These chains include not only product manufacturing but also the front-end customer contact and support services and consist of several layers, including parent companies, subsidiaries, and subcontractors.

With the liberalization of foreign trade regimes and reduction of barriers to FDI following the collapse of central planning, the indigenous IT and automotive sectors developed earlier in the Region's countries had no chance of withstanding international competition unless they were taken over and restructured by foreign investors. Where soft budget constraints and high barriers to import competition remained, post-Communist supply chains had survived. Belarus manufacturers of automotive parts could continue feeding plants in Russia relatively safely behind high tariff and nontariff barriers. IT producers from Bulgaria and Latvia could do the same.

Not surprisingly, these activities turned out to be neither expanding nor sustainable. Once reforms began to take hold in CIS countries and their markets became less distorted, they had to face competition from other suppliers. The IT sectors in Estonia and Lithuania, on the one hand, and in Latvia, on the other, offer two contrasting developments showing the importance of FDI. Both countries inherited from the Soviet era a relatively well-developed IT industry that used to work for both the civilian and military sectors. However, while the Latvian electronic sector has not done well, electronic products in Estonia and Lithuania, where local firms have successfully integrated into global IT networks, have been among the best export performers. Success in the IT sector hinges critically on the presence of multinationals. Again, the evidence is overwhelming. Firms such as Nokia, Thomson, Siemens, Philips, IBM, General Electric, and their suppliers have driven modernization and development of IT sectors in all countries that have attracted sizable FDI inflows (FIAS 2003).

While the IT network is of a more recent vintage than the automotive sector (and indeed provides input into many other sectors, including the automotive network), both networks share an important characteristic: their development in a local economy requires foreign capital and know-how, because both networks are capital-intensive and, especially the IT network, knowledge-intensive. Building a competitive IT or automotive sector from scratch, without external involvement, is almost impossible today.

Developments in the automotive sector show that, without the involvement of multinational corporations, local firms are likely doomed to failure. Before the collapse of Communism, many of them produced motor vehicles mostly on the basis of licenses (for example, Fiat-Lada in Russia, Polish Fiat, and Renault-Dacia in Romania). Czechoslovakia, with a strong tradition in automotive manufacturing going back to the beginning of the last century, produced an array of motor vehicles. So did the former Soviet Union and Yugoslavia. The Czech Skoda, Yugoslav Yugo, Polish Fiat, Romanian Dacia, and Soviet Lada (a modified Fiat model) were marketed in Western Europe without much success, despite their low prices. Except for Lada or Volga in

Russia, they are no longer manufactured. Skoda flourishes as a brand name, but as an integral part of the Volkswagen Group.

Multinational corporations have been responsible for restructuring companies and subsequently engendering impressive performance in the automotive network. Examples abound. In the Slovak Republic, Volkswagen (automobiles), Siemens (cable harnesses, lights), INA Werke Schaffeler (ball bearings), and Sachs Trnava (coupling assemblies for passenger cars), just to name a few, have become household names. Piston engines for VW-Audi automobiles assembled in Hungary have set the stage for Hungary's spectacular entry into supply chains in the automotive sector. Skoda Auto of the VW Group and other car producers in the Czech Republic have attracted large international firms specializing in automotive parts and components (see box 7.4).

FDI: The Driver of Network Trade Expansion

There is abundant evidence suggesting strong links between FDI and the scope of incorporation of local IT and automotive manufacturing capacities into global production networks. Hungary, the largest exporter of network products and parts among the Region's countries, accounting for 27 percent of the Region's total network exports in 2003, was the first to open up and actively seek FDI. Hungary's FDI stock, accumulated mainly in 1990–95, amounted to 40 percent of the total FDI stock in all transition economies by the end of 1995. By 1997, the list of the top 100 Hungarian companies was filled with easily recognizable names of subsidiaries of multinational corporations.[5]

Although a relatively small economy, Hungary surged ahead of other former centrally planned economies in attracting large inflows of FDI during the early stages of the transition. In 1990–93, Hungary absorbed 45 percent of total FDI inflows to 25 countries of the Former Soviet Union and Central and Eastern Europe. Its share in these flows subsequently fell during 1994–96, once other transition economies had become attractive to foreign investors. Yet, over the whole 1990–96 period, almost one-third of total FDI flows to the Region were directed to Hungary.

The question is why? The pace of moving away from central planning and macroeconomic stability provides a good explanation of why the EU-8 economies performed better than the CIS economies in terms of attracting FDI, but it fails to explain the variation within the EU-8. After all, these countries had many similar features, including the speed of liberalization, endowments of production factors, and proximity to EU markets. Why, for instance, did the Czech Republic

BOX 7.4

Automotive Components Clusters in the Czech Republic and the Slovak Republic

Thanks to a long tradition and successful privatization of Skoda (which in 1991 became part of the Volkswagen Group [VW]) and other automotive state-owned enterprises, the Czech Republic is the largest producer of cars in the Region. The $2.6 billion in VW investments in Skoda Auto has provided a stimulus to the expansion of the automotive industry and attracted other global motor vehicle producers (including PSA Peugeot and Toyota). Large international firms specializing in automotive parts and components have quickly followed either through purchasing and modernizing local firms to perform multiple operations or through undertaking greenfield investments. As of 2002, there were 270 firms operating in the Czech Republic, representing 45 percent of the top 100 world suppliers of automotive parts and components.

Geographical proximity to Germany, Hungary, and the Slovak Republic meant that auto parts producers operating in the Czech Republic became suppliers to auto manufacturers in many European countries. Their clients, however, are not located solely throughout Europe. VW's Beetle plant in Mexico uses wiper systems manufactured by PAL Praha, a subsidiary of Canadian multinational Magna.

The proximity and links to the German automotive industry explain the largest presence of German-based firms in the sector. Such brand names in automotive components as Robert Bosch, employing around 5,000 workers in its Czech subsidiaries, or Siemens, with about 10,000 em-

attract less FDI in 1990–95, despite lower inflation and debt stock? Or why did Poland, with much stronger GDP growth performance, attract less FDI than both Hungary and the Czech Republic?

The short answer is that Hungary was immensely successful in turning its liabilities into assets. First, Hungary was saddled with a huge international debt at the outset of its full-fledged transition to competitive markets, but, in contrast to Poland, it had never sought rescheduling nor had it defaulted in its payments to private or public creditors. Therefore, its creditworthiness was high.

Second, earlier dealings with the international financial community had helped Hungarians develop considerable financial management and negotiating skills. Therefore, despite heavy indebtedness, Hungary was perceived as a reliable and creditworthy partner. However, sustainability of capital flows requires sustainability of reform efforts. Without continued liberalization, the virtuous circle would have come to a screeching halt. Privatization policy and measures aimed at deepening the financial sector created a favorable environ-

ployees, continue to expand their activities. So do firms not only from other EU countries (especially Italy and France) but also from other countries, including the United States, Canada, Korea, and, more recently, Japan.

The Slovak Republic's impressive performance in the automotive network has also been driven by multinational corporations, such as Volkswagen, Siemens (cable harnesses, lights), INA Werke Schaffeler (ball bearings), and Sachs Trnava (coupling assemblies for passenger cars), just to name a few. Siemens has ownership shares in 14 Slovak companies, which employ more than 8,900 people. Two-thirds of the total of SKK's $16 billion revenues in 2002 came from exporting. Siemens' subsidiaries have been involved in a variety of export activities, all centered around providing inputs into global networks of production and distribution. Osram Slovakia (part of Siemens group) contributed to the growth of exports of electrical lighting and signaling equipment, which is being sold to the EU-15 countries and the Czech Republic. Siemens has also been the driving force behind exports of pumps—one of the fastest-growing product categories exported to the EU-15.

SAS Automotive, formed in Bratislava in 2000, has been very closely integrated for their customers, as well as for their suppliers abroad. It supplies VW with completely assembled cockpits. Modules consist of dashboards, electronic components, air-conditioning, airbags, steering rods, and pedals. The module must be assembled error-free and delivered directly to the production line of the specific car within two hours of receiving the order. Logistics ensure the supply of more than 100 parts from various European countries and their effective storage and removal from the warehouse.

Sources: The Auto Parts Market; U.S. and Foreign Commercial Service; U.S. Department of State, Washington, DC, 2002; Kaminski and Javorcik 2004.

ment for FDI. So did an active policy of selling firms to strategic investors on a case-by-case basis.

Third, high indebtedness, combined with a policy decision not to reschedule the debt, brought about a quick change in policy attitudes toward FDI and gave an extra incentive to establishing a relatively transparent legal system, with the privatization policies favoring sales to the highest bidder, no matter whether domestic or foreign. There were no lengthy national debates over the alleged dangers of foreign penetration (as in the Czech Republic or Poland), and Hungary was the first to open the so-called strategic sectors (banking, telecommunications, energy, and utilities) to foreign investors.

Last but not least, Hungarian firms had had a history of direct links with Western firms. They had been involved in subcontracting since 1968. This had created a good foundation for foreign investors wanting to respond to new opportunities created by the collapse of Communism and for Hungarian managers wanting to seek foreign partnership. Investments by large multinationals paved the way for other investments. These would include investments made by competing multinationals in similar lines of products and subcontractors following major multinationals in purchasing their products.[6]

The massive entry of multinationals dramatically affected Hungary's trade in general and network trade in particular. Both network imports and exports skyrocketed in 1995–99, recording average annual growth rates of 32 percent and 52 percent, respectively (table 7.3). However, despite FDI stocks that were almost twice as large as those in the Czech Republic, the value of Hungarian exports of automotive and IT parts and products in 1996 stood at 34 percent of Czech exports. By the following year, it was already 49 percent higher, despite very impressive growth of Czech exports. While the value of Czech network exports rose from $3 billion in 1996 to $3.7 billion in 1997, Hungarian network exports jumped from $1 billion to $5.5 billion during the same period. By 1999, their value had doubled, and Hungary accounted for more than one-third of the Region's network exports.

Differences in FDI inflows appear to explain differences in the dynamics of network trade among countries in the Region. The other members of the High Performers group (HP-7) also witnessed stronger export performance after attracting FDI inflows in the second half of the 1990s. As happened earlier in Hungary, subsidiaries of large multinationals proliferated and served as an engine behind the growth of network trade. The Czech Republic, Estonia, Poland, the Slovak Republic, and Turkey had average annual growth rates of network exports at double-digit levels throughout the 1995–2003 period, but—except for the Slovak Republic—they were significantly higher in 1999–2003 than in 1995–99. Automotive network exports have been responsible for a significant share of Turkey's exports.

TABLE 7.3

Dynamics of Producer-Driven Network Trade and Its Share in Manufactured Goods, Excluding Chemicals of HP-7, 1996–2003 (%)

| | Average annual rate of growth of network | | | | Share in manufactured goods | | | | | |
| | Exports | | Imports | | Exports | | | Imports | | |
	1995–99	1999–2003	1995–99	1999–2003	1995	1999	2003	1995	1999	2003
Czech Rep.	16.8	21.7	5.9	13.4	15.5	24.3	34.4	22.2	24.1	31.3
Estonia	14.6	17.5	8.8	8.6	25.1	27.8	29.9	30.1	27.9	31.5
Hungary	52.1	12.5	31.9	7.9	18.1	52.2	53.8	22.6	39.0	41.8
Poland	17.0	22.7	20.3	−2.0	11.9	19.5	26.2	21.6	31.2	19.2
Slovak Rep.	29.3	25.0	15.3	13.9	11.2	30.5	40.5	24.0	31.0	34.7
Slovenia	2.3	8.1	3.3	−8.0	19.7	21.5	22.0	31.8	32.1	28.0
Turkey	18.0	24.2	17.3	6.6	8.0	13.9	21.6	19.4	34.6	31.8

Source: UN COMTRADE database.

Considering the Region as a whole, one finds a strong positive correlation between FDI stock in manufacturing and producer-driven network exports. As can be seen from data in table 7.4, there is a full correspondence between ranking of the Region's economies in terms of network exports per capita and FDI stocks in manufacturing per capita. Further down the ladder, Belarus and Bulgaria are outliers, albeit for different reasons. Belarus' network exports are significantly larger than FDI stock would suggest, whereas the reverse is true for Bulgaria.[7]

This, however, does not change the overall conclusion about a strong predictive power of differences in FDI in manufacturing to explain the variation in network export performance. The value of the correlation coefficient for FDI stock in manufacturing per capita (end of 2003) and producer-driven network exports in 2003 is 88 percent (figure 7.1). The value of the correlation coefficient between

TABLE 7.4
Overview of Trade in Producer-Driven Networks in 1996, 1999, and 2003
% and $ millions

	FDI stock in manufacturing per capita ($) 2003	Networks' exports per capita ($) 2003	Share in ECA networks' exports 2003	Share of networks in manufactured imports 2003	Index 2003[a] 1995 = 100	Share of networks in exports of manufactured goods (chemicals excluded)			Import intensity	
						1995	1999	2003	1999	2003
Hungary	1,694	1,847	27.4	41.8	1,463	18.1	52.2	53.8	56	49
Czech Rep.	1,338	1,391	20.8	31.3	579	15.5	24.3	34.4	46	43
Slovak Rep.	624	1,339	10.6	34.7	1,102	11.2	30.5	40.5	59	49
Slovenia	824	1,094	3.2	28.0	165	19.7	21.5	22.0	56	48
Estonia	548	844	1.7	31.5	442	25.1	27.8	29.9	67	54
Poland	547	275	15.4	30.2	608	11.9	19.5	26.2	117	52
Lithuania	314	220	1.1	26.5	349	18.5	13.8	19.1	75	42
Belarus	54	127	1.8	15.5	151	n.a.	32.1	25.3	29	29
Croatia	694	69	0.5	27.9	205	5.7	5.5	8.0	136	146
Romania	262	59	1.9	18.8	609	4.1	5.7	9.7	149	90
Latvia	230	32	0.1	25.4	101	10.9	3.3	4.9	432	261
Bulgaria	428	22	0.3	25.2	112	7.6	4.9	3.9	197	226
Serbia & Montenegro	217	15	0.2	26.5	158	10.5	12.8	11.2	116	155
Russian Fed.	75	15	3.1	24.8	93	12.7	8.9	9.4	60	89
Macedonia, FYR	60	11	0.0	28.0	50	6.9	3.2	2.4	160	208
Ukraine	43	9	0.8	23.0	66	8.3	5.8	4.0	81	109
Kazakhstan	74	4	0.1	23.3	100	3.8	2.9	3.0	436	669
Kyrgyz Rep.	3	3	0.0	26.0	163	6.7	22.5	11.1	155	225

Sources: Trade figures: UN COMTRADE Statistics. FDI figures: cumulative net FDI inflows 1990–2003 calculated on data from IMF International Financial Statistics, combined with information on the shares of FDI in the manufacturing sector taken from various national sources.

Note: Table includes countries with the value of networks' exports exceeding $10 million in 2003.
a. Index in terms of value of exports of producer-driven exports.

FIGURE 7.1

FDI and Exports of Producer-Driven Network Products ($)

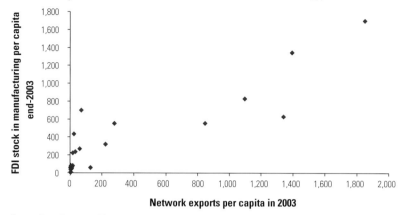

Sources: Trade figures: UN COMTRADE Statistics. FDI figures: cumulative net FDI inflows 1990–2003 calculated on data from IMF International Financial Statistics, combined with information on the shares of FDI in the manufacturing sector taken from various national sources.

the share of producer-driven network exports in exports of manufactures (excluding chemicals) in 2003 and the FDI stock in manufacturing (end of 2003) is slightly higher, at 90 percent. Considering that several countries in the Region—Poland, Romania, Russia, and Ukraine—have relatively large domestic markets, this is a rather surprisingly strong positive correlation between FDI inflows and exports of network products.

There are stark differences among countries in the Region, as well as Turkey, in the extent of participation in these two networks. On the export side, the HP-7 plus other new EU members accounted for 92 percent of the Region's total network exports in 2003. Adding Bulgaria and Romania, which are EU accession countries, raises the share to 94 percent. With a share of around 4 percent, CIS economies are yet to become involved in intraproduct trade. On the import side, the EU-8 and Turkey took 82 percent of network imports into the Region in 2003, while the corresponding figure for the CIS was around 13 percent.

IT Final Products and Automotive Parts: New Drivers of Networks' Exports

In line with global trends, trade in IT network products has displayed stronger dynamics than that in the automotive network. The share of IT network exports in producer-driven supply chains increased in most countries in the Region. Most spectacular was the increase in Czech IT exports, which grew from $0.7 billion to $5.1 billion between 1999 and 2003. This was still, however, around 50 percent of the value of Hungarian IT exports, which accounted for 45 percent of the Region's total IT exports in 2003, down from a peak of 54 percent in 1999. Around two-thirds of the Region's IT exports have originated in these two countries since 1999. Except for several CIS countries and Albania, network exports grew at double-digit rates over 1999–2003. Strong growth in the automotive network has been responsible for the fall in the share of IT products and parts exports from the Slovak Republic and Turkey. Note that IT exports from both countries grew at a hefty annual rate of around 25 percent. By any standards, this has been an impressive growth performance.

TABLE 7.5

Trade in IT Network in Comparative Perspective and Exports of Automotive Parts in 1999 and 2003 (%)

	Share of IT in producer-driven network				Share of parts in IT				Share of parts in automotive				Memo-randum: Average annual growth rate of IT
	Exports		Imports		Exports		Imports		Exports		Imports		Exports
	1999	2003	1999	2003	1999	2003	1999	2003	1999	2003	1999	2003	1999–2003
Hungary	52	58	52	57	30	21	52	57	71	79	66	58	19
Czech Rep.	13	36	45	52	56	26	45	52	47	57	59	59	65
Slovenia	9	12	27	26	35	25	27	26	37	47	41	42	18
Croatia	33	61	28	35	37	49	28	35	96	84	15	14	40
Slovak Rep.	14	12	31	27	46	44	31	27	30	37	68	72	26
Estonia	80	72	62	53	58	54	62	53	52	45	26	21	19
Poland	30	22	43	38	40	42	43	38	41	66	60	41	20
Bulgaria	28	64	38	39	49	41	38	39	66	60	20	18	43
Lithuania	57	41	41	34	73	73	41	34	28	14	27	17	25
Romania	42	43	70	54	78	19	70	54	83	89	59	36	40
Latvia	58	61	47	40	57	25	47	40	62	56	25	21	29
Serbia & Montenegro	3	9	37	45	46	34	37	45	80	85	20	24	56
Russian Fed.	37	22	50	41	54	43	50	41	50	43	45	24	–2
Kazakhstan	49	41	36	33	17	15	36	33	21	24	17	26	10
Macedonia, FYR	7	14	30	52	26	63	30	52	70	86	19	23	19
Albania	47	57	29	33	10	54	29	33	21	73	16	16	–3
Belarus	9	9	34	37	36	31	34	37	31	29	60	57	3
Armenia	15	69	48	50	76	83	48	50	79	90	14	15	18
Ukraine	29	24	40	30	51	43	40	30	78	66	34	30	–2
Moldova	67	29	56	35	17	36	56	35	16	34	34	26	–12
Azerbaijan	32	14	53	32	42	29	53	32	4	4	26	43	–17
Kyrgyz Rep.	8	3	46	30	26	40	46	30	53	57	49	43	–24
Georgia	19	29	44	38	20	62	44	38	15	13	8	21	3
Turkey	30	24	52	37	6	5	52	37	47	34	48	50	25

Source: UN COMTRADE Statistics. For Ukraine and Serbia and Montenegro, available data are for 2002.

Two different patterns of specialization appear to have been emerging. While most of the Region's economies that got involved in automotive networks moved toward specialization in automotive parts, participation in IT networks has relied more on assembly operations. For the major IT producers in the Region—the Czech Republic, Estonia, and Hungary—the share of final products in IT exports has significantly increased, indicating the shift toward final production. Countries that succeeded in expanding exports of final products have also increased imports of IT parts. On the other hand, countries that remain outside IT supply chains (that is, CIS and SEE) tend to specialize in parts production.

Producer-Driven Network Trade and Reintegration of EU-8 Countries

Given geographical proximity, it comes as no surprise that around three-fourths of producer-driven network trade is with the EU-15.[8] However, while the share of the EU-15 continued growing and the network trade of CIS economies almost disappeared, there are signs that some of the Region's countries, all former CMEA members, increasingly trade among themselves and that the most successful among them increasingly rely on supplies from the Region.

"Reintegration" varies in scope and intensity across networks. Although the share of the Region's economies in total trade of automotive parts of the Czech Republic, Hungary, Poland, and the Slovak Republic—which account for more than 80 percent of the Region's trade—declined between 1999 and 2003, the value of this trade was more than 50 percent above its level in 1999. "Regional" imports of parts of such countries as Hungary or the Slovak Republic at least doubled in terms of value. The rebound of trade in parts between the Czech Republic and the Slovak Republic augurs well for future growth. There are no signs, however, of any increase in network exports between the EU-8 and the CIS. The share of the CIS in automotive parts trade with the EU-8 fell from 2 percent in 1999 to 1.8 percent in 2003 in exports and from 1.2 percent to 0.8 percent in imports. Increasingly, however, motor vehicles manufactured in the EU-8 are sold in markets within the Region. The share of these markets in total Czech exports of motor vehicles was 21 percent in 2003, up from 16 percent in 1999.

Interestingly, IT network trade displays a much stronger bias in favor of local suppliers and consumers. It appears that some producers in these countries have become part of supply chains feeding parts for further processing in Hungary, a regional powerhouse in IT manufacturing that accounts for almost half of IT exports from the Region. Hungary has emerged as a focal point using inputs manufactured in other EU-8 economies. Its rise to prominence in this new role has been not only swift but also spectacular. In 2002, Hungary accounted for 40 percent of intra-EU-8 IT imports, up from 5 percent in 1995. Hungarian IT network imports from other EU-8 economies increased from $66 million in 1999 to $436 million in 2002. Its imports from the Czech Republic increased from $5 million in 1999 to $200 million in 2002, from Poland from $20 million to $125 million, and from the Slovak Republic from $7 million to $23 million. Parts were dominant in these imports, with the average share of Hungary's imports from the EU-8 amounting to 62 percent in 2002: they accounted for 79 percent of imports from the Czech Republic, 38 percent from Poland, and 93 percent from the neighboring Slovak Republic.

Two-way trade in IT products has picked up also in other country pairs, but not with or among CIS economies. Trade in parts has been a driver of a rapid expansion in intra-EU-8 trade in the IT network. EU-8 markets took almost 10 percent of their own total exports of IT parts and accounted for 6 percent of their imports in 2002. Considering that the respective shares were at around 4 percent three years earlier, this is a significant change. Trade in parts between the EU-8 and the CIS is practically nonexistent, although the EU-8 share in CIS total imports of IT network products increased from 4 percent in 1999 to 5.2 percent in 2002. However, this is not two-way trade and, therefore, does not indicate a network-type arrangement.

Producer-Driven Network Trade and Twin Gaps: Factor Content and Trade Balance

Network trade appears to have profoundly affected factor intensities of exports as well as trade balance. Countries whose firms have become parts of a new division of labor based on producer-driven network trade have also experienced the shift toward capital-intensive and skilled-labor-intensive products. In addition, they have witnessed closing the gap between network product imports and exports.

Despite their endowments of educated and skilled labor, expansion in unskilled-labor-intensive products has characterized the adjustment in foreign trade flows following the implementation of stabilization-cum-transformation programs in many of the Region's transition economies. Some countries have witnessed a closing of this gap; others' exports are still heavily tilted toward unskilled-labor-intensive products (for example, Uzbekistan) or dominated by natural-resource-based products (for example, Russia).

It appears that countries that became part of producer-driven networks are those where skilled labor and capital-intensive goods account for the largest share of total exports. The value of the correlation coefficient between network exports per capita and the shares of skilled labor and capital-intensive products in total exports of 81 percent in 2003 is high. Furthermore, economies with higher network trade per capita have also registered a stronger growth in skilled labor and capital-labor-intensive exports. The correlation between the change in the value of these exports between 1995 and 2003 and network exports per capita is positive at 74 percent. Finally, as illustrated in figure 7.2, countries with larger FDI stocks per capita are also those with a higher share of skilled labor and capital-intensive products in total exports.

The networks' export orientation appears to be increasing. The initial participation in network trade is associated with increased imports. However, with time, successful entry into networks has led to falling growth rates of imports and strong growth of exports. As evident from table 7.6, each of the HP-7 economies had "network trade deficits" before FDI in these sectors resulted in restructuring or setting new production activities. Each HP-7 economy ran also sizable "deficits" in network trade in both 1995 and 1996, with imports four times (Turkey) or more than twice (Estonia, Hungary) the value of exports. With time, these deficits turned into surpluses for most HP-7 economies: Hungarian exports exceeded imports in 1997, Czech in 1998, Slovak a year later, and Estonia's in 1999. The remaining HP-7 economies remain in "the red," but exports have grown faster than imports. Except for Poland, IT imports have been responsible for these countries' deficits.

FIGURE 7.2

FDI Stock per capita and Share of Skilled Labor and Capital-Intensive Exports in 2003

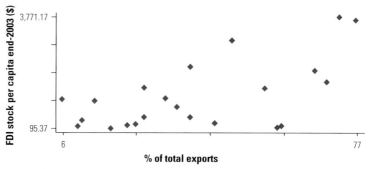

Sources: UN COMTRADE; IMF International Financial Statistics.

Hence, "network firms," once firmly established, have become mostly net foreign currency earners, not only through their own foreign trade activity but also by attracting other foreign investors or developing backward linkages with local producers. Because foreign-owned firms do not operate solely in network sectors, an important question to which we now turn concerns their overall impact on trade balance and economy.

Foreign-Owned Firms and Trade Balance

The presence of foreign firms has a profound effect on a host country's participation in international trade, because it is often associated with an increase in both exports and imports. Empirical evidence suggests that firms with foreign capital tend to be more export-oriented than domestic firms and are responsible for a larger share of exports in many transition economies; see chapter 4. The contribution of foreign firms to host-country exports may not be immediate. A surge in FDI inflows frequently results in a spike of imports because multinationals bring capital equipment for their newly established production plants. Because it takes several years to establish links with local suppliers, in the initial period of operation, they may also rely on imported intermediate inputs before switching to local sourcing.

TABLE 7.6

Producer-Driven Networks' Exports of HP-7 in Percentage of Imports of Networks' Products, 1995–2003

	1995	1996	1997	1998	1999	2000	2001	2002	2003
Total "producer-driven" networks									
Czech Rep.	66	65	83	109	108	107	115	139	123
Estonia	55	47	55	63	70	112	87	70	66
Hungary	61	43	106	116	124	123	118	121	124
Poland	46	37	34	38	40	59	69	74	78
Slovak Rep.	60	63	67	86	107	119	99	104	135
Slovenia	69	75	75	78	66	77	83	88	85
Turkey	33	26	19	26	34	25	73	83	72
Total Region and Turkey	47	44	48	58	65	68	78	85	83
Automotive networks									
Czech Rep.	112	108	128	170	169	176	171	187	164
Estonia	58	48	41	32	37	39	41	39	40
Hungary	68	53	113	119	125	129	136	129	123
Poland	68	49	40	43	49	87	98	97	99
Slovak Rep.	103	74	93	109	132	150	122	131	164
Slovenia	81	85	88	93	82	97	100	109	101
Turkey	47	32	20	26	50	31	106	113	87
Total Region and Turkey	66	59	55	68	81	83	97	102	95

Source: UN COMTRADE statistics.

While the imports take place straightaway, there may be a delay in exporting, leading initially to a (possibly) sizable trade deficit associated with FDI. However, from the point of view of the balance of payments, this initial deterioration in the current account position is offset by inflows into the capital account.

Receiving foreign investment often helps local companies become exporters. Entering foreign markets is costly because potential exporters are initially disadvantaged relative to indigenous firms because they have to bear transport costs and overcome tariffs, and they are less familiar with the tastes of local customers and local regulations. Thus, only firms with above-average productivity are able to compensate for this disadvantage and successfully make sales in foreign countries (Clerides et al. 1998, Bernard and Jensen 1999). The ability of the firm to export is likely to increase with foreign ownership, even without any changes in technology or organization. This happens when foreign ownership offers access to marketing and production channels of a parent company. Because establishing a presence in foreign markets requires not only marketing skills but also considerable resources, foreign ownership increases prospects for exports. In addition, change of ownership may be a necessary condition for a firm to become a supplier in a global production and distribution network.

The data confirm that firms with foreign capital tend to be more foreign-trade-oriented than domestic enterprises and are therefore bound to make a relatively larger contribution to integration of a host country into the world economy. As illustrated in figures 7.3 and 7.4, foreign firms exported on average a larger share of their output in each year during the 1995–2001 period in the Slovak Republic and the 1996–2000 period in Lithuania. These two countries are no exceptions, as a similar pattern was observed in many other EU-8 countries. The difference in export intensity between domestic and foreign firms may be partially the result of the fact that foreign investors acquire more productive and successful local companies, which tend to be exporters. However, even if this is the case, this usually does not impede the capacity of the acquired firm to export. To the contrary, it usually makes it even more competitive in both domestic and external markets. For instance, an econometric analysis of Indonesian data suggests that a foreign acquisition of a local plant leads to an increase in the share of output exported by between 10 and 20 percentage points, depending on the industry and the time period considered. This increase in the average export share is a result both of increased export intensity of previously exporting firms and of acquired firms entering foreign markets for the first time (Arnold and Javorcik 2004).

FIGURE 7.3

Export Intensity of Domestic and Foreign Firms in the Slovak Republic, 1996–2001

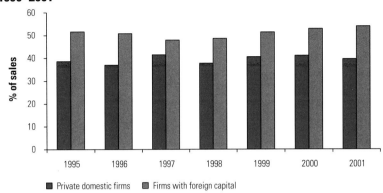

Source: World Bank staff calculations.

FIGURE 7.4

Export Intensity of Domestic and Foreign Firms in Lithuania, 1996–2001

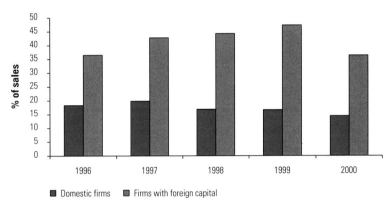

Source: World Bank staff calculations based on data from the Lithuanian Statistical Office.

As noted, the initial spike in imports associated with FDI inflows tends to disappear over time as multinationals develop linkages to local suppliers in a host country. The Czech Republic may serve as an example. The results of a World Bank survey suggest that multinationals operating in that country were actively engaged in local sourcing in 2003 and expected this trend to continue in the future. Ninety percent of interviewed multinationals reported purchasing inputs from at least one Czech company. Czech companies constituted the most important supplier group, followed by other European suppliers (located in the EU-15 or the EU-8) and other multinationals operating in the Czech Republic. When asked about the share of inputs purchased from each type of supplier (in terms of value), the multinationals indicated sourcing on average 48.3 percent of inputs from Czech enterprises, as compared with 33.3 and 12.6 percent from firms in the EU-15/EU-8 and foreign firms located in the Czech Republic, respectively. The share of inputs coming from the other regions appeared to be negligible (Javorcik and Spatareanu forthcoming). Besides having positive implications for the trade balance, local sourcing undertaken by multinational companies may bring an additional benefit in the form of technology spillovers to domestic producers (see box 7.5).

Why Some Countries Got Involved and Others Are Yet to Tap into Networks

The preceding analysis suggests that (i) participation in international production and distribution networks has been an important way of

---

BOX 7.5

Empirical Evidence on FDI Spillovers

Spillovers from FDI take place when the entry or presence of multinational corporations increases productivity of domestic firms in a host country and the multinationals do not fully internalize the value of these benefits. Spillovers may take place when local firms improve their efficiency by copying technologies of foreign affiliates operating in the local market, either based on observation or by hiring workers trained by the affiliates. Another kind of spillover occurs if multinational entry leads to greater competition in the host country market and forces local firms to use their existing resources more efficiently or to search for new technologies (Blomström and Kokko 1998).

When local firms benefit from the presence of foreign companies in their sector, we refer to this phenomenon as horizontal spillovers. To the extent that domestic firms compete with multinationals, the latter have an incentive to prevent technology leakage and spillovers from taking place. This can be achieved through formal protection of their intellectual property, trade secrecy, paying higher wages, or locating in countries or industries where domestic firms have limited imitative capacities to begin with. Recent economic research based on firm-level panel data, which examined whether the productivity of domestic firms is correlated with the extent of foreign presence in their sector or region, however, casts doubt on the existence of horizontal spillovers from FDI in developing countries. For instance, Aitken and Harrison's analysis (1999) of Venezuelan data, work by Djankov and Hoekman (2000) on the Czech Republic, and Konings' (2001) study of firms in Bulgaria, Romania, and Poland in the early 1990s either fail to find a significant effect or produce the evidence of negative horizontal spillovers. An exception is a study by Javorcik and Spatareanu (2003), which finds positive intraindustry spillovers in Romania in the late 1990s. The picture is more optimistic in the case of industrialized countries, as demonstrated by Haskel,

entering foreign markets for the Region's countries and that (ii) FDI has been the driver behind the Region's involvement in international production chains. Indeed, the data presented indicate that countries heavily involved in network trade are the countries that have received large FDI inflows. Thus, examining the reasons why some countries have not been successful in attracting FDI can explain why they have been left out of international production and distribution networks, particularly because many determinants of FDI inflows also determine the country's ability to participate in international trade.

The cross-country differences in the amount of FDI received over the past decade have been startling. According to the data presented in table 7.7, while Tajikistan received only $11 of FDI per capita as of end-2003, the corresponding figure for the Czech Republic was 342 times larger, at $3,771. All of the HP-7, with the exception of Turkey,

Pereira, and Slaughter (2002) and Keller and Yeaple (2003), who give convincing evidence of positive FDI spillovers taking place in the United Kingdom and the United States, respectively.

While foreign affiliates may want to prevent knowledge leakage to local firms against whom they compete, they may have an incentive to transfer knowledge to their local suppliers in upstream sectors. The phenomenon, referred to as "vertical spillovers," can take place through several channels. Multinationals may transfer knowledge about production processes, quality control techniques, or inventory management systems to their suppliers. By imposing higher requirements with respect to product quality and on-time delivery, they may provide incentives to domestic suppliers to upgrade their production facilities or management. The pressure from multinationals is often the driving force behind obtaining the quality certifications, as 17 percent of Czech companies surveyed by the World Bank reported getting an ISO certification in order to become suppliers to multinationals (Javorcik and Spatareanu forthcoming). Finally, the increased demand for intermediate products resulting from multinational entry may allow local suppliers to reap the benefits of scale economies.

The case study of a Czech producer of aluminum castings for the automotive industry may serve as an illustration. When the company signed its first contract with a multinational customer, the staff from the multinational visited the Czech firm's premises for two days each month for an extended period of time to assist with the quality control system. Subsequently, the Czech firm applied these improvements to its other production lines (not serving this particular customer), thus reducing the number of defective items produced and improving its overall productivity (Javorcik 2004a).

The evidence consistent with the presence of spillovers taking place through contact between multinationals and their local suppliers has been found by Schoors and van der Tol (2001) in Hungary and Javorcik (2004a) in Lithuania. The magnitude of the effect is economically meaningful, because a one-standard-deviation increase in the foreign presence in the sourcing sectors is associated with a 15 percent rise in output of each Lithuanian firm in the supplying industry.

Source: World Bank staff.

have been very successful in attracting FDI inflows. The Czech Republic, which topped the list, was closely followed by Hungary. Estonia
received $3,013 in FDI per capita, while Slovenia received $2,028.
The Slovak Republic's inflows of FDI, which only recently became
very sizable, have been catching up fast. Among CIS countries, only
Azerbaijan and Kazakhstan managed to attract significant foreign
investments, albeit mainly in oil sectors, which accounted for 98 and
66 percent of total inflows, respectively. None of the other CIS countries have performed well in this area.

What explains success or failure in attracting FDI inflows? An
obvious critical factor is political stability. Its absence almost always
discourages FDI inflows, all other things being equal. For instance,
until around 1995–97, the politically unstable Caucasus, not to mention the former Yugoslav republics, attracted very little FDI. Lack of

TABLE 7.7
Stock of Foreign Direct Investment per capita, end-2003 ($)

	IMF	EBRD	UNCTAD
Czech Rep.	3,771	3,939	4,022
Hungary	3,697	2,335	4,241
Estonia	3,013	2,027	4,823
Croatia	2,147	1,712	2,547
Slovenia	2,028	1,875	2,184
Slovak Rep.	1,647	2,161	1,904
Latvia	1,461	1,461	1,430
Poland	1,431	1,166	1,365
Lithuania	1,091	1,184	1,436
Azerbaijan	1,049	934	1,049
Kazakhstan	1,001	1,078	1,178
Bulgaria	824	676	650
Romania	482	455	572
Macedonia, FYR	476	505	500
Albania	343	351	344
Bosnia & Herzegovina	280	258	279
Armenia	279	283	275
Georgia	261	222	202
Russian Fed.	223	67	366
Belarus	180	222	192
Moldova	156	227	186
Ukraine	131	115	144
Kyrgyz Rep.	95	84	99
Turkmenistan	44	280	270
Tajikistan	11	32	35
Serbia & Montenegro	n.a.	260	410
Uzbekistan	n.a.	42	36
Turkey	216	n.a.	234

Sources: IMF International Financial Statistics—cumulative net FDI inflows 1990–2003; UNCTAD FDI database—FDI
stock end-2003; EBRD Transition Report Statistics—cumulative net FDI inflows 1990–2003.

political stability may also explain the poor performance of Turkey in attracting FDI. However, political stability is not a sufficient condition, as the example of many countries show. Belarus and the Kyrgyz Republic enjoyed stability, but no significant FDI inflows.

Empirical studies of capital flows seem to agree on two observations: official flows lead or stimulate countries' reform efforts, whereas private capital flows, with FDI as their most important component, follow or respond to reform measures. Empirical research shows that liberal reforms provide a more powerful explanation of variation in FDI flows to former centrally planned economies than to other developing countries, although there are many other factors involved, as the early success of Hungary illustrates.[9] Indeed, leaving aside investment in nonrenewable natural resources, which are partly (albeit not fully) immune to the nature of economic regimes, there has been a rather strong positive relationship between the size of FDI inflows and progress in dismantling central planning.

Structural reforms and sound macroeconomic fundamentals are also clearly necessary conditions for attracting flows of foreign direct investment. Among various determinants of FDI examined in empirical studies, the strength of macroeconomic fundamentals as measured by GDP growth or low inflation has been found to be consistently important.

Macroeconomic stability alone, however, is not sufficient to attract foreign investors. The critical variable is institutions or, more specifically, the pace of progress in establishing market-supporting institutions that assure protection and enforcement of property rights (which were discussed in detail in chapter 4). The empirical research supports this observation. Garibaldi et al. (2002) show that the quality of institutions explains the variation in FDI flows to transition economies. In a similar vein, in the econometric analysis of factors affecting the decision of multinational firms to establish a presence in transition countries in the first half of the 1990s, Javorcik (2004b) demonstrates that greater progress in the reform process, higher effectiveness of the legal system, and a lower level of corruption all encourage FDI inflows.

In order to capture the impact of political (in)stability and the quality of institutions, we plotted indicators of governance, derived from the World Bank database, and cumulative net FDI inflows per capita. The quality of governance is defined here as an average value of the indicators of political stability, government effectiveness, and regulatory quality. These three aspects of the business environment are critical to FDI inflows.[10] The indicators pertain to 1996, 1998, 2000, and 2002, and range from –2.5 (lowest score) to +2.5 (highest score). The rationale behind averaging over the seven-year period is that a good climate has to exist for a sufficiently long time to affect investors' decisions.

The variation in the quality of governance corresponds very closely to the variation in cumulative FDI net inflows per capita over 1990–2003 (figure 7.5). There is a strong correlation between cumulated net FDI per capita and the aggregate measure of the quality of governance, with a value of the correlation coefficient of 83 percent. The EU-8 and Croatia both have FDI per capita exceeding $1,000 and positive values of the quality of governance. The quality of governance is in the negative territory, that is, below 50 percent of the best-quality governance for all other countries. Investments in the oil sector explain the high FDI stock per capita in Azerbaijan and Kazakhstan in relation to their relatively low scores in quality of governance.

Although the quality of governance matters less for countries that happen to be amply endowed in natural resources, especially oil and natural gas, the exclusion of FDI in extractive industries does not significantly change the overall picture. The value of the correlation coefficient increases from 83 percent to 85 percent. Taking into account only FDI stock in manufacturing lowers the correlation coefficient to 78 percent, which may be explained by the fact that investors in services are sometimes lured not by an attractive business environment but by arrangements granting them exclusive rights. The examples include privatization of telecommunications in Albania and Armenia (see chapter 6 on the services sectors).

It may also suggest that considerations other than the quality of governance in a host country may be more important in manufactur-

FIGURE 7.5

Quality of Governance over 1996–2002 and Cumulative FDI Inflows in the Years 1990–2003 ($)

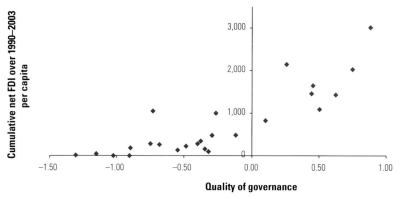

Sources: FDI data from IMF International Financial Statistics; population data from World Bank Development Indicators.

ing than in services. Proximity to markets, which is strongly related to geography, may explain a relatively larger FDI stock in manufacturing in some countries than the values of governance indicators might imply. Examples abound. Armenia is ranked roughly on par with Albania, but the latter has accumulated a 25 percent larger FDI stock. While the values of the governance indicator for the Kyrgyz Republic and Moldova are roughly the same, the latter's FDI stock in manufacturing is 17 times higher, while the total is less than three times higher. These deviations notwithstanding, the power of governance to explain the variation in FDI inflows is strikingly high.

Geographical disadvantage may be overcome in two ways. First, good governance can compensate, although not fully, for distance to major markets. Thus, the only way for landlocked, remotely located countries to attract larger FDI inflows is to improve the quality of governance and cooperate on arrangements that would reduce the transaction costs associated with moving shipments through their respective territories. Second, acceding to regional trade agreements may increase the size of the market. Ireland's impressive growth performance, which raised its GDP per capita from 64 percent of the EU average in 1983 to 122 percent in 2002, can be attributed directly to sound macroeconomic policies and its ability to act as a magnet for U.S. investment, thanks to a friendly business environment and duty-free access to the European Union market (Barry 2000).

Trade transactions costs associated with FDI also depend crucially on the trade-facilitating infrastructure, such as the performance of the customs administration and the quality of transportation and communications networks. Long delays at the border and high variance in clearing times make it difficult for potential foreign investors to commit to a particular delivery time. Corruption at border crossings increases the costs of doing business, thus lowering the competitiveness in world markets of locally produced goods. The poor condition of transport networks increases the cost and time needed for shipping goods. High costs of communications, whether through fixed-line telephony, cellular network, and Internet increase the costs of doing business (see chapters 4 and 5 for more details).

The quality of services infrastructure is another crucial component of a business-friendly climate that facilitates both FDI inflows and participation in international production networks. Well-designed liberalization of services sectors can lead to higher competition, greater range of services available, and more efficient services provision, which in turn decreases the costs of doing business and attracts new entry by both domestic and foreign entrepreneurs (for more information on the role of services, see chapter 6).

Many other factors may influence attractiveness to FDI. For instance, investors operating in high technology sectors may be looking for availability of skilled labor and protection of intellectual property rights. Those interested in simple labor-intensive assembly operations will be more sensitive to labor costs and labor market flexibility.[11]

Lessons for Countries Left outside Global Production Chains

The experience of countries that have successfully taken advantage of opportunities offered by global markets suggests that two elements have to be in place—successful implementation of first-generation reforms (liberalization of prices, foreign trade, and exchange regimes) and consistent movement toward a rule-based institutional regime with the capacity for their enforcement. The former is relatively easy to implement, provided there is an absence of political opposition, whereas the latter requires advanced institutional capacity of the state, as discussed in chapter 4.

What other policies could be used to facilitate participation in international production networks? Three policy options are possible: (1) export processing zones (EPZs); (2) duty drawbacks or other systems offsetting import tariffs; and (3) economywide trade liberalization combined with trade facilitation measures. The problems with EPZs are threefold: first, many countries have established them, but only a few have succeeded in encouraging exports. Second, EPZs are not amenable to horizontal and vertical spillovers. Last but not least, EPZs signal to international investors a weakness in the business climate; see chapter 4.

As to the second option, although elaborate systems including effective implementation of duty drawbacks may offset the bias in favor of production for domestic markets, they require sophisticated administrative capacities. These are lacking, as demonstrated by almost universal complaints across CIS about delays in rebates of VAT and duties. Hence, the best option is economywide trade liberalization, combined with trade-facilitation measures. Establishing a business-friendly and efficient services environment can be facilitated by either adopting reforms that would have the additional benefit of speeding up accession to the WTO or, for WTO members, leveraging their obligations under WTO rules to accelerate reforms.

Locking in the reform path through international agreements has helped EU-8 countries achieve these goals. First, in order to become eligible for accession to the EU, they had to remove, albeit gradually, barriers to their trade with the EU, including behind-the-border measures, and they had to introduce trade-facilitating measures, such as reforms of customs administration, as well as other reforms, to converge to the *acquis communitaire*. Taken together, these measures have contributed to the emergence of well-functioning services blocs and a business-friendly environment, which are a necessary condition—though not a sufficient one—to participate in a fragmentation-induced division of labor. Thus, it is no surprise that all HP-7 countries, except for Turkey, have recently acceded to the European Union. The absence of commitment to reform had slowed down the reform process of Bulgaria and Romania and adversely affected FDI inflows into their economies, hindering their integration into international production and distribution networks.

Second, in addition to the EU accession process acting as an anchor of domestic institutional and policy reforms, the emergence of a "Pan-European" free trade area for industrial products—encompassing the EU-15, EFTA, EU-8, and Turkey—has been a magnet for FDI and has created enormous opportunities for industrial exchanges (Kaminski 2001 and 2004a). The Pan-European Cumulation of Origin Agreement, which went into effect as of January 1, 1997, has allowed for "diagonal cumulation" of rules of origin (parts manufactured in any of the participating countries count as local input in entering any of these markets) across all participating countries. It has also accelerated and coordinated the schedule of removing tariff rates on industrial products.

What lessons can be drawn from the EU-8 experience for countries that have been left outside the global production chains? *The first lesson is the need for combining a strong commitment to reform with an outside mechanism that will enhance the credibility of the governments introducing domestic structural reform and provide an external stimulus to the process.* WTO accession, which is at various stages in Azerbaijan, Belarus, Bosnia and Herzegovina, Kazakhstan, Russia, Tajikistan, Ukraine, and Uzbekistan, can be used as such a commitment-creating device. However, domestic reforms alone will not be sufficient to increase the integration of geographically disadvantaged states. Even if a land-locked country had a world-class customs service, its trade flows would still be impeded by the necessity to ship products through neighboring countries with slow and corrupt border controls.

The second policy message is the need for adding both multilateral and regional dimensions to the reform process. In sum, reforming countries should rely on *a two-pronged strategy encompassing improvements in both domestic and external conditions by using WTO rules as a tool to leverage both domestic and regional reforms.*

Indeed, governments should leverage their obligations under WTO rules to accelerate domestic reforms. The credibility of government actions is a crucial factor in stimulating adjustment at the micro level. If firms do not believe in the permanency of liberalization or governments are pursuing other policies that make sustaining reforms difficult, firms may choose not to adjust. Instead, they are likely to devote resources to lobbying for overturning the reforms. Tying the reform process to a multilateral or regional agreement may also help implement reforms, thanks to lower period-by-period adjustment costs and strengthening complementary institutions and policies by establishing external (regional) checks.

Countries can make greater use of regional bodies to economize on the costs of implementing WTO rules. For instance, many members of the Eurasian Economic Community (EURASEC) or the CIS face pressures to reform customs administrations and domestic standards regimes.[12] Seeking regional cooperation in customs administration and in the dissemination of information about international standards and foreign governments' technical regulations, will, therefore, bring overall gains to regional partners.[13]

The following areas lend themselves to regional cooperation:

- Border and customs procedures: The improvements in national customs procedures, although highly desirable, will have a positive but limited impact without similar improvements in neighboring countries. Hence, there is the need for close cooperation. The same applies to transit rules.

- Conditions of transit: Although transit has been a subject of bilateral and regional discussions, the principle of national treatment should be extended to all service providers and enshrined into regional agreements.

- Technical standards: Each country should move quickly on its own to establish a market-based system of technical standards. However, this will yield higher returns if other countries within the regional grouping move in step and cooperate closely. Benefits of such cooperation will be particularly visible in small economies, which can substantially lower costs to domestic producers if, for instance, a conformity assessment is provided on a regional rather than national level.

- Services: Issues pertaining to services sectors should be addressed in their entirety and brought under a regional umbrella. As a first step, measures restricting market access should be listed and bound (that is, subject to a standstill). This is a long-term objective, as it involves regulatory overhaul of sectors with often-powerful vested interests.

Changes in regulatory policies in services sectors can potentially have the largest positive impact on the reforming economy. Efficient provision of services is not only a source of foreign currency earnings and employment; their availability and low pricing also lower the costs of exports and imports alike. Considering that services contribute on average around 10–20 percent to the production costs of a product and account for all trading costs (transport, trade finance, insurance, communications, distribution, and services), savings indeed can be substantial (Hodge 2002). So can gains in competitiveness in international markets of both services and goods. Moreover, their supply is decisive for domestic firms to participate in the most rapidly expanding division of labor based on fragmentation of production, simply because without high-quality "service links," production will not be moved to a country.

Endnotes

1. See Blonigen (2001) for a literature review.
2. For an extensive discussion of issues involved, see Jones and Kierzkowski (forthcoming).
3. For instance, according to Hill (1989), the average Japanese automaker's production system consists of 170 first-tier, 4,700 second-tier, and 31,600 third-tier subcontractors.
4. Our definition of the IT network encompasses office equipment, telecommunication equipment, and electronics. It covers only trade in goods.
5. See the top 100 list in *The Wall Street Journal Europe's Central European Economic Review* (July and August 1998, Vol. VI, Number 6), compiled by Dun & Bradstreet Hungary, Inc. Among the 20 largest firms in terms of sales, there were at least seven companies that were part of large multinationals. These included IBM Storage Products (#2); Volkswagen's Audi Hungaria Motor (#6); General Motor's Opel Hungary (#7); Philips (#12); General Electric Lighting (#15); Lehel Hutogepgyar (#39), owned by Electrolux; and Japan's Magyar Suzuki (#16).
6. For more details, see Kaminski and Riboud (2000).
7. Both countries, however, had unimpressive growth performance. While one may have doubts as to the sustainability of Belarus' network exports mainly directed to the relatively highly protected automotive sector in Russia, Bulgaria's prospects, mainly in IT networks, appear to be promising. Note that the share of network products in Belarus' manufactured exports declined between 1999 and 2003 and that the share in Bulgaria's increased.
8. For a discussion of the role of MNCs and network trade in "reintegrating" the EU-8 among themselves, see Kaminski and Ng (2005).

9. See, for instance, Claessens et al. (1998), Garibaldi et al. (2002), and Broadman et al. (2004).

10. We exclude the indicators of rule of law, control of corruption, and voice and accountability, because they are strongly correlated with the three measures used. Hence, taking them into account in a single aggregate indicator of governance would not bring new information. (See chapter 3 for further discussion of these factors.)

11. The results of Javorcik and Spatareanu (forthcoming) suggest that FDI inflows are deterred by rigid regulations on hiring and firing workers.

12. The EURASEC members include Belarus, Kazakhstan, the Kyrgyz Republic, Russia, and Tajikistan.

13. For a more extensive discussion along these lines, see World Bank (2005d).

PART IV

CONCLUSIONS

CHAPTER 8

Policy Agenda, Reform Linkages, and Action Plan

Based on the underlying economic and political dynamics of the transition process that is still under way in the countries of Eastern Europe and the Former Soviet Union, the opportunities for trade in the global marketplace will continue to increase for the countries of the Region. As the international economy continues to globalize, however, competition from other regions in the world will only become stronger. This poses a challenge to the Region's countries' abilities to use trade and international integration as an engine for growth and the reduction of poverty.

The experience to date in the Region shows that success in this environment requires a *combination* of not only implementing sound, market-based trade policies and trade-related institutions but also establishing a strong, complementary "behind-the-border" incentive framework in the domestic sphere. The previous chapters developed a detailed set of policy recommendations. Here, the principal recommendations that deserve priority attention are outlined, as well as linkages among the reforms and how they might be best sequenced in their implementation. The "division of labor" for the responsibilities of the various stakeholders with policy-making roles in furthering the Region's transition is identified, as is an action plan. A one-page Policy Matrix that summaries this information is at the end.

Priority Policy Recommendations

Priority Trade Policy Reforms

- *WTO accession is a critical policy objective for the 10 countries in the Region that are not yet members.* Many countries in the Region—especially in the CIS and SEE—must *address the challenge of how to rationalize the large number of existing bilateral FTAs* and to *broaden them to include such matters as trade facilitation as well as liberalization of services.*

- In a few countries—notably in the CIS—trade is restricted by high average tariffs and nontariff barriers (NTBs). *These should be appreciably reduced over the medium term.*

- In several other countries, there is still a large gap between "bound" and "applied" tariff rates: *all tariffs in the Region should be bound closer to the level of applied tariffs.* Not doing so undermines the economic effectiveness of commitments already made in trade agreements.

- *Tariff regimes also should be simplified and the structure of rates reduced in dispersion.* This will make customs administration more transparent and improve the predictability of the trade policy regime. It will also reduce opportunities for discretionary behavior and incentives for corruption.

- Reforms are needed to reduce the bias in investment decisions across sectors and reduce disincentives for greater product diversification. To this end, *the widespread practice of discrimination against export activities that exists in many countries of the Region should be eliminated.*

- To improve market access, reforms are needed in developed countries' *extensive use of "nonmarket"-designated antidumping actions against the Region's economies*, as well as in their *protectionist agricultural policies.*

Priority Behind-the-Border Reforms

Enhancing Competition and Governance

- The Region's governments should work toward *eliminating fundamental economic and policy barriers to new business entry, especially structural conditions that engender a lack of or weak competition among businesses.*

- *Barriers to exit of commercially nonviable firms also need to be eliminated*, through reducing subsidies and eliminating the practice of tolerating arrears (with the government, banks, and among firms).

- *Competition authorities should be given greater authority and competencies to assess, penalize, and, if necessary, remedy dominant firm structures, as well as other forms of restrictive business practices, such as collusion, anticompetitive mergers and acquisitions, and predatory pricing.*

- Improving governance will require efficient institutions that facilitate effective resolution of commercial disputes. *Policies aimed at the simplification and cost reduction of formal legal procedures as well as bolstering out-of-court mechanisms will strengthen contract sanctity and property rights and improve the level of investor confidence in the Region.*

- Sound governance will also require mechanisms to ensure *greater transparency and accountability of public officials' conduct.*

Improving Trade Facilitation

- In trade facilitation institutions, the priority reforms are *to improve coordination among agencies, both within and across countries; simplify customs procedures; make customs codes and associated regulations, rules-based, transparent and commercially oriented, with proper incentives for employees; and introduce the use of IT into customs systems.*

- As to further development of trade-related infrastructure, the critical areas for improvement are *modernization of ports and IT capacity. Meeting this challenge will require continued privatization or private-public partnerships* to entice new investments.

Liberalization of Services Sectors

- *Deregulation of services* should be the rule rather than the exception, and include the implementation of market-reinforcing reform of regulatory procedures and rules, including rate levels and structures. Where regulation is warranted, *independent regulatory authorities* with the proper competencies and resources should be established.

- *Territorial restrictions or other artificial barriers to competition either within a services sector or across services sectors, for example for intermodal competition, should be eliminated.*

- *Private participation in the provision of services,* either through greenfield investment or privatization of incumbent providers should be encouraged. This will require reductions in or elimination of limits or prohibitions on trade and private investment (whether from domestic or foreign sources) in network services.

- Deeper cooperation between the countries in the Region, such as in *regional approaches to deregulation (or more efficient regulation) of utility services,* could help reduce implementation costs and increase the overall benefits of regulatory reform.

Enhancing Intraindustry/Network Trade through Greater FDI

- The policy regime governing FDI should be *brought in line with international best practice,* which typically includes (i) adhering to "national treatment" for foreign investors; (ii) prohibiting the imposition of new, and the phasing out of existing, trade-related investment measures (TRIMs), for example, local content measures; and (iii) providing for binding international arbitration for investor-State disputes.

- Actions should be taken that ensure *transparency, predictability, and consistency of the FDI policy framework across different levels of government* and different industry sectors.

Fostering Resource Flexibility in Markets

- To reduce poverty impacts from changes in prices and outputs engendered by trade flows, measures should be implemented to *promote labor mobility* (for example, enhancing wage differentiation and adaptability and improving the effectiveness of social safety nets) *and to facilitate the reallocation of capital* so as to encourage new investment and job-creating opportunities.

Linkages Between and Sequencing of Reforms

- Many of the *policy reforms are mutually supportive and reinforcing.* Their implementation should capitalize on these linkages. For example, further tariff reform will enhance import competition, which in turn improves efficiency and increases export penetration.

- *Some policy actions can be done in the short term.* These include, for example, increasing Technical Assistance (TA) for institutional capacity building in the poor CIS countries.

- *Other reforms require balancing "winners and losers" or the marshaling of significant resources. These necessarily can be implemented only in the medium term.* For example, a few powerful vested interests will stand to lose from competition as liberalization in certain services sectors takes place and these losses must be balanced against the diffused gains enjoyed by the public. Investment in the modernization of ports will require large amounts of capital resources.

- *Sequencing of reforms can be critical, not only for their proper implementation, but also to build public support for the reform program and to maintain its momentum.* For example, steps should be taken to enhance labor mobility and strengthen social safety nets while liberalizing imports, or regulatory reform and strong competition policy institutions should be established as services sectors are liberalized.

Division of Labor among Stakeholders

What the Developed Countries Can Do

- Improve market access for many of the Region's countries' agricultural products through reform of the EU's Common Agricultural Policy (CAP) program and of other related Organisation for Economic Co-operation and Development (OECD) programs; rationalizing the Generalized System of Preferences (GSP) program.

- Change the "nonmarket" designation for several of the Region's countries—primarily in the CIS—in enforcement of antidumping (AD) policies to reduce excessive, protectionist use of AD procedures.

- Facilitate WTO accession for current non-Members. The CIS countries have fewer trade preferences from the EU, for example. However, the solution is not enlargement of the number of such preferences. Rather, it is for these countries to liberalize multilaterally through WTO accession and thus enjoy the benefits of "most favored nation" (MFN) treatment.

What the International Community (Donors and International Organizations) Can Do

- Many countries in the Region, apart from the EU-8 and the two EU accession and EU candidate countries, are in need of technical assistance and capacity building to strengthen trade-related institutions and policy implementation and management, for example, in customs regimes; in WTO and EU accession; in the harmonization of regional trade agreements (for example the 29 bilateral FTAs in SEE); in competition policy; and in governance reform.

- Special attention for TA should be paid to the poor countries in the CIS, which "fall through the TA cracks." Because they are neither classified as "least developed countries" nor have realistic prospects for EU accession, they are often overlooked in qualifying for such assistance.

What the Region's Governments Can Do

- Virtually all of the remainder of the reform agenda will largely depend on the implementation efforts of the Region's countries themselves.

- In the area of trade policy, this would include tariff reductions; termination of NTBs; elimination of disincentives to exporting; pursuit of WTO accession; and rationalization, harmonization, and modernization of existing RTAs.

- The more challenging tasks will be the vigorous implementation of economywide behind-the-border reforms to: enhance competition and governance in domestic markets and foster greater flexibility in labor and capital markets; improve trade facilitation infrastructure and institutions; liberalize the services sectors and reform of associated regulation; and improve the climate to attract FDI.

SUMMARY OUTLINE OF PRIORITY POLICY RECOMMENDATIONS

Region's Subregion*	REFORM AREAS I. Trade Policy Regime		
	Reform	**Principal Responsibility**	**Term**
EU-8	As part of EU WTO negotiation objectives, push proactively to reduce global trade barriers in manufacturing, services, and agriculture in Doha Round	EU-8 governments	S/M
SEE	Bosnia and Herzegovina and Serbia and Montenegro: pursue WTO accession vigorously	BiH/SaM governments	S/M
	Bulgaria, Croatia, and Romania: align tariffs with EU/pursue EU accession vigorously	BG/CR/RM governments	S
	Bind *all* tariffs at applied levels	SEE governments	S
	Eliminate remaining NTBs; also policies that create anti-export bias	SEE governments	S
	Rationalize, consolidate, and modernize 29 bilateral FTAs	SEE governments, w donor TA	S
	Strengthen regional cooperation on Trade and Transport Facilitation (TTF) utilization (for example, customs)	SEE governments, w donor TA	M/L
CIS	AZ, BEL, KZ, RU, TAJ, TKM, UKR,UZ: pursue WTO accession vigorously	Named CIS gov'ts w donor TA	S/M
	Non-WTO members: appreciably reduce tariffs; bind at applied levels; simplify tariff design; and reduce dispersion of rates	CIS governments	S
	Eliminate NTBs; also policies that create anti-export bias	CIS governments	S
	Rationalize, consolidate, and modernize CIS/CAR (Central Asian Republics) RTAs and bilateral FTAs	CIS governments w donor TA	S/M
	Establish mechanism for regional cooperation on TTF development and utilization	CIS governments w donor TA	M/L
	Reform of nonmarket antidumping designation and reduce protectionist policies (for example, in agriculture)	EU, OECD, other governments	S
	II. Behind-the-Border Policy Regime		
	Reform	**Principal Responsibility**	**Term**
EU-8	Continue to strengthen competition policy agencies' competencies and resources; focus on anticompetitive conduct (for example, mergers, pricing)	EU-8 governments	S/M
	Continue to improve judicial-legal institutions to protect property rights and resolve commercial disputes and public administration reform to reduce corruption	EU-8 governments	S/M
	Continue modernization of TTF infrastructure	EU-8 governments	S/M
SEE	Increase removal of economic and policy barriers to entry and exit (for example, subsidies; arrears)	SEE governments	S
	Strengthen competition policy agencies' competencies and resources; focus on anti-competitive structures (for example., dominant firms) as well as on conduct (mergers; pricing)	SEE governments	S/M
	Ensure public procurement is transparent and open to foreign competition	SEE governments	S
	Improve judicial-legal institutions to protect property rights and enhance public administration reform to reduce corruption	SEE governments w donor TA	S/M
	Implement reforms for greater labor and capital mobility to enhance flexibility in factor markets (for example, wage-setting rules/social benefits/pension and corp. governance)	SEE governments	S
	Further develop TTF infrastructure (esp. ports and IT applications to customs)	SEE governments	S/M
	Cont. reg. reform, public-private partnerships, privatization/liberalization of services	SEE governments	S/M
	Establish mechanisms for regional cooperation in infrastructure/services regulation	SEE governments	S/M
	Improve FDI policy regime to comport w. int'l. best practice (for example, national treatment)	SEE governments	S
CIS	Systemic removal of economic and policy barriers to entry and exit (for example, subsides; arrears)	CIS governments	S
	Establish modern bankruptcy/insolvency institutions, including judges, trustees	CIS governments w donor TA	M
	Build independent competition policy agencies w. political teeth, legal basis, adequate competencies/resources: focus on anticompetitive structures as well as conduct	CIS governments w donor TA	M
	Establish judicial and legal institutions to protect property rights and resolve disputes	CIS governments w donor TA	M
	Reform public administration system to reduce corruption	CIS governments w donor TA	M
	Open up public procurement to competition—private domestic and foreign vendors	CIS governments	S
	Develop and implement reforms for labor and capital mobility for flexible factor markets (for example, reform wage-setting rules/social benefits/pension and corp. governance)	CIS governments	S
	Develop TTF infrastructure (esp. ports and IT applications to customs) and institutions	CIS governments	M
	Establish independent regulatory agencies; liberalize/deregulate services sectors	CIS governments w donor TA	M
	Privatize "nonstrategic" services sectors (for example, telecom, transport, energy, banking)	CIS governments	S
	Reform FDI policy regime to comport w. int'l. best practice (for example, national treatment)	CIS governments	S

Note: * Summary policy recommendations do not necessarily apply equally to all countries in each group. S–short-term (1-2 yrs); M=medium term (3-5 yrs); L=longer term (5-10 yrs). AZ = Azerbaijan; BEL = Belarus; BiH = Bosnia and Herzegovina; FDI = foreign direct investment; FTA = free trade agreement; IT = information technology; KZ = Kazakhstan; NTB = non-tariff barriers; OECD = Organisation for Economic Co-operation and Development; RTA = regional trade agreement; RU = Russian Fed.; SaM = Serbia and Montenegro; TA = technical assistance; TAJ = Tajikistan; TKM = Turkmenistan; UKR = Ukraine; UZ = Uzbekistan; WTO = World Trade Organization.

Bibliography

ADB (Asian Development Bank). 2001. "Almaty-Bishkek Regional Road Rehabilitation." http://www.adb.org/Documents/Profiles/LOAN/32463013.ASP.

———. 2004. "Rebuilding the Silk Road: Encouraging Economic Cooperation in Central Asia: The Role of the Asian Development Bank." http://www.adb.org/documents/brochures/silk_road/silk_road.pdf.

Aitken, Brian J., and Ann E. Harrison. 1999. "Do Domestic Firms Benefit from Direct Foreign Investment? Evidence from Venezuela." *American Economic Review* 89 (3): 605–18.

Anderson, James H., David S. Bernstein, and Cheryl W. Gray. 2005. *Judicial Systems in Transition Economies—Assessing the Past, Looking to the Future.* Washington, DC: World Bank.

APEC (Asia-Pacific Economic Cooperation). 2004. "APEC Symposium Urges Greater Use of Paperless Trading Systems for Import/Export Business." July 28. http://www.apec.org/apec/news_media/2004_media_releases/280704_paperlesstradingsys.html.

Arnold, Jens, and Beata S. Javorcik. 2005. "Gifted Kids or Pushy Parents? Foreign Acquisitions and Plant Productivity in Indonesia." Policy Research Working Paper 3597, World Bank, Washington, DC.

Australia, Commonwealth of, Ministry of Foreign Trade and Economic Cooperation. 2001. "Paperless Trading: Benefits to APEC—The Potential of the APEC Paperless Trading Initiative." http://unpan1.un.org/intradoc/groups/public/documents/APCITY/UNPAN007623.pdf.

Babetskii, Ian, Oxana Babetskaia-Kukharchuk, and Martin Raiser. 2003. "How Deep Is Your Trade? Transition and International Integration in Eastern Europe and the Former Soviet Union." Working Paper 83, EBRD, London.

Baldwin, Richard E. 1994. *Towards an Integrated Europe.* London: Centre for Economic Policy Research.

Barry, Frank. 2000. "Convergence Is Not Automatic: Lessons from Ireland for Central and Eastern Europe." *The World Economy* 23 (10): 1379–94.

Baumol, William. 1967. "Macroeconomics of Unbalanced Growth." *American Economic Review* 57 (3): 415–26.

Belkindas, Misha V., and Olga V. Ivanova, eds. 1995. "Foreign Trade Statistics in the USSR and Successor States." Studies of Economies in Transformation 18, World Bank, Washington, DC.

Bergstrand, J. H. 1985. "The Gravity Equation in International Trade: Some Macroeconomic Foundations and Empirical Evidence." *Review of Economics and Statistics* 67 (3): 474–481.

Bernard, Andrew B., and J. Bradford Jensen. 1999. "Exceptional Exporter Performance: Cause, Effect, or Both?" *Journal of International Economics* 47 (1): 1–25.

Bićanić, Ivo, and Marko Škreb. 1991. "The Service Sector in East European Economies: What Role Can It Play in Future Development?" *Communist Economies and Economic Transformation* 3 (2): 221–34.

Blomström, Magnus, and Ari Kokko. 1998. "Multinational Corporations and Spillovers." *Journal of Economic Surveys* 12 (3): 247–77.

Blonigen, Bruce A. 2001. "In Search of Substitution between Foreign Production and Exports." *Journal of International Economics* 53 (1): 81–104.

Brainard, S. Lael. 1997. "An Empirical Assessment of the Proximity-Concentration Tradeoff between Multinational Sales and Trade." *American Economic Review* 87 (4): 520–44.

Broadman, Harry G. 1994. "GATS: The Uruguay Round Accord on International Trade and Investment in Services." *The World Economy* 17 (3) (May): 281–91.

———. 2000. "Competition, Corporate Governance and Regulation in Central Asia: Uzbekistan's Structural Reform Challenges." Policy Research Working Paper 2331, World Bank, Washington, DC.

———. 2004. "Global Economic Integration: Prospects for WTO Accession and Continued Russian Reforms." *The Washington Quarterly* 27 (2) (Spring): 79–98.

Broadman, Harry G., ed. 2002. *Unleashing Russia's Business Potential: Lessons from the Regions for Building Market Institutions.* Washington, DC: World Bank.

Broadman, Harry G., and Francesca Recanatini. Forthcoming. "Where Has All the Foreign Investment Gone in Russia?" *Eurasian Geography and Economics.*

Broadman, Harry G., Mark Dutz, and Maria Vagliasindi. 2002. "Competition in the 'Old' and 'New' Economy in Russia's Regions." In *Unleashing Russia's Business Potential*, ed. H. Broadman. Washington, DC: World Bank.

Broadman, Harry G., James Anderson, Constantijn A. Claessens, Randi Ryterman, Stefka Slavova, Maria Vagliasindi, and Gallina Vincelette. 2004. *Building Market Institutions in South Eastern Europe: Comparative Prospects for Investment and Private Sector Development.* Washington, DC: World Bank.

Campos, Nauro F., and Fabrizio Coricelli. 2002. "Growth in Transition: What We Know, What We Don't, and What We Should." *Journal of Economic Literature* 40 (3): 793–36.

Carlton, Dennis W., and Jeffrey M. Perloff. 2000. *Modern Industrial Organization,* 3rd edition. Chicago: Addison-Wesley Professional.

Caves, Richard E. 1996. *Multinational Enterprise and Economic Analysis,* 2nd edition. Cambridge: Cambridge University Press.

Chen, M., and M. Ravallion. 2004. "Welfare Impacts of China's Accession to the WTO." In *China and the WTO: Accession, Policy Reform and Poverty Reduction Strategies,* ed. D. Bhattasali, S. Li, and W. Martin. Chapter 15. Washington, DC: World Bank.

Claessens, S., D. Oks, and R. Polastri. 1998. "Capital Flows to Central and Eastern Europe and the Former Soviet Union." Policy Research Working Paper 1976, World Bank, Washington, DC.

Clerides, Sofronis K., Saul Lach, and James R. Tybout. 1998. "Is Learning by Exporting Important? Micro-Dynamic Evidence from Colombia, Mexico, and Morocco." *Quarterly Journal of Economics* 113 (3) (August): 903–47.

Csaki, Csaba, and Holger Kray. 2005. "Romanian Food and Agriculture from a European Perspective." Working Paper 39, World Bank, Washington, DC.

Csaki, Csaba, John Nash, Achim Fock, and Holger Kray. 2000. "Food and Agriculture in Bulgaria: The Challenge of Preparing for EU Accession." Technical Paper 481, World Bank, Washington, DC.

Cukierman, Alex, Geoffrey P. Miller, and Bilin Neyapti. 2001. "Central Bank Reform, Liberalization, and Inflation in Transition Economies: An International Perspective." Discussion Paper 2808, CEPR, London.

Cuthbertson, Sandy, and Chris Jones. 2000. "Trade and Export Promotion Study." Center for International Economics for the Asian Development Bank, Kyrgyz Republic Ministry of Finance, and Kyrgyz Republic Ministry of External Trade and Industry. Sydney.

Deardorff, Alan. 1997. "Determinants of Bilateral Trade: Does Gravity Work in a Neoclassical World?" In *The Regionalization of the World Economy,* ed. Jeffrey A. Frankel. Chicago: University of Chicago Press.

de Melo, Martha, Cevdet Denizer, and Alan Gelb. 1996. "From Plan to Market: Patterns of Transition." Policy Research Working Paper 1564, World Bank, Washington, DC.

Diamond, Jared. 1997. *Guns, Germs, and Steel: The Fates of Human Societies.* New York: W.W. Norton.

Djankov, Simeon, and Bernard Hoekman. 2000. "Foreign Investment and Productivity Growth in Czech Enterprises." *World Bank Economic Review* 14 (1): 49–64.

Dobson, Paul W., and Michael Waterson. 1996. "Vertical Restraints and Competition Policy." Research Paper 12, Office of Fair Trading, London, United Kingdom.

Dollar, David. 1992. "Outward-Oriented Developing Economies Really Do Grow More Rapidly: Evidence from 95 LDCs, 1976–1985." *Economic Development and Cultural Change* 40 (3): 523–44.

Dollar, David, and Aart Kraay. 2001. "Trade, Growth and Poverty." *Finance and Development* 38 (3). http://www.imf.org/external/pubs/ft/fandd/2001/09/dollar.htm.

———. 2002. "Growth is Good for the Poor." *Journal of Economic Growth* 7 (3): 195–225.

Dunning, John H. 1993. *Multinational Enterprises and the Global Economy.* Wokingham, England: Addison-Wesley.

EBRD (European Bank for Reconstruction and Development). 2003. *Transition Report 2003.* EBRD, London.

———. 2004a. *Transition Report 2004.* EBRD, London.

———. 2004b. "Private Sector Participation in Infrastructure." In *Transition Report 2004.* EBRD, London.

EBRD-World Bank. 2002. "Business Environment and Enterprise Performance Survey." Accessible at http://info.worldbank.org/governance/beeps2002/.

EC (European Commission). 2004. "Helping to Tackle Non-Tariff Trade Barriers in South East Europe." Report to the Stability Pact Working Group on Trade (September).

Edwards, Sebastian. 1993. "Openness, Trade Liberalization, and Growth in Developing Countries." *Journal of Economic Literature* 31 (3): 1358–93.

———. 1998. "Openness, Productivity, and Growth: What Do We Really Know?" *Economic Journal* 108 (447): 383–98.

EIU ([The] Economist Intelligence Unit). 2004. "Uzbekistan Country Profile 2004." London.

EUROPA. 2004. "Glossary." http://europa.eu.int/scadplus/leg/en/cig/g4000.htm.

Falcetti, E., M. Raiser, and P. Sanfey. 2002. "Defying the Odds: Initial Conditions, Reforms, and Growth in the First Decade of Transition." *Journal of Comparative Economics* 30 (2): 229–50.

Faye, Michael L., John W. McArthur, Jeffrey D. Sachs, and Thomas Snow. 2004. "The Challenges Facing Landlocked Developing Countries." *Journal of Human Development* 5 (1) (March): 31–68.

Feenstra, Robert C., James R. Markusen, and Andrew K. Rose. 2001. "Using the Gravity Equation to Differentiate among Alternative Theories of Trade." *Canadian Journal of Economics* 34 (2): 430–47.

Finger, J. Michael. 1993. *Antidumping: How It Works and Who Gets Hurt.* Ann Arbor: University of Michigan Press.

Fink, Carsten, Aaditya Mattoo, and Randeep Rathindran. 2003. "An Assessment of Telecommunications Reform in Developing Countries." *Information Economics and Policy* 15 (4): 443–66.

Fischer, Stanley. 1991. "Growth, Macroeconomics, and Development." In *NBER Macroeconomic Annual 1991,* ed. Olivier Blanchard and Stanley Fischer, 329–64. Cambridge, MA: MIT Press.

Foreign Investment Advisory Service. 2003. "Latvia: Toward a Knowledge Economy: Upgrading the Investment Climate and Enhancing Technology Transfers." World Bank, Washington, DC.

Francois, Joseph, and Kenneth Reinert. 1996. "The Role of Services in the Structure of Production and Trade: Stylized Facts from a Cross-Country Analysis." *Asia-Pacific Economic Review* 2: 35–43.

Frankel, Jeffrey A. 1997. *Regional Trading Blocs in the World Economic System.* Washington, DC: Institute for International Economics. http://bookstore .iie.com/merchant.mvc?Screen=PROD&Product_Code=72.

Frankel, Jeffrey A., and David Romer. 1999. "Does Trade Cause Growth?" *American Economic Review* 89 (3): 379–99.

Freinkman, Lev, Evgeny Polyakov, and Carolina Revenco. 2004. "Trade Performance and Regional Integration of the CIS Countries." Working Paper 38, World Bank, Washington, DC.

Fuchs, Victor. 1968. *The Service Economy.* New York: Columbia University Press.

Garibaldi, Pietro, Nada Mora, Ratna Sahay, and Jeromin Zettelmeyer. 2002. "What Moves Capital to Transition Economies?" Working Paper WP/02/64, IMF, Washington, DC.

Gereffi, Gary. 1999. "International Trade and Industrial Upgrading in the Apparel Commodity Chain." *Journal of International Economics* 48 (1): 37–70.

Hamilton, Carl B., and Alan L. Winters. 1992. "Opening Up International Trade with Eastern Europe." *Economic Policy: A European Forum* 14 (April): 77–116.

Harrison, Ann. 1996. "Openness and Growth: A Time-Series, Cross-Country Analysis for Developing Countries." *Journal of Development Economics* 48 (2): 419–47.

Harrison, Glenn W., Thomas F. Rutherford, and David G. Tarr. 2003. "Trade Liberalization, Poverty and Efficient Equity." *Journal of Development Economics* 71 (1): 97–128 (June).

Hart, Oliver, and Jean Tirole. 1990. "Vertical Integration and Market Foreclosure." Working Paper 548, Department of Economics, MIT, Cambridge, MA.

Haskel, Jonathan E., Sonia C. Pereira, and Matthew J. Slaughter. 2002. "Does Inward Foreign Direct Investment Boost the Productivity of Domestic Firms?" Working Paper 8724, NBER, Cambridge, MA.

Helpman, E., and P. Krugman. 1985. *Market Structure and Foreign Trade: Increasing Returns, Imperfect Competition, and the International Economy.* Cambridge, MA: MIT Press.

Hendley, Kathryn, and Peter Murrell. 2002. "Dispute Resolution in Russia: A Regional Perspective." In *Unleashing Russia's Business Potential,* ed. H. Broadman. Washington, DC: World Bank.

Hertel, Thomas W., Fan Zhai, and Zhi Wang. 2004a. "Implications of WTO Accession for Poverty in China." In: Bhattasali, D., S. Li, and W. Martin, eds. *China and the WTO: Accession, Policy Reform and Poverty Reduction Strategies.* Washington, DC: World Bank.

Hertel, Thomas W., Maros Ivanic, Paul V. Preckel, and John A. L. Cranfield. 2004b. "The Earnings Effects of Multilateral Trade Liberalization: Implications for Poverty." *World Bank Economic Review* 18: 205–36.

Hill, Robert C. 1989. "Comparing Transnational Production Systems: The Automobile Industry in the USA and Japan." *International Journal of Urban and Regional Research* 13 (3): 462–80.

Hodge, James. 2002. "Liberalization of Trade in Services in Developing Countries." In *Development, Trade, and the WTO: A Handbook*, eds. B. Hoekman, A. Mattoo, and P. English, 221–34. Washington, DC: World Bank.

Hoekman, Bernard. 2002. "Economic Development and the WTO after Doha." Policy Research Working Paper 2851, World Bank, Washington, DC.

Hoekman, Bernard, and Sübidey Togan. 2005. *Turkey: Economic Reform and Accession to the European Union.* Washington, DC: World Bank.

Hoekman, Bernard, and Sübidey Togan, eds. Forthcoming. *Turkey: Towards EU Accession*. World Bank and CEPR.

Hooley, Graham, David Shipley, Jozef Beracs, Tony Cox, John Fahy, and Kriztina Kolos. 1996. "Foreign Direct Investment in Hungary: Resource Acquisition and Domestic Competitive Advantage." *Journal of International Business Studies* 27 (4): 683–709.

Horst, Thomas, 1972. "Firm and Industry Determinants of the Decision to Invest Abroad: An Empirical Study." *The Review of Economics and Statistics* 54 (3): 258–66.

———. 1974. *At Home Abroad: A Study of the Domestic and Foreign Operations of the American Food-Processing Industry*. Cambridge, MA: Ballinger Publishing Company.

Hummels, David L. 1999. "Have International Transportation Costs Declined?" Working Paper, University of Chicago, Chicago, IL.

Hungary, Ministry of Economy and Transport. 2003. "Hungarian Transport Policy 2003–2015." Ministry of Economy and Transport, Budapest, Hungary,

———. 2004. "New Hungarian Transportation Policy at the Beginning of the EU Membership." Government of Hungary, Budapest, Hungary.

Hunya, Gabor. 2002. "Restructuring through FDI in Romanian Manufacturing." *Economic Systems* 26 (4): 387–94.

IBM Consulting Services and Christian Kirchner. 2004. "Rail Liberalisation Index 2004. Comparison of the Market Opening in the Rail Markets of the Member States of the European Union, Switzerland and Norway." Berlin: IBM.

IIED (International Institute for Environment and Development). 2004. "Liberalization, Gender and Livelihoods: The Cashew Nut Case in Mozambique and India." www.iied.org/NR/agbioliv/ag_liv_projects/t3proj01.html.

IMD. 2000. *World Competitiveness Yearbook*. Lausanne: IMD.

IMF (International Monetary Fund). 2004. *Direction of Trade Statistics Yearbook 2004.* Washington, DC: IMF.

Jansen, Marion, and Hildegunn Kyvik Nordas. 2004. "Institutions, Trade Policy and Trade Flows." Staff Working Paper ERSD-2004-02, World Trade Organization, Geneva.

Javorcik, Beata Smarzynska. 2004a. "Does Foreign Direct Investment Increase the Productivity of Domestic Firms? In Search of Spillovers through Backward Linkages." *American Economic Review* 94 (3): 605–27.

———. 2004b. "The Composition of Foreign Direct Investment and Protection of Intellectual Property Rights: Evidence from Transition Economies." *European Economic Review* 48 (1): 39–62.

Javorcik, Beata Smarzynska, and Mariana Spatareanu. 2003. "To Share or Not to Share: Does Local Participation Matter for FDI Spillovers?" Policy Research Working Paper 3118, World Bank, Washington, DC.

———. "Disentangling FDI Spillover Effects: What Do Firm Perceptions Tell Us?" Forthcoming-a. In *The Impact of Foreign Direct Investment on Development: New Measures, New Outcomes, New Policy Approaches*, eds. M. Blomstrom, E. Graham, and T. Moran. Washington, DC: Institute for International Economics.

———. Forthcoming-b. "Do Foreign Investors Care about Labor Market Regulations?" Weltwirtschaftliches Archiv.

Jayanthakumaran, Kankesu. 2003. "Benefit-Cost Appraisals of Export Processing Zones: A Survey of the Literature." *Development Policy Review* 21 (1): 51–65.

Jensen, Jesper, Thomas F. Rutherford, and David Tarr. 2004. "The Impact of Liberalizing Barriers to Foreign Direct Investment in Services: The Case of Russian Accession to the World Trade Organization." Policy Research Working Paper 3391, World Bank, Washington, DC.

Jones, Ronald W., and Henryk Kierzkowski. Forthcoming. "International Fragmentation and the New Economic Geography." *North American Journal of Economics and Finance.*

Jones, Ronald W., Henryk Kierzkowski, and Chen Lurong. Forthcoming. "What Does Evidence Tell Us about Fragmentation and Outsourcing?" *International Review of Economics and Finance.*

Kaminski, Bartlomiej. 2001. "How Accession to the European Union Has Affected External Trade and Foreign Direct Investment in Central European Economies." Policy Research Working Paper 2578, Development Research Group-Trade, World Bank, Washington, DC.

———. 2004a. "Production Fragmentation and Trade Integration in Enlarged Europe: How MNCs Have Succeeded Where CMEA Had Failed." *Papeles del Est: Transiciones Postcommunistas* No. 9. Warsaw.

———. 2004b. "Armenia's Integration into the Global Economy: Emerging Patterns of Competitiveness and Barriers." Draft, ECA, World Bank, Washington, DC.

Kaminski, B., and M. de la Rocha. 2003a. "Policy-Induced Integration in Balkans: Policy Options and their Assessment." In *Trade Policies and Institu-*

tions in the Countries of South Eastern Europe in the EU Stabilization and Association Process, Volume 1, Regional Report, World Bank, Washington, DC.

———. 2003b. "Stabilization and Association Process in the Balkans: Integration Options and Their Assessment." Policy Research Working Paper 3108, World Bank, Washington, DC.

Kaminski, Bartlomiej, and Beata S. Javorcik. 2004. "The 'EU' Factor and Slovakia's Globalization: The Role of Foreign Direct Investment." *Czech Journal of Economics and Finance* 54 (9–10): 456–72.

Kaminski, Bartlomiej, and Francis Ng. 2004. "Romania's Integration into European Markets: Implications for Sustainability of the Current Export Boom." Policy Research Working Paper 3451, Development Research Group-Trade, World Bank, Washington, DC.

———. 2005. "Production Disintegration and Integration of Central Europe into Global Markets." *International Review of Economics and Finance* 14 (3): 377–90.

Kaminski, Bartlomiej, and Michelle Riboud. 2000. "Foreign Investment and Restructuring: The Evidence from Hungary." Technical Paper 453, ECA PREM Series, World Bank, Washington, DC.

Kaminski, Bartlomiej, and Beata Smarzynska. 2001. "Integration into Global Production and Distribution Networks through FDI: The Case of Poland." *Post-Communist Economies* 13 (3): 265–88.

Kaminski, Bartolomiej, Zhen Kun Wang, and Alan Winters. 1996. "Foreign Trade in the Transition: The International Environment and the Domestic Policy." Study of Economies in Transition, World Bank, Washington, DC.

Kaufmann, Daniel, Aart Kraay, and Pablo Zoido-Lobatón. 2002. "Governance Matters II: Updated Indicators for 2000–01." Working Paper 2772, World Bank, Washington, DC.

Keller, Wolfgang, and Stephen Yeaple. 2003. "Multinational Enterprises, International Trade and Productivity Growth: Firm-Level Evidence from the United States." Working Paper 9504, NBER, Cambridge, MA.

Knickerbocker, Frederick T. 1973. *Oligopolistic Reaction and Multinational Enterprise.* Division of Research, Graduate School of Business Administration. Boston, MA: Harvard University.

Konings, Jozef. 2001. "The Effects of Foreign Direct Investment on Domestic Firms: Evidence from Firm-Level Panel Data in Emerging Economies." *Economics of Transition* 9 (3): 619–33.

Kormendi, Roger C., and Philip G. Meguire. 1985. "Macroeconomic Determinants of Growth: Cross-Country Evidence." *Journal of Monetary Economics* 16 (2): 141–63.

Kornai, Janos, Eric Maskin, and Gerard Roland. 2003. "Understanding the Soft Budget Constraint." *Journal of Economic Literature* 41 (4): 1095–1136.

Kwoka, John, and Lawrence White, eds. 2003. *The Antitrust Revolution: Economics, Competition and Policy.* 4th ed. Oxford: Oxford University Press.

Labys, Walter C., and Montague J. Lord. 1990. "Portfolio Optimization and the Design of Latin American Export Diversification Policies." *Journal of Development Studies* 26 (2): 260–77.

La Porta, Rafael, Florencio Lopez-de-Silanes, Andrei Shleifer, and Robert W. Vishny. 2000. "Legal Determinants of External Finance." *Journal of Finance* 52 (3): 1131–50.

Larive International. 2000. "Sector Study Internet and e-Commerce, Balkan Region." Study for International Finance Corporation (November). Zeist, The Netherlands.

Levine, Ross, and David Renelt. 1992. "A Sensitivity Analysis of Cross-Country Growth Regressions." *The American Economic Review* 82 (4): 942–63.

Limao N., and A. J. Venables. 2001. "Infrastructure, Geographical Disadvantages, Transport Costs and Trade." *World Bank Economic Review* 15: 451–79.

MacBean, Alasdair I. 1966. *Export Instability and Economic Development.* New York: George Allen and Unwin.

Madani, Dorsati. 1999. "A Review of the Role and Impact of Export Processing Zones." Policy Research Working Paper 2238, World Bank, Washington, DC.

Marchetti, Juan. 2004. "Developing Countries in WTO Services Negotiations." Staff Working Paper ERSD-2004-06, WTO, Geneva.

Markusen, James R. 1984. "Multinationals, Multi-Plant Economies, and the Gains from Trade." *Journal of International Economics* 16 (3–4): 205–26.

———. 2002. *Multinational Firms and the Theory of International Trade*, Cambridge, MA: MIT Press.

McCulloch, Neil, L. Alan Winters, and Xavier Cirera. 2001. *Trade Liberalization and Poverty: A Handbook.* London: CEPR and U.K. Department for International Development.

Messerlin, Patrick A. 2001. *Measuring the Costs of Protection in Europe: European Commercial Policy in the 2000s.* Washington, DC: Institute for International Economics.

Messerlin, P., and S. Miroudout. 2004. "Harmonization of FTAS in South Eastern Europe: The Options Ahead." Paper presented at the Stability Pact Working Group on Trade meeting, Budapest (March).

Michaely, Michael. 1998. "Ukraine: Foreign Trade and Commercial Policies." Working Paper, World Bank, Kiev.

Michalopoulos, Constantine. 1999. "The Integration of Russia and Ukraine in the World Trading System." In *Prospects for European Integration after Ten Years of Transition.* Ministry of Economic Affairs of the Netherlands, The Hague.

———. 2001. "L'Integration des Economies en Transition au System du Commerce Mondial." *Revue d'Economie Financière.* Special Issue.

———. 2003a. "The Integration of Low-Income CIS Members in the World Trading System." Paper prepared for the Lucerne Conference of the CIS-7 Initiative, World Bank, Washington, DC (January 20–22).

———. 2003b. "Trade Performance and Regional Integration of the CIS Countries." World Bank, Washington, DC (September).

———. 2004. "The Integration of CIS-7 Countries into the World Trading System." In *The Low-Income Countries of the Commonwealth of Independent States: Progress and Challenges in Transition,* ed. Clinton Shiells and Sarosh Sattar. Washington, DC: International Monetary Fund and World Bank.

Michalopoulos, Constantine, and Vasileio Panousopoulos. 2002. "Services Trade in the Balkans." Technical Paper 530, World Bank, Washington, DC.

Michalopoulos, Constantine, and David G. Tarr. 1994. "Summary and Overview of Developments since Independence." In *Trade in the New Independent States,* ed. C. Michalopoulos and D. G. Tarr. Study of Economies in Transformation 13, World Bank, Washington, DC.

———. 1996. *Trade Performance and Policy in the New Independent States.* Washington, DC: World Bank.

———. 1997. "The Economics of Customs Unions in the Commonwealth of Independent States." *Post-Soviet Geography and Economics* 38 (3) (March): 125–43.

Michalopoulos, Constantine, and David Tarr, eds. 1994. *Trade in the New Independent States.* Washington, DC: The World Bank.

Michalopoulos, Constantine, and L. Alan Winters. 1997. "Summary and Overview." In *Policies on Imports from Economies in Transition,* Peter D. Ehrenhaft, Brian Vernon Hindley, Constantine Michalopoulos, and Alan L. Winters. Study of Economies in Transformation 22, World Bank, Washington, DC.

Mikhailov, L., L. Sycheva, E. Timofeev, E. Marushkina, and S. Surkov. 2001. "1998 Russia's Banking Crisis and Stabilization Phase." http://www .banks-rate.ru/mikhailov/crisis1998/Sum_eng.pdf.

Miranda, Jorge, Raul Torres, and Mario Ruiz. 1998. "The International Use of Anti-Dumping: 1987–1997." *Journal of World Trade* 32 (5) (October): 5–71.

Molnar, Eva, and Lauri Ojala. 2003. "Transport and Trade Facilitation Issues in the CIS-7, Kazakhstan, and Turkmenistan." Paper prepared for the Lucerne Conference of the CIS-7 Initiative (January 20–22).

———. 2004. "Transport and Trade Facilitation Issues in the CIS-7, Kazakhstan, and Turkmenistan." In *The Low-Income Countries of the Commonwealth of Independent States: Progress and Challenges in Transition,* ed. Clinton Shiells and Sarosh Sattar. Washington, DC: International Monetary Fund and World Bank.

Ng, Francis, and Alexander Yeats. 2001. "Production Sharing in East Asia: Who Does What, for Whom, and Why?" In *Global Production and Trade in East Asia,* eds. Leonard K. Cheng and Henryk Kierzkowski. Boston, MA: Kluwer Academic Publishers.

———. 2003. "Major Trade Trends in Asia: What Are Their Implications for Regional Cooperation and Growth?" Policy Research Working Paper 3084, World Bank, Washington, DC.

Nicita, Alessandro. 2004. *Who Benefited from Trade Liberalization in Mexico? Measuring the Effects on Household Welfare.* Policy Research Working Paper 3265, World Bank, Washington, DC.

Noland, Marcus. 1999. "Competition Policy and FDI: A Solution in Search of a Problem?" Working Paper 99-3, Institute for International Economics, Washington, DC.

Odling-Smee, John. 2003. "Economic Performance and Trade in the CIS." Paper prepared for delivery at the international conference dedicated to the 10th Anniversary of the National Currency of the Kyrgrz Republic in Bishkek (May 10), International Monetary Fund, Washington, DC.

Olcott, Martha B., Anders Ashlund, and Sherman W. Garnett. 1999. *Getting It Wrong: Regional Cooperation and the Commonwealth of Independent States.* Washington, DC: Carnegie Endowment for International Peace.

Overman, Henry G., Stephen Redding, and A. J. Venables. 2001. "The Economic Geography of Trade, Production, and Income: A Survey of Empirics." http:// econ.lse.ac.uk/staff/ajv/hosrtv.pdf.

Palmeter, David N. 1998. "The WTO Antidumping Agreement and the Economies in Transition." In *State Trading in the Twenty-first Century,* ed. Thomas Cottier and Petros C. Mavroidis. Ann Arbor: The University of Michigan Press.

Perry, Martin K. 1989. "Vertical Integration: Determinants and Effects." In *Handbook of Industrial Organization,* Vol. 1, ed. Richard Schmalensee and Robert D. Willig, chapter 4. Amsterdam: North Holland.

Piazolo, Daniel. 1996. "Trade Integration between Eastern and Western Europe: Politics Follows the Market." Working Paper 745, Kiel Institute of World Economics, Kiel, Germany.

Polyakov, Evgeny. 2001. "Changing Trade Patterns after Conflict Resolution in the Caucasus." Policy Research Working Paper 2593, World Bank, Washington, DC. http://econ.worldbank.org/files/1713_wps2593.pdf#xml =http://econ.worldbank.org/cgibin/texis/webinator/econsearch/xml.txt? query=Caucasus&db=db.econ&id=3930d07881566444.

Porto, Guido. 2003. "Trade Reforms, Market Access and Poverty in Argentina." Policy Research Working Paper 3135, World Bank, Washington, DC.

———. 2004. "Informal Export Barriers and Poverty." Working Paper 3354, World Bank, Washington, DC.

Ramasastry, Anita. 2000. "Assessing Insolvency Laws after Ten Years of Transition." *Law in Transition.* EBRD, Spring 2000: 34–43.

Redding Stephen, and Anthony J. Venables. 2003. "Geography and Export Performance: External Market Access and Internal Supply Capacity." Working Paper 9637, NBER, Cambridge, MA.

Rodriguez, Francisco, and Dani Rodrik. 2001. "Trade Policy and Economic Growth: A Skeptic's Guide to the Cross-National Evidence." In *NBER Macroeconomics Annual 2000,* ed. Ben S. Bernanke and Kenneth S. Rogoff. Cambridge, MA: MIT Press.

Rodrik, Dani, Arvind Subramanian, and Francesco Trebbi. 2002. "Institutions Rule: The Primacy of Institutions over Geography and Integration in Economic Development." Discussion Paper Series 3643, CEPR, London.

Roland, Gérard. 2000. *Transition and Economics: Politics, Markets and Firms.* Cambridge, MA: MIT Press.

Rose, Andrew K. 2002. "Do WTO Members Have a More Liberal Trade Policy?" Working Paper 9347, NBER, Cambridge, MA

Rutherford Thomas, David Tarr, and Oleksandr Shepotylo. 2005. "Poverty Effects of Russia's WTO Accession: Modeling 'Real' Households and Productivity Effects." Working Paper 3473, World Bank, Washington, DC.

Sachs, J. D., and A. Warner. 1995. "Economic Reform and the Process of Global Integration." *Brookings Papers on Economic Activity.* Brookings Institution, Washington, DC.

Salop, Steven C., and David T. Scheffman. 1983. "Raising Rivals' Costs." *American Economic Review* 73 (2): 267–71.

———. 1987. "Cost Raising Strategies." *Journal of Industrial Economics* 36: 19–34.

Scherer, F. M., and D. Ross. 1990. *Industrial Market Structure.* Boston: Houghton Mifflin.

Schoors, Koen, and Bartoldus van der Tol. 2001. "The Productivity Effect of Foreign Ownership on Domestic Firms in Hungary." Paper presented at the International Atlantic Economic Conference in Philadelphia, PA (October 11–14).

Schwartz, Eric. 1998. "Foreword." In *Litigation and Arbitration in Central and Eastern Europe,* David W. Rivkin and Charles Platto. The Hague: Kluwar Law International.

Stevens, Christopher, Matthew McQueen, and Jane Kennan. 1999. "After Lomé IV: A Strategy for ACP-EU Relations in the 21st Century." Paper presented at the Joint Commonwealth Secretariat-World Bank Conference on the Small States, St. Lucia (February 17–19).

Tarr, David G. 1998. "Design of Tariff Policy for Russia." In "Russian Trade Policy Reform for WTO Accession," H. G. Broadman. Discussion Paper 401, World Bank, Washington, DC.

Tarr, David, and Peter D. Thomson. 2004. "The Merits of Dual Pricing of Russian Natural Gas." *The World Economy* 27 (8): 1173–94.

Tarr, David, Glenn Harrison, Thomas Rutherford, and Angelo Gurgel. 2003. "Regional, Multilateral and Unilateral Trade Policies of MERCOSUR for Growth and Poverty Reduction in Brazil." Policy Research Working Paper 3051, World Bank, Washington, DC.

Tinbergen, Jan. 1962. *Shaping the World Economy.* New York: The Twentieth Century Fund.

Transparency International. 2005. "Corruption Perception Index." http://www.transparency.org/publications/annual_report.

TTFSE (Trade and Transport Facilitation in Southeast Europe). 2003. "Progress Report 2003." http://www.seerecon.org/ttfse/.

Tumbarello, Patrizia. 2004. "Regional Trade Integration and WTO Accession in the CIS: Which is the Right Sequencing? An Application to the CIS." Working Paper 05/94, IMF, Washington, DC.

Tybout, James. 1997. "Manufacturing Firms in Developing Countries: How Are They Different and Why?" Department of Economics Working Paper 97-19. Georgetown University. Version of 2000 at http://www.worldbank.com/wbi/mdf/mdf2/papers/benefit/finance/tybout.pdf.

UK Trade & Investment. 2003. "Turkmenistan." http://www.uktradeinvest.gov.uk.

UNCTAD (United Nations Conference on Trade and Development). 1996. *World Investment Report 1996: Investment, Trade and International Policy Arrangements.* United Nations, New York and Geneva.

United Nations. 1997. *World Investment Report 1997: Transnational Corporations Market Structure and Competition Policy.* United Nations, New York and Geneva.

———. 2001. "Transit Systems of Landlocked and Transit Developing Countries: Recent Developments and Proposals for Future Action." United Nations, New York and Geneva.

———. 2002a. "E-Commerce and Development Report, 2002." UNCTAD/SDTE/ECB/2. United Nations, New York and Geneva.

———. 2002b. *World Investment Report 2002: Transnational Corporations and Export Competitiveness.* United Nations, New York and Geneva.

———. 2004. *World Investment Report 2004: The Shift towards Services.* UN, New York and Geneva.

UNESCO (United Nations Educational, Scientific, and Cultural Organization). 2002. "Landlocked Countries: Opportunities, Challenges, Recommendations." UNESCO TRADE/2002/23 (March 14), United Nations, Paris.

Vedev, Alexei. 2004. "Russian Banking System: The Current State and the Prospects for Future Developments." Draft. http://we.worldbank.org/WBSITE/EXTERNAL/TOPICS/TRADE/0,,contentMDK:20341369~menuPK:167367~pagePK:64020865~piPK:51164185~theSitePK:239071,00.html.

Vernon, R. 1966. "International Investment and International Trade in the Product Cycle." *Quarterly Journal of Economics* 80: 190–207.

Vincelette, Gallina, and Maryann Feldman. 2004. "Path of Investment: Lessons about FDI in Maryland." Monograph, Johns Hopkins University Institute for Policy Studies, Baltimore, MD.

Viscusi, W. Kip, John M. Vernon, and Joseph E. Harrington. 2000. *Economics of Regulation and Antitrust,* 3rd Edition. Cambridge, MA: MIT Press.

Wallsten, Scott J. 2000. "The Effects of Government-Industry R&D Programs on Private R&D: The Case of the Small Business Innovation Research Program." *RAND Journal of Economics* 31 (1): 82–100.

Wang, Zhen Kun, and Alan L. Winters. 1991. "The Trading Potential of Eastern Europe." Discussion Paper 610, CEPR, London.

Williamson, Oliver E. 1985. *The Economic Institutions of Capitalism: Firms, Markets, Relational Contracting.* New York: Free Press.

Wilson, John S., Xubei Luo, and Harry G. Broadman. 2004. "Trade and Transport Facilitation: European Accession and Capacity Building Priorities." Draft paper prepared for the workshop on "Transport Costs and their Impact on International Trade," European Conference of Ministers of Transport and OECD Research Center, Paris (October 21–22).

Wilson, John S., Catherine Mann, and Tsunehiro Otsuki. 2004. "Assessing the Potential Benefit of Trade Facilitation: A Global Perspective." Policy Research Working Paper 3224, World Bank, Washington, DC.

Wilson John S., Catherine Mann, Yuen Pau Woo, Nizar Assanie, and Inbom Choi. 2002. *Trade Facilitation: A Development Perspective in the Asia-Pacific Region.* Singapore: Asia Pacific Economic Cooperation.

Winters, L. Alan, Neil McCulloch, and Andrew McKay. 2004. "Trade Liberalization and Poverty: The Evidence So Far." *Journal of Economic Literature* 42 (1): 72–115.

Woo, Yuen Pau, and John S. Wilson. 2000. "Cutting Through Red Tape: New Directions for APEC's Trade Facilitation Agenda." Asia Pacific Foundation of Canada, Vancouver.

World Bank. 1991. "The Demise of the CMEA: Implications for Hungary." Report 9074-HU, World Bank, Washington, DC.

———. 2000a. "Bulgaria Country Economic Memorandum (CEM)." World Bank, Washington, DC.

———. 2000b. *Making Transition Work for Everyone: Poverty and Inequality in Europe and Central Asia.* Washington, DC: World Bank.

———. 2000c. "Trade and Transport Facilitation in Southeast Europe Project—Albania." Project Appraisal Document. Report 20828-ALB (October 5). http://www.seerecon.org/ttfse/ttfse-coredocs.htm#PID.

———. 2000d. "Trade Facilitation in the Caucasus—Final Report." World Bank, Washington, DC (October).

———. 2001. "Federal Republic of Yugoslavia Breaking with the Past: The Path to Stability and Growth." 2 vols. Report 22267-YU, World Bank, Washington, DC (July 15).

———. 2002a. "Armenia: Trade Diagnostic Study." World Bank, Washington, DC.

———. 2002b. "Kyrgyz Republic—Telecommunications Project." Implementation Completion Report. World Bank, Washington, DC.

———. 2002c. "Trade and Transport Facilitation in Southeast Europe Project—Federal Republic of Yugoslavia." Project Appraisal Document. Report 23888-YU (May 7). http://www.seerecon.org/ttfse/ttfse-core docs.htm#PID.

———. 2002d. "Trade Policy and Poverty." Poverty Reduction Strategy Paper (PRSP) Source Book. World Bank, Washington, DC.

———. 2002e. *Transition—the First Ten Years: Analysis and Lessons for Eastern Europe and the Former Soviet Union.* Washington, DC: World Bank.

———. 2003a. "Azerbaijan: Building Competitiveness." 2 vols. Report 25818-AZ, World Bank, Washington, DC.

———. 2003b. "Croatia: Country Economic Memorandum." 2 vols. World Bank, Washington, DC.

———. 2003c. "Ethiopia: Trade and Transformation: Diagnostic Trade Integration Study." 2 vols. World Bank, Washington, DC. www.integrated framework.org.

———. 2003d. "Georgia: An Integrated Trade Development Strategy." Report 27264-GE, World Bank, Washington, DC.

———. 2003e. "Project Appraisal Document on a Proposed Loan in the Amount of US$140.0 Million to the Russian Federation for a Customs Development Project." World Bank, Washington, DC.

———. 2003f. "Trade and Transport Facilitation in the Caucasus—Georgia Policy Note." World Bank, Washington, DC (November).

———. 2003g. *Trade, Investment, and Development in the Middle East and North Africa: Engaging with the World.* MENA Development Report. Washington, DC: World Bank.

————. 2003h. "Trade Policies and Institutions in the Countries of South Eastern Europe in the EU Stabilization and Association Process." World Bank, Washington, DC.

————. 2003i. "Water Resources Management in Southeastern Europe." 2 vols. World Bank, Washington, DC.

————. 2004a. "Bosnia and Herzegovina: Country Economic Memorandum." World Bank, Washington, DC.

————. 2004b. "Doing Business" database. http://rru.worldbank.org/.

————. 2004c. "Global Economic Prospects 2004." World Bank, Washington, DC.

————. 2004d. "Kyrgyz Republic: Country Economic Memorandum." 2 vols. Report 29150-KG, World Bank, Washington, DC.

————. 2004e. "Moldova: Investment Climate Assessment." World Bank, Washington, DC. (May).

————. 2004f. "Moldova: Trade Diagnostic Study." Report 30998-MD. World Bank, Washington, DC.

————. 2004g. "New Silk Road Linking China to Western Europe to Be Completed within 10 Years." Press Review, World Bank, Washington, DC (October 28).

————. 2004h. *Reforming Infrastructure: Privatization, Regulation, and Competition.* Policy Research Report 28985. Washington, DC: World Bank.

————. 2004i. "Romania: Country Economic Memorandum." 2 vols. World Bank, Washington, DC.

————. 2004j. "Russia: The Transport Sector." World Bank Policy Note, World Bank, Washington, DC (August).

————. 2004k. "Serbia and Montenegro: Country Economic Memorandum." World Bank, Washington, DC.

————. 2004l. "Tajikistan: Trade Diagnostic Study." World Bank, Washington, DC.

————. 2004m. "The Republic of Moldova: Trade Diagnostic Study." World Bank, Washington, DC (December 23).

————. 2004n. "Trade and Regional Cooperation between Afghanistan and its Neighbors." World Bank, Washington, DC (February 18).

————. 2004o. "Trade and Transport Facilitation in Central Asia: Reducing the Economic Distance to Markets." World Bank, Washington, DC.

————. 2004p. "Trade Performance and Regional Integration." World Bank, Washington, DC.

————. 2004q. "Ukraine: Trade Policy Study." 2 vols. World Bank, Washington, DC (November 10).

————. 2004r. *World Development Report 2005: A Better Investment Climate for Everyone.* Washington, DC: World Bank.

————. 2005a. "Azerbaijan: Transport Sector Overview." World Bank, Washington, DC.

————. 2005b. *Growth, Poverty, and Inequality in Eastern Europe and the Former Soviet Union.* Washington, DC: World Bank.

———. 2005c. "Hungary: Transport Sector Overview." World Bank, Washington, DC.

———. 2005d. "Kyrgyz Republic: Country Economic Memorandum: Enhancing the Prospects for Growth and Trade." Report 29150-KG, ECA, World Bank, Washington, DC.

———. 2005e. "Moldova: Transport Sector Overview." World Bank, Washington, DC.

———. 2005f. "Poland: Transport Sector Overview." World Bank, Washington, DC.

———. 2005g. "Trade and Transport Facilitation Audit of the Baltic States (TTFBS): On a Fast Track to Economic Development." World Bank, Washington, DC (February).

———. 2005h. "Kazakhstan: Transport Sector Overview." http://lnweb18 .worldbank.org/ECA/Transport.nsf/Countries/Kazakhstan?Opendocument.

———. 2005i. "World Development Indicators" database. World Bank, Washington, DC. http://devdata.worldbank.org/data-query.

World Economic Forum. 2001. *Global Competitiveness Report 2001–2002.* Geneva: World Economic Forum.

———. 2003. *Global Competitiveness Report 2003–2004.* Geneva: World Economic Forum.

World Trade Organization (WTO). 1999a. "Accession of the Kyrgyz Republic to the Customs Union between the Russian Federation, Belarus and Kazakhstan." Notification, WT/REG71/N/1 (April), WTO, Geneva.

———. 1999b. "Technical Note on the Accession Process." WT/ACC/7 (March), WTO, Geneva.

———. 2003. "Turkey: Trade Policy Review." WT/TPR/S/121 (September), WTO, Geneva.

———. 2004a. *World Trade Report 2004: Exploring the Linkage between the Domestic Policy Environment and International Trade.* Geneva: WTO.

———. 2004b. "WTO Workshop for Central and Eastern Europe, Central Asia, and the Caucasus on the Agreement on Technical Barriers to Trade." http://www.wto.org/english/news_e/events_e/events2004_e.htm.

Index